Bremen

Hanover

WESER R.

Magdeburg

EAST GERMANY

Leipzig

ELBE R.

NE R.

Cologne

Bonn

Frankfurt

Prague

CZECHOSLOVAKIA

WEST GERMANY

Nuremberg

ALSACE-LORRAINE

Strasbourg

Munich

DANUBE R.

Vienna

AUSTRIA

RHINE R.

SWITZERLAND

YUGOSLAVIA

Trieste

Venice

va

Milan

Turin

Marengo

PO R.

I T A L Y

ADRIATIC

SEA

éjus

Nice

TIBER R.

CORSICA

ELBA

DITERRANEAN

SEA

Rome

By Norah Lofts:

ETERNAL FRANCE

HOW FAR TO BETHLEHEM

THE CONCUBINE

THE HOUSE AT SUNSET

THE HOUSE AT OLD VINE

THE TOWN HOUSE

HEAVEN IN YOUR HAND

SCENT OF CLOVES

AFTERNOON OF AN AUTOCRAT

WINTER HARVEST

ELEANOR THE QUEEN

BLESS THIS HOUSE

THE LUTE PLAYER

A CALF FOR VENUS

SILVER NUTMEG

TO SEE A FINE LADY

JASSY

I MET A GYPSY

HERE WAS A MAN

WHITE HELL OF PITY

REQUIEM FOR IDOLS

COLIN LOWRIE

BLOSSOM LIKE THE ROSE

HESTER ROON

THE BRITTLE GLASS

THE GOLDEN FLEECE

By Margery Weiner:

ETERNAL FRANCE

MATTERS OF FELONY:
A Reconstruction

THE PARVENU PRINCESSES:
Elisa, Pauline and Caroline
Bonaparte.

THE FRENCH EXILES:
1789–1815

*Translated by Margery
Weiner:*

THE ART OF CUISINE
by Henri de Toulouse-
Lautrec and Maurice
Joyant.

The Mainstream of the Modern World Series

EDITED BY JOHN GUNTHER

ETERNAL FRANCE

The Mainstream of

DOUBLEDAY & COMPANY, INC.

the Modern World

ETERNAL
FRANCE

A History of France 1789-1944

NORAH LOFTS *and*
MARGERY WEINER

Garden City, New York, 1968

Contents

BOOK I

1. The Revolution   1

2. The Consulate and the Empire   33

BOOK II

1. The Fall of the Empire. The Restoration.
   The Hundred Days   63

2. The Reign of Louis XVIII   81

3. The Reign of Charles X   95

BOOK III

1. Louis Philippe   109

2. The July Monarchy   124

3. 1848   141

BOOK IV

1. The Second Republic   147

2. The Second Empire   161

BOOK V

1. *The Third Republic*   195

2. La Belle Epoque   226

3. *War*   245

4. *Between the Wars*   266

5. *Again War*   298

INDEX   315

ETERNAL FRANCE

Book I

Chapter 1. THE REVOLUTION

Every year, on a summer day, an unwary visitor to France will find himself confronted with closed banks and shuttered shops. Unable to obtain money, possibly even without food, he must take what comfort he can from the sight and sound of the festivities with which the French celebrate the fall of the Bastille on July 14, 1789. The same thing might happen to the unwary one in the United States on Thanksgiving Day, or in England on a Bank Holiday, but the French are remembering one incident in a series whose all-over effect changed the whole world. The movement which we now call the French Revolution started something so far-reaching, both in area and time, that its full effects cannot be reckoned until the last pigmy in the Kalahari desert, the last painted native in New Guinea, has been given the chance to adopt or to discard its doctrine of Liberty, Equality, and Fraternity.

The outbreak of violence on that July day was not expected, nor its implication fully understood by the man most threatened by it—Louis XVI, King of France, whose diary on some days of crisis bears the laconic entry, "Hunted." His comment, upon hearing of the attack on the Bastille, showed surprise and shock. "But this is a revolt!" he said. The Duc de la Rochefoucauld-Liancourt who was with him, christened the whole movement when he replied, "No, sire. It is a revolution."

It was a revolution; its origins, its avoidability or its inevitability have been and still are the subject of debate; its course has been and still is, a fertile field for novelists, dramatists and historians, whose human eyes are limited in focus, whose human minds are affected by theory, prejudice and fashion. Only one thing emerges as uncontroversial—it happened and, in happening, formed a watershed in world history, comparable to the breakup of the Roman Empire.

It affected France first; it affected France most; for there the "principles of '89" is still a potent phrase. Most things flourish best in their native soil, their native air. And now, in the latter half of the twentieth century, when France has once again risen from anguish and defeat, and once again takes her place with the great powers of Europe, it is necessary to know her past in order to understand her present.

It is equally reasonable to say that in order to understand the French Revolution it is necessary to understand something of the conditions in which it was born.

Land! Urbanized as we are, we still speak of our father*land*, our mother*land*, *land* that I love, *land* of Liberty. The phrases come easily, often unthinkingly; but land is the thing upon which all things living, except marine life, finally depend; and how land is cultivated and handled and made productive must, in the ultimate issue, take precedence of all else. The man has not yet been born who could eat a dollar, a dividend slip or a diamond.

In 1787, an Englishman named Arthur Young, an ardent agriculturist and an experienced observer, having ridden all over England, went to ride through France. One day, in his journal, he wrote, "Heaven grant me patience while I see a country thus neglected, and forgive me the oaths I swear at the absence and ignorance of the possessors." He was shocked to find so many French peasants without shoes or stockings: "It reminded me of the misery in Ireland." Young may not have been a completely unprejudiced observer: after several successive days of traveling thirty, even forty miles a day, his horse broke down and he blamed the careless French ostlers, but he knew about land and came from a country where agriculture was making great strides. When he wrote, "Banishment alone will force the French nobility to execute what the English do for pleasure—reside upon and adorn their estates," he put a finger on one of the ills of pre-Revolutionary France.

Since 1614, when Louis XIII dismissed the States-General, the kings of France had ruled as despots, and banishment from court was a fate to be dreaded by anyone who aspired to power or office. Even Louis XVI, not by temperament a dictatorial man, once said, "The sovereign authority resides exclusively in my person." In such circumstances the King and the court exercised a centripetal force; if one wished for advancement for oneself or one's sons, or even a good marriage for one's daughter, it was necessary to be at Versailles, part of the great formal puppet show, to be conversant with the complicated etiquette, to wear clothes exactly suited to one's rank and to the occasion.

Not every landlord was an absentee or a place-seeker or a heartless grinder of poor faces; the Duc de la Rochefoucauld, taking a keen interest in agriculture, draining a marsh to turn it into good land, was not an isolated example. In the years immediately preceding 1789 progressive ideas had made headway; some of the heaviest burdens and impositions of a medieval feudal system had been lightened. And this fact in itself was a contributory factor to the Revolution. De Tocqueville summed it up: "It often happens that a people which has supported without complaint the most oppressive laws, violently throws them off as soon as their weight is lightened." For a short period, until in the 1780s there came a series of bad harvests, the position of the French peasant had improved rather than deteriorated. The bad harvests brought hardship and discontent; no man likes to be worse off this year than he was last; but the French Revolution was far from being merely a Peasants' Revolt; it involved the middle class, the bourgeoisie, men who by industry and the exercise of intelligence had gained wealth and professional status and then found themselves confronted by a blank wall. A rigid system which ordained that only the wellborn could hope to attain high office in the state, preferment in the Church, commissioned rank in army or navy was not only dangerously wasteful of talent, but dangerously exasperating to those disbarred. Napoleon only managed to scrape into the military school at Brienne because his father, poor as he was, could make claims to gentle birth. Only very occasionally could an exceptionally gifted person break out of this class bondage; he was then, very often, ennobled, and lost to the potentially stable middle class into which he had been born.

Of the hardships and the festering discontents in the country over which he ruled, Louis XVI knew little. His court, like those of his predecessors, was isolated at Versailles, and its mental energy was more concerned with intrigue, fashion and etiquette, who raised hat to whom, who was entitled to a chair, a stool, than with outside problems. In the whole nineteen years of his reign Louis made only one visit to the provinces. Lyons, Bordeaux, Marseilles and the other growing cities of France were as unknown to him as Madrid or Rome. The suggestion—wrongly attributed to Marie Antoinette, and possibly entirely apocryphal—that those who had no bread could eat cake, even if invented, is significant of the gulf that gaped between the ruler and the ruled.

Louis XVI had had no training in kingship; he, his two brothers and his sister had been orphaned early in life. Their parents, excellent characters, had died before they could put into effect their intention to rear their children to be good Christians, well educated, conscious of the responsibility that comes with privilege. The children were reared in a licentious court by their grandfather, Louis XV, who was far too busy with his pleasures and his paramours to find time for training the young. And who else in that gay, frivolous society could be bothered? Madame de Pompadour? Any of her successors? Though they were surrounded by luxury, their upbringing was bleak, their education superficial. In some ways the boys resembled one another, all having the Bourbon profile with its aquiline nose and heavy lip, all having the family dignity, affability, egotism, good health and hearty appetite. From their Polish grandmother they had inherited the Slav characteristics of fatalistic resignation in the face of adverse circumstance, and great resilience. Louis, doomed to the saddest end, was pious, phlegmatic, well-meaning, unintellectual; he had no use for books, which might have remedied some of the deficiencies in his education; he liked doing things with his hands and became a competent locksmith; he was fond of hunting. Provence was clever and proud of it; he resented his place as second son and was jealous of his elder brother; he was given to intrigue. Artois was handsome, slimmer than the others, possessed of great charm but prone to a frivolity that often nullified his kindliness and generosity.

Each in turn was to be King of France, though in 1789 this prospect seemed unlikely.

Louis, at the age of sixteen, had been married to an Austrian princess, Marie Antoinette, and seemed to have been lucky in the royal-marriage lottery. His bride was young and pretty, well brought up, and the daughter of that redoubtable woman, Maria Theresa of Austria who, in addition to ruling her realm and waging wars, had borne and reared nine children. It took Louis seven years to consummate the marriage, but when he did it was fruitful; of four children there remained an heir and a daughter. The seven-year delay had, however, driven Marie Antoinette to seek release from frustration in frivolous ways which had lost her popularity and brought stern admonitions from her mother. She had friends who loved her and to whom she was devoted; she also had virulent enemies, both political and personal, who were not above plotting against her. She was extravagant, but her extravagances were exaggerated, and the rigged scandal of the Diamond Necklace made ordinary people detest her and blame her for the bankruptcy of the country.

France had been on the verge of bankruptcy before Marie Antoinette was born. Louis XIV's wars had brought him glory, but they had been ruinously expensive; his palace at Versailles, considered the most splendid edifice in Europe, had cost outrageous sums; his religious policy had sent half a million industrious, productive citizens into exile. Louis XV's wars had also been expensive and had ended with the loss of French colonies in India and Canada. At one point in his reign the suggestion that the whole nation should declare itself bankrupt had been considered. The efforts of a Scotsman, John Law, to rescue the ailing economy had resulted in a financial crash similar to the bursting of the South Sea Bubble. Financial instability was part of Louis XVI's heritage and French intervention in the War of American Independence had put a final strain on the resources of a country whose external trade was dwindling, whose internal trade was hampered by heavy customs barriers between area and area.

When, in 1788, Louis summoned the States-General to meet in

the spring of the following year, he was acting under pressure from one of the most powerful forces—financial necessity. In Paris alone there were 120,000 unemployed begging their bread, and bread was in such short supply that a loaf cost fourteen and a half sous, while a man in work earned fifteen sous a day. Bread—someone said—is used by the rich only to mop up the gravy; for the poor it is a staple food; bread or the lack of it, and its price, has powerfully influenced history.

Lack of money and shortage of bread do not in themselves bring about revolutions. "Revolutions begin when a number of eccentric opinions discover for themselves a common centre." For some time before 1789, eccentric opinions had been expressed, by Voltaire wittily attacking the established order, by Rousseau claiming that government should be a social contract between governors and governors. The existing order of things had been challenged even in the realm of light entertainment. Beaumarchais' *Marriage of Figaro* was kept off the stage for three years but, when at last it was produced, Figaro's speech to Count Almaviva ("Because you are a *grand seigneur* you think you're a great genius. Birth, fortune, rank and office—everything to make you proud. What have you done to deserve it all? You took the trouble to be born and that's all. As for the rest you are a very ordinary man.") was greeted with genuine applause.

Reform was in the air, by some assuming the urgency of a crusade, by some admitted as a practical necessity, by some viewed with distaste and fear. Prior to 1789 there was no machinery for bringing reform into action. The King chose—and dismissed—his ministers; they made the laws and fixed tax levels. There were regional *parlements*, in no way resembling the English Parliament; they did not represent the people but were bodies of lawyers and magistrates who registered and enforced laws. In a country the size of France and communication so slow they were necessary. The *parlements* had a theoretical right to remonstrate to the King about the laws they must enforce but, since the King did not recognize this right, the claim was meaningless.

The machinery by which reform could be achieved was helped into being by Necker, the minister who insisted that representation at the States-General should be in some proportion to population and the amount of taxes paid. As a result the Third Estate—neither nobles nor clergy—was twice as large as it had formerly been.

So long had elapsed—175 years—since the States-General had met that no one was quite certain of the deputies' powers or even what they should wear, but when, on May 5, 1789, they assembled in the Salle des Menus Plaisirs at Versailles, one thing was immediately plain; sitting in session altogether the Third Estate could outvote the other two on any issue, particularly as they could count upon the support of many of the clergy, the humble parish priests who knew, and often shared, the poverty of the ordinary people.

The suggestion of one sitting was innovation; formerly each Estate had sat separately, reached its decision and announced it: the new idea was resisted by those with privileges to defend; but the deputies of the Third Estate included Mirabeau who, though a noble, was a liberal-minded man, passionately eager for reform; the Abbé Sieyès; and Maximilien de Robespierre, a young barrister from Arras, all determined men. On June 20, in heavy rain, finding the door of the assembly room locked against them, the deputies of the people adjourned to the nearby covered tennis court to hold a session on their own. The choice of place was suggested by a Dr. Guillotin whose name has another, undeservedly dark, association. A mechanical beheading device had been known in Sparta, had reached Italy by the thirteenth century and Edinburgh by the fifteenth, but it had always been particularly favored as a device for severing the heads of the wellborn. Dr. Guillotin, egalitarian and humane, supported it as a swift, relatively painless method for removing any head.

In the bare tennis court the deputies took the famous Tennis Court Oath; they would meet, they swore, wherever circumstance should demand, and they would not separate until the country had been granted a constitution. Having taken this oath they cried, "*Vive le roi!*" Not one of them then, not even Robespierre, was anti-Royalist.

Had Louis XVI been politically alert or even opportunist, he would have seen that here was a chance to place himself at the head of a party which, though intent upon reform, was fundamentally loyal. Confused and ill-advised, he let it slip. A week later he faced the general assembly of the Three Estates and having studied the *cahiers de doléances*—lists of grievances sent in from local communities—he promised a program of reform. This he immediately nullified by ordering that the Three Estates should return to the traditional method of meeting in separate sessions; if they did not, he said, he would dismiss the States-General. Mirabeau called out, "We are here by the will of the people; we will leave here only at the point of the bayonet."

The King accepted, or seemed to accept the situation; the deputies remained in one body, now calling itself the Constituent Assembly, and prepared to draw up a constitution for the country.

The dominating figure in the Assembly was Mirabeau, a man of paradox; an aristocrat who could say, "Woe to the privileged orders. Better to be a man of the people than of the nobility; privilege will come to an end but the people is eternal." A man born with an oral defect that made it doubtful whether he would ever speak at all, who became a great orator; a man hideously scarred by smallpox who was as attractive to women as they were to him. He believed in reform, but also in royalty: "Royalty is the only safety anchor which can save us from shipwreck." He was one of the few who held Marie Antoinette in high esteem, but she never trusted him, probably sharing the view of so many aristocrats that he was a renegade, a traitor to his class.

Louis at this moment, with what can only be called a genius for mistiming, dismissed Necker, the minister whose financial wizardry had propped up the country's tottering finances and whose insistence on some sort of proportional representation had given the Third Estate its power. Necker had also advocated personal economies and the Queen had resented and ignored the doctrine. Necker's dismissal and his replacement by a man known to be a reactionary was regarded as sinister. Women who knew what cajolery is possible when the candle is blown out, blamed the Queen.

In mourning for Necker's dismissal, the theatres of Paris closed their doors—always a sign of impending trouble, and all over the country disturbances broke out. Those in Paris were fomented and financed by the Duc d'Orléans, head of the junior branch of the Bourbon family, which had a long tradition of opposition to the ruling house.

Louis never lacked courage, nor was he inclined to panic, but now, urged by the fears and warnings of those about him, he ordered troops, mainly Swiss and German mercenaries, to be stationed at Versailles. This move roused suspicion, and rumors began to circulate that the members of the Assembly were about to be arrested. A few men were killed in brushes with the troops; Paris prepared to retaliate.

Throughout the night of July 13, citizens who possessed weapons patrolled the streets while others raised barricades of paving stones at strategic points. More arms were needed and in the morning the people set out to find them. One likely source was the fortress of the Bastille. This ancient building, with its thirty-foot-thick walls, its seventy-foot-wide moat, had a sinister reputation. In the past it had been a prison for political offenders, a place into which a man might vanish and be seen no more. It was now little used and its demolition was already planned. The Parisians knew this; it was as the symbol of tyranny—as well as an armory—that they moved against it. Its taking was an altogether tamer business than the word "storming" evokes. The crowd shouted, "*Vive le roi!*" and promised that, if no one resisted, no one should be hurt: the governor surrendered and the crowd surged in. They found seven prisoners, none political; two madmen, four forgers and a nobleman convicted of incest. By this time, however, the heat of the day and the excitement that invades mobs had engendered lawlessness and a desire for bloodshed. The governor and the guards were butchered.

It was this day's doings that provoked the King's comment about revolt which the more foresighted Liancourt amended to revolution.

There was one man in France who knew that mob rule must lead to disaster and that insurrection should be checked. He was Charles Maurice de Talleyrand-Périgord who, but for his lameness, would have been in the army. Instead he became a cleric and, by 1789, as Bishop of Autun, was already a considerable force in

Parisian society, seemingly destined to follow that long line of ecclesiastical statesmen who are such a feature in French history. He was witty, charming, skeptical, the most shrewd politician of his day; he believed, with Mirabeau, that what France needed was a constitutional monarchy based on the English pattern. Louis XVI did not like him; pious himself, he suspected the Bishop of Autun of being a freethinker, and it was through the King's younger brother, Artois, that Talleyrand sent his message at this critical moment—force should be used in quelling this unruly Parisian mob. Louis, with his humanitarian repugnance to bloodshed, ignored this advice.

There were, however, in Paris, many moderate-minded citizens who were less squeamish; they felt that their homes and their businesses were threatened by mob violence and must be protected. They banded together to form the National Guard, choosing for their leader the immensely popular Marquis de Lafayette, who had come back from the American War of Independence with dreams of becoming a French George Washington. The fact that Lafayette was disliked at court may have endeared him to the ordinary decent citizens fumbling their way, as always, between privilege on the one hand and license on the other.

To Lafayette France owes its *tricolore*, the blending of the Bourbon color, white, with the red and blue of Paris. In flags and cockades and sashes the three colors broke out all over Paris and then as the provinces copied the capital, all over France. On July 17, when the King visited Paris—and men held their children shoulder-high so that they might see him—he wore the *tricolore* emblem and there must have been many who, seeing it, hoped that the combination of colors was prophetic of unity of purpose, of reform without upheaval.

Necker was recalled to office without ever having really left it. The government of Paris was reorganized as a commune with an elected mayor; like the formation of the National Guard and the adoption of the *tricolore*, the system of communes spread rapidly. So did something known as the "great fear." There were rumors of bands of brigands on the move, rumors of foreign invasion, rumors that Artois—known to be a reactionary—had put himself at the head of the army. There was panic, and under its prod men moved apparently like a stampeding herd, but with a difference. Châteaux were burned and pillaged because they were strongholds of which brigands, invaders, Artois' army might take possession; but the basic sound sense of the French countryman was still evident. Everywhere particular care was given to the destruction of any kind of document that might establish one man's lordship over another. Records of feudal rights, of dues, of obligations, of debts—into the fire with them.

At Versailles the Constituent Assembly solemnly, in careful phrases, dismantled the old feudal system; in far country places those who had suffered under it destroyed its legal evidence by the countryman's weapons, fire and ax. (In England, in 1381, the peasants in revolt showed the same antipathy to parchment and paper.)

Louis knew that Artois was unpopular and suspect; concerned for his safety, he suggested that he should leave the country. Artois went; others went with him, among them the Polignacs, friends of the Queen, whom the people regarded as her evil advisers, responsible for much in her behavior that they deplored. These first exiles called their leaving the "joyous emigration," regarding it as a temporary affair which would end when this tiresome business between the King and his people had been settled.

The Constituent Assembly sat on, planning a new world without privileges, or tithes or titles. All citizens were to be equal, to be equitably taxed. "Men are born free and remain free and equal in rights. They have a right to liberty, security and property, to freedom of religion, of speech and of the press. . . . The people are sovereign and above all equal," ran the Declaration of the Rights of Man, a document of importance, not only because it formed the basis for every constitution in France until 1848, but because it was a blueprint adopted by every country in Europe which sought political freedom.

(The French are popularly supposed to be a gay people; the Founding Fathers of America are commonly thought of as dour and puritanical; yet the latter included among man's rights the right to pursue *happiness*, and the French omitted it. Could it be that they sensed that for them happiness would be far to seek?)

Louis was, naturally, hesitant to give his blessing to a declaration which destroyed his absolute power; the Paris mob was, naturally, impatient. Rumor, as always, was busy. It was said that although the King had accepted and worn the *tricolore* in Paris, in Versailles it was being trodden underfoot; it was said that the King, encouraged by dissension within the Assembly, refused to ratify its decrees. A busy and well-fed community might have shrugged off such rumors or waited for their confirmation, but the people of Paris were still unemployed and still hungry. Much had happened since May when the States-General met; much had happened since July when the people had first shown their claws, but nothing yet had provided jobs, or loaves. To people who had expected immediate improvement in their condition, some of the work of the Constituent Assembly, such as doing away with the ancient provinces of France, Normandy, Brittany and the rest, and the reorganization into Departments, named for the most part for the rivers running through them—Seine, Lot, Doubs—seemed remote and academic. A journalist named Jean-Paul Marat poured out inflammatory articles in his paper, *L'Ami du Peuple;* the Duc d'Orléans hinted that if his cousin Louis had objections to becoming a constitutional king, he himself had none.

By October patience was running out; even the season may have influenced men's moods; winter, always hardest on the poor, was imminent. On the fifth, despite the rain, the crowd set off to trudge the twelve miles to Versailles, "to see the King," they said.

It is fashionable at the moment to stress the middle-class character of the Revolution; men of the middle class, lawyers, journalists, together with members of the aristocracy such as Mirabeau and Lafayette, formed its spearhead, shaped its policies and on the whole controlled it; but there were situations and elements which at times could not be controlled. There were between six and seven thousand women in the crowd that set off for Versailles on that wet October day; many of them, doubtless sober, worthy women inspired by some residual belief in the near-divinity of kings; the King had only to be told that one must queue for a whole day to buy a loaf of bread. But there were others who carried broomsticks, skewers and kitchen knives. One woman sharpened her knife on a handy milestone, and said, referring to the Queen, "How glad I should be if I could open up her belly with this knife and tear out her heart." And when two young girls, chosen to represent all, one a flower girl, the other a sculptor's apprentice, had been admitted to the King's presence and emerged without any written promise, but with a report of a kindly reception, they were punched and kicked and, but for intervention, would have been hanged in other women's garters.

Lafayette and the National Guard rode with the crowd and did their best to control it. The King did his best, but the limitations of his understanding are exposed cruelly in his answer to one of the delegates' demand for bread: "I have no bread in my pocket, but you can go to the pantries . . ."

He and his family were forced at last into a carriage and made a slow journey through the rain and the mire to the long-disused palaces of the Tuileries. Damp, dust and spiders had encroached; the young Dauphin said to his mother, "Everything is dirty here, Mama." But Louis, asked what repairs and redecoration he wished for, said, "Let each lodge as he can. I am well enough."

Well enough? Mirabeau for one did not think so. "Do they not see," he wrote to one of the King's friends, "the abyss which is opening at their feet? All is lost; the King and Queen will perish, and you will see, the mob will tear them limb from limb. You do not fully understand the dangers; nevertheless you must make them see it! . . . If you have any means of inducing the King and Queen to listen to you, persuade them that they and France are doomed if the royal family does not leave Paris."*

Mirabeau went on to suggest that Louis should go to Normandy; that he should sedulously avoid any association with the *émigrés*— now mounting in number—and, above all, turn a deaf ear to any suggestion of intervention from abroad.

This was sound advice from a man who saw the shape that the force he had helped to unleash was about to take. There may even have been a touch of deathbed prescience about it; Mirabeau preceded his King to the grave, but, like Talleyrand's advice about

* Quoted by G. Salvemini, *The French Revolution 1788–1792*.

using force against mob violence, Mirabeau's went unheeded. Perhaps because Paris now seemed to be restored to order, even giving demonstrations of loyal enthusiasm for the King and Queen; perhaps because of Louis' inborn inertia which, if it prevented his fleeing to Normandy, also prevented his encouraging any attempt at counterrevolution mounted by Royalist partisans; perhaps, and probably most likely, because the Queen was not in favor of retreat. She was, after all, the daughter of Maria Theresa of Austria, who had outfaced Frederick the Great.

Louis' passive policy seemed to be justified when, on the first anniversary of the fall of the Bastille a celebration was held on the Champ de Mars to mark the federation of the National Guards. Twenty thousand delegates came to represent the three million citizens now under arms, and a crowd of four hundred thousand citizens came to watch. Talleyrand, Bishop of Autun, celebrated Mass; the delegates swore on the altar to support the new constitution; the King was acclaimed. The bright July day was filled with the sense of past difficulties overcome and with hope for the future. Idealism stirred again.

But there remained the financial difficulties. The Assembly issued paper money, *assignats*, the value of which was rapidly reduced by the continuing inflation and the activities of forgers. Then, as security for the assignats, they turned to the most readily available source—Church property. Anticlerical feeling was ripe for exploitation; the literate section of the community had read Voltaire; the upper ranks of the clergy were closely associated with the aristocracy, all the 143 bishops in France were of noble birth. And the Church was very rich. Half the great vineyards of France were in the hands of the monks. But the mere confiscation of wealth did not satisfy the zealous anticlericalists; they insisted upon the Civil Constitution of the Clergy which made all clerics servants of the state and broke the links between the Gallic Church and Rome. This measure put Louis XVI into a most painful position. Thus far he had been so compliant and phlegmatic that the American, Gouverneur Morris, had asked in wonderment, "What is to be expected of a man who in such a situation can eat, drink, sleep soundly, laugh and enjoy the best of health?" Other people, even the King's friends, asked the same question. Nobody then knew anything about glandular deficiency but, whatever the state of his thyroid, Louis' conscience was active; how could he ratify such proposals and continue to regard himself as "His Most Christian Majesty"? He held out as long as he could and then gave way upon an issue where a bold stand might have served him, for the parish priests had served their people well and were revered, and the ties with Rome went back to the time of Clovis, the pagan who, newly converted and instructed about the Crucifixion, uttered the touching exclamation, "If only I had been there, with my Franks!"

The Assembly demanded that every priest should take an oath of allegiance to the Civil Constitution. Of the bishops only seven obeyed—Talleyrand among them; of the lower orders about a third similarly trimmed their sails. Louis XVI was careful, for what remained of his life, to accept ministration only from men who had not taken the oath.

In the Assembly old faces vanished, new ones appeared. Necker resigned, and in 1791 Mirabeau died, taking with him his ability to have a foot in both camps, his desire for reform without excess. Of the old guard only Talleyrand and Lafayette showed the tough adaptability necessary to survive every change.

Mirabeau's advice to the King to leave Paris had been rejected, but now, in June 1791, Louis, realizing at last that he had become a puppet, decided to leave the country. The story of the escape of the royal family in disguise from the Tuileries at night, the whole thing arranged by the Queen's Swedish friend, Axel Fersen—the pursuit, the arrest, the dreary, humiliating journey back—has all the quality of melodrama. Even then, being ignominiously hustled back to Paris, Marie Antoinette showed how little she understood the temper of the crowd. She thought that by holding up her young son for the people to see, she could calm them. They were calling her "bitch" and "slut" and "whore"; the gesture evoked more virulent insults, questioning the boy's paternity.

Back in the Tuileries—where some wit had fixed a "To Let" notice on the gate—the nature of their imprisonment became more sinister; formerly it had amounted to little more than what is now known as "house arrest"; now it became stringent. By attempting to flee the country Louis had forfeited much of the people's good will, and somewhere on the road back from Varennes the almost superstitious awe of royalty, which had in the past hedged about and protected kings far more selfish and aggressive, had been lost forever.

The Assembly, still proceeding upon constitutional lines, temporarily suspended all the King's functions.

Louis was stunned to find himself so much hated. To his brother, Provence, who had succeeded in escaping and was busy mustering an army of *émigrés* across the Rhine, he wrote that he had become the slave of his oppressors but that, so long as he was King of France, he would do nothing to dishonor himself. He could have understood it, he said, had he been a Nero or a Tiberius, but what had he done to be so hated, he who had always cherished the French people who had once loved their kings? The pathetic question answers itself; he was a weak man in a situation where strength was called for.

Exactly one year and three days after the Feast of the Federation at which the King had been acclaimed, the Champ de Mars was the scene of a gathering of a very different sort—a great popular demonstration of extremists demanding his deposition. The appearance as well as the attitude of the crowd had changed; cravats and collars had been abandoned; in reaction against knee breeches, men wore trousers and called themselves *sans-culottes*; the red cap of liberty was fashionable wear.

On this occasion authority acted; the National Guard fired upon and dispersed the crowd. Lafayette lost his popularity, but the truth of Talleyrand's words was proved; disorder could be checked by force. And since in the Assembly the Republican element was still weak and divided, there was a chance of compromise. Many people still hoped for constitutional monarchy, others saw the value of the puppet king as a hostage and a guard against foreign attack.

This was a threat of which the Assembly was extremely conscious. Ever since Artois had left France in July 1789, he had been working upon the other sovereigns in Europe to intervene on Louis' behalf. When Provence escaped he added his pleas to those of his brother and succeeded in extracting from the Holy Roman Emperor—Marie Antoinette's nephew—and from the King of Prussia, a half-hearted promise. They would intervene if the other European monarchs concurred. Although this was vague it roused the deepest resentment in the French.

In September 1791, Louis was restored to his functions and took the oath of fealty to the new Constitution: "I swear to be faithful to the nation and to the law, to use the power which has been delegated to me to maintain the decreed constitution." That power was so diminished as to be virtually non-existent; Louis now held what authority he had from the nation, not by divine right, no longer King of France, but King of the French.

Now that the Constitution was framed, the Assembly changed its name to Legislative Assembly; it was to be composed of 745 members, elected on a restricted and indirect franchise. The King retained the power to dismiss ministers.

The freedom of the press led to the proliferation of newspapers; the freedom of speech resulted in the mushrooming of political clubs. Of these the most important—the one which was soon to lend its name to a whole party—held its meetings in an old monastery of the Jacobins, conveniently near the Riding School where the Legislative Assembly sat, and the lodging in the Rue St. Honoré of a prominent member, Maximilien de Robespierre. Its nearest rival was the Cordeliers, frequented by Jacques Danton, a lawyer, a great orator and rabble-rouser, but far more human than Robespierre; Camille Desmoulins, a very influential pamphleteer and journalist; and Marat, once a doctor, an evil and violent man.

The revolutionary theories originating in these clubs were disseminated by discussions in the cafés; Jacobin clubs were formed in the provinces and closely affiliated with the one in Paris. Even the world of fashion adopted the theme of revolution; one wore the *tricolore* red, white and blue, even on one's slippers; one adopted hairstyles called *aux charmes de la liberté* or *à la nation*. Kitchens were not exempt; plates were decorated with slogans, "Let us live free or die"; with crowing cocks announcing, "I watch for the nation"; with the traditional naked Cupid, renamed

"Love sans-culotte." Here is proof that revolutionary fervor was not confined to the "have-nots"; the really poor, the unemployed cannot, at whim, change their coiffures and their crockery.

With so much drama in real life, audiences fell away from the theatres. It was fashionable nowadays to attend the sessions of the Assembly to sit—sucking oranges and ices—and enjoy a pleasurable shudder as the deputies discussed the penalties to be imposed upon those *émigrés* who refused to return. It was exciting to watch the battle for supremacy between the Jacobins and the Girondists, the party that took its name from the area in the basin of the Gironde from which most of its members came. Of the two parties the Girondist was the more moderate. Most exciting of all was the declaration, in April 1792, of war on Austria. The ministry responsible for this move was headed by J. P. Brissot, and the fact that a journalist, son of an innkeeper, now held a post formerly occupied by dukes and cardinals, was a measure of the distance France had traveled in three years.

This decision to strike the first blow at the most threatening of enemies was made without due consideration of circumstance. The army was in a deplorable condition; the navy, once strong enough to challenge Britain's, even worse. Both had been officered by men of noble birth, most of whom had seen it as their duty to emigrate, to take what was called "the path of honor." They had taken their skill and their experience with them.

The vacant places were filled by volunteers who rushed from all quarters to the defense of their country. They were ignorant and untrained, but they brought boundless enthusiasm and an "invisible asset."

"The song that nerves a nation's heart is in itself a deed," Tennyson wrote. The men mustering for war in 1792 were the first to march to a new rhythm. Rouget de Lisle called his song, "The War Song of the Army of the Rhine." As the "Marseillaise," it was to be marched to by millions; later governments, frightened of its inflammatory effect, were to ban it; it lived on; it became so much a part of France that it is safe to say that when "*Allons, enfants de la patrie*," is heard no more the last Frenchman will be dead.

To Louis XVI, his brothers' attempt to rouse Europe to come

to his rescue had always been embarrassing. The limited power of veto restored to him when he took the oath to the Constitution did not extend to vetoing entry into a war upon which the whole nation was determined, nor was he able to interfere when the Assembly—fearing their subversive influence—decided to deport all the clergy who had refused to swear allegiance to the Civil Constitution. With only the clothes they wore and their breviaries, they were thrown out: many of them took refuge in Protestant England, where they were kindly received and charitably dealt with; they were Catholics, but they were also men who had put principle before all else.

This war went badly for the French; enthusiasm was no substitute for experience, competent logistics and discipline. When the French were defeated on the Belgian border they murdered not only their prisoners but also their general. In similar fashion, when news of the defeat reached Paris, the Jacobins turned upon the Girondists, and the populace turned upon the King.

At this point Louis' bad judgment and bad luck came into disastrous collision. It was proposed that a camp of 20,000 men should be established near Paris as defense against invasion. This was a matter upon which the King had the right of veto, and he exercised it. The people of Paris drew their own conclusion and stormed the Tuileries. They forced the red cap of liberty on his head; he remained imperturbable, and finally the people retired, baffled.

Then the Duke of Brunswick sent a message: Should the King be harmed, he would destroy Paris. A great cry, "*La patrie en danger*," went up, and once again the crowd closed in on the Tuileries. They massacred the loyal Swiss Guards and crowded in the royal apartments from which the King and Queen had just fled, vainly seeking shelter in the Assembly's hall. From there, with their two children and the King's sister, they were taken to genuine imprisonment in the Temple, to be kept under day and night surveillance by ruffianly guards, who delighted to subject them to every possible humiliation.

This violent reaction to a threat from outside had been led by the Jacobins; the Girondists went the way of all moderates in time of crisis; overnight thousands of formerly uncommitted citizens became Jacobins. The King was again suspended from all his functions; the Legislative Assembly was replaced by a National Convention, with all executive power concentrated in the hands of five men, of whom Danton as Minister of Justice was one. The Paris commune also fell into the hands of the extremists.

None of these changes affected the progress of the war; Longwy fell, and then Verdun. Lafayette and his staff went over to the Austrians, only to be imprisoned. The King of Prussia began his march upon Paris. Panic and its close accomplice, blood lust, induced mania in a city now crowded with *sans-culottes* and *fédérés* from country districts come to join the army.

In September came the massacres when the prisons holding "the enemies of the Revolution" were broken into. Many of the prisoners were non-juring priests who had failed to escape. Without pretense at trial, the prisoners were slaughtered mercilessly and rather less expeditiously than if they had been cattle. Among the days' victims was the beautiful, gentle Princess de Lamballe, who had voluntarily come back to France in order to be with her friend, the Queen. Her head, on a pike, was paraded under the windows of the Temple, and the crowd shouted that if Marie Antoinette would not come and look at it, they would force her to come down and kiss it.

None of this did anything to halt the enemy; that was left for Danton to attempt. He rallied the responsible element, the peasants and the middle class. "The tocsin which sounds is not a signal for alarm," he declared; "it is the sound of the charge against the country's enemies. To defeat them we need daring, more daring, always more daring and France will be saved."

Spurred by his energy and confidence, the ragged army, ill led and worse equipped, went out and won the Battle of Valmy; not a great battle in terms of men and material, but a decisive one. It made France feel that she was still strong, her citizen army a match for any other. The army pushed on to occupy Savoy, Nice and Mainz; it regained Longwy. By the end of October the threat of invasion was ended. In November, Dumouriez' victory at Jemappes opened the road to Belgium. At the end of the year, the Convention, intoxicated by success, invited all peoples to wage war against their kings and to embrace the principles of revolution.

That invitation showed a lack of statesmanship; it did nothing to help France and it did inspire in other governments a great distrust, conducive to war. It also injured the cause of reform by associating it with revolution; even so well-meaning a person as Queen Victoria could confuse the two at times.

The Convention had already abolished the monarchy and declared France a Republic, "one and indivisible." The King was there, though, alive in his prison, an anachronism and an embarrassing one. Could he be brought to trial? Upon what charges? A commission set to work to find answers to these questions, while the Convention gave its attention to lighter matters, such as the terminology suitable to a Republic. Forms of address such as *monsieur* and *madame* went the way of lordly titles; male citizens were to be *citoyens*, females *citoyennes*. There was to be a new calendar, with September 22 the year's beginning, and months named, poetically, for their salient seasonal feature, Vendémiaire, month of the vintage, for example. (Was this merely French, or the eighteenth century's feeling for beauty; one cannot help but feel that in a comparable revision nowadays the months would be given numbers.) The poet who named the months was later guillotined. The Convention also decreed, somewhat ambivalently, that all *émigrés* were to be perpetually banished and that any *émigré* caught with a weapon in his possession would be condemned to death; that roads and education should be improved and that the river Meuse should be open to all shipping.

The question of what to do with the harmless fat man now known as Louis Capet could not be shelved forever; it cropped up so often and led to such long and heated debates that eventually the Convention was obliged to impose a limit to the time spent on the subject. The Abbé Gregoire said, "Kings are in the moral order what monsters are in the physical. . . . The history of kings is the martyrology of nations." Young Antoine de Saint-Just, slim and elegant and, despite the fashionable slovenliness, still a dandy, said, "The King must be killed . . . for royalty is an eternal crime . . . the King must not have a long trial . . . he must be killed."

There were many such speeches, but the Convention hesitated. The French are, above all, a logical nation; and there must have been many who, pondering Saint-Just's speech, wondered whether a man born royal and therefore by inference born criminal, should be punished for his crime. In addition those in power had no means of knowing how the country as a whole felt; they feared a Royalist reaction. Brissot, whose short hour of glory had passed, said, "The whole history of our assemblies can be summed up in one word—that word is fear."

As in the case of Mary Stuart, incriminating documents, said to compromise Louis, were found. Robespierre, rapidly attaining ascendancy, said, "Louis cannot be judged because he is already condemned. . . . If he can still be made the cause of a trial he can be acquitted; but if Louis can be presumed innocent what will happen to the revolution?" A tricky, lawyer's question; if Louis were innocent why was he not at Versailles?

The trial began in December 1792. The King made a poor appearance; denied the use of a razor for three days he wore the beginning of a beard on cheeks that now sagged flabbily; his brown coat was shabby. Impartial observers noted that he had not lost his dignity; there still clung about him the ghost, the vanishing shadow of royalty. He had been allowed counsel to defend him . . . but against what? For being born to the throne? Being passive? Being stupid? When the prosecution declared "Louis, the French nation is your accuser," the impersonal nature of the trial was revealed; it was not Louis who was on trial, it was the system of monarchy.

Louis had been reading an account of the trial of Charles I of England—so had many other people, copies were on sale in the lobbies outside the hall in which the trial was held. Had he compared his case with that of the small, intransigent Stuart who had *not* been passive and lethargic and had brought about a civil war?

Outside, in the streets, there were Royalist demonstrations. People sang of another King who, abandoned by all but the faithful, had yet been saved. But there was no rallying point for this emotional force, nobody came forward to save *this* King.

In the Convention one member said, "I am tired of my part of despotism—tormented by the tyranny I am forced to exercise . . ." But Robespierre was there, ready to quell any protest, to stiffen any weakening will.

The verdict was guilty of conspiracy against the national safety. Then for three days the penalty was debated; should Louis be imprisoned, kept in irons or without? Should he be banished? Should he be killed? Tom Paine, the English author of *The Rights of Man*, who, banished from his own country, had come to France and now sat as deputy for the Pas de Calais, voted for imprisonment; but Robespierre was for death, Danton too, and Camille Desmoulins and Marat. *La mort sans phrases*. There was one vote for death which even to the extremists seemed shocking—that of Louis' cousin, the *ci-devant* Duc d'Orléans, and now known as Philippe Egalité.

Louis went to the guillotine on January 21, 1793. He made an attempt to address the crowd, "Frenchmen, I die innocent. I pardon the authors of my death. I pray God that the blood about to be spilt will never fall upon the head of France. . . ." Somebody signaled to the drums to resume playing and the rest of his words were drowned. When his head fell, Sanson the executioner lifted it by the hair and displayed it to the crowd.

For a time Marie Antoinette—far more virulently hated—remained in the Temple with her children and Madame Elisabeth, the King's sister; then she was removed to the Conciergerie prison and finally, after a trial that reads like an exercise in pornography rather than of justice, sent to the guillotine. Madame Elisabeth followed her. The little Dauphin was taken away to be taught to revile the parents he had loved, to swear drunken oaths, to become a travesty of a child and then, in 1795, to disappear. The truth about his fate was never known. Certainly a child did die of disease and ill-treatment, but some people believed that this was not the Dauphin; years later there were rumors of his survival. Of a happy family only one survivor is certain, Marie-Thérèse, Madame Royale, who remained a prisoner in the Temple.

The courts of Europe, stunned and horrified, wore mourning for Louis XVI, but their mood soon changed to alarm. In February 1793, France declared war on England and Holland, then on

Spain, thus collecting a formidable coalition of enemies. In March, Dumouriez, once the hero of France, suffered a defeat in the Netherlands and went over to the enemy, taking with him a young general of his staff, Louis Philippe, son of the regicide Philippe Egalité.

Louis XVI's last expressed hope—that his blood should not fall on France—was not fulfilled. His death, so far from bringing internal peace, fomented civil war. In the west the Catholic and Royalist Vendée rose "For God and the King." After a war, bloody and cruel on both sides, the Vendéens suffered defeat, followed by savage reprisals which did little to reconcile them to the Republic. In the south the great cities of Marseilles, Bordeaux and Lyons rose in a revolt inspired by the Girondists. In Paris a young girl from Normandy, Charlotte Corday, plunged a knife into Marat's heart as he lay in a bath, soaking his stinking sores.

And nothing so far, not the death of a king, war within and without or political upheavals, had solved the everyday problem of finding food to eat. In Paris the bread riots continued and the Convention was forced to fix the maximum price for a loaf.

Things were obviously not shaping as they should. Was this because there were traitors at work? If so they must be sniffed out. "We must establish the despotism of liberty in order to crush the despotism of kings." To conduct this witch hunt the Convention appointed a Committee of Public Safety and endowed it with practically unlimited power. On the slightest suspicion of being unsympathetic to the régime, or on no suspicion at all, on an enemy's whisper, a man could be arrested, given a travesty of a trial and sent to the guillotine. This was the time of the Terror.

The Terror was not the Revolution, though it is the part upon which popular attention has been focused through literature. It lasted only thirteen months and, by the sorry arithmetical standards of the twentieth century, the number of its victims seem few; but the eighteenth century was still capable of being shocked by mass slaughter. The daily procession to the guillotine, of the tumbrils bearing moderates, aristocrats, extremists, bourgeoisie, humble people, young and old, innocent and guilty, made such an impression of horror upon the watching world that the echo of the emotion has reverberated down the years. It is possible that the excesses of this period will be remembered when Belsen is forgotten.

The Girondists, who had dominated the Assembly in 1792, now regarded as lukewarm in the cause, went to the guillotine; so did Philippe Egalité who had once thought to be King of France and had voted for his cousin's death. Even Danton, who had rallied the country to repel the invader and inspired the army to its first victory, was sent to his death; he had reacted against the ruthlessness of the Committee of Public Safety; and he stood between Robespierre and absolute power. Before he knelt to be beheaded, Danton said to the executioner, "Show my head to the people; it is worth it."

A tiger, once loosed, is as likely to savage its trainer as the bystander; in the end the guillotine claimed even Robespierre. As he had served Danton, Fouché and Barras served him. Was he "mortal, angel or demon?" Early in his career Mirabeau had said of him, "He will go far because he believes what he says." In the house where he lived he was regarded as a model lodger. He wears in history a tag, "the sea-green incorruptible," because of his aquamarine colored coats and his moralistic tendencies. He died more slowly and horribly than most of his victims, shot through the jaw some hours before he went to the guillotine, and obliged to suffer the taunts of those who only yesterday had feared him. One of these, knowing Robespierre as an atheist, looked down on him where he lay and said, "Yes, Robespierre, there is a God."

The Convention went on with its work; the plan for a new Constitution, published in 1793, shows significant trends; a hint of direct, universal suffrage and the process of the referendum, but such things must be deferred "until the peace." The war took precedence of all. Every able-bodied man between the ages of eighteen and twenty-five was now conscripted, and new methods of strategy were evolved. Lazare Carnot, by his energy and enterprise earned for himself the title, "Organizer of Victory."

Victory, though it can be planned for, cannot be assured at long range; always something depends upon the man on the spot.

Such a man, in December 1793, drove the English out of Toulon where they had established themselves. He was an artillery officer of whom his commanding officer wrote, after the action, "This young officer deserves careful attention for, whatever line he adopts, he is destined to throw a great weight into the balance." Hindsight so often has an ironic eye. *Whatever line he adopts!* The name of the young officer was Napoleon Bonaparte.

In addition to waging war, the Convention showed prodigious energy in social and civil affairs, creating institutions which survive to this day; the Institute of France, the Ecole Polytechnique for the training of officers and mathematicians; the Ecole Normale for teachers and professors; the Schools of Mines, Public Works, Arts and Crafts, Oriental Languages, the Conservatoire of Music. These, with the introduction of the decimal system, free compulsory primary education, the abolition of slavery and the freedom of black citizens as well as white, are part of the legacy of the Convention to the world. For these ideas were carried, first by the French soldiers and then by the written word, throughout the length and breadth of Europe; every modern state owes something to them. It may not be too fanciful to suggest that Russia, which most firmly repelled the invaders and most sternly repudiated the new French theories, paid in the end for the delay.

Through the war and through the innovations, ordinary life went on. Looking back one tends to think of the Revolution, especially under the Terror, as a time of chaos. But people were born, married, avoided trouble as best they could, pursued their ordinary lives and died. The diary of a governess to a middle-class family records birthday parties and happy family outings at the very time when people in Paris were requesting the removal of the guillotine because of the stench of stale blood. (Cattle, being driven in to their own place of slaughter, would not cross the blood-soaked square.) The one thing that few could ignore was the steady rise in prices, due in part to the fact that the peasant, the real producer, tended in the face of inflation to hoard his surplus. A liter of olive oil priced in 1790 at 1.8 livres, sold in 1795 for 62. The city of Lyons was once, for five days, entirely without bread of any kind.

In another sphere there was also a dearth. The revolutionary years produced no drama, no belles-lettres, no work of criticism or of history of any importance. It was as though the whole creative impulse had been expended in the Revolution itself. Presently, in 1797, Chateaubriand was to publish his *Essay on Revolutions*, but at this period he was an *émigré* in England, scribbling away to earn enough to keep body and soul together, as other *émigrés* taught dancing and penmanship, or made straw hats. (Madame Tussaud was an *émigrée*, a maker of wax death masks.) One poet, a lyricist, was at work at this time; his name was André Chénier, and at the age of thirty-two he went to the guillotine; the bulk of his work was not published until long after his death.

What the revolutionary period was rich in was journalism and oratory, both fleeting things. Today's newspaper wraps tomorrow's fish; and without any recording device oratory is lost; fancy alone can recall the impact of speeches by Mirabeau, Robespierre and Danton.

Other arts suffered the same eclipse; the court, the wealthy, had been patrons of the arts; now they were gone, and what artist or sculptor could give of his best with a *sans-culotte* looking over his shoulder, avid to spot, or to imagine some anti-revolutionary tendency? When painting finally revived it did so in the person of Jacques-Louis David, who was a member of the Convention. He sketched Marie Antoinette on her way to the guillotine, her hair shorn, an old woman at thirty-eight. This drawing, in terrible contrast to portraits—Vigée le Brun's, for example, all silk and laces—must have been acceptable to the most rabid anti-Royalist. But there is a theory that any work of genius contains something not consciously intended, and by that measure David's sketch is a work of genius; for this woman, stripped of everything, even her love for her son made the basis of suggestions of the utmost obscenity, still has dignity.

The Republic, newborn and with nothing in the immediate past to lean upon, looked back to the ancient models of Greco-Roman classicism and adopted their styles of dress, named their children Aristide, Leonidas, Gracchus. With the fall of Robespierre and the end of the Terror, there came a great upsurge of pleasure-seeking; 300 dance halls and 32 theatres flourished in Paris. At the popular *bals à la victime* the relatives of those who had been guillotined wore crape on their arms and a thin scarlet ribbon about their necks. When the salon—that unique French institution where the cultured met for discussion—revived, the talk was more frivolous and less intellectual than in pre-Revolutionary days.

In the Year III by the new calendar the Convention drew up a new constitution which provided for the division of the legislature into two houses, the lower the Council of Five Hundred, the upper the Council of Ancients. They hoped to make it impossible for one man ever to gain such ascendancy as Robespierre had held over the single Assembly. The members were to be elected by property holders—a far cry from the universal suffrage visualized in 1793; two thirds of the members of the new houses must be chosen from men already sitting on the Convention. Executive power was entrusted to five Directors to be chosen by the two houses. The preamble to the new constitution reiterated the Rights of Man, but admitted that a man had duties as well as rights, "No one is a good citizen who is not a good son, a good friend, a good husband." This sentence showed that the Convention was alive to the deterioration of family life which had followed the legislation permitting civil marriage and divorce. One year in Paris alone there were 6000 divorces, and the foundling homes were full.

The populace did not take kindly to the self-perpetuating clause in the Convention's proposal; they wanted a real change of government. Hunger and unemployment remained; an artisan was actually worse off than he had been in 1789. Immediately after Robespierre's death the law regarding the maximum price of bread had been abolished; the cost of living still soared. With an ironic *volte-face* the mood of the people changed and became Royalist in feeling. Riots began again, and a full-scale uprising threatened.

It fell to Barras—a former noble and a member of the Convention who had played his part both in the Terror and in the fall of Robespierre—to deal with this situation. He remembered a young soldier whom he had met in Toulon, who was now attached to the Topographical Bureau of the Ministry of War. His name had been suggested for the Army of Italy and again for the Vendée, where revolt still smoldered. Neither appointment had actually been made, and the young officer, restless from ambition, was seriously thinking of going to Turkey where the Sultan welcomed such as he. However, he was still in Paris when Barras remembered him.

In appearance Napoleon Bonaparte was not impressive; his hair, ill-combed and badly powdered, hung lankly to his shoulders; his face was thin and yellowish in complexion; his boots were clumsy and unpolished, his coat so threadbare that the seams showed white. But there was something arresting and memorable about his expression, an intensity and magnetism in his gaze. He was twenty-six when on the 13 Vendémiaire—October 5, 1795—he moved against the rioters, and, backed by a troop of cavalry under Captain Murat, loosed the "whiff of grapeshot." The insurrection collapsed; the Directory was saved. For Napoleon reward was swift and sure; first the command of the Army of the Interior, then of the Army of Italy. For him the days of penury and obscurity were over.

France was still at war. Belgium had been conquered, so had Holland and Luxembourg. Peace had been made with Prussia, Holland and Spain. England, though beaten on land, had been successful at sea and now had Russia and Austria, whose empire extended into Italy, for allies. The war there dragged on; 30,000 hungry, ragged men in the army were better, from the government's point of view, than a similar number unemployed and hungry at home; the blockade imposed by the English was a more acceptable excuse for shortages than political ineptitude, and war served its familiar function of distracting attention from domestic ills. The conquest of Italy was an old dream of the French, and the liberation of conquered provinces from their oppressor was an aim entirely in keeping with the ideals of the Revolution.

Before he left to join the famished, near-mutinous Army of Italy, Bonaparte took two days off in order to get married. He had fallen in love with Josephine de Beauharnais, whom the guillotine had widowed. She was a Creole from Martinique, where her family owned a plantation. (An old fortuneteller there had told her that she would wear a crown, and predicted for one of her cousins a fate equally dramatic and in the circumstances unlikely. Both predictions were completely justified by events.) Josephine was no longer very young; her children, Eugène and Hortense, were in their teens, but she had—and would retain all her life—a grace and a charm of manner that had nothing to do with age or even with beauty. She was not in love with Napoleon when she married him; she thought him "a funny little man," but she needed a husband to pay her debts and to rehabilitate her reputation —she had been Barras' mistress. Bonaparte needed a wife because he was young and, like all his family, highly sexed, but he married Josephine because he loved her. She was the great and abiding passion of his life.

By the time that Bonaparte set out for Italy the Directory was firmly established, with Barras as paramount Director. The Royalist revival had been quelled by prompt action, and the heart had been taken out of the movement by the reported death of the little boy who would have been Louis XVII. This left the Comte de Provence as heir, and who but the most rabid ultra-Royalist would wish to see him on the throne? From exile in Verona he had issued a declaration of great political ineptitude, outlining his plans should he be restored; he would bring back the old régime; he would punish everyone who had served the Revolution, he would—this perhaps most alarming of all—take away from the multitude of small men who had bought them, all the lands that had formerly belonged to the Church and to the aristocracy.

The Directory was established, but it had troubles to face. It embarked upon a deflationary policy which inflicted even more hardship upon the poor and emphasized the difference between them and the *nouveaux riches,* a growing class of shrewd or fortunate men who had profited by the changes. An ex-Jacobin, François Babeuf, formed a Society of Equals, based on the doctrine that every man had an equal right to a share in all property. He was arrested and guillotined, but amongst the underprivileged his teaching was remembered and formed the core of revolutionary socialism in days to come. Ordinary decent people were disgusted by the corruption of the Directory, Barras himself was a notably immoral man; every instance of scandalous behaviour was eagerly remarked, on the one side by the die-hard Royalists, on the other by ex-Jacobins. In 1796 it was found necessary to establish a Ministry of Police for the special purpose of muzzling public opinion: but no amount of police supervision could prevent prices from rising, unemployment from spreading or dissatisfaction from increasing.

However, in Italy the war went well. In his opening address to the soldiers Bonaparte told them that he realized how hungry and ill-clad they were, and that he proposed to lead them into the richest plains in the world. His confidence and his special ability to handle men put new spirit into them. Victory followed victory; Dego, Mondovi, Lodi—where he laid the guns with his own hands—then Castiglione, Arcola and Rivoli. Bonaparte made a triumphal procession through Milan. He had, as he wrote to his brother Joseph, "acquired more glory than is necessary for happiness."

What was necessary for his happiness was that his wife should join him and share the glory. Throughout the arduous campaign he had written to her almost every evening, passionate, touching love-letters. Finally, reluctantly, she came, and met his suspicious and critical family who hated her before they saw her and, confronted by her, refused to be charmed. They were Corsican and, by their standards, a woman was to be judged by her potential fertility; Josephine was too old, and soft and frivolous as well.

Austria now feared that the French might push on toward Vienna, and proposed a peace; Bonaparte, on his own initiative, signed the Peace of Campo Formio which left Venice to Austria but established two new republics, the Cisalpine and the Ligurian.

Bonaparte's promise of rich loot awaiting had been fulfilled; for months, wagons, heavily laden with treasure, had been lumbering toward Paris; the core of the Louvre collection was acquired in this way. Now, with the peace signed, Bonaparte could follow, traveling more swiftly.

At home affairs were still troubled. After the Jacobin Babeuf had come a Royalist attempt at a *coup d'état* in Fructidor (September) 1797. Success, with the Councils holding a Royalist majority, seemed assured but the army's intervention, bloodless

on this occasion, was decisive. The conspiring Directors were allowed to escape but some members of the Councils were sent to
French Guiana, the "dry guillotine." The Directory survived, but
two further attempts to overthrow it made its weakness all too
apparent. Would it be able to maintain itself?

Chapter 2. THE CONSULATE AND THE EMPIRE

The Directors were well aware of the danger to themselves of having, in Paris, a national hero whose popularity was growing. They decided to appoint him to the command of the army which was to invade England. The peace of Campo Formio had robbed England of an ally, but it had not ended the war. Bonaparte accepted his new post reluctantly; he believed that "the real moment for preparing for this invasion has passed, perhaps forever." He and Talleyrand hatched between them the alternative plan of striking at England through her possessions in the Far East. Talleyrand knew England; he had lived there first as an unofficial representative of the Constituent Assembly, later, after the September massacres, as an *émigré*. With the outbreak of war he had gone to America where he stayed for two and a half years. At the end of that time his friends at home had managed to get his name removed from the list of the proscribed. After this long period in the shadows he was Foreign Minister—a post he was soon to resign when his uncanny political foresight warned him that the day of the Directory was done.

The East had always held a special lure for Bonaparte, and the prospect of conquering Egypt and using it as a jumping off place for India was far more attractive than invading England or staying in France, where, as he said to Bourrienne, his secretary, "There is nothing to be done. I can see that if I remain here I shall soon be finished."

He set out for Egypt in May 1798. With him he took scientists and archaeologists capable of studying the ancient land, writers and artists to make records of the discoveries. He was alive to the fascination of the past. (His remark to his army before the Battle of the Pyramids—"Soldiers, forty centuries are watching you," is now said to be apocryphal. Perhaps he *thought* it.) The Turks then in control of Egypt were defeated in this battle; but Nelson at

the Battle of the Nile destroyed the French fleet and left the
army cut off from supplies—and from news. Bonaparte took advantage of the free hand given him by the Directory and, in
emulation of Alexander the Great, set off on the land route for
India. The old fortresses of Gaza and Jaffa fell to him but Acre,
held by Sir Sydney Smith, resisted. Bonaparte returned to Egypt
and won the Battle of Aboukir. Then, from papers sent him by
the English, he learned the latest news from France and knew
that the time had come for his return: the Directory was again
in trouble.

In this decision there was a personal element, too. From his
family he learned that in Paris Josephine was flaunting a love
affair. This was not to be taken lightly by a man who, for all his
father's pretensions to gentility, was at heart a *petit bourgeois*, a
man with Corsican views about wifely fidelity, a man who
genuinely loved his wife. The knowledge of Josephine's faithless-
ness had a psychological effect upon him, the results of which were
felt by France and the world. He wrote to his brother Joseph
that nothing remained but to become completely selfish. In future
head would rule heart.

He slipped away with only a few companions, Berthier his indispensable chief of staff, Generals Lannes, Marmont and Murat—
Murat still hoped, despite Bonaparte's opposition to the match,
to become his brother-in-law—and the academicians. As they
avoided the English frigates and landed at Fréjus, Napoleon
was planning to divorce his wife, but face to face with her he fell
victim to the old magic. He forgave her, but he never fully trusted
her again.

The Directory, threatened by plots from Royalists and from
left-wing extremists, now faced the danger which had brought the
monarchy down—bankruptcy. It had inherited some acute financial problems, foremost a top-heavy military expenditure. It was
saddled with the cost of protecting three Italian republics, two in
the north and one in the south, but this protection had been ineffec-
tive. In the spring of 1799 French armies were thrown back in
Italy. There was an Anglo-Russian invasion of Holland. Money
was needed to continue the war but the collection of taxes fell

short of estimate. Revolutions do not lend themselves to stable finance. An attempt to enforce a capital levy failed; the Frenchman can be as stubborn in defense of his money as in defense of his country. Economically France was at a standstill, with only the profiteers busy exploiting the situation. By the time the Directory decided upon a forced loan it was already too late. It was 17 Brumaire, the month of mist, and ever since his arrival in Paris on the 24 Vendémiaire, month of vintage, the General had been busy, intent this time not to save but to overthrow the Directory.

Publicly, dressed in civilian clothes, he made a parade of his civilian interests; he addressed the Institute not on the subject of battles in Egypt but on the possibilities of cutting a Suez canal and other scientific matters. In private there was much questionable activity, accomplices to be sounded out, a pretext found for destroying the government, plans made for another, this time successful, *coup d'état*.

On the 18 Brumaire, in an address to the troops, he leveled an angry accusation: "What have you done with the France that I left you so brilliant? I gave you peace and I find war. I gave you victories and I find only defeats. I gave you all the riches of Italy. I find laws of spoliation and poverty. What have you done with the hundreds of thousands of Frenchmen who were my friends and shared my glory? They are dead."

A letter of resignation from his Directorship was placed before Barras and he was asked, politely but firmly, to sign. There is some evidence that he was bribed as well as coerced; he signed and left for his country estate.

Next day, at St. Cloud, where the two houses had been persuaded to go because of a suspected Jacobin plot, it was literally a matter of touch and go. Cries of "Down with the dictator" and "Outlaw him!" and references to Caesar and Cromwell unnerved Bonaparte who made a wild and incoherent speech. But his brother Lucien was there, President of the Five Hundred, and so was Murat who, with his grenadiers, came in to clear the hall at the President's command. The deputies in their Republican togas, "rushed for the doors, leapt out of the windows, and swiftly scattering through the gloom of the trees and bushes were lost to view and to history."*

Now it was for Bonaparte to regenerate France as he had regenerated the Army of Italy.

The Abbé Sieyès, an experienced constitution-maker, had ready a new form of government, based on classical pattern; but his suggestion of placing power equally in the hands of three Consuls was brushed aside by Bonaparte who proposed instead a First Consul, himself, and a Second and Third, Cambacérès and Lebrun, both able jurists. The consuls were to nominate ministers and a Council of State which would initiate legislation. This body was to be supplemented by a Tribunate and a Legislative Assembly, which alone would have the power to vote taxes.

Despite the First Consul's personal popularity, these administrative shufflings were regarded by the common man with apathy or skepticism. There had been so many changes and so little real difference in the last ten years.

France was now in the hands of one who, being a man, had human faults and failings, but was possessed of that something more which is genius. He saw that what France needed above all was unity and, by placing himself above all parties, he was able to offer a point of reconciliation between the warring factors. France also needed order and efficiency and these he gave her. One, most concrete, example is the way in which he dealt with the taxes. The Bourbons had employed 200,000 tax collectors, he employed 6000, who collected twice as much revenue though farmers paid only a quarter of what they had done in 1789. He founded the Bank of France. He put into practice theories of education, long given lip service but never yet applied. Everyone must go to school and everyone must study science and mathematics as well as the "humanities." School hours began and ended to the sounding of a drum, and a military precision governed the timetable; in the grammar schools where Latin was taught the same page was being studied by children of comparable ability at the same time, on the same day, throughout the whole of France.

The energy of a man capable of working eighteen hours a day, with meals snatched in a matter of minutes, infused everything. A

* H. A. L. Fisher, *Napoleon.*

commission of lawyers tackled the chaos of the legal system and evolved the Code Napoléon, effective to this day. Amnesty was granted to the *émigrés*, priests were favorably treated. Even such matters as manners and morals were not overlooked.

These had so far declined in the last ten years that theatres in poorer quarters had been obliged to post notices asking clients, *de ne pas faire vos ordures dans les loges*. Under Barras, himself corrupt, a man in Paris had been able, without incurring censure, to marry the niece of a wealthy woman, divorce the girl, marry the aunt, who was eighty-two, and, when she died, remarry the niece. Such latitude did not appeal to the First Consul, nor did the fashionable immodesty in women's dress. The notorious ladies of the Directory, such as Madame Tallien, were not admitted to the salon of Madame Bonaparte, whose own lapse from virtue was forgotten, and whose company was much sought.

In all the business of reorganization Bonaparte had the assistance of able men. Talleyrand remained at the Foreign Office; Gaudin, a gifted financier had charge of Finance, Carnot, "organizer of victory" was Minister of War. The Ministry of Police was presided over by Joseph Fouché, ex-priest and regicide, supple-minded, more humanitarian than any other Minister of Police, but a man almost totally lacking in scruple. Fouché could be relied upon to sniff out any opposition amongst the jealous or the ambitious or—rarer men—those like Carnot who were ideologically against the rule of the one "strong man." And Fouché's watchfulness was necessary, because events did not allow Bonaparte to forget that he was a soldier first of all.

The year 1799 brought defeat for the French army in Italy where war had broken out, and Bonaparte decided to go campaigning again; in May 1800, he crossed the Alps by the Great St. Bernard Pass, reoccupied Milan, re-established the Cisalpine Republic, retook Genoa and in June won a great victory over the Austrians at Marengo. He did not linger in Italy; by July he was back in the Tuileries; in his own words, "It is not enough to be in the Tuileries; one must stay there." And for fifteen years, from the old palace of the Kings of France, the Corsican general continued his work of remaking a nation.

The army had faith in its "little corporal," the workers believed

in the man who had set industry moving, the peasant approved of
the administrator who had guaranteed his holding. With these behind him he could push on with public works, canals and roads,
and the beautification of Paris, which he meant to make the envy
of the world.

There were those who did not accept him; liberal elements who,
though they had helped with the *coup d'état* that had brought him
to power, were dissatisfied with the result, and Royalists so naïve
that they thought General Bonaparte might play the same part in a
Bourbon Restoration as General Monck had done in putting a
Stuart back on to the English throne in 1660. Had these optimists
ever looked at the man? How could that intense, brooding stare
ever have regarded any future but his own?

Such encouraging reports reached Louis XVIII that he wrote
a personal letter to the First Consul. He said that, as a Frenchman, he had great esteem for Bonaparte; he said that he was sure
that the victor of Lodi, Castiglione and Arcola, the conqueror of
Italy and Egypt, would not prefer an empty celebrity to the true
glory. He suggested that together Bonaparte and Louis XVIII
could ensure glory for France.

He may even have been right; Louis had learned a good deal
since he issued his declaration from Verona, but he had not yet
learned that there are men born not to be partners in any enterprise.
Even Talleyrand, shrewd as he was, hoped that direct relationship
between Bonaparte and Bourbon might lead to something, though
at this point he suggested giving Louis a throne other than that
of France.

Napoleon felt confident that he could ensure the glory of
France with no help from anyone; he wrote to Louis bluntly,

"You must give up any hope of returning to France; you would
have to pass over a hundred thousand dead bodies. Sacrifice your
private interests to the peace and happiness of France. . . . History will not forget."

He added that he would do what he could to make Louis' retirement "pleasant and undisturbed." He proposed to allow him a
pension.

The Royalist response to this rebuff was swift and dramatic—
though not the work of Louis XVIII. The First Consul, his wife,

his sister Caroline, now married to Murat, and Hortense, his step-daughter, were on their way to the Opera, in December 1800, when a keg of gunpowder exploded under the carriages as they reached the Rue St. Nicaise. Bystanders were killed and injured: the Consular party was unhurt and next day, when General Bonaparte held a review at the Tuileries, people showed, by the reception they gave him, that France had no wish to lose her idol.

This attempt at assassination was followed by executions and deportations, but some Royalist feeling survived, with the under-lying question, if Bonaparte could be eliminated who but Louis XVIII could replace him? Already men were beginning to think in term of personalities. The Royalists continued to plot ineffec-tually against a man who day by day, by his achievements, settled more firmly in the saddle, and in the esteem of France as a whole.

By 1802 he could give the country what it most wanted—peace. In that year the Treaty of Amiens ended the struggle with England as the Treaty of Lunéville in 1801 had ended that with Austria.

The immediate result was a great influx of visitors. To men of culture at that time France was a second home, from which the Revolution and the war had exiled them. Now they came back, to visit the country they loved and to see the treasures of art which had been collected at the Louvre; to see, if they were lucky, the man who had not only made himself master of France but had become identified with her.

One of these was the Englishman, Charles James Fox, now perhaps more remembered as a liberal statesman and a heavy gam-bler than as a judge of character. Fox saw Napoleon as "a young man a good deal intoxicated with his success and surprising eleva-tion." The remark showed an unusual percipience; few other peo-ple saw the First Consul as a man not yet fully assured that the high destiny of his romantic dreams was fact. As with all who cherish inordinate ambition, Napoleon had known his moments of despair. His youth had been penurious, full of strain, cheered only by the thought of what the future *might* hold; now that possibility was translated into actuality small wonder that he was intoxicated and surprised. Napoleon thought Fox "an ornament to humanity."

Even in the midst of his elation it was impossible for Napoleon to ignore the fact that all was not yet wholly well. Egypt, once conquered, was lost again; Nelson had won the Battle of Copenhagen, and in France itself religious discord militated against the longed-for unity. France was still at heart a Catholic country. The Revolution had been anticlerical: a pretty prostitute had been enthroned at Notre Dame as the Goddess of Reason. But, as the Jews in ancient days had found in the golden calf no permanent substitute for Jehovah, so the French found in the Goddess of Reason no real substitute for the power and majesty and ritual of the Holy Catholic Church, the one institution which had survived the breakup of Rome and the Dark Ages which had followed.

Some part of Bonaparte's success was due to his ability to understand and up to a point to share the feelings of the ordinary man; he knew how people felt about their religion; he also saw that the Church stood for the order and discipline which to him were desirable. He, therefore, made a Concordat with the Pope. The Catholic Church was re-established and Catholicism acknowledged to be the creed of the majority, though minorities were not to be robbed of their freedom to worship as they wished. The Pope agreed to recognize those clergy who had taken the oath to the Civil Constitution and did not insist upon the condition which would have brought all compromise to nothing—the return of the ecclesiastical property, now in the hands of land-hungry peasants or profit-seeking speculators.

There were those who grumbled at the Concordat, Gallicans like Talleyrand, anticlericals like Fouché, but the general feeling of the nation was summed up in the words of the Archbishop from the pulpit of Notre Dame who said, after the singing of a Te Deum, that this was an occasion which "reconciles France with Europe and Europe with herself."

Bonaparte showed a desire to be recognized by a wider world where no reconciliation was needed. When George Washington died he put the whole French army into mourning and issued an Order of the Day:

"Washington is dead. This great man combated tyranny. He consolidated his country's liberty. His memory will always be dear to the French people as well as to all the free men in the two hemispheres, and especially to the French soldiers who, like him and his American troops, are fighting for liberty and equality."

Later that year France made a treaty of friendship—in force to this day—with the United States; the preamble runs:

"There shall be a firm, inviolable and universal peace and a true and sincere friendship between the French Republic and the United States of America."

In 1803 America bought from France, for $15 million, the province which the French had colonized, named Louisiana after Louis XIV, lost to Spain and then regained.

Open cordiality toward America, which was still regarded by many English people as a rebel colony, was not calculated to sweeten relationships between France and her old enemy, and Bonaparte knew that permanent peace was unlikely while France held all the best ports between Genoa and Rotterdam. The Peace of Amiens was a lull which gave him time to deal with internal affairs and to improve his fleet. It also returned to France some of her island possessions in the West Indies. In one of these, San Domingo, a slave rebellion had broken out and had been successful. In 1801, while the treaty was being negotiated, the world saw an ironic situation; the self-appointed liberators of all oppressed people sent an expedition to the island to put down the oppressed who had managed to liberate themselves there.

General Leclerc, the husband of Bonaparte's favorite sister, Pauline, was in command of the expedition which encountered an enemy more deadly than the ex-slaves. Yellow fever decimated the army and widowed Pauline. When news of Leclerc's death reached Paris the First Consul ordered ten days' mourning for his brother-in-law. It was the exact period recognized as a time of mourning for members of *royal* families.

This indication of the direction in which Bonaparte's thoughts were turning was amplified by his approach to Louis XVIII, urging him to renounce his claim to the throne, "freely, entirely, absolutely." He pointed out, with brutal frankness, that the nation had an invincible repugnance to government by a Bourbon prince, that the present government of France based its rights on public law and that a renunciation would calm both *émigrés* and Catholics and block at the source England's threat of aggression. To this he added that he was not the maker of the Revolution but the product of it, that he had not destituted the Bourbons, on the contrary he had avenged the throne. He repeated his offer to provide for the Bourbon family.

Louis XVIII's reply showed that he had acquired some political acumen since he had issued his declaration from Verona. He expressed his esteem for Bonaparte's military talents and his gratitude for such of his administrative acts as had benefited Louis' dear people: but he made the subtle point that "Bonaparte makes a mistake if he believes that he can invite me to give up my rights. Rather does he himself underline them."

This repulse and a new Royalist plot decided Bonaparte to deal once and for all with the underground monarchists. The leader of the plot, Georges Cadoudal, was executed; General Pichegru avoided this fate by committing suicide; Moreau, too formidable a general to be shot, was allowed to escape into exile.

Bonaparte then committed the crime that has been denounced as a blunder. The young Duc d'Enghien, the last of the brilliant family of Condé, which had rendered such great service to France, was kidnaped from just across the frontier, brought to Paris, accused of plotting against the First Consul, given a summary trial and shot. There was no proof that he had been involved in the plot. In the horrified courts of Europe his death was regarded as murder, and hostility toward Bonaparte stiffened. On May 18, 1803, war again broke out between France and England. Neither side had observed the conditions of the Treaty of Amiens; England had not evacuated Malta, France had not evacuated Holland, and she had seized Piedmont.

Despite his remark made five years earlier about the time for an invasion being already past, Bonaparte now assembled a flotilla of flat-bottomed boats at Boulogne. This threat to invade, whether real or a feint, was taken seriously by the English; for years afterward naughty children were told, "Old Boney will get you." The invasion never took place; but on May 18, 1804, exactly a year from the declaration of war, an invasion of another character occurred and the Bonapartes moved into the narrow circles of royal families in Europe.

Of the throne Napoleon had said scornfully that it was "a plank covered with velvet," but he had progressed toward it steadily. A change of title could not enhance his power; he had already been made First Consul for life, with the right to choose his successor, he already had almost complete control of the three legislative bodies. But Napoleon understood the French people and realized that they would welcome some symbol of grandeur and glory, something decorative to fill the vacuum which the fall of the monarchy had left at the top of the social structure. Also—though as yet he had no heir—there was something stabilizing about the hereditary system, more stabilizing than the process of naming one's successor.

The Senate went in a body to St. Cloud to proclaim Napoleon Bonaparte Emperor of the French. The new constitution of the Year XII used a quaint and incongruous formula; "The government of the republic is vested in an Emperor." All authority was his because by the will of God—but not by divine right—he was the sole representative of the sovereign people. The other clauses of the constitution followed that of the Year X, with the powers of the Senate slightly extended at the expense of those of the Tribunate.

Louis XVIII sent a letter of protest to all the sovereigns of Europe who could do nothing except hope that they might defeat the new Emperor in battle; a recent coalition had already brought Russia and Austria into the war.

Napoleon now faced a personal problem; his was a barren marriage. Should it remain so, the constitution gave him the right to choose his heir from his brothers' sons, and the choice was narrow. Joseph had two daughters and seemed unlikely to have other children; both Lucien and Jerome had made marriages of which Napoleon disapproved. But Louis had married Josephine's daughter Hortense, and though miserably unhappy, that marriage had produced sons. Napoleon was fond of his stepdaughter and she of him; in fact her fondness and sympathy, and her brother Eugène's staunch fidelity, tell us something about Napoleon himself, and are in pleasant contrast to the tiresome, jealous, bickering behavior of his blood kin.

Josephine had done her best to provide an heir; she made repeated visits to Plombières to drink the waters that were supposedly a cure for sterility. She was by this time genuinely in love with the man whom she had married as an expedient, and longed to bear him a son. Her failure to do so created a nagging sense of frustration under all the splendor of her new state. The Pope himself came to Paris to place the crown on Napoleon's head, and Napoleon had then crowned Josephine. At the ceremony his sisters Elisa, Pauline and Caroline, now all Imperial Highnesses, had so resented being obliged to carry her train that they did it clumsily and almost pulled her over backward. Theirs was not the only jealousy present; Murat was not alone in thinking that the crown would have looked equally well on his head.

In May 1805, Napoleon was crowned again, in Milan Cathedral as King of Italy; he then turned his attention to the defeat of Austria and in a series of victories occupied Augsburg, Munich and Salzburg, and, after the victories of Elchingen and Ulm, Vienna itself. Then in December came the Battle of Austerlitz, the victory most dear to him, the one to which he always harked back. This defeat of the combined Austrian and Prussian forces marked the end of the Holy Roman Empire which Charlemagne had founded; henceforth there would be only an Emperor of Austria. By the Peace of Pressburg, signed in the Palace of Schönbrunn, Venice was ceded to Italy, of which country Eugène de Beauharnais was appointed Viceroy. Austerlitz was the French Emperor's own battle, one that made him an Emperor in the traditional sense, not merely a man vested in authority by a new Republic. The sun of Austerlitz, glinting out unexpectedly on an overclouded day, the sword of Austerlitz, remained for him, forever, symbols of success, portents of destiny.

But there had already been a portent of another kind. In October, on the day after the capitulation of Ulm, Nelson, far away at Cape Trafalgar on the Spanish coast, had destroyed the French and Spanish fleets and ended all hope of French colonial power in the near future. The French Empire in Europe was landlocked; the fleet of the gray, fog-bound island—still half a century away from being an Empire itself, was in control of the seas and therefore of trade routes.

Napoleon saw that without a fleet France could not blockade England, but he could and would ruin her trade with Europe; from Berlin he issued the Continental Decrees which forbade France and all her dependent states to trade with England. The English retaliated by prohibiting all trade with France. The heyday of the smuggler dawned. The English still wanted French brandy, silk, gloves, lace; the French still needed the wool which England produced herself and the cashmeres, the tea and the sugar which she brought from the East and West and reshipped. Neutral American ships were liable to be searched by both English and French. By 1810 the trade embargo had done such damage that certain French ports were given licenses which allowed them to admit some English goods.

While the war, and the blockade, went on, Napoleon established his family; Joseph was King of Naples, Louis King of Holland; Caroline and Murat received the Grand Duchy of Cleves and Berg; Pauline, now remarried to the Italian Prince Borghese, was given the titular Duchy of Guastalla. The mother of them all was known as Madame Mère and drew an allowance which permitted her to save, in thrifty Corsican fashion, against any change in fortune. Riches and dukedoms were showered on the marshals and dignitaries of the Empire, and the places of the Bourbon courtiers were filled by flamboyant newcomers struggling to adjust themselves to the strict rules of etiquette which were again in fashion. Napoleon intended his court to be the match for any in Europe.

The old royal families of Europe regarded him as a parvenu, but after Austerlitz he was a parvenu with power, one with whom they must of necessity come to terms. The acceptance of Eugène de Beauharnais as a husband for the Princess Augusta of Bavaria was an event of both political and social significance. It is possible that Eugène's marriage set something stirring at the back of Napoleon's mind, fully occupied at the moment, but given to cherishing dreams.

Poland now engaged his attention. That unhappy country had

been so often divided—generally to Russia's advantage—that its very name had become associated with the word "partition." Poland chafed under the Russian yoke and Russia was an ally of England; it was logical for Napoleon to offer himself as a liberator. He captured Warsaw, where he met the young and beautiful Polish Countess Marie Walewska, who became his mistress. After Warsaw came the battle of Eylau, another victory but not an easy one. After it Napoleon wrote to Josephine, "I am still at Eylau. The countryside is covered with dead and wounded; it is not the best part of war. One suffers and is distressed to see so many victims."

It was said of him that he was indifferent to the loss of men, that he spoke coldly of being able to expend 25,000 men a month. This letter shows that he was aware of the deaths and the wounds: and men who are recklessly wasteful of soldiers' lives seldom retain for long the devotion and loyalty of the troops they lead.

The Russian campaign ended with another great victory, that of Friedland in June 1807; after that the Russians were eager to negotiate. Napoleon and Alexander met at Tilsit and on a raft in the river discussed peace terms. The young Czar, a highly impressionable man, fell under Napoleon's spell and never entirely shook himself free, though they were to fight another day.

Napoleon returned to Paris in July, after an absence of ten months. He was rapturously acclaimed; he had waged war successfully, and people hoped that it might be the last. Victory was glorious, victory was necessary, but thousands of families were mourning the men who had not come home.

The Emperor himself had some mourning to do; the son of Louis and Hortense, who had been marked to succeed him, had died of croup. Napoleon offered a prize for anyone who could discover a cure for this ailment. There was a second son, one vulnerable life to carry on the dynasty should the Emperor die in battle, or be assassinated, or fall victim to some incurable ill. The alienation between Louis and his wife made it doubtful if they would have other children. And it was increasingly evident that, despite the Plombières waters, Josephine's childbearing days were done. The children of Napoleon's sisters were not named as potential heirs in the constitution, but, nevertheless, Caroline Murat had two sons and was convinced that their claims were at least as good as that of Hortense's child.

Talleyrand and Fouché, temporarily halting their enmity to each other, agreed with Caroline. They both fancied themselves as kingmakers and saw that, if Napoleon's death should leave a child as heir, Murat as regent would be far more malleable than Joseph. Napoleon, back from the war, uninjured and at the very height of his powers, dealt with the intriguers. Talleyrand was dismissed from the Ministry of Foreign Affairs, but not from public life; he was appointed Vice-Grand Elector and was still consulted. Fouché was sternly and explosively reprimanded, but allowed to retain his post as Minister of Police.

Through it all, Napoleon knew that there was one possible solution to this problem of the succession. He was thirty-eight years old, so vigorous and energetic that during his absence from Paris he had not only fought battles, exercised diplomacy, and conducted a love affair, but attended to such details as the creation of a new chair at the Collège de France and the reorganization of the Paris Opera. Such a man had only to marry a healthy young woman and surely, surely might hope for a son of his own. But he hesitated; his heart was concerned, and just possibly his latent superstition; his luck had begun with his marriage; the Army of Italy had called Josephine "Our Lady of Victories." Moreover, with her natural grace and tact and fundamental goodness of heart, she was an admirable Empress. Unfaithful to her he might be, but he shrank from the thought of divorce. He turned his attention to other matters, to governing France and creating economic prosperity.

Keeping himself and his brother on a cadet's meager pay, he had often been hungry. He knew the value of bread. He said, "I fear insurrections due to economic causes although I am not afraid of political risings." In principle he upheld the liberty of labor and believed that government should favor workers against employers, lest the tyranny of employers should lead to the revolt of the employed. Yet he instituted a system of strict control of labor by the police and the issue of work permits. Associations of workingmen were banned, and all control of labor was made easier because ever since 1803, any man who wished to change his job or his place of residence had been obliged to obtain a passport.

Economically, the blockade, hampering as it was, had not worked to the disadvantage of France. England was the most highly industrialized country in the world and, with English products now inaccessible, France, the foremost industrial power on the continent of Europe, found ready markets. And the luxury goods, like the silk of Lyons, which had been out of fashion during the Revolution and could now only be exported by smuggling routes, were greatly in demand from a court where any foul-mouthed old soldier who had happened to attain high military rank was required to present himself in satin knee-breeches, and to bring his wife in a rich gown. Josephine set a high standard of fashion; with Leroy, her dressmaker, and David, the artist, she evolved the Empire style with its high waist, little puffed sleeves, graceful, clinging skirt. Then, for ceremonial wear there was the long court train and the ruff made of lace or tulle, stiffened by wire.

There was also the spurious but immediate prosperity that all wars bring; there was the demand for arms, munitions and uniforms. Few people, gainfully employed after a period of dearth, look farther into the future than the next payday.

Nevertheless, this money, so freely spent, must come from somewhere. Until 1807 Napoleon and his Minister of Finance, Gaudin, could rely upon direct taxation, but in that year the national income fell. Napoleon was suspicious of paper money and of loans; he had seen the effect of the *assignats;* so he introduced a tax on land values and restored the system of indirect taxation, the old, hated levies on such commodities as liquor, salt and tobacco, now renamed—*droits réunis*—and collected as inland customs duties. The new name did nothing to disguise the character of these impositions and the dissatisfaction they aroused mounted as time went on.

Alongside the need for money went the need for men, and more men. The armies of the Empire which swept across Europe were recruited under the Loi Jourdan of 1798, only slightly modified. All men between the ages of twenty and twenty-five, with certain well-defined exceptions, were subject to military service; between 1800 and 1814 two and a quarter million men were recruited; of these nearly a million were mobilized in one year, 1813. But, at least, in this army promotion was by merit, not by birth and any soldier who distinguished himself had a career open to him. Napoleon understood men: "In ambition is to be found the chief motive force of humanity and a man puts forth his best powers in proportion to his hope of advancement." Before a battle an officer rode down the lines, calling out, "The Emperor will reward the man who advances."

The rewards varied; promotion, the star of the Legion of Honor, a sword, a coveted if painful tweak of the ear; in the hope of one of these men plunged into the thick of the fight, and the old spirit of 1792 with its ardent response to the cry *"La patrie en danger,"* evolved in time into a fanatical, personal devotion to the Emperor.

Napoleon knew how to manipulate men through their weaknesses. They were ambitious, greedy for money or for land, they were snobs. He used the members of the old aristocracy who returned from exile so impoverished that they were glad to take service with one whom they regarded as an upstart. They added glitter and style to his court, and, skillfully handled, they served his plan to fuse the aristocracy of birth with the aristocracy of achievement. The Marshals of France—the Augereaus, Neys, Lannes—rich in money and titles, mingled their blood with that of the great families of a former day—the La Rochefoucaulds, the Rohans, the Montmorencys. Napoleon hoped that the next generation would combine the virtues of both contributing streams. And until the pedigree of man is taken as seriously as that of the race horse or the poodle, who can say whether he was right or wrong?

Had Napoleon been more of the cynic that he sometimes imagined himself to be, he would have foreseen the result of loading his new nobility with wealth and honors to the point where they had nothing more to hope for, and the effect of marrying his Marshals into families which still looked upon him with secret contempt. In the salons of the fashionable Faubourg St. Germain the talk was increasingly reactionary, and the society that he created around himself was composed of "secret royalists and sated upstarts." The true imperialists were in the ranks of the army. And as time went on the court became a barrier between him and his people; his isolation, though never so complete as that of the Bourbons, was increased by his prolonged absences from France. In his long climb upward from obscure artillery officer to Emperor of the French, personal magnetism had played no small part, and this elusive quality operates best at close range.

From an administrative point of view he could afford to absent himself, for by a careful process of restoring what had been good in the pre-Revolutionary régime and retaining the best of the Revolution's innovations, he had forged a government machine that worked so well that when a second generation of officials, less efficient than their predecessors, took over, they had only to follow the lines laid down to keep administration running smoothly. The Emperor was the source of power, he had diminished that of the Council of State and finally suppressed the Tribunate; he could truly have said, with Louis XIV, "I am the State." But his power was well delegated and ran down from the top through well-charted channels to end in innumerable small offices where some knowledgeable and responsible petty bureaucrat could say within his limited sphere, "I am the administration." The system survived the man who made it and enabled France to weather many a "wind of change" which would have brought a less well-organized country to disaster. French politicians could afford to experiment and to veer about because, whatever form government assumed, whatever name it adopted, in thousands of dingy offices the real business of administration would go on as usual.

To regard Napoleon as a despot is to site him out of his age. Except in England and America it was an age of despots and the power the French Emperor took to himself was no greater than that possessed by Frederick William of Prussia, Alexander of Russia, or Francis II of Austria.

Napoleon made mistakes. The Continental Decrees damaged England as they were intended to do, but they also harmed France and were a source of constant irritation to her satellite countries. And the break with the Papal authority caused earnest French Catholics to look at the Empire with cooler and more critical eyes.

Pius VII had done everything he could to please the man who had restored France to the Catholic Church; he came to officiate at the Coronation and remained in Paris for six months. The happy relationship lasted until 1805 when, in spite of the Pope's protest, French troops occupied Ancona. Definite rupture came after the Battle of Austerlitz when Napoleon decided that he was now Emperor of Rome as well as of France. In 1808 came the occupation of Rome and in the next year the annexation of the Papal States. To this the Pope retaliated by excommunicating Napoleon. Excommunication might seem to those who had worshiped at the shrine of the Goddess of Reason a medieval weapon, blunt and rusted with age, but the true Catholic saw it differently; an excommunicated man was one from whom God must, pending repentance, withhold all blessing. Faith in the Emperor's future was shaken. Napoleon, in whom success had bred the inevitable *hubris*, imitated the action of an earlier ruler of France, arrested the Pope and imprisoned him at Savona and then, in 1812, when Pius was old and frail, at Fontainebleau. Meanwhile the favor that had been shown to Catholics after the Concordat was withdrawn.

Ordinary life went on. Napoleon loved music and the theatre, and both, under his patronage, flourished, though literature still lagged. The strict censorship was not conducive to the free expression of ideas, and it may not be irrelevant to note that in his youth Napoleon had cherished literary ambitions. It is just possible that, even in a man whose other aspirations had been fulfilled, the jealousy of the writer *manqué* lingered and turned him against pen wielders. He banished Madame de Staël, the foremost woman writer of her age, and Chateaubriand, once his ardent admirer, was alienated by the execution of the Duc d'Enghien.

If literature languished, science flourished. Napoleon delighted in innovation and invention, and had such a passion for even trivial-seeming detail that in a hospital he once pointed out the advisability of always taking fresh sheets from the bottom of the pile in order to equalize the wear. Among the things he encouraged was the technique of producing sugar from beet; for this alone Europe, later to be subject to other and more stringent isolation from the product of the sugar cane, should remember him with gratitude. And now in Persia and Afghanistan, in the East that he dreamed of conquering and never reached, the cultivation of the humble vegetable is spreading and the factories are going up.

Ever since the War of the Spanish Succession, France had maintained an interest in the affairs of the Iberian peninsula but, until 1807, Spain and Portugal, pursuing their medieval way of life, had stood aloof from the rest of Europe. Their long coastline was a gap in the military and mercantile ramparts, and in 1807 Napoleon sent Junot to occupy Lisbon. The Portuguese royal family—including a mad grandmother—left for Brazil, one of their colonies, there to establish the short-lived "Amazon Throne"; the Spanish ruling house was less easily dislodged but it was already torn by dissensions which, cleverly exploited, led to the abdication of the King and his son. Murat took northern Spain and moved toward Madrid. Then, with the complete indifference to human feelings which he could on occasion display, Napoleon moved his pawns about the board. Joseph became King of Spain, Murat replaced him on the throne of Naples. This move reckoned without the Spanish people, once great and powerful and proud; proud still. They refused to accept Joseph Bonaparte as their King and embarked upon a long guerrilla warfare; the conditions under which desperate men, unbelievably ill-equipped, fought are preserved in pictures by Goya, who saw them with his living eye.

The Spanish guerrillas succeeded in chasing Joseph out of Madrid, and the English were glad to seize a chance of coming to grips with the French on land; they won a battle at Vimeiro and liberated Portugal. Napoleon saw that his personal intervention would be needed in Spain; he saw, too, that before he moved he must secure his rear.

The Czar of Russia was now his friend and ally; they had discussed together such glittering schemes as the partition of Turkey and the conquest of the East yet now, when they met again at Erfurt, in Germany, Alexander did not commit himself—as Napoleon had hoped—to engage Austria and Prussia while he was in Spain.

A picture painted of the meeting at Erfurt explains much. Symbolically, in the center stands Talleyrand, loyal to no man, a weathercock, but, like a weathercock, always ready to answer the wind—the wind, in Talleyrand's case being whatever he thought best for France.

Napoleon knew that he no longer had Talleyrand's allegiance, and that he had given him reason for enmity, but he took him to Erfurt because he was unequaled as a diplomat and had some influence over the Czar. Talleyrand used his influence in a way directly opposite to that which Napoleon had hoped. He told Alexander that the French people were tired of war, which meant, by implication, tired of the Emperor. Alexander preferred the role of the liberator of Europe, the savior of the French people, to that of open ally to Napoleon. Therefore he did not give any of the firm promises that Napoleon asked for, and he rejected the other proposal which the Emperor, with almost touching naïveté had entrusted Talleyrand to make. This was that in the event of Josephine's being divorced Napoleon should marry one of Alexander's sisters.

The spell cast at Tilsit still had some potency, but it was not strong enough to make the Czar feel that this self-made Emperor was a fit match for a daughter of the Romanoffs, particularly if that Emperor, his Empire built upon successful war, now reigned over a country wishful for peace, as Talleyrand had suggested.

Erfurt, for all its dazzle, was a failure and Napoleon acknowledged it, probably unconsciously, in a letter which he wrote to Josephine. "The Emperor Alexander dances, but I do not—forty is forty."

In fact he was thirty-nine, but after midday shadows run forward quickly. He was thirty-nine, much of Europe lay at his feet, and he had no heir. He was the father of one illegitimate child, which proved that the sterility of his marriage could not be blamed upon him. He was thirty-nine but still capable of making one of those grueling fast journeys which confounded his enemies. At the end of October he left Erfurt, on December 4 Madrid was recaptured and Joseph back on his throne, on January 23 Napoleon was in Paris again. Too old to dance maybe, but still full of dynamic energy and with a good deal of future ahead.

Five days after his return from Spain he made a final break with Talleyrand, took from him his keys of office and dismissed him. To Talleyrand, with his foresight and subtlety, the dismissal may not have been unwelcome for, when the wind next veered, as he was sure it would, he could justly claim that he had dissociated himself from a régime and a policy which in his opinion was doing France no good.

Spring of 1809 shook out its green banners over a Europe once again torn by strife. As Napoleon had feared, Austria had joined with England in another coalition—the fifth. The French occupied Vienna for a second time. Shortly after, at Aspern-Essling, Napoleon's troops were so hard-pressed that their reputation for invincibility was shaken and hope flared in the hearts of their enemies. It died down again when two months later there was a great French victory at Wagram.

Shortly after Wagram the English in Spain won the Battle of Talavera. Wellington (he did not become Duke of Wellington until 1814, rising from plain Arthur Wellesley through a confusion of titles; for clarity's sake it is better to refer to him by his final one) was another man of thirty-nine, born in the same year as Napoleon. He was not only a brilliant soldier, but a cautious one. After the victory he withdrew to Portugal, to the great disgust of the Spaniards and of hotheads in England. He could foresee that the victory over Austria would free French troops for the Spanish front. He could also see that Spain was a poor country, unable to support for any length of time an army whose only other source of supply was from the sea. Heedless of those who believed that victory should be followed by advance, he retreated and began to build the fortifications of the famous lines of Torres Vedras.

The French in central Europe were moving through less barren land but, even so, as the theatre of war moved farther from France, lines of supply and communication were overextended. And as battle followed battle, the demand for manpower grew. By 1809 only a third of the men in the French army had ever fought in any previous campaign, and Napoleon became increasingly dependent upon foreign contingents, Italians, Swiss, Germans and Poles—mercenaries frequently brave and prepared to earn their money, but lacking in the emotional attachment to a man, a cause or a country which can in a crisis make all the difference. Frenchmen were being called to the colors before their time was due; some went unwillingly, some did not go at all. People were tiring of a war that went on and on, and deserters and conscription dodgers found more sympathizers prepared to shelter them.

Still, the end of the war on one front was near. The English made an abortive expedition to Walcheren—scene of so many disasters for them—and Francis of Austria, despairing of immediate help from his ally, was compelled to make peace. There was now a new face on the scene, that of the Austrian Minister, Metternich, whose diplomatic skill was rivaled only by that of Talleyrand. He also had the advantage of knowing Napoleon well, for he had been Austrian ambassador to Paris.

Napoleon was now to make not only a peace but a marriage.

He had at last made up his mind to divorce Josephine. From Erfurt in the autumn of 1808, months before his fortieth birthday, he had written of himself as *being* forty, a sure sign of his awareness of speeding time. On August 15, 1809, he had his fortieth birthday, the turning point in a man's life. He was not too old to father a son; he could always assure himself that he was sacrificing his own feelings for the good of his country, yet the decision was a painful one. He had not been faithful to Josephine, but his hesitation over taking this step, the way in which he broke the news to her, his behavior in the difficult period preceding the divorce, his care for her material well-being and her dignity after it, prove that he had feelings which were being sacrificed. Josephine received the situation with tears, with swooning fits, with conduct that indicated that hope died slowly and hard and then, in the end, with resignation.

The Emperor of Austria was hardly in a postion to reject Napoleon's proposal; the marriage would gain for Austria that invaluable commodity—Time. It seemed to fit the pattern of advantageous matches traditional in the House of Hapsburg. The Archduchess Marie Louise was just suited to Napoleon's purpose, young, buxom, a potential mother and of royal blood so that, after the pompous ceremony in March 1810, it was possible for him to speak of his late uncle, Louis XVIII, and his late aunt, Marie Antoinette. Something of that "Austrian woman's" immense unpopularity cast its shadow on this new Empress who had come from Austria. Almost all the women of Paris, making a self-case of Josephine's plight, sympathized with her, and the soldiers especially deplored the change. To them Josephine would always be associated with the victories of the Italian campaign, with luck, with the star in the ascendant, and perhaps with youth. For Time had touched even the Emperor. He was no longer the lean young man who had fought at Rivoli and Arcola. Despite abstemious diet he was growing stout, his eyes had lost luster and his hair was thinning. There was a change of character, too, a general slowing down, less passion, less imperiousness; he was still capable of great physical endurance, though perhaps it demanded more effort. Modern medical science suggests that already he was suffering from failure of the pituitary gland.

In the next year the divorce was justified; Marie Louise bore a son, heir to the throne, and the immediate recipient of one of his father's titles—King of Rome.

Except in Spain where Wellington emerged from behind his fortified lines to win the battles of Busaco, Fuentes de Oñoro and Albuera, the years of 1810 and 1811 were years of peace. Napoleon for the most part remained in Paris or in one of his suburban palaces. He had never spared himself either physically or mentally; into forty-odd years of life he had crammed more effort and achievement than could be expected of ten ordinary men in a long lifetime; marriage to a young wife is not always a rejuvenating business, and the break with Josephine had been an amputation. Even at the baptism of his longed-for son it was observed that the Emperor's face was overcast until the moment came for him to lift the child and show him to his people; then it became transfigured with joy and pride.

Napoleon was not alone in showing signs of strain. The economic scene was darkening. The cumulative effects of the Empire's policy of overreaching itself, the continued drain of the Spanish war, and the injury to trade and commerce wrought by the Continental System were making themselves felt. The great French commercial ports were ruined and external trade stagnant. There was also one of those mysterious waves of recession, not confined to France; and the harvest in 1811 was bad. The price of bread rose and

Napoleon was forced to fix a maximum price, a step which he hated and deplored, knowing as he did that food, not policy, is the concern of every household every day.

Driven by sheer necessity, the Emperor demanded more and more money, more and more men from his satellites, and these demands roused resentment and antagonism even from members of his own family. Murat from Naples grumbled to the man who had made him King that he had not been put on a throne in order to obey. Napoleon retorted, "If I have conquered kingdoms it was in order that France should get advantage from them and, if I do not get my wish, then I shall be obliged to incorporate these kingdoms within France." He had, in fact, already done that in the case of Holland, where the always difficult Louis had chosen to abdicate rather than give up his independence. Murat took warning—but he waited.

The powers of Europe waited, too. As the situation in France grew worse and less controllable, they watched, undeceived by the Emperor's attempts to impose a synthetic gaiety by more balls, more reviews.

In 1810, Alexander of Russia showed his hand. The Treaty of Tilsit, though made amicably and in an atmosphere of mutual admiration, had taken from Russia the greater part of Poland for the creation of the Duchy of Warsaw; in Russian minds this still rankled. Equally resented was the Continental System, which ruined Russia's trade with England. Alexander announced that in future he would ignore the blockade and let Russian merchants trade where they chose. Caulaincourt, French ambassador to Russia, returned to France and had a serious talk with the Emperor. Caulaincourt was not, in ability, the equal of Talleyrand or of Fouché—who in 1810 had followed Talleyrand into disgrace—but he was devoted and his honesty could be relied upon. Napoleon listened when Caulaincourt warned of dangers to come.

Napoleon had never been one to sit and wait for trouble to find him; swift decision and rapid movement had served him well in the past. On May 9, 1812 he set out for Russia.

He left behind him a country afflicted by scarcity, unemployment and economic crisis; but he took with him the Grand Army, 600,000 men, the pick of his troops, the largest force ever mustered in the history of the world. Dresden welcomed and fêted them; except for the absence of the Russian Czar it was Erfurt all over again—"The Kings sit down to dinner; the Queens stand up to dance." Marie Louise had accompanied him so far, but on May 29 he took leave of her and rode off, a somber figure in the plain green coat which contrasted so sharply with the brilliant uniforms of his staff. Ahead lay the Niemen, his Rubicon.

By August he was in Smolensk, where news reached him of further English victories in Spain. Wellington had won battles at Ciudad Rodrigo, at Badajoz and Salamanca, and then again withdrawn to Portugal. Joseph Bonaparte had once more abandoned his capital. This was unwelcome news, but the Grand Army was moving steadily eastward, meeting with little opposition. The Russians were following an old, tried policy—the brief skirmish and the retreat, seldom offering the head-on battle in which the French excelled. There was limitless space into which to retreat. In September there was a battle at Borodino, and Napoleon rewarded Ney for his brilliant cavalry action by giving him the title of Prince of the Moskowa. After the battle the Russians withdrew again and the French marched on, with their lines of communication lengthening dangerously and men wearying of the seemingly endless marches across flat plains from which the retreating Russians, like an outgoing tide, had swept all that an advancing army far from its base needed. No food for men or horses, no shelter from the increasing cold. The vital lines behind the army lengthened; and so did the nights.

It was mid-September, the real turn of the year, when the French reached Moscow, the old capital of Russia, the place from which Napoleon had imagined himself dictating terms of peace. The old campaigners in the Grand Army had followed their leader into many cities, but never one like this; empty of people, void of stores and silent save for the crackle of fires which filled the air with acrid stench and destroyed the buildings in which weary men had hoped to rest.

Still, Moscow was taken and Napoleon was convinced that Alexander would come to terms, but Alexander had said that if necessary he would withdraw as far as Tobolsk.

Napoleon waited for five long weeks, busying himself with anything, even the affairs of the Comédie Française in order to conceal from those about him and from himself that in moving against Russia he had made a mistake, in entering Russia another, that every victory east of the Niemen had been a Pyrrhic one and that he and his army were stranded in a wasteland, with the Russian winter closing in. On October 10 the first snow fell—only a light fall, but ominous.

On October 19 the Grand Army left Moscow and began its long retreat. Hunger went with them, so that they were reduced to eating their own skeleton horses; frostbite went with them, they were not clad or shod to face the winter; and the plains which had seemed so empty as they advanced were now full of skirmishing Cossacks on their tough little ponies, still avoiding pitched battle but swooping in to cut off stragglers or to take advantage of any catastrophe such as the crumbling of the ice on the Berezina River as the French made their crossing.

It is sometimes said that Napoleon deserted his stricken army; actually he stayed with them, sharing the hardships and danger until December 9 and some of the men still loved him well enough to spend their last energies at the end of each disastrous day in a hunt for fuel for his fire. When he left them he did so for the same reason that he had left the army in Egypt—affairs in Paris needed attention.

News between France and the front traveled slowly and unsurely. Dispatch riders had grueling journeys to make, hazards of weather to face, were set upon by Cossacks and by wolves. Those riding west carried no news of great victories or of looted treasure on the way home such as would have put heart into the French people; those riding east presently carried disturbing stories. The one which showed Napoleon that he must go, unencumbered and at full speed, to Paris concerned the activities of a General Malet, imprisoned in 1808 for subversive activities and no longer quite sane. He had escaped from custody, announced that the Emperor was dead and nearly succeeded in seizing power, reestablishing the Republic and suing for peace. Everyone he had approached seemed to accept this proposition—no one thought of Marie Louise as regent nor the King of Rome as Napoleon II.

The near success of Malet's plot exposed the shallowness of the roots of this wide Empire.

Napoleon left what remained of the Grand Army in the command of Murat, an experienced soldier, his brother-in-law, the man he had made King. Murat was the deserter: muttering about the impossibility of serving a madman, he set out for Naples, intent, at all costs, upon saving his own throne. The task of getting the army home fell to the man who had never wavered, never would waver in his loyalty, Eugène de Beauharnais, Josephine's son.

By traveling day and night Napoleon managed to reach Paris on December 18. Before his arrival Malet and eleven other plotters had been executed, and Napoleon went feverishly to work to repair the damage done and to strengthen the structure of the Empire.

The Senate promised him 350,000 men to fill some of gaps in the ranks of the Grand Army which had set out 600,000 strong and come back a mere 50,000. The spirit of *la patrie en danger* revived as a new coalition against France, the strongest yet, was formed among Prussia, Russia, Sweden and Great Britain.

There was hope yet; genius was still genius; with an army hastily mobilized and insufficiently trained, Napoleon won two engagements against the Prussians and Russians, at Lützen and at Bautzen. Then there was a breathing space—everywhere except in Spain where Wellington moved again and won the Battle of Vittoria. There was hope that Austria, not in this latest coalition, would act as a mediator to bring about peace.

In June 1813, Napoleon and Metternich met again, this time in Dresden, where they talked for nine hours. There was deadly realism in Napoleon's remark, "Your sovereigns, who were born upon the throne, can allow themselves to be beaten twenty times, and can always return to their capitals. I cannot do that; I am a self-made soldier." But alongside this realism there was a staggering naïveté. From his own blood kin he had been given countless examples of greed and jealousy and opportunism; now, from his father-in-law he hoped for clemency. By the end of the long talk he knew differently and said that he was willing to accept the terms upon which Austria was prepared to act as mediator. Then came a curious turn of fate—though even fate needs human hands to do its work: his reply, with all its concessions, reached Austria exactly one day too late. Overnight she had declared war.

There followed the battle of Dresden, another victory for the French. But in Spain Wellington had defeated Soult and this time following victory with advance was moving toward the Pyrenees.

In October was fought what the Germans call the battle of the Nations. At Leipzig the French were called upon to face the massed armies of Prussia, Russia, Austria and Sweden. The Swedish troops were commanded by Jean-Baptiste Bernadotte, the French Marshal who had been elected Prince Royal of Sweden. Had Bernadotte, a Frenchman, not brought forces from the land of his adoption to fight against his old rival, the issue might have been different: as it was, Leipzig was a decisive defeat for Napoleon.

His prestige was still so tremendous that the Allies offered him generous terms in return for peace, terms which would, it was said, "have delighted Louis XIV." They demanded that France should withdraw to her natural frontiers. Napoleon knew how the French felt about the territorial gains that had been made under the Revolution, the Directory, the Empire; all bought with French blood. To bargain them away would cost him his throne. He had already told Metternich at Dresden that he would not yield an inch of conquered land: and one lost battle had not changed his mind. He refused the terms, preferring to go back to Paris and ask, as he said, with regret, "for fresh sacrifices at the hands of my generous people."

Murat sent an imploring message from Naples:

"Make peace, make it at any price. Gain time and you will have gained all. Your genius and time will do the rest. If you refuse the wishes of those who are your friends, of your subjects, you will be lost and you will have caused us all to be lost."

The self-interest of the man who had abandoned the sorry remnant of the Grand Army was blatant. Napoleon replied caustically,

"I don't imagine that you are one of those who think the lion is dead."

Not dead, perhaps; had the lion been dead, Murat would not

have been proffering it advice; but he did consider it toothless, clawless, moribund. And he himself was still King of Naples, and determined, if possible, to remain in that position. He lost no time in going over to the Austrians.

Eugène de Beauharnais, the man upon whom Napoleon had bestowed no crown, was left to stem, as best he could, the tide of the Austrian advance.

Book II

Chapter 1. THE FALL OF THE EMPIRE. THE RESTORATION. THE HUNDRED DAYS

The love affair between France and Napoleon was now, at the beginning of 1814, on the wane, and to outsiders he and the country were no longer identifiable as one. He admitted this when, urging the country to resist the Allies massing on the frontier, he added,

"Tell France that, whatever may be said to her, it is against her as much as against me that war is being made, and that she must defend not my person, but her national existence."

The Allies implied that they were moving, not against France, but against the man who had led her to glory and then to catastrophe. This was psychological warfare and was not without effect. In the Legislature, Laîné was emboldened to describe the country's state in terms he would not have used a year earlier:

"Our ills are at their height; the country is menaced on all our frontiers; we are experiencing a penury unexampled in our history as a state. Commerce is dead, industry dying."

Napoleon dismissed the Legislature and exiled Laîné, but he could not recall the spoken words nor prevent their finding an echo in the minds of the discontented and the disillusioned all over France. The failure in Russia had made war detestable. While the soldiers of France had marched through city after city in Europe and the Emperor dictated his terms to the conquered, the moans of the bereaved, the groans of the taxpayer had been lost in the general jubilation. Now the mood of the country had changed; there were people who agreed with what Murat said as he abandoned the remnants of the Grand Army: "It is no longer possible to serve a madman; there is no hope of success in his cause."

The truth was that there had always been cracks in the imposing structure of Empire, but the stucco of success had hidden them; the stucco was flaking off and the French were no longer united by anything but their wish for peace. From the gray Atlantic coast to the warm Mediterranean shore, that was the dominating desire, peace, immediate, at any price.

In their hopes of what peace would bring, men differed. There were the genuine Republicans who had disapproved of the Empire —though willing to accept office and honor from the Emperor; they hoped for a revival of the Republic. There were the Royalists who had always hated the Corsican upstart and saw in the forces menacing France, the armies of two Emperors and two Kings who, if successful, would restore the monarchy in France. There were hordes of ordinary men, little concerned with ideologies, who thought of the material advantages that peace would bring in her hand; the end of the ruthless conscription that ripped sons away from the family business, the family farm; the end of the taxes which had rocketed until they had become as heavy as in feudal days; the end of the Continental System so ruinous to trade. It was now a quarter of a century since the Revolution which had seemed to promise so much and the ordinary man, whose sense of being wronged had been lulled for a while by the drug of military glory, looked about him and saw poverty and unemployment; the ordinary woman knew that bread was as scarce and as dear as ever.

It was with this divided, peace-avid country behind him that Napoleon turned to face the invaders. He could count upon the patriotism that would override dissension and war-weariness; *la patrie en danger* was a call that would not go unanswered; the French would allow no enemy to walk into France. He could count upon the "old mustaches" in the army, those seasoned men who looked upon him as General Bonaparte rather than as the Emperor; he was theirs; they were his. But there were not enough of them. In the army, too, high noon was over. Too many of his veterans had been lost in the snows, the icy waters of Russia; too many of the raw young conscripts had never had a chance to fall under his personal spell; worst of all, too many of his high-ranking officers were no longer young and, laden with honors, rich with booty, wished for peace—for how, without peace, could a man settle down to enjoy his hard-earned reward of rank, estates and wealth? With the old ones, too, there was another thing, a triviality, a mere superstition, but soldiers are only men and all men at times are irrational. Josephine had been lucky; she'd been thrown off, and how much luck had the Emperor enjoyed since? It all counted.

Years before, Rochambeau had written to Lafayette, "It is always good to think the French invincible but . . . there are no men easier to defeat when they have lost faith in their leaders."

If Napoleon himself had lost faith in his lucky star—and the flames of Moscow, the ice of the Berezina, the battle of Leipzig might hint that it was on the wane—he gave no outward sign. France was threatened by invasion for the first time in twenty years and he set about repelling the invaders with energy and determination, though to an experienced soldier the mere sight of the army must have been dismaying. Many of the recent recruits were "little more than children."

But they fought well, contesting every yard in those most disheartening of contests, rear-guard actions. The Prussians moved toward Champagne; the Austrians—Marie Louise's own people— came from the Lyonnais and with them came Alexander of Russia, Napoleon's onetime friend and admirer; from the Pyrenees, Wellington advanced.

From Châtillon, 130 miles from Paris, the Allies offered peace on precisely the same terms that Napoleon had rejected less than six months ago after Leipzig; France must relinquish all her territorial gains. To accept would carry the same penalty, the loss of his throne, the disinheritance of his son. Self-made men, more than others, are obsessed by a desire that their offspring should benefit by their exertions. Napoleon, exceptional in so much else, was not exceptional in this. Sooner than hand over France's gains, mortify the French people, be dethroned and lose all hope of the little King of Rome becoming Emperor of France, he would fight on.

So he refused the peace offer, and with increasing despair the

French fought on. Spring of 1814 saw the Allies closing in on Paris; on the first day of April, with a soft rain falling on just-breaking leaves, Alexander of Russia and Frederick William of Prussia rode into the city from which, obeying Napoleon's order, Marie Louise had fled in the night, with attendants, officials, the crown jewels and thirty-two little barrels full of gold.

The Paris crowds who in a few years had seen so much, stared at the Prussians and the Russians. Everywhere proclamations were already posted, announcing that the Allies came not as conquerors but as liberators, to free the oppressed French people from their Emperor. In the crowd there were those who remembered how the armies of the Revolution and of the Empire had entered other cities with similar avowals of good intent; and there were those who did regard the Allies as liberators. These flung flowers and greenery to be trampled by the hoofs of the horses ridden by Prussians and by Russians and by strange-looking men from the Caucasus, from Siberia and Mongolia. In the evening the Cossacks built their little straw huts in the Champs-Elysées and raided the Bois de Boulogne for firewood.

Most people were stunned and confused—at this point even the Emperor's whereabouts were unknown—but there was one man in Paris who knew exactly what to do and how to go about it. Talleyrand had awaited this day and had deliberately remained in Paris, to welcome and to entertain Alexander, to pull strings, to limp into the Senate and persuade it to vote for the deposition of the Emperor and the setting up of a provisional government with himself at its head.

The Allies were glad enough to negotiate with him; had he been stupid instead of subtle, uncouth instead of charming, raw instead of vastly experienced, they would still have welcomed his collaboration; for France beaten was still a problem and the Allies were far from unanimous in their approach to it.

Despite all that had happened since Tilsit, Alexander of Russia was still dazzled by Napoleon and disposed to treat with him as one Emperor to another. The Russian "scorched earth" policy had been successful, had started the decline, and the Czar could afford to be magnanimous.

Francis of Austria was in a personal quandary. His chief minister, Metternich, was determined to be rid of Napoleon, but to do so meant depriving Marie Louise of her throne and her son of his crown.

The English wished to remain strictly faithful to Pitt's policy of non-intervention in the internal affairs of France; they refused to impose upon her any régime not acceptable to the country as a whole. Did Talleyrand speak for France?

Only Prussia's attitude was uncomplicated; a war was fought to be won, and after victory came the spoils.

Talleyrand's hardest task was to convince Alexander that France had completely rejected Napoleon; that to set up a regency for the King of Rome would be farcical, since it would leave real power in the ex-Emperor's hands; that France desired the return of the Bourbons. Talleyrand believed that France could regain her natural place in Europe only under a King who, once restored, would not risk being driven out again by adopting an aggressive policy. In the cause of persuasion he staged a demonstration at the Opera which the Czar attended; ladies wore the Bourbon white and distributed white cockades, and one of the actors sang a song in praise of Alexander who "had brought the Bourbons back again." To Talleyrand it was immaterial that the ordinary man was so indifferent to the Bourbon dynasty that its very name had sunk into oblivion. While Royalists embraced one another and declared that the Restoration had come, people in the streets were saying, "The Bourbons? Never heard of them."

Napoleon had reached Fontainebleau on the day after the Allies entered Paris. From there he sent word to Alexander that he was now prepared to open discussions on the basis of the terms offered at Châtillon. It was already too late; the demand now was for unconditional abdication; and when he learned that his generals would no longer accept his orders and that Marshal Marmont, the friend of his youth whom he trusted, had defected, he saw that he had no alternative. In the red-damask hung study where decisions had been reached, from which decrees had issued, he wrote out the Act of Abdication himself.

"The Allied powers have proclaimed that the Emperor Napoleon is the only obstacle to the re-establishment of peace in Europe,

the Emperor Napoleon, faithful to his oath, declares that he re-
nounces for himself and his heirs, the thrones of France and Italy,
and that there is no sacrifice he will not make, even to that of his
own life, in the interest of France."

When he wrote those words his face was livid, his hair in disorder; the great dream was over. Yet the words were handled in
masterly fashion, not one wasted and every one aimed at the susceptible ear and heart. He stresses that he is not abandoning France,
not abdicating of his own free will, but under pressure. Twice he
refers to himself as Emperor. He says he will sacrifice his life for
France. Nobody now wished for his death, nor would it profit
France; all that anyone wanted was that the war should stop and
not begin again.

It was, one cannot help but feel, the Act of Abdication that
had been demanded, but couched in such terms as would rally men
to him. France was to be allowed, the Allies said, to choose her
own destiny. . . . He may well have believed that France might
opt for him. As she might have done, given time, given the
means, by election or referendum.

Instead there was Talleyrand, bearing down hard on the word
"legitimacy." Russia, Prussia, Austria and England were all ruled
by legitimate monarchs to whom the very word "Republic" was
anathema. Behind Talleyrand was the die-hard core of Royalists
with its secret society, the Chevaliers de la Foi, now ready to come
into the open. Those who on one day had said, "The Bourbons?
Never heard of them," had their memories prompted. The legitimate Bourbon King, Louis XVIII, was the Comte de Provence
who, in 1789, had supported the Third Estate; he was a man of
liberal and constitutional opinion. There was talk about the re-
blooming of the lilies of France and of the traditional love of
France for her Kings.

Chateaubriand wrote a brilliant pamphlet, *Bonaparte and the
Bourbons* which fomented monarchical fervor. The Senate and
the Legislature decided to call "the head of the House of Bourbon
to the throne."

Louis was in England, nursing his gout, but his fifty-seven-year-
old brother, the Comte d'Artois, and his two sons, the Ducs
d'Angoulême and de Berri were already behind the Allied lines.

On April 12, a radiant spring morning, Artois, on a white horse, made his entry into Paris which he had not seen for twenty-five years. He wore the uniform of the National Guard and looked astonishingly youthful. His grace and affability were in strong contrast to the strained and somber looks of those who rode with him, the Marshals of a vanished Empire, Marmont, Moncey and Ney, who had hurried to switch their allegiance from Emperor to King.

There was a touch of eighteenth-century courtesy—so soon to vanish—in the decision of the Allies to withdraw all their troops from the streets, so that all about him Artois saw only French faces, heard only the French tongue. As he rode, distributing gracious smiles and words, the enthusiasm grew, became exuberant. In the working-class areas his reception had been tepid, but in the center of the city sheets had been taken from beds and hung from windows as flags, and the white lilies were everywhere. Men shouted, women wept. Artois himself had tears in his eyes, and the papers next morning reported him to have said, "Nothing has changed in France unless it is that there is now one Frenchman the more."

That evening there was almost one Frenchman the less. Sometimes, in his frustrated youth, Napoleon's thoughts had turned to self-destruction; now they did so again. Not after a disastrous battle, not after signing his abdication, but after Artois had arrived and been welcomed. With this proof of his rejection by France the ex-Emperor tried to escape the prospect of a mock kingship of Elba by swallowing poison; the drug had lost its potency and he survived. He made no second attempt. Perhaps—always interested in the lives and achievements of other military geniuses—he remembered Clive of India who had also tried to kill himself and failed and lived on to taste triumph. In any case he settled down and waited, despite the general eagerness to be rid of him, to hear from England the exact details of his future rights and income. His mother's blood showed there. He did not, at this time, talk of himself or his past with its vanished glories; he spoke of the future and foretold that Louis XVIII would not be able to hold together the divergent parties in France, and that he must inevitably fall.

On April 20 Louis' gout had abated sufficiently to allow him to travel. He drove from Buckinghamshire to London and was met by cheering crowds and by the Prince Regent, now anxious to make amends for lack of courtesy to not-always-welcome guests. There had been a time when the French exiles, in retaliation for real or imagined slights, had shown friendliness to Caroline, the Regent's wife, whom he hated. All differences were forgotten now as the crowds sang "The White Cockade";

"England no more your foe, will bring you aid,
When France shall welcome home the White Cockade."

The English, no less than the French, were tired of war and happy to see a dynamic, unpredictable soldier replaced by this elderly, sensible, dignified man.

On the same day Napoleon set out for Elba. He walked down the steps at Fontainebleau, said an eyewitness, with the same calm as he had mounted the steps of the throne. In the Court of Departure, so called in memory of this event, he said farewell to the troops. They had been his own; now they were the King's; he had a toy guard of 400 men, granted him by the Powers as a defense against the Barbary pirates.

"Soldiers of my Old Guard," he said, "I am going to bid you farewell. For twenty years I have always found you on the path of honor and glory."

Twenty-five years earlier those émigrés who chose exile and penury rather than a compromise with the Revolution, had spoken of taking the path of honor. Now here was the phrase again, the same words for two very different concepts which had for so long divided France and were to divide her far into the future.

"Remember me," Napoleon said, and embraced the golden eagle on the standard that had terrorized Europe. Many of the men were in tears, but there was no demonstration. The soldiers shared with civilians a mood of half-stunned resignation. So they let him go.

They remembered him, though, and passed on their memories to their sons, a folklore of the living, half fact, half myth. Any ruler of France in the immediate future would be bound to compete with a dangerously attractive legend that would brighten as old men forgot the wounds and the hardships and remembered only the glory.

As Napoleon posted across Europe with his British and Austrian escort—once, in the Royalist South, reduced to the ignominy of wearing Austrian uniform in order to escape from a hostile mob—it was too early to assess the benefits which the First Empire had brought to France, alongside the wars; the sound organization of internal affairs which would survive every change of régime, the well-founded institutions and the educational system.

On May 3, 1814, Louis XVIII rode into his good city of Paris. In his appearance there was little to attract; he was so fat that his breeches were as wide as skirts; his gouty feet were encased in shapeless felt boots. He wore a blue coat, the Order of the Holy Ghost, two spuriously military gold epaulettes and a white-plumed hat. But he had his share of the Bourbon dignity and his white hair, his benevolent smile, even his obesity, well-equipped him for the part of the father figure for whom France, most feminine of nations, now longed. She had erred, she had taken a masterful lover, who had first exalted and then humiliated her; she was ready to lay her penitent head against Louis' well-cushioned knee.

Yet, even at this early moment, in the crowds that welcomed him, differing opinions made people see him with different eyes. Vigée Lebrun, the Royalist who had painted Marie Antoinette and her court, saw a King, Louis the Desired, coming into his own again, to the great and general joy of the crowd. The Bonapartist Duchesse d'Abrantès saw him as a King imposed by the Allies, returning to France in "an English coat, an English hat, with an *English* cockade which the Prince Regent himself had pinned on. . . ."

Louis faced a formidable task; he was sixty; he had been an exile for twenty-two years; he was following as ruler one of the most dominating personalities of all time. The prospect would have daunted anyone less convinced of his right to be King. Louis was convinced; he always had, even as a child, resented the rule of primogeniture, for he believed that he was in every way more fitted to be King than his brother. He had shown—while his brother was still alive—that he was willing to take his place;

when he fled from France he had placed himself at the head of
the army of *émigrés* and acted as though he were already King.
Once he wrote to his friend, the King of Sweden, that he lived
on hope.

Now that hope had flowered, and the man whom Marie Antoinette had once called Cain was riding in to claim what he had
always felt should have been his and what, since the reported
death of little Louis XVII, had been his in the eyes of all Royalists.
Paris welcomed him; he attended a Te Deum at Notre Dame
and then rode on to the Tuileries where, as in other places,
seamstresses had worked all night, stitching woven Bourbon lilies
over the Imperial bees on carpets and hangings. The bands played
and the crowds hummed the song *"Vive Henri IV,"* for though
people had forgotten, or pretended to forget, the later Bourbons,
everybody remembered that good King of France who had expressed a wish that every Frenchman should, every Sunday, have
a chicken in the pot.

By Louis' side, and entertaining very different emotions, was
his niece, Marie-Thérèse. For her Paris held nothing but unhappy
memories; it was the place where she had been imprisoned, had
seen father, mother and brother taken away one by one. Nothing
in later life had offered any compensation; her marriage with her
cousin, the Duc d'Angoulême, was bleak and sterile. The people
of Paris might regard her with awe—the surviving "orphan of the
Temple"—or, remembering how her parents' heads had fallen
into Sanson's blood-stained basket, with latent guilt and the
desire to make amends: she could never regard them with anything but hatred. She rode through Paris with a stiff, awkward
demeanor; her looks faded, her eyes reddened from much weeping.
She had no smile for the crowd; no pleasure in her position as
first lady in France. Later she was to tell her coachman that
never, never on any account, was he to drive her carriage across
the Place de la Concorde where the guillotine had once stood.

Louis XVIII began his reign by issuing a Charter. This was
the eighth written constitution since 1791, but it was the first
attempt to install representative government since the days of the
Directory. In it he described himself as King by the Grace of

God, and by dating it as the nineteenth year of his reign, emphasized that he had been King since the death of his nephew. Although this Charter was adopted—with a few modifications—from a Constitution devised by the Senate, Louis always regarded it as *his*, given by *him* to *his* people. From this view he never deviated.

Almost twenty years earlier, Lord Macartney, a British emissary had reported of Louis XVIII: "The King is undoubtedly intelligent; he is very well informed and purveys his knowledge with an easy manner; nor is he lacking in judgment when he is not influenced by the prejudices of his upbringing. Even those prejudices have been considerably modified by misfortune and reflection."

Louis was still intelligent, and the ensuing twenty years had taught him some useful lessons. His Charter guaranteed the people of France equality before the law, individual liberty, liberty of the press and religious liberty, though Catholicism was to be restored as the religion of the state. Louis, from exile, had promised the Pope that this should be so, should he ever rule in France. But the Church was not to receive back its land; a further clause in the Charter guaranteed the inviolability of property; those who had bought land from the Church or from the confiscated estates of the nobility, could keep them. This clause was a disappointment to the *émigrés* who had returned in the full expectation that their lands would be restored. Louis decided, wisely, that it was better to antagonize a hundred thousand *émigrés* than to provoke thirty million Frenchmen, among whom the lands were now divided and subdivided, to revolt.

Another clause in the Charter affected most French families; "the conscripts now assembled are free to return home and those who have not yet joined up, to stay there." And all the honors, ranks and pensions awarded by former régimes were to be preserved, all the debts incurred by the Empire or former régimes were to be honored.

The government was to consist of two Chambers, the House of Peers, nominated by the King, and the Chamber of Deputies, elected on a very limited franchise. The King held executive power, the right to make war or peace, to appoint ministers, to initiate laws, to adjourn or dismiss the Assembly whose main function was to debate and, if it wished, to reject measures laid before it, and to impose taxes.

The Charter was, all things considered, moderate and sensible and designed to stabilize the country. In his speech from the throne on June 4, Louis struck the note to which he hoped the nation would attune itself. (Because there had been no time for elections, the old Senate took the place of the House of Peers, and the legislature stood in for the Chamber of Deputies.) Vain of his scholarship, Louis had prepared the speech himself, and he delivered it in a beautiful, sonorous voice that did much to compensate for his ungainly appearance. "War," he said, "is universal, so is reconciliation." He urged the nation to adopt the forgetfulness that Louis XVI had recommended in his will, and he assured the French people that the glory of their arms had not been dimmed and that by conciliation and reconciliation France would retain her place among the nations.

He meant well; but he had been absent from France for many years, seven of them spent in England where constitutional government had had a century and a half in which to settle down into routine. France was different. Oil and vinegar, vigorously shaken, will make an emulsion that gives the appearance of being one entity; so had the French nation been, shaken by disaster, longing for peace; but left to settle, the emulsion will separate again into its diverse ingredients. Louis issued his Charter to a country already divided; aristocrats bent on regaining their former privileges and estates, feeling that the monarchy owed them something since they had suffered with it in exile; ordinary people, equally intent upon retaining what they had gained; and the army, now recovering from shock.

Peace had permitted and the national economy had demanded, a stringent reduction in the armed forces. A number of men and officers had been put on half pay. Under Napoleon, the army had been a career, a way of life, so the men now deemed redundant had lost more than mere money, they had lost objective. This they might have borne, grumbling, had Louis XVIII not reconstituted the Royal Household Corps.

There was an echo here; Louis had always held that one of his brother's cardinal mistakes had been the disbanding of his personal guard. He wished for a guard of his own and, though in political matters he was determined to be impartial, in such a personal matter he felt that he should be allowed to follow his own wishes. So he instituted the Maison du Roi, and of whom should that be composed but of those loyal friends who had gone into exile, and suffered, and come back only to find that a clause in the Charter left them still dispossessed?

So the soldiers of the Empire, men who had fought on all the battlefields of Europe, sat about idle in the cafés and glowered at these new, privileged soldiers who had seen no service since 1789 or, if they had, it had been with the enemies of France. When the unemployed soldiers played cards and held a King they slapped it down saying, "Pig of clubs. Pig of spades, of hearts, of diamonds." Somebody with a real diamond scratched on a shop window, "Long live the Emperor," and other diamond owners, coming along, added, "Approved," "Approved," "Approved."

A lively court, full of people whose sayings and doings provided food for gossip, might have done something to mitigate the dull boredom which so soon overtook the new reign, but under the rule of the unyielding Marie-Thérèse correctness and exclusiveness, not entertainment, was the aim. The dukes and duchesses of the Empire, the Marshals of the Empire, retained their titles; but they were not received. Louis himself was inclined, through indolence and ill-health, to yield in too many matters to Artois, more rigid and conservative, whose smiles were no longer directed at the people, but reserved for those who had been his companions in exile.

There was peace, which all had longed for, and a constitutional government; there were good will and good intentions, but a nation which for twenty-five years had been accustomed to excitement found life dull.

Life on Elba, too, was dull.

Napoleon threw himself with energy and interest into the organization of his doll's-house domain. He built a house, wielding pick and shovel and lunching with the workmen off a crust and a hard-boiled egg in the way that had endeared him to his soldiers. He converted an old military store into a theatre and encouraged the ancient industry of mining the iron from which the island took its name. But despite all this, and the presence on the island of his favorite sister, Pauline, always ready to arrange some entertainment, it was a trivial, makeshift life, a cruel parody. Also—no small matter to Letizia Bonaparte's son—Louis XVIII had not paid, and showed no sign of paying, the annuity that had been promised.

At home Louis practiced his doctrine of conciliation. In his eyes Talleyrand was a renegade priest, a traitor to his own class, a turncoat, but he dismissed all that in a simple sentence: "A great deal has happened since we last met." He appointed him to the post of Foreign Minister and, in this capacity, as representative of the *vanquished* nation, Talleyrand went to the Congress of Vienna where the victors were gathered to settle the affairs of Europe. With superb skill Talleyrand so manipulated things that within a short time the victors regarded him as one of themselves and it was thanks to him that, within six months of the abdication, France had resumed her position in Europe as though there had been no cataclysmic war.

At the Congress Talleyrand urged the removal of Napoleon from Elba to some more remote place, the Azores or even St. Helena; Metternich was opposed to the suggestion. Already a gulf separated the Allies, Russia and Prussia on one side, Austria and Britain, with France which, but for Talleyrand's cunning, would have counted for little, on the other. Metternich, who had never underrated Napoleon's appeal to the French, saw the advantage of having him handy enough to be used as a threat to any too-recalcitrant nation and, should the gulf widen into war, there would be use for the man himself. The Congress, with all the accompanying social gaieties, dragged on.

Louis XVIII gave further proof of his determination to put the country's welfare before his personal feelings. He appointed another renegade priest, Baron Louis, as Minister of France, ignoring the apostasy and choosing the astute financier, the best man for the job. And, in order to make things run smoothly, he deprived himself of the company of his current favorite, the Duc de Blacas, who had shown himself too ultra a Royalist for even the Royalists to stomach. So Louis sent him as ambassador to Rome, where he amused himself by making the lives of the Bonapartes living there in exile as miserable as possible.

Talleyrand's feeling that Elba was rather too near to France was amply justified. Spies—some of them working for both sides —kept a constant flow of information—some of it misleading—moving between island and mainland. Napoleon was aware that the monarchy, if respected, was not loved and that the nation was finding it difficult to adjust itself. Louis was told that the ex-Emperor was growing decrepit. One spy discovered the fact that Napoleon was in communication with a man in Grenoble who was in touch with an ardent Bonapartist in charge of a famous regiment in that area. This vital piece of information went in a letter to the Minister of the Royal Household who passed it on to the Minister of Police. He filed it.

On March 5, 1815, news reached the Tuileries that Napoleon had landed near Cannes with a few hundred soldiers whose numbers were swelling to thousands as they moved inland. One did not need to be a committed Bonapartist to thrill to the story of how, faced with an opposing force, he had dismounted, thrown open that familiar overcoat and cried:

"Soldiers of the Fifth of the Line, you recognize me! If there is one among you who wishes to kill his general, his Emperor, let him do so. Here I am!"

They ran forward, not to kill but to embrace him. Then they fell in and marched behind him to Grenoble.

Napoleon knew the value of a dramatic gesture, but he also knew that France was not composed solely of soldiers, Bonapartists, or romantics to whom a romantic gesture made an appeal. To these others his arrival would bring dismay, fear for the future, fear of war. In Grenoble he made a speech calculated to allay such fears and to explain the reason for his return. And every word of that speech was as nicely chosen as the words of his act of abdication.

He had come, he said, to save France from the outrages of the returned nobles, to secure to the peasant the possession of his land, to uphold the rights won in 1789. France had made trial of the Bourbons; it had done well to do so, but the experiment had failed. The Bourbon monarchy had proved incapable of detaching itself from its worst supporters, the priests and nobles. Only the dynasty that owed its throne to the Revolution could maintain the social work of the Revolution. As for himself, he had learned wisdom by misfortune; he renounced conquest. He should give France peace without and liberty within . . . He should henceforth govern as a constitutional sovereign, and seek only to leave a constitutional crown to his son . . .

On how many sunny lunchtimes with the workmen, on how many evenings in the new theatre had this masterly speech been mentally rehearsed? It promised peasants and workmen what was already theirs under the Charter; it offered to the middle classes a greater share in the government than they had yet received. And over and above all was that appeal to the emotions. Here I am!

Resistance was negligible. Marshal Ney set out from Paris declaring that he would bring Napoleon back in an iron cage; face to face with him, he fell weeping into his arms. Somebody posted a notice in the Place Vendôme—"Napoleon to Louis XVIII: My good brother, it is useless to send me any more soldiers. I have enough."

The eagle flew from steeple to steeple. The Duc d'Angoulême and his intrepid wife—in Napoleon's opinion the only *man* among the Bourbons—tried in vain to rally the Royalist city of Bordeaux to the King's cause. By March 12 Napoleon was within a day's march of Paris and Louis XVIII had himself hoisted into his carriage and fled with his household troops to the north, stopping only when he reached Ghent, across the Belgian border.

In the Tuileries the tacked-on lilies were ripped off to reveal the bees.

Napoleon had learned from adversity; he no longer promised a marshal's baton in every knapsack, but a vote in every civilian briefcase. Universal suffrage and a truly parliamentary régime were offered to France at the Champ de Mai, one of those grandiose parades so dear to the French. The *tricolore* once more ousted the white flag of the Bourbons, the hated Maison du Roi was disbanded and replaced by the Imperial Guard. For a hundred days he worked feverishly to unite and inspire the nation, for he knew that the peace implied by his speech at Grenoble was not in his power to bring about. Already the powers had declared him to be outside the pale of law, and Wellington was posting to Belgium to organize the Allied forces for the inevitable war.

Opinions differ about the campaign that followed, the battles of Quatre-Bras, Ligny and Waterloo. Some hold that Napoleon was no longer the man he had been, that he had lost the power of rapid decision, that his confidence was gone: others believe that the putting into the field of an army raised in so short a time and not led by first-class men—for there were few of the old marshals who could be trusted—yet capable of making Waterloo, in Wellington's words, "a damned close run thing," is proof that genius lingered. The French were outnumbered; they had no ally to come in as Blücher and his Prussians did, a little late, toward the end.

Waterloo was decisive; once again Napoleon retreated into France, pursued by his foes. Once again he abdicated.

He made one last visit to Malmaison, where Josephine had died in May 1814, and where her roses still bloomed and her ghost lingered. He tried to plan the future which was to be decided for him by others. He considered asking permission to go to America, where in a free new world so many people were starting life afresh. He meditated throwing himself upon the chivalry of the Prince Regent and becoming a private citizen of England. But the Hundred Days had proved how potentially dangerous he was; how right were those, like Talleyrand, who wished him far away. This time a remote island in the South Atlantic awaited him; St. Helena, slow decline of body and spirit, death.

On St. Helena, in genuine captivity this time, he had resort to the weapon which according to the cliché is mightier than the sword and which, in other circumstances, in a different age, might have served him better. He had once said, "What a romance my life has been." So he wrote about it in *The Memorial of St. Helena*, attributing all his doings to humanitarian and liberal motives, representing himself as a martyr in the cause of mankind's freedom.

It was too late for this theory to benefit him, but it might serve his son, now called Duc de Reichstadt and being drilled into the conventional shape of an Austrian prince. The boy died too soon to benefit—but another of his name reaped the harvest of the legend. For the legend, thus forged, lived on, and, when France was settled again, and flowers bloomed on the graves of the dead, the nation forgot what it owed to the dull, painstaking Bourbons, discounted the victories of peace and remembered other victories, Arcola, Austerlitz, Wagram and Jena. The legend was burnished not only by the "old grumblers" of the army but by the writings of such men as Béranger and Victor Hugo. Had Napoleon died in one of his successful battles he would have wielded as little postmortem political influence as Nelson; but he was beaten, he was caged, and to romantic writers "the beaten man is a story forever," as Masefield says.

France's tendency, paradoxical in a freedom-loving nation, to turn, from time to time, to the rule of the one strong man, is due, in part, at least, to the Napoleonic legend.

In 1815, as in 1814, France had troubles to face. This time there was no question of consulting her about her future government. Willy-nilly the monarchy returned, a warmed-up dish. Louis XVIII issued, from Ghent, one of his sensible statements:

"I hasten to place myself for a second time between the Allies and the French—my government may have made mistakes—experience alone can avoid them—I want everything that will save France." To those Frenchmen, and there were many, who had been led astray, he promised pardon excepting only those directly concerned with what he called "the plot." But even this clemency could not prevent amongst Frenchmen a feeling that the King's return was the result of the Allied victory and that the Bourbons were, in a sense, alien.

Coming back in the summer of 1815 to the Tuileries where, once again, the lilies hid the bees, Louis XVIII faced more difficulties than had confronted him in the spring of the previous year.

Chapter 2. THE REIGN OF LOUIS XVIII

This time there was no pretense that the Allies were in Paris as anything but conquerors. They marched in with their guns loaded and the fuses lit. The scarlet uniforms of the British mingled with the Prussians' blue, the white, crimson-faced jackets of the Austrians and the Russians' green tunics. Bugle calls and sharp orders in alien tongues broke the silence of a city under military occupation for the first time in its history.

Soldiers swarmed all over Paris. The rank and file were fascinated by the Boulevard du Temple with its carousels, marionettes and booths. The officers patronized the cafés, the gambling places and the brothels in the arcades under the Palais Royal, a center of vice that even Napoleon, disapproving of it, had never succeeded in suppressing.

The British, under the stern discipline of Wellington, behaved in a manner that soon made them tolerated; the Scots with their kilts and high feathered bonnets were even popular. With the Prussians it was different; they had suffered invasion themselves and were out for revenge. In Paris and the country districts that they occupied there was murder and pillage, rape and arson. In brutality they outdid the Cossacks whose Hetman went to bed in his spurs. Marshal Blücher wanted to blow up the Pont d'Iéna and was only dissuaded by the protests of Louis XVIII.

Following the invasion of the armies came the invasion of tourists, all eager to see Napoleon's improvements. Paris was all enclosed by its customs wall with its 58 barriers, but within there were great new buildings to be stared at; the Madeleine, the Palais Bourbon, new home of the Chamber of Deputies, the Bourse, the long, colonnaded Rue de Rivoli, new quays and bridges, the still unfinished Arc de Triomphe. These were all impressive, since Napoleon believed that to be great was to be beautiful. More valuable, if less obvious, were his contributions to the city's amenities, the abattoirs, the vast covered food markets and an adequate water supply.

While all this lively commotion filled the streets, in quiet places the business of government was resumed. Louis XVIII again applied his policy of conciliation and retained Fouché as Minister of Police though he had held that office during the Hundred Days. As he had promised from Ghent, the King appointed a president of the Council where all administrative affairs would be discussed. Talleyrand, with the portfolio of Foreign Affairs, naturally became its chief; Baron Louis remained as Finance Minister and Marshal St. Cyr became Minister of War. The Bourbon princes, tainted by reaction, were excluded from the Council.

The future of the army demanded immediate attention. Drawn up beyond the Loire under the command of Marshal Davout, it constituted a threat because of its bellicose attitude toward the King and toward the Allies. There was danger that Davout might combine with the Royalist chiefs in the west and continue fighting. Talleyrand's persuasive tongue went to work on Davout and brought him to agree to the disbanding of the troops in return for the promise that they should be generously treated. Under the new command of Marshal MacDonald, the disbanding went on so slowly that in fact France kept her military force.

The next business was to order elections. The age limits were lowered, from forty to twenty-five for candidates, from thirty to twenty-one for electors, but the franchise still rested on so narrow a tax qualification that out of a population of thirty million rather fewer than a hundred thousand citizens could vote.

The elections were held under the shadow of a ruthless White Terror in the south and west and the Chamber of Deputies that resulted was made up of Royalists so extreme that Louis, remarking that its like could not be found anywhere, nicknamed it the *Chambre Introuvable*.

The majority of its members were obscure country gentlemen, inactive under the Republic and the Empire and now filled with a burning desire to reverse the injuries inflicted during the last quarter of a century upon their caste and their Church. Most of them were strangers to Paris, their ignorance of the city and its ways matched their political inexperience, but their opinions, if not their manners, made them welcome in the salons of the Faubourg St. Germain, where the women of the aristocracy were considerably more Royalist than the King, or even, possibly, than Artois himself.

The Chamber of Peers, on the other hand, chosen by the King, was of a liberal and progressive nature—a comfort to Talleyrand and Fouché, who were confounded by the character of the Chamber of Deputies. In the pre-Revolution days liberal and thoughtful aristocrats—allowed privilege but no political power—had looked enviously upon the English House of Lords; now, possessed of some authority, they naturally sought to extend it to the utmost; but they did France no harm because their aim was not to turn back the clock but to consolidate their new political power. Most of them were conditioned by heredity and tradition to put service before personal advantage. It is noticeable that the Restoration assemblies were free of the politico-financial scandals which have bedeviled later periods.

Elected assemblies come and go, political complexion can change overnight, but treaties of peace, dealing with wider issues, have more permanent effects. The Allies still saw France as the real enemy of peace in Europe; the ease with which Napoleon had staged his comeback had shaken their faith in Louis' ability to control his people. The Hundred Days must be paid for; this time there must be guarantees of good behavior. In Paris the ambassadors of Russia, Prussia, Austria and Great Britain were to form a quadripartite council to act as watchdog. France was to pay indemnities of some forty million pounds to defray the cost of maintaining an Allied force of 150,000 men in her northern provinces for a period not exceeding five years. Also—a humiliation more keenly felt and less reasonably bewailed—France was to restore all the works of art which Napoleon had collected as spoils from conquered countries. The Prussians did not wait for the treaty to be signed before rushing to the Louvre to grab what was due to them. The official who superintended this recovery of treasure was named Ribbentrop!

Prussia would have liked, indeed pressed for, the surrender of the provinces of Alsace and Lorraine; the other Allies resisted this demand. They were aware that the loss of the Rhine frontier and of Belgium, which the return to the frontiers of 1792 had involved, had hurt France sorely. That wound, more than a year old, still bled; to insist upon her giving up her two most valued provinces might, even now, provoke her to war.

The final Act of the Congress of Vienna, hastily signed, together with the Second Treaty of Paris, shaped the future of Europe for the next hundred years and ushered in a period of peace that outlasted the most hopeful expectations. Even Talleyrand could hardly have foreseen that the Congress of Vienna, and those congresses which succeeded it, would set a pattern for the regulation of international affairs by discussion which became part of nineteenth-century diplomacy and is still, in the twentieth, regarded as ideal.

Talleyrand, who had served France so well through all the interminable sessions of talk, did not hold the pen when the moment for signing came. He lost the confidence of his friend, Alexander of Russia, by arranging a secret alliance between France, Great Britain and Austria. He sensed the menace of Prussia. At home his moderate government had not been able to withstand the pressures from that reactionary Chamber of Deputies. So he offered the King his resignation and it was blandly accepted. Such blatant ingratitude—after all, who had organized the Bourbon Restoration?—could hardly surprise his tempered, cynical mind, but he was humiliated and resentful. He never again held office under the Restoration. His enemies called his treatment rough justice. Talleyrand nursed his grudge.

Peace and order in France were essential, not only for the well-being of Europe, but for her own. There was that swingeing indemnity to be paid. The Allies realized that Louis XVIII was a man who respected his obligations (Napoleon might have disagreed with them!) but they had little faith in Artois and his friends and realized that the White Terror might have spread across France but for the presence of the Army of Occupation. One and a half million men, occupying sixty-one of France's departments, ensured peace; but there was still to be some bloodshed.

Louis had promised pardon to those who had gone over to the Emperor during the Hundred Days; it would have been impossible to punish them all, but there were token sacrifices of those whose behavior was too flagrant to be forgiven. Whenever one of these was brought to trial there were mutterings and grumblings from the people and from the soldiers. Louis XVIII would have given much to avoid the trial of Marshal Ney, "the bravest of the brave"; he knew it would be a political disaster. Ney was given chance after chance to escape, and ignored them all; so he was executed, to the horror of those who had cast off the Emperor yet held his Marshals dear.

The government might argue that, if Ney's execution was a blunder, so had been that of the Duc d'Enghien; that one death balanced the other. But this Old Testament eye-for-an-eye argument did not appeal to the people or do anything to make the régime popular.

On one thing, however, Louis could congratulate himself; he had chosen Talleyrand's successor wisely and well. His new minister was Armand-Emmanuel du Plessis, Duc de Richelieu who, to the prestige of a famous name—Cardinal Richelieu had been Louis XIII's great minister—added a handsome face, a commanding presence and a character of such outstanding integrity that Wellington said of him that his word was as good as a treaty.

He was fifty when he took office and he had spent his last twenty-five years in Russia, where Alexander had liked and trusted him well enough to make him Governor of the Crimea. After the Restoration he had returned to France for family reasons, and he intended to go back to his post in Russia, but Alexander joined with Louis in urging that it was his duty as a patriot to take the post vacated by Talleyrand. Richelieu argued that, after so long an absence from France, he was virtually a foreigner —this could hardly have pleased Louis to whom the same thing applied. He also said that his experience in autocratic Russia had not fitted him to handle political parties. Both objections were met with the counter-argument that his greatest asset was his dissociation from any former régime.

Ultra Royalists in the country welcomed Richelieu's appointment; he was one of them; he had been exiled and impoverished by the Revolution; surely he would sympathize with them. The returned émigrés were no longer clamoring for the restoration of their lands; they realized that it would disrupt the social fabric of the country (when a French peasant landholder dies his property is divided amongst all his children; in twenty-five years land-holders had proliferated), but they did hope for monetary compensation.

They suffered another disappointment. Wherever Richelieu's sympathies lay, his hands were tied. There were the debts of the Empire to be paid; there were the indemnities. There was no money for the ex-landowners and the question of compensation was raised again and again in the ensuing years, and as regularly shelved. The returned *émigrés* became increasingly embittered and their feeling that they were victims of injustice, that they were now underprivileged, did much to prevent the unification of the country which was Richelieu's main aim.

This aim he kept in view when refusing demands for a general reprisal against revolutionaries and Bonapartists, but neither he nor Louis XVIII could prevent the Chamber of Deputies from passing laws which exiled all those surviving regicides who had voted for the death of Louis XVI, and banished the Bonaparte family from France forever.

Richelieu applied his energy and talent to the payment of the indemnity and to persuading the Allies to withdraw their troops before the five years had elapsed. In 1816 the Allies did consent to cut down the occupying force by one fifth, but this was not on account of the political changes which had now established a Chamber more representative of public opinion, but because the grape harvest had failed which, coinciding with another economic crisis, had brought great distress to France.

Eighteen sixteen brought a cause for rejoicing to all Bourbon adherents—the marriage of the Duc de Berri, Artois' son. As a penniless and exiled prince he had vainly sought a bride in every court in Europe; now he married his cousin Marie Caroline, daughter of another restored Bourbon, King of the Two Sicilies. De Berri had already proved—without benefit of clergy—that he was capable of begetting children, so it was hoped that this would prove a fruitful marriage and ensure succession to the throne. Even to those who had little interest in the dynasty the wedding gave something to stare at and to talk about.

And so, shortly afterward, did the appearance upon the Paris streets of a novelty. It was a wooden horse, similar to those on a roundabout but with a head that swiveled so that it could be steered, and with two wheels in place of four legs. This was called a "velocipede," and it and its inventor were subject to howls of derision. All modern cyclists should know the name of M. Garcin and be thankful for his pertinacity in the face of ridicule.

The benefits of peace were soon apparent; the population increased because men who might have fallen in battle stayed at home and reared families. Trade revived with the reopening of the seas to shipping and of foreign markets for such luxury goods as silk and wine. New, fast-moving steamships made the export of perishable foodstuffs possible.

Yet neither the fields of France nor her factories were producing to capacity. The wars had demanded all her effort, while in England the agricultural and industrial revolutions had gone ahead. The French peasant still worked with a wooden plow, or even with spade and hoe and, since holdings were usually small, he could not afford to experiment or develop as people like Coke of Holkham were doing across the Channel. Those who owned more—often members of the bourgeoisie who had bought land as a safe investment or to assure an improved social status—had, as a rule, neither the necessary knowledge nor the wish to introduce innovations.

Industry, so long geared to the demands of war, lacked capital, skilled labor and raw materials; the very thing that was plentiful, unskilled labor, delayed modernization; why mechanize when men were so cheap? Many industries were still carried on in the home and workers in these industries were naturally hostile to the idea of machines which would replace them or huddle them into factories, as had happened in England.

With France, however, this comparative backwardness mattered less than it would have done in many other countries. France is large and has a wide diversity of climate and soil so that it is virtually self-supporting. The Restoration government did much to improve roads—neglected even by Napoleon except where they were of military importance, and this enabled regional products to circulate more freely. In 1815 it needed eighty-six hours to cover the 350 miles between Paris and Bordeaux, in 1830 the journey could be made in forty-five. Travel, however, was still expensive, out of reach of the working man, so regional differences in tradition, costume and manner persisted. There was little similarity between the Provençal in the lazy south, watching his grapes and olives ripen and the Auvergnat, wresting a living from his poor soil; and neither had much in common with the silk worker of Lyons. The newspaper which breeds conformity and shapes opinion could have small influence upon largely illiterate people dependent upon what was said by the curé from the pulpit on Sundays or by the gossips on market days.

For the great mass of the people, now that the Revolution had righted the worst of their wrongs and the war was over, politics meant little. The Chamber of Deputies in Paris might spend two years in heated argument as to who should and who should not be eligible to vote; but Richelieu, staying in a country place, wrote:

"You would not believe how little impression is made here by all those discussions which have so much agitated the salons of Paris. I can assure you that to change or not to change the electoral law is all the same to the vast majority of Frenchmen."

Realists have always held that a hungry man offered a sandwich or a vote would opt for the sandwich; and the ordinary man of this period, if not actually hungry, was busy staving off hunger. It was as well for Richelieu and Louis XVIII that the ordinary man was not clamoring for a vote, for at the end of the two years of debate the franchise was still limited to men who paid 300 francs annually in direct taxes, and candidates for election must be men who paid 1000 francs. With minor modifications this electoral law remained in force for thirty years.

Intellectual life surged ahead with remarkable vigor. Paris was full of young men of ability and ambition debarred by the age limit for deputies from participating in active political life—they could not emulate Danton, Robespierre or Desmoulins, nor could they hope to be, like Marmont, a general of division at twenty-six, or like Ney, a Marshal of France at thirty-five. They must find other outlets. François Guizot, himself one of the young men of the time and destined for a long and brilliant career, recalled those days when intellectual liberty flourished and flowered:

"Who does not remember the great intellectual movement which arose and flourished rapidly during the Restoration? The human spirit, but lately absorbed and confined by the rude toil of war, rediscovered its wide and generous activity. Poetry, philosophy, history, moral and literary criticism, every branch of intellectural activity, received a new and bold impetus."*

Restoration France produced Ampère's work in electricity, Sadi Carnot's in thermodynamics, Lamarck's in natural history; Orfila busied himself with toxicology, Laënnec with the stethoscope. Niepce and Daguerre made the first experiments with photography.

Printing presses were kept busy, issuing new works, reprinting the classics. Literary fashion changed. Classical tradition held that death or any fierce action must take place off stage. Victor Hugo, one of the most brilliant exponents of the new style wrote a play, *Cromwell* which shocked and disgusted those reared in, and still attached to, the old tradition; he defended himself in his preface:

"Authors have the right to dare, to risk, to create, to invent their own style."

A nation which had seen so much actual bloodshed turned away from the insipid and writers went for inspiration, as Louis Cazamian says: "To the far-distant in time and space, to the foreign and the exotic, the strange and the mysterious, to night, ruins, the symbols and images of death, to the wild and primitive, and nature."

Scott's historical novels, widely and passionately devoured, stimulated an interest in history—that history which lay between the present and the classical times of Greece and Rome to which the Empire had looked so often. Interest in the Middle Ages became fashionable. The *émigrés* who had been in England had sampled the wares of the Gothic revival.

Archetype of the new school of romantic writers was Chateaubriand with his aristocratic birth, extreme good looks, attraction for women and foreign travels. A Breton from St. Malo, it was natural that he should seek adventure overseas, but his proposed exploration of the polar regions took him no further than Baltimore

* Quoted by G. Bertier de Sauvigny, *La Restauration.*

and Philadelphia, where, though his actual acquaintance with the native Indians may have been slight, he acquired enough interest in them to write *Atala, René* and *Les Natchez*, books which had a profound influence upon his generation, indeed upon his century, since so many subsequent writers were affected by them. His *Génie du Christianisme* played its part in Napoleon's decision to restore Catholicism and make his peace with the Pope. His greatest work is *Mémoires d'Outre-Tombe*.

With the return of the Bourbons, Chateaubriand abandoned literature for politics and political writing. He typifies that association between literature and politics that is characteristic of the period. Guizot and Thiers were both historians before their energies were diverted to politics. Lamartine, the great lyric poet whose *Méditations Poétiques*, published in 1820, freed French poetry from the stranglehold of classicism, was to have an outstanding political career.

Richelieu was not a literary politician; his aims were practical and immediate—financial stability and the removal from French soil of every foreign soldier. In 1818 he attended the Congress of Aix-la-Chapelle and returned home with the welcome news that the five-year occupation period had been reduced to three. In Paris there was a great outburst of rejoicing, but Talleyrand marred Richelieu's well-earned triumph by gibing that he was the Czar's tool, an insinuation which ill-intentioned and ill-informed people, especially in the provinces, were quick to seize upon.

The election of 1818 swung to the left. Back to the Chamber came Lafayette whose enmity to the King dated to the time when his ambition to be the George Washington of France had run counter to Louis' ambition to be its King. Other prominent members of the Assembly were Casimir Périer, the banker Lafitte and, later, Benjamin Constant, all champions of popular sovereignty and individual liberty, all opposed to the Church and to militant nationalism.

Faced with this opposition, Richelieu thankfully gave up the office he had never wanted and which only his patriotism had induced him to accept. He had filled the post with distinction and retired into private life no penny the better off. The achievement of his aims was his only reward. He had freed his country from foreign occupation, carried on Talleyrand's work of reinstating France among the nations of Europe, set the national finances on a sound basis and paid the war indemnities promptly, but these things weighed light against party friction.

Louis chose his latest favorite, Elie Decazes, as the new head of government, but he was not long in office. In February 1820 the Duc de Berri was assassinated, not, as might have been expected, by a jealous husband, but by a fanatical Bonapartist who had once worked in the stables at Elba and whose wish was to destroy the Bourbon race. De Berri, with his last breath, made a plea for mercy for his murderer, but people were too much shocked by the senseless crime to heed it. There was a wave of emotional, pro-Bourbon sympathy, which was fortified when, seven and a half months later, the Duchess gave birth to a child, the Duc de Bordeaux, Child of France, "the child of the miracle."

Feeling about the assassination was so strong that the public demanded some scapegoat in addition to the murderer; popular sentiment pointed to Decazes. Louis was compelled to part with the man he looked upon as a son. He installed him comfortably as ambassador to England, and appealed to Richelieu to resume his post, which he did with his former reluctance and sense of duty.

The pro-Royalist feeling lasted long enough to affect the election of 1821 which returned a largely right-wing Chamber; but reaction had evoked reaction and now the left, led by Lafayette, was better organized, more active and less inclined to compromise. Lafayette still possessed what Thomas Jefferson had called "his canine appetite for publicity"; he was always ready to stand forth as a champion of any anti-government cause and to involve himself in any subversive activity.

In the new Chamber both extremes of right and left were powerful and vociferous and, despairing of reconciling them, Richelieu again resigned. He did not long survive his retirement; when he died in 1822 he left behind him the memory of one of France's most high-minded ministers, leader of one of the best governments she has ever enjoyed.

The choice of his successor this time showed how far the ailing old King had fallen under the influence of Artois. It had been a sour joke in Paris that there were two kings, Louis at the Tuileries, Artois at the Louvre. Artois and his men—in the Chamber of Deputies, the Comte de Villèle, in the Chamber of Peers, De Polignac, hated for his name which reminded people of Marie Antoinette's favorite. Now it was Villèle who took Richelieu's place. Artois had urged the appointment, assuring Louis that a right-wing government would render the rest of his days free from trouble. It was not, of itself, a bad choice of minister. Villèle, though a southerner, was calm and imperturbable, lucidly intelligent and an able financier.

The old King, failing now, inclined to fall asleep even at council meetings and able to move about only in a wheel chair, was subject to another influence, that of Zoë Talon, Comtesse du Cayla, a beautiful thirty-seven-year-old brunette, to whom a friend of Artois had introduced Louis, hoping that she might fill the void in his life left by the departure of Decazes. It was, of necessity, a platonic relationship. The Comtesse visited the Tuileries once a week, on Wednesday, and then only to play chess, but she wrote to Louis every day, letters inspired by Villèle. Soon her hold over him was absolute.

Louis had never thought highly of his brother's political acumen and had once said that if Artois could find no one else against whom to plot he would conspire against himself but, now that the shadows were closing in, the future whittled down to a few more tomorrows, he increasingly left matters to Artois and his friends.

Yet he lived to see the French army march again.

It was a different army, reformed and reconciled to the régime through the work of Marshal St. Cyr. Men were recruited for a term of six years, with six years in the reserve. The émigré officers had been gradually paid off and many important commands given to former general officers of the Imperial army.

This army moved in a cause unlikely to appeal to liberal opinion; it went to quell an insurrection in Spain and to bolster up King Ferdinand; but the Royalists were anxious to show that under the Bourbons the army was as good as it had been under the Empire, and the soldiers themselves were eager for action, for glory.

In fact the expedition, though led sensibly and well by the Duc d'Angoulême, was little more than a military parade; but there was one significant incident. At the Spanish border the army was met by a group of Bonapartist exiles waving the *tricolore*. French soldiers, marching for the first time in thirty-four years under the Bourbon lilies, did not hesitate, at the word of command, to fire upon those under the flag of the Revolution and the Empire.

By 1824 it was plain that Louis' life was ending but, though his flesh might weaken, his prejudices remained; he dismissed Chateaubriand who, under Villèle, had attained the rank of Foreign Minister and Chateaubriand went over for a time to the liberal opposition and plied his eloquent pen in their cause.

In March the King forced his decrepit body to face the task of opening the new Chamber returned by the last election. He had always been careful to surround the elected representatives of France with all the symbols of dignity with which he enveloped himself and this opening session lacked nothing of pomp and grandeur. There were the peers of France in their ermine-trimmed mantles, the diplomatic corps, the Marshals of France. And there, on his magnificent throne, draped with crimson velvet and topped with ostrich plumes, was the King of France. He made an admirable effort; he spoke of "the primary needs of France after its long trials," he named them, peace and stability. He drew up the balance sheet of the past and offered a prospectus for the future; but his voice failed and became a confused and painful whisper. Men of all parties listened in silence; even politicians are human at times. This was a dying man, and he had ruled the destiny of France through nine critical years . . .

Six months later, after a final three days of agony, Louis Xavier Stanislas de Bourbon, by the grace of God King of France and Navarre, who had frustrated the Revolution's intention that his brother, Louis XVI, should be the last of the Louis', died, and the crown of France, with all that it carried of glory and ancient heritage and present problems, passed to his brother, Charles Philippe, Comte d'Artois.

Napoleon had died in 1821, and a few months before he died Wellington said: "We made a tremendous mistake in getting rid of Napoleon. He is the man we ought to have had. As long as the

Bourbons hold four thrones there will be no peace in Europe. None of that family is any good."

A sweeping statement and one which ignored Louis XVIII's real achievement; finding France invaded he left her liberated, finding her poor he left her with finances improved, her credit re-established by a régime of strict probity and economy; finding her an autocracy he left her with her feet firmly set on the path of democracy. He died in his bed, in his own Palace of the Tuileries, and was succeeded by his brother as peacefully and automatically as though there had never been a break in the monarchy.

He was fortunate in his ministers, but that was thanks to his good judgment. His weaknesses were human; if he was inclined to be lazy that was because his youthful vigor had all been expended before he came to the throne and because throughout his reign he was engaged in an exhausting internal struggle between what he had been—a man reared in the hothouse atmosphere of Versailles—and the man he had become, shaped by the vicissitudes of exile; if he was inclined to have favorites it was because he was lonely and enjoyed the company of those with whom he could cast off that monumental dignity, show off his knowledge and indulge his taste for salacious gossip. The way in which he could forget his favorites, once they were out of sight, indicated a lack of genuine warmth in his nature, and the courtiers, contrasting him with the generous, kindly Artois, said, "Louis may be a greater king, but the other is the better man."

It was now for the better man to show that he could be as good a King.

Chapter 3. THE REIGN OF CHARLES X

Only in fiction would one expect to find a woman's deathbed repentance having profound influence on a country's history; yet the piety of the man who was now King of France at a time when the fierce struggle between clerical and anticlerical factions was coming to a climax, dated back twenty years, to the death of his mistress in 1804. With her last breath Louise d'Esparbès, Comtesse de Polastron, implored her lover to belong henceforth to God alone; Charles "wept and he believed," like Chateaubriand when he discovered the genius of Christianity. His conversion was sincere and lasting.

This love affair of his had already changed him from a frivolous man, aware only of his privileges, to one conscious of his responsibilities and of his ignorance, who could speak sadly of having been brought up so ill that he could never read four pages at a time without boredom.

Exile had changed him too; when he fled from France he is said to have taken with him enough shoe buckles to allow him to wear a different pair each day for a year; having tasted the very lees of humiliation and actually been imprisoned for debt he returned so marked by poverty that, to the end of his days, he had his boots resoled and his cuffs turned.

He was sixty-six when he became King, a simple, kindly and generous man, of equable temper, averse to distressing others and generally benevolent; but his loyalty to old friends—admirable in a private man, a possible drawback to a statesman—led him to cherish and consort with those who had been his fellow exiles and uncompromising Royalists who could not stomach the new order under which the King's rule was circumscribed by Parliament and freely criticized by the press. Politically these men were still of the *ancien régime*, of the Versailles that had vanished, and they embroiled Charles in spite of his sincere intention to fulfill his duties as a constitutional king.

When Charles made his formal entry into Paris, he rode, despite the rain, on horseback as Napoleon was accustomed to do. Ten years had passed since he had come as his brother's herald and the damage of the years was slight. He had retained his easy grace, his lithe figure and his superb health. His hair had whitened, that was all. With him rode several generals wearing the old Imperial uniform. Optimists in the crowd saw in this a sign of reconciliation between Bourbon and Bonapartist.

The reign opened with a brilliant social season; the Royalists showed their delight at Charles' accession by a series of balls; sixty-three successive nights of dancing in the winter of 1825. Ladies wore delicate, filmy dresses that still showed the influence of Leroy, and had wreaths of real flowers on their curls; or, at the splendid costume balls which testified to the new interest in the medieval, they wore rich silks and velvets.

One of the most splendid of these balls was given by Charles' cousin, Louis Philippe, Duc d'Orléans. Louis XVIII, with his cold good sense, had recognized that collateral branches of a family often suffer the occupational disease of envy and tend to become the focus of disaffection. It took him some time to allow Louis Philippe to return to France at all, and when he did showed him no favor. Charles, warmer-hearted, less farsighted, reinstalled his cousin in his old family home, the Palais Royal. Louis was right, Charles wrong, as events would prove.

Politically, the opening acts of the reign won approval and did much to dispel the preconceived image of Charles as a reactionary, priest-ridden bigot, who would put his Catholicism first and his royal responsibilities second. He declared his adherence to the Charter and professed liberal principles. But he retained Villèle in office despite his unpopularity.

This unpopularity Charles began to share when, at the beginning of the parliamentary session, he announced two projects dear to his heart; one concerned matters of sacrilege and the other the payment, at last, of compensation to the émigrés. He claimed that this latter measure was an act of justice and reparation which Louis XVIII had always wished to see effected as soon as the country's finances allowed.

Neither measure was outrageous; the first imposed more severe punishments for theft from churches and made the desecration of the Host a capital crime; the second proposed a far-from-generous payment to those *émigrés* who had followed their princes abroad, and only about 70,000 of them were still alive. But the one ran counter to the anticlerical feeling in the country, the other threatened the taxpayer's pocket.

It was unfortunate for Charles that such controversial problems, left over from his brother's reign, should demand solution so early in his own. It was also unfortunate that there should be at this point so many discontented and disillusioned young men about with nothing to do except to be anti-establishment in any form. Napoleon's educational reforms had the immediate effect of too many young men with qualifications chasing too few jobs in professions that were overcrowded. Often, after years of study and sacrifice from his family, a young man found himself unemployed, disillusioned, an easy prey for disaffection. It is a social pattern that can be observed at firsthand in many places in the world today.

Charles' reign should have seen the firm re-establishment of family life; the King was a widower, with neither favorite nor mistress, the Angoulêmes were models of rectitude, the Orléans a devoted couple with a large family; men were no longer away at the wars. But the gulf between the generations yawned, young men thought their fathers had submitted too easily to imperial autocracy and were now submitting too easily to Bourbon domination.

The young were restive; and the Bonapartists resented the fact that when, for reasons of economy, the army was reduced, most of the officers retired were old soldiers of the Empire. By a most unlucky coincidence, or through sheer stupidity, the ordinance for their dismissal was published on the anniversary of the Battle of Austerlitz, a day of the utmost sentimental significance to every Bonapartist, and one to which even the most level-headed Frenchman could hardly be completely indifferent.

Louis XVIII had never been formally crowned, not because he wished to break with tradition but because he lacked the physical stamina to endure so long a ceremony. To Charles it seemed right and proper that he should be crowned at Rheims, the place which had seen the coronation of thirty-two French Kings; and why should not His Most Christian Majesty invite God's blessing on his reign when even Napoleon had done so, and brought the Pope himself to bestow it?

Charles gave further evidence of his loyalty to old friends. The Archbishop of Rheims who officiated at the ceremony was the man who had been his confessor during his exile at Holyrood, the man who had received Louise's confession and brought her lover back to the Church. But though to the pious Charles and those who thought with him, the Coronation was a traumatic experience, there were those who looked upon it as mummery, savoring strongly of the old régime. There was irony in it too; Talleyrand who, at Napoleon's coronation had carried the mantle, now had the task of putting on the King's shoes, made of violet velvet and embroidered with the golden fleur-de-lis.

After the Coronation the rift between Charles and his people—a rift not entirely of his making—began to widen. Discontent found voice in the popular press of the opposition, often so virulently partisan as to have scant regard for truth; and when, in March 1827, the King reviewed the National Guard, composed largely of his bourgeois adherents, he was met with a hostile demonstration, to which he replied by dismissing the Guard, an action which was to have fatal consequences.

Like other governments in trouble at home, this one sought to distract public attention to affairs abroad. In October 1827, the French sent a fleet to join those of Russia and England to support the Greeks in their fight for freedom against the Turks. At Navarino, the Turko-Egyptian fleet was beaten, but though French prestige was enhanced Villèle's home government gained no popularity.

Villèle's next move was an attempt to offset the large liberal majority in the upper house by a massive creation of new peers. Then, finally, he decided to dissolve parliament in the hope that an election would produce a safe majority for his government.

The election which followed, nicknamed the election "of anger and vengeance," showed some ominous signs. There were street riots which the cavalry were called out to quell. There was the birth of a new left-wing organization that called itself *Aide-toi-et-Dieu-t'aidera* (God helps those who help themselves), of which Lafayette was a prominent member.

When the election was over and Villèle surveyed the new Chamber he found little comfort; those who supported his policies were exactly matched in number by those who did not, liberal and splinter groups of every shade of opinion. Deadlock.

Very reluctantly Charles decided that the time had come to dismiss Villèle. The Duchesse d'Angoulême warned him, "You are dismissing M. de Villèle; it is the first step down from your throne."

Others shared her dismay, but the opposition rejoiced, and France lost a man who had rendered her unique service and who might, with his financial skill, have helped her weather the coming economic squalls.

Charles made an honest effort to behave constitutionally. Did he ever remember that he had once declared that he would sooner hew wood than reign under the conditions that ruled the King of England? He chose as his new Minister the Vicomte de Martignac who, like all the Restoration ministers, possessed great personal qualities but lacked the art of parliamentary manipulation. All those concerned during these years with the government of France were pioneers, breaking fresh ground, often stony ground; there was no inherited system. Charles himself was in many ways equipped to be a monarch on the English pattern, but the time was not ripe; good will, impeccable family life, the ability to make public appearances and gracious speeches were not enough in a country where the ferment of revolution had not yet worked itself out.

Martignac attempted the impossible, the circus performer's feat of riding two horses, one foot on the liberal left, the other on the monarchy. He maintained a precarious balance for eighteen months.

In the summer of 1829 the King made a tour of Alsace and Lorraine where the warmth of his reception led him to believe that the ordinary people were on his side. Encouraged by this, and by the fact that the country's finances were in better heart, he decided to change his tactics. He was irritated by Martignac's continual appeasement of the left, he was tired of his own policy of compromise; he would have a new minister, one calculated to interpret his wishes exactly, one to whom he could give his full confidence. He chose Prince Jules de Polignac, whose very name was hated by the people. They looked on him as conservatism incarnate.

To this injudicious choice Charles added others; Bourmont, who had changed sides on the eve of the Battle of Waterloo, was made Minister of War; La Bourdonnaye, who had been an ardent supporter of the White Terror in 1815, was Minister of the Interior.

"Here again," shrieked the press, "is the court with its old grudges, emigration with its prejudices, the priesthood with its hatred of liberty, come to throw themselves between France and her King. All that has been conquered by forty years of work and misery is being violently imposed on her. Unhappy France! Unhappy King!"

Charles' heart, rather than his head, dictated the choice of de Polignac, who was not only one of his oldest friends but the nephew of his dead mistress. Like his immediate predecessors de Polignac had great personal qualities and, as an *émigré*, then as ambassador to London, he had seen representative government at work: but of his fifty-eight years thirty had been spent abroad so that he, like Richelieu, was a stranger to his own country, and he had the added disadvantage that a long prison sentence, earned by his implication in the Cadoudal plot, had left him melancholy and inert.

The times called for energetic action; the opposition was now determined upon nothing less than the downfall of the dynasty. Lafayette stumped the country, collecting adherents for *Aide-toi-et-Dieu-t'aidera*. Talleyrand, sensing a change of weather, turned his coat once more; the ultimate good of France was still his aim and little good could come to her while an aging King, surrounded by aging and intransigent men, pulled in one direction, the people in another. Talleyrand joined with two rising young journalists, Thiers and Mignet, and with that veteran statesman, Baron Louis, to form the nucleus of an Orleanist party whose views and aspirations were expressed in a new paper, the *National*, which was subsidized by the banker Jacques Lafitte. The paper quickly became influential. There was talk now of the parallel between Bourbons and Stuarts; the similarity was remarkable; execution; restoration; succession by a brother; people were reminded that James II and Charles X were alike in their religious policies; and that James had been deposed and succeeded by a member of his own family after a bloodless revolution. The French had not far to look for a member of Charles' family to succeed him; Louis Philippe was there in the Palais Royal, behaving with the utmost discretion . . .

Charles was angered by the open emergence of the Orleanist party and by the increasing hostility of the press. Before he made his speech from the throne in March 1830, he talked with Villèle, whom he had dismissed from office but continued to consult in private. Villèle advised him to make a conciliatory speech; this advice he ignored. From the throne he said bluntly: "If guilty maneuvers produce for my government obstacles I do not wish to envisage, I shall find the strength to overcome them in my resolution to maintain public order, in a just confidence in the French people and the love they have always borne their Kings."

It was now a long time since the French people had so loved a king as to be blind to his policies and their own self-interest. And had Charles been a thousand times more popular than he was, between him and the people there were now the Chambers, all too ready to catch the minatory note in that speech, to resent it and to reply to it. They said that an indispensable condition for the conduct of public affairs was an identity of view between government and governed. Did this exist? They said that the people were anxious because their liberty was threatened.

The Chambers did not speak for all the people, Charles had many supporters, but they spoke for Paris and in 1830 it was Paris, not the provinces, which made and unmade governments.

Charles was not, at heart, the bigoted tyrant that the Chambers, the Orleanists, the hostile press represented him to be, but, like Pascal's wicked animal, he was prepared, if attacked, to defend himself. Also there was no need for him to read more than four boring pages of history to know what had happened to his elder brother. The ghost of Louis XVI walked the palace corridors that summer. Louis had compromised; Charles would not.

He dissolved parliament, as Napoleon had dismissed the Legislature when it told him what he did not wish to hear. He fixed new elections for June 23 and July 3 and ordered the convocation of the new Chambers for August 3.

The times for him were truly "out of joint." The delegates were sent home on May 16, and on June 10, brought by that marvel of the century, the telegraph, came news of a kind that had bolstered many a toppling government; a French expedition to Algiers, ostensibly to punish an insult offered to a consul of France, had been successful and was throwing open the way to the fulfillment of a long-cherished dream—the establishment of a French colony.

In this election Charles himself, King of France, went to the hustings and admonished the electors to do their duty. "I know I shall fulfill mine," he said. The electors thought they knew what that meant; he would fulfill his duty to the Church and to the reactionary right with which he was now identified.

On July 19 all the votes were in and counted. A landslide to the left! Charles could either accept that with good grace or resist.

There is a point at which all men are "suppled and tamed" by experience and age; there is another when not only the arteries harden. Charles had reached that stage. He made a fighting speech to the Council:

"The spirit of revolution exists in the fullest sense in the men of the left; it is the monarchical system they wish to overthrow. Unhappily I have more experience on this point than you, gentlemen, who are not old enough to have seen the Revolution. I remember what happened then. The first time my brother made concessions was the signal of his undoing . . . If I yield up this time to their demands they will end up by treating us as they treated my brother . . ."

His was not the first nose to sniff revolution in the air; Lamartine had scented it, so had all the promoters of the *National;* yet Polignac still assured the King that there was no danger or, if there was danger, the military force in Paris was well able to deal with it. This was an optimistic judgment, since there were only 7000 troops in the capital. Nevertheless it was assuring, and so was the clause in the Charter which ran:

"The King is the supreme head of the State, commands the forces on land and sea . . . enacts the regulations and ordinances necessary for carrying out the laws and the safety of the State."

Charles genuinely believed that the state was in peril; he genuinely believed that under the Charter he had the power, indeed the duty to act. He proceeded to do so, mistakenly perhaps, but with courage.

On Sunday, July 25, after hearing Mass, he signed four ordinances presented to him by his Council.

The first suspended the liberty of the press and decreed that no journal or pamphlet of fewer than twenty-five pages could be published without official authorization; the second dissolved the newly elected Chamber, which had not yet met; the third narrowed the scope of the franchise by restricting it to the wealthiest 25 per cent of the nation; the fourth fixed new elections for September.

As he signed Charles said, "Gentlemen, the more I think about it, the more I am convinced that it is impossible to do otherwise."

The ordinances were published on Monday in the *Moniteur* and provoked instant response from the opposition. In the *National* Thiers called on France to resist and said that obedience was no longer a duty. On Tuesday the shops were shut, barricades were up in the streets and the appointment of Marshal Marmont to command the Paris garrison was the signal for rioting to start in the working-class districts.

Marmont was aware of his own unpopularity; he was himself opposed to the ordinances; he was paralyzed by the fear of again failing the authority which had given him his command. This state of mind was not conducive to the vigorous action which the situation demanded. On July 18 he wrote to the King at St. Cloud using, by accident or design, words with a sinister similarity to those addressed to Louis XVI in 1789: "It is no longer a riot; it is revolution. It is urgent that your Majesty takes steps for pacification. The honor of the crown can still be saved. Tomorrow will be too late. . . ."

Because de Polignac had not informed him of the true state of things in Paris, and because he thought that Marmont was exaggerating in an effort to get the ordinances withdrawn, Charles ignored this warning, and Marmont, his letter unanswered, deployed his inadequate forces. The deputies sent a delegation to de Polignac, who refused to receive it. Fighting began in the streets.

It was hot weather, rioters' weather. Many of Marmont's troops, already short of food and ammunition, went over to the insurgents, some of whom struggled to hoist the *tricolore* on the towers of Notre Dame, while others advanced upon the Tuileries. The *polytechnicien*, in bicorne and frock, marched side by side with the workman in his blouse, the tramp in rags by the young fashionable in his redingote, the greasy smuggler by the National Guardsman, the student by the veteran of Waterloo. Their weapons were as varied as their dress; sabers, lances, shotguns, muskets and strange archaic weapons snatched from theatrical stores. On that blistering day they drank, we are told, only cocoa and licorice water. They needed no stimulant; they were drunk on "a headier wine."

There were three days of it, *les Trois Glorieuses*. Glorious for old men, marching again under the forbidden *tricolore* to the forbidden strains of the "Marseillaise"; glorious for young men, now given for the first time an opportunity to live romantically. "I will show you how to die," cried a young locksmith's apprentice as, clutching the *tricolore*, he was shot down on the Pont de Grève. "Remember that my name is Arcole." The bridge was renamed in his memory. Those who fell in these three days could be regarded as martyrs in the cause of liberty.

Old Talleyrand looked from his window in the Rue St. Florentin, saw the troops fleeing, looked at the time and murmured, "At five past twelve on July 29, the senior branch of the Bourbons has ceased to reign."

At St. Cloud, Charles, no longer in ignorance, said, "I am now in the position of my unhappy brother in 1792. In three days it will be all over with the monarchy."

These were significantly different epitaphs. It was not all over with the monarchy: Talleyrand, who had avenged Napoleon's insults by engineering the Restoration, now intended to avenge himself for Bourbon neglect by promoting the cause of Louis Philippe, Duc d'Orléans.

When, as eventually they must, the rioters dispersed in search of food and sleep, they came face to face with posters, unsigned, but known to be the work of Thiers.

"Charles X cannot return to Paris; he has shed the people's blood."

"The Duc d'Orléans is a prince devoted to the cause of revolution."

"The Duc d'Orléans has carried the *tricolore* under fire; only the Duc d'Orléans can carry it again; we want no other."

"The Duc d'Orléans has spoken; he accepts the Charter as we have always wanted it."

"It is from the people that he will hold his crown."

Thiers well knew the value of reiteration in propaganda; even those who read with difficulty came to recognize the oft-repeated name.

Paris was as full of news as of posters; even those who had cautiously stayed indoors soon heard how event tumbled after event. They heard that the Duc d'Angoulême had replaced Marmont—but not that Angoulême had seized the Marshal, as he struggled for his sword, by the throat and hissed, "Do you want to do to us what you did to that Other?" They heard that at St. Cloud the King had imperturbably played his usual evening game of whist; that the King had left for the Trianon; that the recent ordinances had been withdrawn; that the ministry was dismissed and the Duc de Mortemart asked to form a new one; that some deputies had formed a provisional government and called Lafayette to head it; that Louis Philippe had been invited to become Lieutenant-General of the Kingdom.

Those who ventured out might have seen Lafayette, wrapped in the folds of the *tricolore*, embrace Louis Philippe on the balcony of the Hôtel de Ville.

Louis Philippe had continued to behave correctly; he had sent Charles two messages, one by Mortemart, saying that he would be cut in pieces before he would take the crown; what the other said is not known, it was concealed in a piece of cheese, and the messenger, when he was arrested, swallowed it.

The newspapers screamed, "Victory is ours!" Whose?

It was not a victory for the Republicans who, under Godefroy Cavaignac, had actually started the riot. Thiers and Talleyrand had seen that a revival of the Republic would be most unwelcome to the powers. It would be some time before memories of the first French Republic could sleep in the chancelleries of Europe. Crowds roaring, "Long live King Louis Philippe," had not been Cavaignac's aim; nor the aim of Lafayette, whose dream of becoming the French Washington receded once more. It is doubtful if many in the shouting crowd had actually set out on July 26 with the conscious intent of bringing Louis Philippe to the throne. What victory there was went to Thiers and Talleyrand and to an *idea*—a popular throne well surrounded by republican institutions.

The last scenes of Charles' reign were swiftly played. At Trianon he laid aside his uniform, orders and insignia; he signed his abdication. There was a moment when, for as long as it took him to sign his name, Angoulême was Louis XIX of France. His abdication made the young Duc de Bordeaux Henri V of France but his rights were ignored in silence, exactly as those of Napoleon's son had been. And when, on August 3, the Chambers met to proclaim Louis Philippe not King of France but King of the French by will of the people, no mention was made of the boy heir; nor did Louis Philippe allow himself to be cut in pieces. Louis Philippe took his cousin's crown; another Bolingbroke superseding another Richard III.

With Bourbon dignity Charles left for the coast and exile. Like a captain abandoning a sinking ship Charles saw all his family aboard first. Then he embarked and resumed the rootless life of exile; first in Lulworth, then in Holyrood, where there was now no Louise to console and cheer, then in Prague and finally in Austria.

When Charles X died in 1836, Leopold of the Belgians, one of the shrewdest men in Europe wrote of him:

"I regret him; few people were ever kinder to me than the good old man. He was blinded by certain absolute ideas, but a good man and deserving to be loved. History will state that Louis XVIII was a most liberal monarch, reigning with great mildness and justice to his end but that his brother, from his despotic and harsh disposition, upset all the other had done and lost the throne. Louis XVIII was a clever, hard-hearted man, shackled by no principle, very proud and false. Charles X an honest man, a kind friend, an honourable master, sincere in his opinions, and inclined to do everything that was right."

Throughout his life Charles was ill-inspired, ill-served and ill-advised; he came to the throne when more was needed in a king than personal virtues and good intentions, when he was too old to adjust himself and when the divisions in the country which Napoleon had forseen were widening. Had he been a little more pliant, France a little more patient, he might have stayed at the Tuileries until death removed him and made way for new men and new policies.

When Charles left France he took with him much of what remained of the eighteenth century, and the country was left to adjust itself to a more pedestrian age. In the last analysis the Revolution of 1830, neither necessary nor unavoidable, was perhaps less against the Bourbon dynasty, or even against Charles himself, than against the approach of a more mundane period; against the shift in prestige from the glowing red coat of the soldier, with all that it implied of glory and excitement, to the somber garb of priest and clerk, that antithesis of scarlet and black so brilliantly expounded by Stendhal in Le Rouge et le Noir, published in the following year.

Louis Philippe, taking his cousin's throne, had the support of those who realized that since a republic was not immediately possible, the choice lay between monarchy and anarchy. Louis Philippe might perhaps have persuaded the country to accept the young Henri V, with himself as regent: he never attempted to do so, either because he was prompted by ambition, or because he believed that only he, the revolutionary prince, combining two ideologies, could satisfy the need of the moment.

France had no clear view of her own needs. Just as a woman seeking some impossible ideal will take and discard lover after lover, so the French sought, in varying régimes, an elusive millennium. They made small allowance for the growing pains of democracy and failed to realize that the welding of monarchical tradition to constitutional rule is a slow and delicate business, demanding beyond all else, compromise and still more compromise.

Book III

Chapter 1. LOUIS PHILIPPE

Louis Philippe's early life had well equipped him to be a citizen king. He had been soundly taught and much influenced by his governess, Madame de Genlis, a woman with leftist views and original ideas about the instruction of the young. He was sixteen when the Revolution began, and in the next year he became, like his father, a member of the Jacobin Club. Still too young for active political life, he had attended the debates in the National Assembly, so he was known and liked by those in power, and not only allowed to retain his army rank but promoted. He was in Holland when his father, Philippe Egalité, voted for the death of Louis XVI.

He fought with distinction at Valmy and then, involved in a plot to overthrow the Republic—a plot made by Dumouriez—he was obliged to flee to Switzerland.

He was like his cousins an exile, but an exile capable of earning his own living. So thoroughly had Madame de Genlis taught him languages and mathematics and habits of industry that he was able to take a teaching post.

When the advances of the French army made it inadvisable for him to remain in Switzerland, he visited the Scandinavian countries and then went to America where he met George Washington, from whom he may have acquired the punctuality, the attention to detail, the love of order and thrift which were his outstanding characteristics. He had great affection for America and predicted that one day she might become a powerful ally of France.

He left America for England, where he became, like his cousins,

the pensioner of the British government. Penury colored his outlook far more deeply than it did that of Charles X with his harmless little foibles of economy in dress: with Louis Philippe it became an obsession for financial security, not only for himself but
for his family, and this led to actions not always advantageous to
his reputation.

In his family life he was fortunate; during his exile he married
Marie Amélie of the Two Sicilies, a woman of sweet disposition.
His sister, Madame Adelaide, was clever and hardheaded, completely devoted to his interests. He had eight children, whom he
loved. After the Restoration and his return to France the recovery
of estates and family wealth made him enormously rich. Now, to
all this was added the throne, the gift of the French people.

He was slightly younger than either of his cousins at their accession, but still well on into middle age—fifty-eight—and there
was little left of the slim, ardent young officer who had entertained
such progressive ideas. Over the years Louis Philippe had come
nearer the political outlook of the ultra Royalists than they guessed
or he dared admit. The Prince in him had outlived the Jacobin, and
the very phrase, *the will of the people* which qualified his monarchy, was a constant reminder of the fate of his father, who had
—despite his support for the Revolution—been executed by the
will of these same people.

Louis Philippe's accession brought to a country already sadly
divided yet another cleavage; the King's men and the Royalists
were no longer one. He could not count, as Louis XVIII and
Charles X had done, on the support of the old aristocracy. They
regarded him as a usurper. Their numbers and their influence had
dwindled, but they were still capable of making themselves heard
and one of the first questions they asked was an awkward one:
"How can one possibly visit this murdering King?"

This was not a rhetorical question; nor were they accusing him,
metaphorically, of killing Charles X. A real murder, with no small
scandal attached to it, was concerned.

On an August morning, a few weeks after the Three Glorious
Days, the Duc de Bourbon, another cousin of the King, was found
dead in circumstances that precluded suicide. The old man—he

was seventy-four—had virtually lost the use of his hands, yet he had been hanged by a handkerchief tied in a very complicated knot, his knees were bent and his feet touched the floor. His huge fortune of 84,000,000 francs was willed to Louis Philippe's fourth son, the Duc d'Aumale.

Many people believed, others pretended to believe, that this was murder, arranged by Louis Philippe, lest the old man should change his will and leave his money to the newly exiled branch of the family. Louis Philippe was in much the same situation as Mary Stuart after Darnley's death; a really stringent inquiry into the circumstances might have cleared his name. An inquiry was begun but, when it threatened to reveal the scandalous details, the King ordered it to be suspended; people drew their own conclusions and the reign began under a sinister cloud. (Access to documents kept secret for a century has convinced modern writers that Louis Philippe was not involved; the suspension of the inquiry does credit to his sense of the seemly.)

Louis Philippe's first political act was to swear fealty to a Charter, not prepared by himself, but drawn up and presented by the Assembly. The variations from the Charter of 1814 were undramatic but they showed a shift in the wind. The Catholic religion was no longer that of the State, but of the majority of the people. Tax qualifications for both candidates and voters were slightly lowered. The King was to share with the Chambers the right of introducing laws, though he retained the preponderant share in the shaping of policy. The peers were to be nominated for one term only. Above all the new King was required to show himself as heir to the Revolution and to ensure that its doctrines and achievements should not dwindle into a mere shuffling of power from one section of the nation to another.

A new king, even a new Charter, were not enough to bring immediate internal peace; the question of whether policy should be dictated by the passions of the mob or by authority was not yet settled; and there was still some blood to be shed. The great Revolution had set a pattern, every shift of power must be followed by a purge. Merely to depose a king and send him into exile seemed a milk-and-water business to a nation that had decapitated

Louis XVI. With the Three Glorious Days come and gone, the people remembered that their national anthem invites them to water their soil with the blood of traitors. The traitors this time were the ministers who had served Charles X.

The National Guard stormed the Chamber of Peers and threatened to take action into their own hands if the ministers were not impeached. Some ministers—with an efficient "early-warning" system, succeeded in leaving the country; others, among them de Polignac, were arrested and tried for high treason. There was little legal justification for such a charge but nobody, least of all the King whom the mob had made, was capable of resisting the popular demand. Nevertheless, the death sentence which would have been as great a political blunder as the executions of d'Enghien and Ney, was avoided. The ministers went to prison and stayed there until 1837, by which time passions had cooled.

Anticlericalism inspired another riot which had as its target the church of St. Germain-l'Auxerrois, parish church of the Kings of France where the Legitimists were attending a Requiem Mass for the Duc de Berri. After desecrating the church the rioters moved on to burn the palace and library of the Archbishop of Paris. It was an isolated incident but symptomatic of the general spirit of unrest and dissatisfaction.

Far more serious—as Napoleon had remarked—were the riots due to economic rather than political reasons. These broke out in Lyons, where the silk weavers were in dispute with their employers. The economic crisis which had contributed to the downfall of Charles X had not ended with his laying aside the crown. Unemployment continued to increase and the national deficit to swell. Changing the sovereign's head on a coin had done nothing to increase its value.

The silk workers, like many others in the nineteenth century, had genuine grievances, but the riots were put down with great severity. The immediate effect of the disturbances was to damage the workers' cause, since the demand for better circumstances became associated with violence and bloodshed. Memories of the brutality which they had suffered festered in the minds of the people of Lyons, who had a long tradition of revolt.

These upheavals and the successive attempts upon the King's

life were evidence of discontent and disappointment over the results of the Three Glorious Days. The French always hoped that
revolution, followed by a change of régime, would usher in the
millennium; when it failed to do so, they felt cheated. They lacked
the patient perseverance which would have allowed time for
growth and development; like overeager gardeners they would
grub up the roots of a new régime without knowing what form
its buds might take. Nor did they realize that at this point even
revolution could mean no more than a shift in power from one
set of politicians to another, or the substitution of this reigning
house for that one.

Not that France was alone in suffering a hangover from the
Great Revolution. The French army had carried the creed of
liberty, equality and fraternity wherever it went. When the army
was withdrawn, these ideals, together with nationalism, had stayed
on, working away underground in countries which, with the fall
of the Empire, had thought their absolutist rule secure. Unrest was
rife throughout Europe. There were insurrections in Poland, in
Belgium and in Italy, each one a source of gratification to the
French, who, given their heads, would have sent aid to those who
were struggling for freedom. Louis Philippe was less romantic and
he was a genuine believer in peace. As a young man, whenever
he was asked to propose a toast, he would raise his glass and say,
"To universal peace throughout the world." He was not the man
to send French armies, under the *tricolore*, singing the "Marseillaise," to carry on the work which the ragged, barefoot Army of
the Revolution had begun. He refused to intervene. He was virtually his own Foreign Minister and he could truly contend that
his travels in many places had given him experience that his
ministers and his people did not possess. He persisted in his policy
of nonintervention, even though he knew that it made him
unpopular and that unpopularity was a thing that the King of the
French could ill afford.

He showed the same good sense in the situation which arose
after the Belgian insurrection. This had originated in the decision
of the Congress of Vienna—more concerned with tidy map making
than with national characteristics—to unite the Dutch and Belgian
Netherlands under one King, the Dutch King William. This forced

marriage, unhappy from the start, reached breaking point in 1830; the Belgian rebels emerged victorious and had a crown to give away.

They offered it to Louis Philippe's second son, the Duc de Nemours.

To refuse it must have gone sorely against the grain. Louis Philippe loved his children; his anxiety to see them buffered against the vicissitudes of life amounted to neurosis; later in life he became unscrupulous about promoting their welfare; but he refused the Belgian crown and gave his support to another possible candidate, Prince Leopold of Saxe-Coburg, the widower of George IV's daughter Charlotte, who had died in childbed. Leopold became King of the Belgians and married Louis Philippe's eldest daughter, Louise, so discretion was in a measure rewarded. Of his eight children, Louis Philippe might reasonably hope three at least would never lack a crust. With any luck his eldest son would inherit the throne of France, Louise was a Queen, and d'Aumale had his fortune.

The Polish insurrection ended less happily, with the rebels crushed, the constitution abolished, the kingdom of Poland abolished and the country absorbed into the Russian Empire. Austria stayed quiet, less concerned with this increase of power and territory for her neighbor, than with what might happen within her own frontiers, or her Italian provinces.

The country least affected by the spirit of unrest abroad in 1830 was Prussia. She was pursuing a profitable policy of peaceful economic penetration, gathering around her in a customs union, the Zollverein, the minor German states which had hitherto looked to Austria for guidance. Economic ties were the first step toward the political bonds and military power with which Prussia was to influence the history of France, of Europe and the world.

Louis Philippe's refusal to let his son take the Belgian crown, his support of a candidate with links with England, the marriage of his daughter to that candidate, all indicate the trend of his thinking at this time. He saw that the best ally for France was England, stable and powerful, unconcerned with the great and growing powers of Europe which still regarded France with mistrust. But

Waterloo was only fifteen years away, and the fostering of friendship between two old enemies was a delicate, difficult task. There
was only one man in France with the experience and skill to be
trusted with the attempt.

Talleyrand, now aged seventy-four, emerged from retirement,
urbane, witty, inscrutable as ever, and went as ambassador to
London. He had been loyal to no master, faithful to no dynasty
but to France he had always been devoted, and it was fitting that
the last four years of effort on his country's behalf should be
crowned with success. Who but Talleyrand could have talked the
powers into accepting the principle of nonintervention in another country's internal affairs, and then talked them into accepting
French intervention in a squabble between Holland and Belgium?
In 1834, having brought France, England, Spain and Portugal together in a treaty of alliance, Talleyrand resigned and retired to
live out his last years in peace. Before he died he turned his coat
again, this time in a personal, not a public matter: he, the apostate
bishop, who had lived most of his life as though he were an atheist,
was reconciled to the Catholic Church. He also wrote a declaration to be read after his will had been read. In it he acknowledged
the debt which he owed to Napoleon and directed his heirs that,
if anyone bearing the name of Bonaparte should ever be in financial
straits, they were to aid him in any way they could. It was a
gesture suitable to the aristocrat that Talleyrand had been born
and, despite his pursuit of political expediency, had remained. In
France ministries came and went in a manner inevitable in a
country where there were so many opinions and few sharply defined parties. Louis Philippe's government lasted three months,
his second, five; his third, potentially more stable, was cut short
by the death of its leader, Casimir Périer, from cholera. In the
eighteen years of his reign he was served by eighteen governments.

If one may judge from two democracies that have survived and
stayed steady—the United States and England—the system seems
to work best where there are two well-balanced parties. Within
themselves the parties change—the Republicanism of today is not
Lincoln's and the views of the twentieth-century Tory would
bring apoplexy to one of the eighteenth, but the mechanism of one
party in power, the other in opposition, is, with all its faults, work-

able. France had many parties, broadly divided into left and right, splinter groups on each side capable of astounding switches of allegiance, such as the linking of the Bonapartists and the Republicans.

The King was uncomfortably placed; the Left, eager to introduce reform at home and to support revolutionary movements abroad, was the element to which he owed his throne; but he found himself increasingly in sympathy with those who felt that the July Revolution had served its turn, that order must be maintained, reform slowed down and peace preserved both at home and abroad.

He was obliged, too, to look beyond his borders. Metternich could, if he chose, produce a Bonaparte—either the young Duc de Reichstadt, or one of the sons of the ex-King of Holland. Fortunately for Louis Philippe, Metternich, while disliking him, disliked the Bonaparte brothers even more, and they lost all hope of Austrian backing when they joined an Italian secret society called the Carbonari.

The aim of the Carbonari was to free the country of foreign rule and to unify it. In 1831 the society became so active that the Pope took fright and invited Austria to extend her influence and to protect the Papal States. Even the peace-loving Louis Philippe could not restrain France from sending a force to support the Italians and to press the Pope to make reforms; the French were still determined to be the champions of liberty. French troops remained in Italy until 1838.

When Périer died untimely, Louis Philippe chose Marshal Soult as his chief minister. Soult had some of Talleyrand's adaptability and capacity to survive. Under Charles X, a pious man, he had been ostentatiously pious; now he reverted to his martial role and by virtue of it dominated men more able than himself. Thiers and Guizot were his most competent colleagues, but he quarreled with them incessantly.

By this time one section of the opposition—the Republicans— were in eclipse; the office of commander of the National Guard had been abolished and Lafayette had withdrawn from the political scene. Now another section—the Legitimists—were to suffer a blow from that most deadly weapon, ridicule.

Far away, in Holyroodhouse the Duchesse de Berri had cheered her exile by reading the novels of Sir Walter Scott and brooding over all the stirring stories and legends about Bonnie Prince Charlie. As a result she decided that the time had come to strike a blow on behalf of her son who, in Legitimist eyes, was Henri V of France. The Vendée, always a stronghold of Royalist and Catholic feeling, was chosen as the place for the venture; Chateaubriand, always romantic, supported it. The rising was ill organized, and at least in one sense, ill timed; for it was discovered that the Duchesse—a widow for ten years—was pregnant. Her claim that she was secretly married made little appeal to the Catholic Legitimists to whom she looked for support, and the whole thing degenerated from a menace to a joke. One hopes that she gained some consolation from the fact that when the Chamber discussed her venture, comparison was made between this and Bonnie Prince Charlie's attempt to take a throne by force.

After this Louis Philippe could feel that he had little to fear from the Royalist exiles; and in 1832 another possible cause for anxiety was removed. Napoleon's son, the Duc de Reichstadt, died in Vienna. His existence may not have caused Louis Philippe many sleepless nights but he had been there, young and charming, half Habsburg by birth, the son of Napoleon, whose legend in France was gathering strength with the passing years. Now Metternich's pawn was removed, and for Louis Philippe there opened an opportunity to associate himself with the hard-core Bonapartists. It was safe, the King felt, to exploit the Napoleonic cult, though carefully calling himself "the Napoleon of peace." Old soldiers might be somewhat confused by the terminology but they welcomed the revival of the name they revered and, by subscribing to the Napoleonic legend, Louis Philippe brought himself into step with the times.

For the man who now lay under the willows at Longwood on St. Helena was providing material for writers, painters, engravers, sculptors. In Germany Heine and Gothe, in Italy Manzoni and Leopardi, in England Byron and Sir Walter Scott, in France

Stendhal, Vigny, Lamartine, Thiers and Balzac had told, or were telling, their tales. Most eagerly read of all were the books written by people with personal knowledge of the Emperor: the Duchesse d'Abrantès told in her *Mémoires* how the young Napoleon had seemed to her when she was a child; de Ségur wrote the *Campagne de Russie*. And towering above other books as its author had once towered above other men, was Napoleon's own monumental *Mémorial de Ste. Hélène*.

Memory of the man and of his victories was kept alive by Horace Vernet's huge canvases showing the battles of Jena, Friedland and Wagram. The crowds who flocked to view these were not composed of Bonapartists alone; they were Frenchmen, looking back with nostalgia upon the days of glory.

There were plays, too, dealing with every stage of that spectacular career; *Napoleon at Brienne, Josephine, or the Return from Wagram, Bonaparte, Lieutenant of Artillery*. They had no need to be good plays; however small the theatrical merit, applause was certain. The *mystique* was so powerful that the actors who played the part of Napoleon were regarded by the credulous as reincarnations. Mademoiselle George had only to appear on the stage to be acclaimed, not for her talent only but because she had been the Emperor's mistress. It was astute of Louis Philippe to identify himself as far as possible with this upsurge of feeling.

The Marshals of France were back in favor, Soult as chief minister and others, furbishing up their battle-worn uniforms and rusted swords, returned to the army to take the place of the officers whom Charles X had appointed. There was a balance about this new amicability; the old soldiers represented the period of Empire, and the King represented the earlier time, he had been a general under the Revolution. But the rifts remained and, at the funeral of Lamarque, a very popular Napoleonic general, the Bonapartists and the Republicans combined to make a demonstration in which 800 people were killed or wounded. Such heavy casualties, with no result, deterred other would-be demonstrators, though later in the year there was an unsuccessful attempt to kidnap the royal family.

In all, so many attempts were made upon the King's person that one of his contemporaries said that he led the life of a mad dog and would end by being struck down.

Yet Louis Philippe worked hard to attain popularity and to project his image as a citizen. Of the trappings of royalty he said:

"The crown of France is too cold in winter, too warm in summer; the scepter is too blunt as a weapon of defense or attack; it is too short as a stick to lean upon; a good felt hat and a strong umbrella are at all times more useful."

In his good felt hat, clutching his strong umbrella, he walked, unattended, about the streets of Paris and all too often evoked not admiration but mockery. His accouterments were ready-made material for caricature and unfortunately his physique lent itself to that unkindly art. His head, broad-based and narrowing at the top, was as nearly pear-shaped as a head could be, and as a pear it appeared in numerous drawings by Gavarni and Daumier and a host of lesser artists. Even his affability and effusive hand-shaking came in for their share of mockery. On one Shrove Tuesday a journal named *La Mode* hired a man to parade the boulevards, disguised as the King, to shake hands with all and sundry and exclaim, "It is with renewed pleasure that I salute you."

The Citizen King considered that a suitable way to celebrate his birthday was to distribute free sausages to the workingmen— a gesture of good will and good sense which his critics found amusing. Yet despite hat and umbrella and sausages, he managed to preserve something of royal dignity which showed itself in the calm with which he bore mockery and insult. Only once did he retaliate, and that was when he took action against a paper, *Charivari*, which had made a particularly vicious attack upon him. With the same calm he faced physical threats. Somewhere within this King-by-the-will-of-the-people, this incongruous Bonapartist, lived the Bourbon Prince.

In 1814 the Emperor's statue in the Place Vendôme had been torn down from its bronze column made from captured Austrian cannon. A new statue was erected on the third anniversary of the Three Glorious Days, another symbolic link between this monarchy and the Empire. To celebrate it, Victor Hugo, now a convert to Bonapartism, wrote one of his most celebrated odes.

It was not enough, however, for the July Monarchy to pay tribute to, and associate itself with, the glories of the Empire; it had to justify itself by some achievements of its own, difficult in an atmosphere so charged with tension and unrest. Soult's ministry did pass two laws, liberal in intent and lasting in effect. One decreed that the members of general councils which governed the Departments should be elected, not appointed—a natural progression from Périer's law making municipal councils elective: the other, carrying on Napoleon's work, ordered that primary schools should be provided for each village, or neighbouring group of villages.

The French who prided themselves, not without reason, on being the intellectual leaders of the world, had been shocked to find that still, in France, there were fewer children who could read and write than there were in the United States, or England, or even Prussia. It had taken the advocates of equality almost half a century to realize that the real barrier between classes is educational rather than financial.

The law concerning education was largely due to François Guizot, Minister for Public Instruction, who had always advocated and labored for educational reform. He was that comparative rarity, a Protestant from the south; he had started life as a journalist and became professor of history at the Sorbonne where he had made a special study of the constitutional history of England, a country for which he had a profound admiration. His founder membership of the *Aide-toi-et-Dieu-t'aidera* movement lost him his chair at the Sorbonne. He became a member of the Chamber in 1830 and three years later attained his aim of bringing education within the reach of everyone.

But, like many other men, as he aged he moved away from the ardently progressive ideas of his youth. (A King of Sweden once said that nobody could be a good conservative in middle age without having been a rebel in youth.) Guizot's growing conservatism matched that of Louis Philippe and made him, with his keen mind and brilliant oratory, a most valuable minister; he was one of the almost permanent figures in all those shifting governments.

Parisian society was vastly amused by the close and affectionate liaison between this serious statesman, with his bourgeois, Calvinistic background and the Princess Lieven, most haughty of aristocrats, whose husband had been Russian ambassador in London. She was too proud to marry him, but she introduced him to circles closed to the ordinary politician, to the world of aristocrats and diplomats. She knew London well and had many contacts there. Later on they were to be very useful to Guizot.

The trend toward liberalism, of which the new educational laws were soundproof, was checked—as so many of its kind have been, and are—by the behavior of the very people most likely to benefit. Renewed rioting in Lyons and Paris made nervous fingers tighten on the rein.

The uprising of the silk workers in Lyons had been stimulated by Godefroy Cavaignac, who had himself been concerned in the Three Glorious Days, hoping that they would produce not another monarchy but a republic. He was now the leader of a new society called the Société des Droits de l'Homme—an echo of Tom Paine's *Rights of Man*. Cavaignac was arrested, the uprising was put down and followed by severely repressive laws, aimed particularly against the association of workers. (In England, so much admired by Guizot, the same treatment was meted out to the "Tolpuddle martyrs.")

In Paris, the insurrection which was the direct consequence of that of Lyons, was equally savagely quelled; the National Guard, not content with restoring order, indulged in some private massacre.

Then in July, when Louis Philippe was celebrating another anniversary of the Three Glorious Days, a hired assassin, Corsican by birth, rigged up the forerunner of the machine gun and fired it. The King, with only a scratch on his forehead, stood up and with Bourbon calm waved his famous hat to reassure the crowd, but eighteen dead and twenty-two injured lay on the pavement, and Marshal Mortier, riding near the King, was killed by a shot through the ear.

Here was ample reason for further repressive legislation; under it the revolutionary spirit of France seemed to collapse. The multi-barreled gun had not killed the Citizen-King, but it had temporarily shot down both liberal idealism and revolutionary fervor. The period of quietude which followed was welcomed by many people because it enabled them to devote themselves to the congenial business of increasing their prosperity.

But there were many for whom prosperity was still an impossible dream.

Wages were lower than they had been under the Empire, and were still going down. When a man, working fulltime, cannot support his wife and children, a particularly vicious spiral is begun; the woman and the children go out to seek employment, they are cheap labor, there to be exploited; the wages of men go down. This situation was not peculiar to France; industrialization in America and England was equally cruel and ruthless.

Out of the appalling conditions, and the growing literacy which made it possible to publish papers aimed at working-class readers, came a new movement—socialism. Louis Blanc in his book *L'Organization du Travail* advocated state socialism and claimed for every man the right to work. Ledru-Rollin, a rabid Republican, and Lammenais, a Christian philosopher turned democrat, clamored for universal suffrage. They and Saint-Simon accused the government of failing to deal with the growing problem of sweated labor, of ignoring the effects of the economic crises on the poorest workers and of allowing wealth to accumulate in the hands of the few. Gradually these ideas produced the nucleus of a parliamentary Socialist party, aimed at the better organization of the state in the interest of its citizens. This party took the place which the Republicans had once held at the extreme left of the opposition.

As yet all was theory; the only law bettering work conditions passed in the reign of Louis Philippe was that of 1841 which forbade the employment of children under eight years of age.

The new ideas, the working-class self-awareness, the trend toward solidarity by the formation of friendly societies and attempt to form trade unions, all made more headway in the towns than in the country where peasants were more preoccupied with the effects of wind and weather than with theories. France continued to be a predominantly agricultural country, but there was a discernible drift toward the towns. The family holding, divided among children and children's children, eventually became too small to offer a livelihood even at subsistence level, and young people moved into towns where some wage, however meager, could be earned. It is unusual, even today, for a French town dweller not to have some family contact with the country.

Despite this movement toward the towns, only Paris and a few other places showed much increase in population; conditions kept the death rate high, and people voluntarily limited the number of their children.

Industrial progress and mechanization were hampered by the lack of coal; as yet only part of France's most important coal field in the Pas de Calais had been tapped and, by 1848, she was using two million tons more than she produced. Most of this was imported from Belgium. Yet industry was spreading, noticeably in the textile and chemical fields. When the firm of Schneider took over the forges and factories at Le Creusot, the beginning of one of the most important French industrial ventures was laid.

This period saw another invasion of France by the English. This time it was the English navvy with his special skill, his conditioned physique, distinctive dress and nomadic ways of life. He came, he camped, he worked in a way that has made his name a synonym for output of energy, and left behind him the shining railway lines that fused all Western Europe into a single industrial and commercial society. The railway widened horizons and made travel cheaper. Linked with the cross-Channel steamer service it carried dairy produce and vegetables for the markets of London.

English capital and material went into the French railroads too and provided a practical example of the worth of Anglo-French co-operation in the economic field. Given his way Louis Philippe would have extended this co-operation to the political sphere, but here he came into conflict with Thiers.

Chapter 2. THE JULY MONARCHY

Thiers and Guizot were the most brilliant of Louis Philippe's ministers. Superficially they had things in common; both born in Provence; both journalists; both historians, Thiers' interest in the French matching Guizot's in the English Revolution. In character and policy they differed greatly; Guizot, the elder by ten years, was cold and reserved; Thiers was cheerful and expansive. Guizot shared the King's anxiety for peace; Thiers believed that only by being aggressive could France take her rightful place in the world.

Thiers' work on the *National*—and his posters—had helped to bring about the July Revolution and to put Louis Philippe on the throne; he expected, and did indeed obtain, high office. Distrusting his policies, the King reluctantly appointed him to be President of the Council and was relieved to receive his resignation after a few months, months given over to an altercation as to whether France should or should not involve herself in Spanish affairs. When, in the late summer of 1836, Thiers resigned, Louis Philippe appointed as his chief minister a man outside the ranks of the July Monarchy men, and chose Comte Molé, a man of conservative trend and likely to be amenable to his King's wishes. Molé's program was so negative as to have little appeal to the deputies and none at all to the people, always eager for activity and excitement.

In October 1836 excitement came.

Anyone watching France, marking the sluggish economy, the jeers and attacks upon the King, the changes of ministers, might have been led to think that the French were ready to discard constitutional monarchy as an experiment that had failed. One whose observations—and some wishful thinking—had reached this conclusion was Louis Napoleon, the only surviving son of the Emperor's brother Louis and of Hortense, Josephine's daughter.

He was now twenty-eight years old and had spent most of his life in exile. In 1836 he was living in Switzerland and, having watched the growth of the Napoleonic legend, thought the time had come to intervene. He crossed the border and, with Napoleon's will in one hand, the sword of Austerlitz in the other, presented himself to the garrison and citizens of Strasbourg.

It was a green-apple harvest. Within two hours he and those who supported him were arrested. Louis Philippe wisely denied him even the publicity of a trial. He shipped him off to the United States on a man-o'-war bound to make its first call at a South American port so that when Louis Napoleon reached his destination everything had cooled down and his news value was low.

That was in October; in November Charles X died of cholera. Henri V was still a minor whom even the most ardent Legitimist could hardly wish to see on the throne yet so, with all his potential supplanters out of the way, Louis Philippe settled down and gradually gave way to the authoritarianism which lay behind his democratic façade. Molé was inert and ineffectual and during the three years of his ministry gave the King ample excuse for taking a hand in the government.

But Thiers and Guizot, for all their differences, were capable of joining forces to attain what they both desired—the downfall of an unpopular minister. In 1839 Molé was compelled to resign, and in his place, with who knows what misgivings, Louis Philippe appointed Thiers. Guizot was sent to London as ambassador, charged to foster, in every possible way, the good will between France and England that was the cardinal aim of Louis Philippe's policy. Thanks to Princess Lieven, Guizot was assured of a warm welcome in London, and his abilities and devotion to English institutions won him respect, but he had been given a task before which even Talleyrand might have quailed; for once again France was looking outside her own borders, Thiers with his aggressive policy was in power, and all the Powers of Europe were on the alert.

Nobody minded the French being active in Algeria. For nine years colonization had been going on quietly there and, when in 1839 a revolt gave France a chance to bring the whole country under control, even Louis Philippe, so opposed to war, saw in the quelling of Abd-el-Kader an outlet for martial spirit and a possible source of popularity for the government.

But Egypt was a very different matter. Egypt was one of England's many back yards because it straddled the landward approach to India; yet, since Napoleon's expedition in 1798, the French also had been interested in Egypt.

In 1832 Mehemet Ali, the Pasha of Egypt, rebelled against the Sultan of Turkey who was his overlord, and not only established the independence of Egypt but annexed Syria. In 1839 the Sultan renewed the war; Mehemet Ali was again successful and the Turkish fleet deserted to him. England chose to give support to the Sultan; Mehemet Ali was a rebel of the kind that a country with colonies of her own could not be expected to encourage. Just as naturally, France sided with Egypt, a country struggling to cast off the dead hand of authority.

Great Britain, Russia, Prussia and Austria formed themselves into a new Quadruple Alliance with the aim of bringing pressure to bear upon Mehemet Ali and persuade him to make peace with the Sultan and return his conquests. The French, with memories of Waterloo still rankling, set up a howl of protest. War threatened; Thiers began to mobilize his country, to strengthen the fleet and to build new fortifications around Paris.

"You have no idea," Louis Philippe wrote to his son-in-law Leopold, "how far public approval supports mobilization; it is universal. I regret that this should go so far as the fury against England is increasing, and one of the matters I most regret is that our whole people is convinced that England wants to reduce France to *the rank of secondary power* and you know what the national pride and vanity of all peoples is. I believe therefore that it is most urgent that the present crisis should be brought to a peaceful end. The more I believe that the union of England and France is the foundation of world peace the more I regret to see so much irritation caused between our two countries. . . ."

Like the plain felt hat on a royal head, some of the King's thoughts were well ahead of his times.

Across the Channel, Victoria was agitated too, but she had even less control over Palmerston, her headstrong Foreign Minister, than Louis Philippe had over Thiers. It was all very well for Leopold to write her one of his minatory letters:

"I cannot disguise from you that the consequences may be very serious, and the more so because the Thiers Ministry is supported by the movement party, and as *reckless of consequences* as your own Minister of Foreign Affairs, even more so. . . . Thiers is strongly impregnated with all the notions of fame and glory . . . part of the Republican and the Imperial times . . ."

What could Victoria do? What could such a letter do, other than alarm and distress her? She might assert herself over the choice of the Ladies of the Bedchamber, but as the Queen of a constitutional country she could not dictate to ministers.

Louis Philippe's regrets over the situation were genuine; he had no wish to see France plunged into war over a question of whether Egypt should be ruled by Sultan or Pasha, or to gratify Thiers and all the old warhorses of France who were rearing their heads and sniffing powder; but he was a Frenchman and at heart as susceptible as any other to anything that looked like a slight upon his country. Leopold—so fond of warning others— received a warning from the King of the French, a warning intended to be passed on. (Leopold's post bag, at times, was a relay station, full of letters addressed to him but directed at others.)

This time Louis Philippe wrote: "If the governments of England and Russia desire or dare to take steps for the abasement of France, war will break out and then I will throw myself into it, *body and soul.*"

Despite this, his real desire was for peace. Pride, national touchiness and the vivid memories of victories under the Empire might lead the still politically immature people to confuse war with progress; their King saw clearly that war at this moment could only be disastrous for France, damaging to her prestige should she lose and damaging to her economy, now on the brink of the "hungry forties," whether she lost or won.

In October, when the Chambers met for the opening of their new session, Louis Philippe showed courage and conviction by refusing to read an inflammatory speech prepared for him by his ministers; instead he indicated his willingness to yield a little.

Other concessions followed; Mehemet Ali agreed to restore Syria to the Sultan and the Sultan agreed to acknowledge him as hereditary ruler of Egypt. The first round of the long-drawn-out wrangle over the Eastern question was over, with small harm done. Once again the Powers had proved that it was possible for international disputes to be settled by negotiations.

Thiers again resigned; his second ministry, like his first, broken on the question of to fight or not to fight. He joined the opposition and remained there for the rest of the reign. He was young enough to feel that he could afford to wait.

Louis Philippe once more appeared to be justified in his belief that he handled foreign affairs better than any of his ministers. Rousseau had said that if citizens observed the laws and respected the ownership of goods and the safety of individuals, external affairs could be left to ministers; Louis Philippe read "the King" in place of "ministers."

Peace had been maintained outside France, order seemed to prevail within and Louis Philippe felt himself to be well enough established to face any risk which might attach itself to bringing about a project long advocated by Thiers, appealing to the French people, and in keeping with his own encouragement of the Bonaparte cult—the bringing back of the Emperor's body from St. Helena.

Guizot in London, instructed to ask for English consent, was surprised to find that Palmerston raised no objection. Possibly Palmerston saw the advantage of playing off a dead Emperor against a living King and keeping France emotionally divided.

On November thirtieth, 1840, the *Belle Poule,* under the command of Louis Philippe's sailor son, the Prince de Joinville, docked at Cherbourg, and Napoleon was home again.

Laurence Sterne said, in another connection, "They order this matter better in France," and here was an occasion, emotional, ceremonial, exactly attuned to the French genius. With pomp and ceremony the body was transferred to the catafalque barge which was to carry it up the Seine to Paris. Veterans of the Grand Army, Grenadiers, Red Lancers, Dragoons of the Empress, Sharpshooters in their black gaiters, made their way to the banks of the river to stand guard for the last time over their

Emperor, with only their old military cloaks to wrap them from the cold of the winter's night. By day, all along the river crowds gathered to watch the slow progress of the barge and to raise a cry, unheard in France for twenty-five years, "*Vive l'Empereur.*"

Paris was ready—as so often in the past—to receive him. The Champs Elysées was decorated with tall obelisks draped in the *tricolore,* alternating with heroic statues and flaming urns; the funeral car was shrouded in violet velvet, lavishly embroidered with Imperial bees and eagles in gold. As the procession moved toward the Invalides, where Louis Philippe was to receive it in the name of France, the sun broke through the wintry clouds. The sun of Austerlitz, said the Parisians; the Emperor's good omen.

The King may have hoped that, once buried on French soil, Napoleon would be forgotten. He may have remembered that when he opened the Château of Versailles as a military museum, Metternich had warned him that he was playing with a fire that could warm only the Bonapartes. He may even have spared a thought for another Bonaparte, the Emperor's nephew, Louis Napoleon who, in the previous August, had made another abortive attempt to raise rebellion and this time had been tried and condemned to life imprisonment in the cold damp fortress of Ham.

Any hope that Napoleon might be forgotten was doomed to disappointment. That night there were two monarchs in France, Louis Philippe at the Tuileries and Napoleon at the Invalides, where the procession past the catafalque had begun. The faint protests of the romantics who regretted that the dead man had not been left in solitude under the willows were drowned by the steady shuffle of feet, approaching, halting, moving on again, by the sound of weeping and of muted voices telling remembered things. All day, all night, for months and years to come people passed as they still pass before the massive sarcophagus of red porphyry.

As the gloom of the December evening deepened over the golden dome of the Invalides the French might well look back on the last quarter of a century and draw up a balance sheet of profit and loss. It may have been unwise of Louis Philippe to encourage by this ceremony a comparison between the glamorous past and the drab present. People were bound to think that once the whole nation had marched as one, and now it was divided by the sordid antagonism between the haves and the have-nots. They were bound to ask themselves if pacifism, a bourgeois mentality, a bourgeois morality, made a fitting substitute for the romantic ideal known as the Empire. Were a middle-class monarchy and a middle-class parliament, lacking in all the external grandeur so dear to the nation, preferable to the genius which had lit all France and dazzled Europe with its wildfire light?

One section of the community would answer these questions with a resounding affirmative: the bourgeoisie was well content with its material progress, its increasing prosperity, its growing political power. Two factors had contributed to the upsurge of the middle classes; one was the peace, which was good for business; the other was the withdrawal of the aristocracy who were out of step with the times and disapproved of Louis Philippe. They retired into their mansions, behind high walls, and social ascendancy passed to the ordinary man who by industry or luck had prospered. It was a situation which any honest, middle-aged member of the middle class would admit that he had hoped would be the outcome of the Revolution.

Certain social patterns were common to all classes. The family was regarded as the primary unit, and within the family marriage was the primary preoccupation. In the aristocracy marriage could link great names and wide estates; in the bourgeoisie it could fuse business interests; in the peasantry it could add an acre to the family holding or bring another pair of hands to the plow. Marriages of convenience were the rule and the matchmakers acted with more regard to material advantage than for the vagrant fancies of the two people concerned. It was the aim of any family with the slightest claim to respectability to provide a dowry, however small, for every daughter. As a rule the standard of marital fidelity was high and there was no divorce; the law permitting it had been revoked at the Restoration and it did not go back on the statute book until 1884.

The average Frenchwoman, assured by legal contract of some control of the dowry she had brought to her husband, and secure in her position as head of her household, neither desired nor sought influence outside her home. The matriarch is usual in France. To this day if you are lost on a French road and meet a couple and, mindful of your manners, with a "Monsieur" and a "Madame," ask for direction, it is Madame who supplies it, very forcefully. In most of the small eating places run by a family, Monsieur could be mistaken for a hireling, but there is never a doubt as to Madame's status; in decent black, with sharp eye and tongue, she rules her little kingdom—and usually has charge of the till. This dominance in a sex until lately underprivileged politically may surprise until one reflects that perhaps the reason why the Frenchwoman was not so clamorous for the vote was that she never felt the need for it.

Even had divorce been permissible under the July Monarchy it would have been frowned upon, for respectability was the *leitmotiv* of the day. So much that has been called "typically Victorian" and attributed to the character of the Queen of England, had its counterpart in Louis Philippe's France. There were the same subdued colors and dowdy fashions in clothes, the same modest hair styles, the same heavy furniture, with yellow Utrecht velvet and mahogany replacing the elegance of damask and giltwood. The spirit of the age expressed itself in the mass production of workingmen's clothes, and in the shrouding folds of the shawl which was to be found in every decent woman's wardrobe.

For men facial hair growths were a symbol of respectability. In France they offered a clue to the wearer's political affinity; the Republican wore a full beard, the Orleanist, in compliment to his King, cultivated side whiskers; the Bonapartist was distinguished by mustache and imperial.

Paris suffered less from the smothering boredom of a regimented social life than did the provincial cities and towns. The capital, then as now, was a world enclosing a number of worlds. The Latin Quarter, the world of students in their almost uniform dress of dark blue trousers, black Quaker jacket, low shoes and woolen stockings was nearly as exclusive, in its own way, as the Faubourg St. Germain, where the Legitimist salons were closed to the politicians of the July Monarchy. The world of aspiring artists and writers, the Mimis and Rodolphes gaily starving in garrets, was poles apart from the prosperous life of the boulevards where the young bloods, politically Anglophobe but in sporting matters Anglophile, aped the Regency whips as they maneuvered their calèches, cabriolets and phaetons with their little "tigers" perched behind, through the press of the traffic.

Elegant young exquisites, in narrow shepherd's plaid trousers, wasp-waisted frock coats and gorgeous embroidered waistcoats on pouter-pigeon chests, brushed past the sober bourgeois as he went purposefully about his business. Men of fashion sauntered along the Grands Boulevards to dine at the Café de Paris—held to be the best restaurant in Europe—or at the Café Riche or Tortoni's where reputations were made or lost, secrets of the boudoir revealed, new fashions and *bons mots* launched upon the world. *La vie Parisienne*, the reputation of Paris as a gay city, originated when life in the rest of France was on the whole dull.

One thing the idler could not do was to gamble in the establishments that had existed for so long under the arches of the Palais Royal. Louis Philippe had spent his youth in apartments that overlooked the galleries and gardens where vice and frivolity flourished and one of his laws forbade gambling within thirty kilometers of Paris. It says much for the innate conservatism of the French that this law is still in force today.

Even with gambling banished there was still plenty left for the Parisian's entertainment. The Opera reached heights of distinction never touched before and attracted singers and dancers from all over the world. In music this was the golden period of Berlioz, Auber, Halévy and Meyerbeer. In the theatre Rachel was deserting the great classical tradition and creating her own. In art Corot, Ingres and the Barbizon school were bridging the gap between traditionalist and impressionist.

But above all the July Monarchy saw the maturing of writers who had been young at its beginning. In France writing and politics are closely intertwined, and writers regarded with respect. It was possible at this time, for all the respectability, for George Sand to adopt masculine dress with her masculine pseudonym, to smoke cigars and flaunt her love affairs, two of them at least with famous men, de Musset and Chopin. In England George Eliot, in her modest, feminine dress, faithful unto death to one lover, found it necessary to explain that her liaison was in fact a "true marriage," lacking only the nuptial ceremony.

When Thiers resigned over the Egyptian crisis in 1839, Louis Philippe recalled Guizot from London and made him his chief minister. Time had modified Guizot's liberal ideas; he was no longer the reformer who had so ardently advocated education for all. He now held that any workingman who wished to advance himself should work harder and heave himself into the middle class. To the middle class his advice was terse and simple, "Enrich yourselves." This slogan appealed strongly to those to whom it was addressed, and also to the King, with his haunting fear of poverty, his dread that his children might one day go hungry. In other ways, too, Guizot's ideas made him acceptable to the King; they shared the belief that a King should play a part in the government, and that the interests of peasant and artisan were adequately represented by the bourgeois members in the Chamber. Louis Philippe had at last found a minister after his own heart for, as he grew older, his vanity and egoism increased; he overestimated his capacity to deal with men and affairs and was more and more inclined to put his dynastic interests before those of the country as a whole. He held steadily, however, to his belief in, and wish for, an Anglo-French alliance, and here again his feelings were shared by Guizot.

War between the two countries was still a threatening possibility when Guizot took office, but by moderation and prudence he managed to avert it, much to the disgust of the hotheads in the nation. In each crisis they saw the chance of avenging Waterloo and, as each crisis passed, they accused the King and his chief minister of being too ready to appease.

Promoting friendship between the two countries was not easy, for the old pattern of rivalry in far places which had brought about the eighteenth-century clashes in India and the New World, was now being repeated as English and French reached out into the half-explored regions of the world. Bougainville had reached Tahiti a year before Cook, yet it was the London Missionary Society that now had charge of the island, and when French Catholic missionaries attempted to land there and share in the harvest of souls, they were driven off with scant ceremony. Such an incident was an affront to French pride.

The English, having abolished slavery in their own colonies, had taken upon themselves the right to search any ship suspected of being a slaver of whatever nationality. Off the coast of Africa French ships had been searched; again national pride was hurt and the French felt that they had lost face when Guizot settled the dispute peaceably.

Guizot knew his King's mind and understood that this desire for peace with England was not solely concerned with politics. Personal, and very human, motives were involved. Louis Philippe's vanity had been injured by the lack of enthusiasm with which the sovereigns of Europe had greeted his accession. To them, as to the Legitimists in France, he was a usurper. The Czar of Russia, Nicholas I, would not even address him with the formula in use between monarchs, "Monsieur my brother."

There was one way by which all these subtle little snubs could be canceled out. There was Queen Victoria, legitimate head of a rapidly expanding empire, a woman of impeccable character, with far-reaching family connections. Whom Victoria could be induced to accept, who could reject? Louis Philippe and his daughter Louise, married to Victoria's "dearest uncle," worked determinedly to bring about a meeting between the two monarchs.

Victoria was agreeable, but she had to wait until Lord Palmerston, high-handed, anti-French, made way for a new Foreign Minister, Lord Aberdeen, who was a personal friend of Guizot and whose appointment promised much less tension and much more warmth in Anglo-French relationships.

Before the meeting could be brought about Louis Philippe suffered a great personal sorrow; his eldest son, the enlightened and popular Duc d'Orléans was killed in a carriage accident.

The King and Queen, devoted parents, were inconsolable. It is significant, that even at such a moment the attitude of the old aristocracy did not soften. They remained aloof, sent no condolences. Among the superstitious the question was asked, Did some malignant fate haunt all the direct heirs of their dynasties? The Bourbon prince, the Duc de Berri, had been assassinated;

Napoleon's son had died untimely; and now Louis Philippe's heir, killed by two runaway horses.

The King's grief must have been tinged with uneasiness. What of the dynasty? True, he still had four living sons, but by the law of primogeniture they must be passed over, and the heir apparent, the Comte de Paris, was still a child. Louis Philippe was sixty-seven; there would be a long regency; and regencies, with their long history of bad government, were not popular. When the Citizen-King went to his grave might not someone override this child's right as he had overridden the right of the young Duc de Bordeaux? Might not people's minds revert to the Legitimist line and think the Duc de Bordeaux preferable to the Comte de Paris?

Between grief and foreboding it is possible that the real loss to France passed unnoticed. Had Orléans lived, his more modern and enlightened outlook might have influenced his father and tempered his policy.

In the summer of 1843 Louis Philippe put aside his grief and his fears for the future and welcomed Victoria and Albert, come to make the long-hoped-for visit. Their yacht brought them to Le Tréport, and then they went inland to the Château d'Eu. The visit was a great success, and all but the most intransigent hoped that it would lessen the friction between France and England. The nineteenth century had run almost half its course, but in the palaces of Europe medieval ideas, a thousand times disproved, still prevailed. Gestures of friendship, acts of civility and matings were still believed to have significance. Nicholas of Russia was to visit England and be warmly welcomed, yet the Crimean War broke out; Victoria was to marry her daughter to the Crown Prince of Prussia, and what came of that marriage the world knows only too well.

Happily unconscious of the futility of it all, Victoria enjoyed her visit and invited Louis Philippe to go to Windsor next year. He enjoyed his visit; he was the first French King to pay a courtesy visit to a British sovereign, the people gave him an enthusiastic welcome and the Queen gave him the Order of the Garter. Time had avenged the poor *émigré* of Twickenham. Singularly few men are capable of measuring their personal achievements by the yardstick of history and it is pleasant to think that Louis Philippe believed that he had "arrived" and that Victoria felt she had found a friend. In 1844 she made a second visit to the Château d'Eu; then in the next year Palmerston was back at the Foreign Office and there was a revival of mutual distrust.

Yet it was Louis Philippe who with his own hand struck down the friendship he had worked so hard to cultivate and gave Victoria reason to denounce his conduct as "very dishonest."

In 1843, with the Queen of Spain a minor and her heir her younger sister, the question of whom these girls should marry had fretted the minds of the ruling families in Europe. Louis Philippe allowed his family feeling to overcome the sense he had shown in refusing the Belgian crown for his son and proposed that as soon as the young Queen was marriageable she should marry his youngest son, the Duc de Montpensier. To the other countries of Europe this smacked dangerously of an extension of French influence in Spain, a second virtual abolition of the Pyrenees. After much argument it was agreed that no member of either the Orléans or Coburg families should be the young Queen's husband. Louis Philippe then suggested that his son should marry her sister. (Another of his brood assured of a crust!) There was more argument and then this proposal was accepted, but on one condition; Queen Isabella must be married and have a child before her sister married. Louis Philippe accepted this condition and gave his word that it should be respected.

In making this promise the King thought that he outwitted Europe. He had private information that the husband chosen for Isabella, the Duke of Cadiz, was impotent; so, though Montpensier would not be a consort, there was every likelihood that his child would eventually succeed to the throne of Spain.

Three years passed. Did Louis Philippe in that time receive private information of a contrary nature? Had his ambition for his family robbed him of all sagacity? He must have known that to go back on his word would affront the other countries, especially England which, in the previous century, had felt strongly enough about the making of a Franco-Spanish bloc to fight the War of the Spanish Succession through eleven blood-soaked years, who more recently had freed the peninsula from French domination, who now held Gibraltar.

Disregarding all this, Louis Philippe arranged that the weddings of the Queen of Spain and her sister should take place simultaneously. Everyone was profoundly shocked. In 1846 even a private gentleman's word was supposed to be as good as his bond; that a King should break his more than justified all those people who had always looked on Louis Philippe as a usurper, a parvenu, a man who would do anything for money.

Victoria, perhaps because she remembered those cozy family meetings, perhaps because she had firsthand experience of the power of ministers, reserved her sternest reproaches for Guizot whose conduct was, she said, "beyond all belief shameful and so shabbily dishonest." She did Guizot an injustice; his affection and admiration for England were genuine, so was his desire for peace; and Louis Philippe, whose notion of constitutional government differed from Victoria's, was quite capable, where his family interests were concerned, of overruling his chief minister.

Louis Philippe lost much and gained nothing. The whole thing ended with one of those instances of rough justice in which history as well as fiction abound. In the shortest possible biological time Isabella gave birth to a child, and the other marriage was important only in its repercussions.

Guizot may have been blameless where the Spanish marriage was concerned, but he was responsible for the increasing loss of confidence felt by the French for their King and his government. Guizot was so strictly honest himself that he was slow to see dishonesty in others; so conscious of his own rectitude that "he covered the petty larcenies and robberies of his colleagues with the mantle of his stern morality." The mantle was not large enough to conceal the corruption and malpractice so widespread among his supporters, many of whom were allowed to hold profitable offices and whose arrogance and ineptitude made them an embarrassment to the man who depended upon them for his majority. In addition to this his manner in the Chamber was unfortunate; he treated his opponents with disdain; he met criticism with insult and sarcasm rather than with reasoned argument, and he made no attempt to conciliate.

Louis Philippe showed little awareness of the discontent mounting in France; since he only read *The Times* he did not know what the French papers were saying, or what the French people were thinking. The economic crisis persisted, people were still poor, and men's minds—deprived of the counter interest that war might have provided—were concentrating upon reform. Of what advantage, they asked themselves, to have shed the blood of a King, of nobles, of priests, to have banished one ruling house, if the result were merely continued misery? The only cure for their ills, the only thing that could bring about real equality and fraternity, was sweeping political change. The Socialist theories once active in the minds of only a few men were now spreading wide and deep, but all clamor for reform met with bleak opposition from the once-Jacobin King and his once-liberal minister. But this time Louis Philippe was as absolutist as Charles X had ever been. He was in full agreement with Horace Vernet, the painter, who said that he could understand an absolute monarchy, even a downright autocracy, but he failed to understand the use of a constitutional King:

"An autocracy means one ruler over so many millions of subjects; a constitutional monarchy means between five and six hundred direct rulers, so many millions of indirect ones, and one subject who is called a king."

Louis Philippe had no intention of being that one subject, but unfortunately for him that was what the French people wanted, and wanted increasingly as he and Guizot set their faces against reform of any kind. Before long all the opposition elements in the Assembly, the left, the left center, the Legitimists and the Republicans, were prepared to bury their differences for a time and to combine against the government, just as Thiers and Guizot had combined to bring about the fall of Molé.

Amidst all the political tug-of-war and the business of the Spanish marriage one event occurred of no immediate importance but momentous for the future. Some very necessary repair work was in progress at the fortress of Ham and, on May 25, 1846, Louis

Napoleon shaved off his mustache, put on a workman's blouse and with a plank over his shoulder walked out of the prison to which he had been consigned for life. He made his way to England.

Eighteen forty-six had seen the breaking of a King's given word; 1847 brought scandals of a domestic nature. The charges varied from electoral mismanagement to receiving bribes; one of the bribed was the Minister of War, another an ex-Minister of Public Works. Gone were the days of men like Richelieu; governments under the Restoration had been inactive and unpopular, but they were incorruptible. Now a new ethic pervailed. The exposures came hard after a number of bogus company swindles which had shaken public confidence and disinclined people to invest their money, thus worsening the economic situation. People told themselves that things were in a bad way indeed.

This conviction was hardened by two entirely fortuitous happenings. One was the murder by the Duc de Praslin of his wife. That such an act should help to discredit Louis Philippe, that good family man, is a profound irony. Less than any other King of France, less than any ruler of his day, had he associated with the aristocracy; he could not be held responsible for their behavior. But against the background of distrust and insecurity of the time the murder had an altogether disproportionate effect. It may not be irrelevant that the murdered Duchesse was the daughter of one of Napoleon's old Marshals. Were the whole upper class, and the government, venal, corrupt and unworthy of respect?

The second event was a bad harvest; it brought distress to many and darkened the nation's mood, for the French have always been prone to blame governments for natural disasters. The mood was not lightened by the publication of massive works like Lamartine's *Histoire des Girondins* and the first volume of Thiers' great history of the Consulate and Empire. France had known great days, look at her now! Past glory emphasized present shabbiness.

On top of all else, trade—though only in Paris—was hit by the death of the King's sister, Madame Adelaide, and the consequent suspension of all gaieties.

Louis Philippe could not be entirely unaware of the way things were shaping, but he lulled any agitation by reflecting upon the length of his reign—eighteen years; he was part of the establishment, and he had the bourgeoisie behind him. It was the bourgeois National Guard that had kept—and would keep—him on the throne. His horizon was limited to the boundaries of the capital, he had always been King of Paris rather than King of France; but he should have known, from firsthand experience, how fickle the people of Paris could be. He chose to ignore what he knew, and he and Guizot watched, with real or affected calm, while the opposition prepared to make, through elections, its appeal to the people.

Chapter 3. 1848

The thought is frivolous but irresistible—how very pleasant it would be if all electioneering campaigns took the form of those in 1848, but perhaps it could only happen in France.

The opposition organized banquets where anyone who could afford a ticket could eat and drink and enliven the political speeches by toasts to the liberalization of the electorate and of parliament; to the July Revolution; to the improvement of the lot of the working classes.

Legitimists, Radicals and Republicans combined in arranging the banquets, but most of those who sat at the long trestle tables were men of the middle class. Peasants and artisans crowded to stand behind the tables and listened to the speeches, sometimes made by tongues liberated by wine. Hope is a tough growth and hope sprang anew; if the conditions which the speeches and the toasts seemed to promise actually came about, who knew? Next year when all these words had been translated into action, the ordinary workingman might afford to sit and eat and drink.

Even of those who were seated not all were entitled to a vote and could therefore have little influence on the elections, but the object of the banquets was to create a climate of opinion sufficiently antagonistic to Guizot to force him and his supporters to make concessions. Thiers took no part in the banquet campaign, preferring to conduct his own opposition inside the Assembly.

At first Louis Philippe and Guizot were scornful of this mingling of politics and feasting; but presently they were bound to see the threat and, when they did so, they acted in a manner which, given their dispositions and beliefs, was predictable. They forbade any further feasting in the name of reform.

A banquet had already been arranged to take place in a working-class district of Paris on February 20, 1848. After a good deal of skillful negotiation, permission was obtained to hold it, in an emasculated form and in another district, more suburban, less inflammable of temper.

The opposition deputies, anxious to observe the letter of the law, decided not to attend, a decision that provoked scathing comment from the press about their retreat in face of Guizot's unusual display of energy; but if the deputies appeared to have abandoned the cause, the democratic and socialist parties were ready to fill the vacant places at the tables where seats cost six francs—with the average male worker earning between two and three in a day, the female worker one franc.

The banquet was canceled. Louis Philippe said, "The Parisians know what they are doing. They will not exchange a throne for a banquet." But Paris was already on the move. Masses of agitators, in orderly fashion, began to parade the streets, shouting "Long live reform," and "Down with Guizot." This was one of the demonstrations beloved by Parisians because it gave them a feeling that they were influencing events.

Had the weather been seasonable for February it might have ended there, with a little shouting and few paving stones prised up ready for the making of barricades. Wars seldom break out until harvests are in, and revolutions seldom take place in cold weather. But February of 1848 was singularly warm. The crowds grew and the noise swelled.

The troops, numbering about 30,000, and the National Guard were called out. In his dealings with the National Guard Louis Philippe had made a grave mistake; fearing hostile demonstrations, he had not reviewed them since 1830; now he paid for his neglect. The trusted, middle-class National Guard, like the mass of the people, wanted reform and the dismissal of Guizot.

Under the threat of defection by the National Guard, the King dismissed Guizot as Charles X had dismissed Villèle, and in this case the Duchesse d'Angoulême's warning could have been repeated. Louis Philippe would not take as his next minister Thiers, whom he detested; he sent for Molé and asked him to form a new government.

The crowd rejoiced over Guizot's dismissal as they paraded the illuminated boulevards and fraternized with the troops and the

National Guard. But the Comédie Française had shut its doors, and that was a sign. As an old man remarked years later, "When the Comédie Française shuts its doors in perilous times it is like the battening down of hatches in dirty weather; there is mischief brewing."

Mischief is always latent in large crowds and this particular crowd was infiltrated by professional troublemakers. Who fired, or ordered to be fired, that first shot in the Boulevard des Capucines? Nobody now can tell; nobody knew then, but it was enough. The troops replied with a volley; forty people were killed, and another revolution had begun.

There was a gunsmith's shop nearby; the people rushed into it, took every weapon and poured out into the street again. "Long live reform" was forgotten, and nobody cried now for Guizot's dismissal; he had already gone. Now the throng sang the "Marseillaise," the marching song of the Revolution, or the "Chant du Départ," the marching song of Napoleon's armies.

Authority seemed paralyzed. The weary troops, discouraged by the defection of the National Guard, broke their ranks and joined with the workers and with the young people, rallied once again by romantic and socialistic ideals. Most of the young had come under the influence of Lamartine and had read the novels of Eugène Sue which preached hatred between the haves and the have-nots in society. For such it was possible to start out in the morning in the spirit of student rag, and by evening be a full-blown revolutionary.

A concentrated effort of the middle class, conscious of its worth and resentful of its political limitations, the working class anxious for better conditions, and the young, always in favor of action and change, brought the July Monarchy down.

It fell in confusion; too late Louis Philippe changed his mind and sent for Thiers to replace Molé. The crowd was already advancing upon the Tuileries and could not be repulsed. The King, who had so often faced personal danger with calm, was not prepared to see men slaughtered and his capital made a scene of carnage; he preferred to go. He said, "I have seen enough blood. All my life I have hated the iniquity of war." His attitude showed consistency, a quality usually underrated. For eighteen years he had insisted—at the risk of unpopularity—upon the maintenance of peace, and now what looked to his enemies like a cowardly withdrawal was probably the most morally courageous act of his life.

Had his two liberal-minded and popular sons, Aumale and Join-ville, been in Paris, they might have persuaded him to a different course; but both were in Algeria. Louis Philippe hastily abdicated in favor of his grandson, the Comte de Paris, and having done that, departed. He and the Queen, in disguise and calling themselves Mr. and Mrs. Smith, set out for England. Their departure lacked —perhaps it was a sign of the times—the dignity which had accompanied the departure of Charles X. Louis Philippe, seemingly blind to the difference, repeatedly muttered, "Absolutely like Charles X. Absolutely like Charles X."

In one way the situation was absolutely similar: just as the Duchesse de Berri had tried to fight for her son's rights, so now did the Duchesse d'Orléans for her son's, and with a similar lack of suc-cess.

For the French people the two dethronements bore a significant difference. Charles X had been King by right of inheritance, Louis Philippe by the will of the people, and what the people had made they could unmake without regrets or feelings of guilt. The Citizen-King had never possessed the aura, the almost mystic quality bestowed by a thousand years of tradition; there was no need for the people to justify their action—a need which even the regicides had felt in 1793 and which had been present, in mitigated form, in the minds of men in 1830. Louis Philippe had been chosen and he had exceeded his mandate by attempting to rule in accordance with Louis XVI's definition of absolute monarchy—"The rights and interests of the people are necessarily identical with mine and rest solely in my hands." Such a statement, coming from a King by divine right, might be arbitrary and resented, but not absurd; the spirit of it, when entertained by a King chosen to rule under a constitution, was ridiculous and dangerous, especially when that King had only been wholly accepted by a section of the people and had nothing to offer to the nation in general except peace, and that not always welcome or appreciated.

A provisional government installed in the Hôtel de Ville announced that the House of Orléans had ceased to rule in France and that the Second Republic was established. It was a moment for which the Republicans had waited eighteen years.

Queen Victoria regarded her former host and hostess as "poor, humbled people." Queen Louise of the Belgians bemoaned her father's fate and summed up, not unastutely, the reason for his failure:

"The exaggeration of the system of peace and resistance, or rather immobility, lost him, as that of war lost Napoleon. Had he less shunned war *on all occasions* and granted in time some trifling reforms, he would have satisfied public opinion. . . . Guizot's accession has been as fatal as his fall, and is perhaps the *first cause* of our ruin, though my father cannot be blamed for keeping him in office, as he had a majority in the Chamber, and an overwhelming one. *Constitutionally* he could not have been turned out. . . ."

An excellent argument; yet in the end Guizot had been turned out unconstitutionally and far too late.

Lord John Russell, the British Prime Minister, took a less emotional view of Louis Philippe's fall: he thought that "selfishness and cunning had destroyed that which honesty and wisdom might have maintained." He was still thinking of the tricky Spanish marriage. He went on to ask who, if Napoleon and Louis Philippe were unable to consolidate the dynasty, would be able to do so? He foresaw history repeating itself with France making a succession of fruitless attempts at civil government and then falling under a military dictatorship.

He failed to appreciate the natural resilience of the French and the stability of their permanent machine for government. Rulers and ministers might come and go, the business of daily administration ground steadily along the lines laid down by the Revolution and the Empire. The changes in France during the nineteenth century which argue frivolity, fatigue, the desire for change for its own sake, argue also the faith, conscious or unconscious, in the strength of administrative machine. Each change was a change of hat, not a major amputation.

Eighteen forty-eight was the year of revolutions in Europe, and the French, despite all their troubles, had less urgent reasons for revolution than many another: they had already an elected house of representatives, on however narrow a franchise; they had a sovereign whose powers were defined by a written constitution, however much he might chafe against his limitations. And, having so much, the more she desired could have been obtained without revolution. For that the personality and character of Louis Philippe were largely to blame. Had he been less vain, less stubborn, a little more aware that no nation stands still for eighteen years . . . fruitless speculation; he was gone and perhaps he was not altogether sorry to have cast off, in his old age, the difficult task of governing the French people.

He left behind problems for his successors—whoever they might be—to solve. The tall chimneys springing up in industrial areas, the derricks of the coal mines, the smoky network of railways were all evidence of the coming of the machine age with its inevitable accompaniment, a growing mass of workers suffering from poor pay, overlong working hours, wretched housing conditions. Country workers, except for the fact that they were less likely to go hungry, were in similar plight; their conditions were worsened by bad harvests and a widespread blight on potatoes.

Opposed to these two oppressed classes stood the bourgeoisie, whose influence had increased with its wealth, who represented capital and had a decisive voice in the country's affairs but, as yet, no great sense of social responsibility.

Once—and not so long ago—peasants, artisans and middle class had combined to form the Third Estate and routed the nobility and the clergy. Centrifugal force had done its work since then. The battleground had shifted; animated by mutual fear, rancor and antipathy, moved by conflicting interests as sharp as those that had once divided the Third Estate from the other two, the proletariat and the bourgeois elements stood ranged, ready for the impending strife.

Book IV

Chapter 1. THE SECOND REPUBLIC

Shelley, himself a poet, claimed that poets are the "*unacknowledged* legislators of the world." Alphonse de Lamartine was a poet prepared to become an acknowledged legislator, to move out into the rough-and-tumble of political life. He took up the burden of guiding the young Republic and making idealism and realism run in double harness.

The events of 1848 had not surprised him. He had foreseen it all. When his book, *Histoire des Girondins* was published, his native city, Mâcon, had honored him with a banquet, at which he made a speech foretelling the end of the July Monarchy. "This royalty will fall, of this you may be sure. It will not fall in its own blood like that of '89, it will fall into the trap it has dug for itself. And after revolutions of liberty and counterrevolutions of glory, you will have the revolution of conscience and contempt."

Revolution had come, and Lamartine, aged sixty, but still handsome and elegant, found himself leading the Chamber and faced with the task of dealing a death blow to the hopes of the Duchesse d'Orléans, who, still in her widow's mourning, "a pretty face under a bonnet," had come to plead the rights of her ten-year-old son, the Comte de Paris.

The poet in Lamartine recognized her appeal as "one of the most touching scenes ever witnessed," but the politician in him refused to be swayed by sentiment; he urged the Chamber to reject the appeal to emotion and chivalry and to form a Provisional Government which "prejudges nothing of our rights, our grievances, our sympathies or our anger nor yet the final government which it may please the country to choose for itself when it has been consulted."

Lamartine signed the proclamation of the Second Republic, "one and indivisible"; he was the mainspring of the Provisional Government of five members; with no weapon other than his burning eloquence he stemmed the rush of workers streaming down from the heights of Paris carrying the red flag. He rode out into the turbulent crowd and made a plea for the *tricolore*, the flag "which has encircled the world with the name, the glory and the liberty of the Fatherland." The red flag, he said, took its color from trailing in the blood of the people.

In the new régime he could have had any office he cared to choose, but with characteristic modesty he accepted the portfolio for Foreign Affairs. His first duty was to assure the suspicious outside world that it had nothing to fear from the new Republic. In a circular to French embassies and legations abroad he laid down in glowing phrases the guiding principles of the Republic of 1848.

He refuted the idea that the proclamation of the Republic was an act of aggression against any form of government in the world. People were subject to the same diversities as individuals, forms of government to varying degrees of national maturity. Nations demand more liberty, more equality and more democracy to the extent that they are inspired by justice and love for the people, to the degree in which they feel themselves more capable of supporting greater freedom.

"Monarchy and republic are not in the eyes of real statesmen absolute principles locked in a death struggle. They were opposing facts which can live face to face in mutual understanding and respect. Between 1792 and 1848 half a century has passed. We wish to march together with the world in fraternity and peace."

These were soothing words, sincerely offered and gladly accepted by those who sensed threat in the very word "Republic," by those occupants of thrones which had trembled in sympathy when Louis Philippe's toppled.

But there was one man, occupying no throne, exiled, not very young, and poor enough to be driven to borrow from courtesans, to whom the word "Republic" was the creak of the hinge of a door marked "Opportunity." Louis Napoleon felt that the time had come to make his third attempt.

Since his escape from Ham he had been living in England. He had resumed his association with the blond and beautiful Miss Howard whose former protectors had endowed her with a handsome fortune which she generously placed at the prince's disposal. He had almost given up hope of any other destiny than life as an English gentleman. The Revolution in France revitalized his ambition. He set out immediately for France, passing in mid-Channel the ship that carried Louis Philippe to exile.

He had adjusted himself, with the born opportunist's skill, to changing times. In 1836 he had come to Strasbourg bearing relics of Napoleon; in 1840 he had come to Boulogne with a tame and rather seedy eagle as a symbol. Now he came with words exactly attuned to the mood of the moment; he had come he said, "with no further ambition than that of serving my country."

The Provisional Government, however, felt itself competent to direct the destinies of France without his help, and his offer was met with a curt request to leave the country within twenty-four hours. He at once returned to London, but he left behind him the faithful Persigny, companion in all his adventures and ready now to form a Bonapartist committee whose aim it was to revive and foster Bonapartist feeling throughout France.

The Provisional Government with its five members—Lamartine, Arago, Garnier-Pagès, all idealistic Republicans, Albert a workingman and Louis Blanc the Socialist, settled to their work.

France had no need to demand of her latest revolution the national independence which was being sought by those European states which had been stirred by her example to revolt. She had no subject minorities; her national consciousness was already highly developed. What she asked was political and social improvement and that it should be immediate.

Of their nature revolutions are swift and violent, and revolutionaries are impatient men, eager to see some return for their expenditure of blood and effort, unwilling to wait for the slow maturing of reform. This impatience was to some degree shared by the Provisional Government. It was anxious to give proof of its generous intentions, but it was inexperienced; it had yet to learn that abstract theories, however admirable and cherished, must be translated into practical politics before they can be effective; it had to learn the truth of Louis Napoleon's words that in France revolutions are easy but reform almost impossible; it had yet to learn that benevolent theorists can make much the same mistakes as benevolent despots.

Within a few days the government instituted universal suffrage, set up a commission to study labor problems, freed the press of restraint, recognized the principle of "the right to work" and founded National Workshops which would guarantee employment and wages to those citizens who had been deprived of a living by the commercial and financial panic which the Revolution had created.

The National Workshops were the brain child of Louis Blanc, who believed that the object of political change should be the advancement of organized labor and the emancipation of the artisan from servitude. The ideals of appropriate employment and adequate remuneration were adopted in the first flush of revolutionary enthusiasm but the establishment of state-directed industries went beyond the moderate liberalism of those members of the government who represented the interests of the urban middle classes rather than those of the workingman.

In fact there was insufficient work and the scheme had been hastily and inadequately prepared. The Workshops were soon swamped both by the unemployed of Paris and by the hungry and the idle who swarmed in from the neighboring Departments. Once again it was found that a change of régime did not immediately result in prosperity; again the workers suffered disillusion, and disillusion bred discontent, which quickened suspicion among the bourgeoisie whose antennae were sensitive to anything that threatened their prosperity.

The Revolution of 1789 had been bourgeois in origin; that of 1848 was proletarian, but post-revolution procedure was almost identical. A constituent assembly was to be elected to determine the future government of France, this time by universal suffrage. Pending the elections, all power was in the hands of the Provisional Government, which meant in effect in the hands of Lamartine. His pre-eminence among his colleagues was due not only to hard work but also to his eloquence. He exercised what Louis Barthou has called "a dictatorship of oratory."

Not all his colleagues were easy shipmates; he had to steer a course between, on the one hand, convinced socialists like Ledru-Rollin, "a rhetorician dominated by the phrases of '93," and Louis Blanc, whose aims for the new Republic were communistic rather than Republican on the one side; and, on the other, the moderate Republicans. The early joy and hope gave way to dissatisfaction. By the middle of April demonstrations of red Republicans were being suppressed by the bourgeois National Guard and for the next fortnight Lamartine's eloquence had the backing of armed force.

The elections at the end of the month were a personal triumph for Lamartine and an overwhelming endorsement of his policy. Universal suffrage returned a Chamber of moderate Republicans willing to give Lamartine the premiership, the presidency of the Republic, any office he cared to choose. It almost seemed that a prophecy made to him by Lady Hester Stanhope might come true. "You will be King . . ." she had told him. But in Lamartine personal ambition took second place to his conception of duty; he was still the idealist rather than the careerist. In the Executive Commission of five members, which took the place of the Provisional Government, Lamartine held no predominant office; Ledru-Rollin remained a member because of his popularity with the masses, but Louis Blanc was excluded.

It soon became apparent that a head-on collision between the new party of order and the socialist democracy of Paris would not be long delayed. The mob had not made a revolution in February in order to see it dwindle in April into anything so tame as a Constituent Assembly. Universal suffrage might gratify men's self esteem but votes did not fill empty bellies.

The moderate Republicans in the Assembly were preoccupied by political considerations not immediately concerned with social justice and the Socialists lacked the power to put their theories into practice.

By May the mob found a means of expressing its smoldering discontent; Lamartine refused to send military aid to revolutionaries in Poland and demonstrations against his decision began. His courage in riding out to face the demonstrators once again quelled the disturbance and he was even allowed to arrest, without trouble, the socialist leaders. It was plain, however, if the new government hoped to establish the economic stability so vital to national survival, that it could no longer tolerate the unrest foaming in the Paris populace.

One obvious source of trouble was the National Workshops. They had been founded with such high-minded intentions and the government had lavished large sums of money on them. The scheme had been an expensive and dismal failure, and the shops themselves had degenerated into centers of discontent and disaffection. They did, however, offer employment of a sort to 100,000 men and a prudent government would have gone about the closure gradually.

This government shared some of the impatience of the mob; the National Workshops were closed between one day and the next, in defiance of the warning of the Minister of the Interior, who foresaw the result of such precipitate action and said, "The insurrection will take place tomorrow." (Not "an insurrection," the vague possibility, but "the insurrection," the expected, near-certainty.)

He was right. Publication of the closing orders acted as a call to arms to the thousands of men thus suddenly deprived of even the most meager livelihood. On June 23 the "*Ça ira*" was again heard in the streets of Paris, mingled with cries of "*Lamartine à la lantern*" and the old demand for liberty or death. The insurgents took control of the eastern parts of the city; up went the barricades again and civil war threatened.

The Executive Commission gave General Cavaignac full powers to put down the revolt; he was brother to Godefroy Cavaignac who in the July Revolution had fought for a republic on the anti-government side of the barricades; now a Cavaignac, on the other side of the street blocks, fought again for a republic, this time in power but threatened by anarchy.

In the past the Paris streets had seen some bitter, bloody battles, but the war waged in the next four days surpassed them all. Both sides committed acts of savagery which even the fury of conflict could not justify. The rising was, in miniature, a foretaste of the "total war" of the next century. When the Archbishop of Paris went out, carrying a crucifix, to appeal for peace he was shot down.

When it was over, with Cavaignac and the National Guard in control, almost 5000 Parisians lay dead on the blood-stained pavements. From his exile Louis Philippe said caustically, "The Republic is lucky. It can fire on the people." It could also make 15,000 arrests and deport 4000 people to Algeria.

The gulf between workers and bourgeoisie was now deeper than ever, and full of blood. The workers turned away in disgust from a régime that gave them bullets instead of bread.

Another general, in 1795, had quelled a riot and been rewarded by all that France had to give. Cavaignac was given power, but he had little capacity for government nor the suppleness necessary to make a political leader. He was a sincere Republican, but by caste and profession he was a rigid upholder of the law.

In the unfortunate, established tradition that after each upheaval somebody must be punished, Lamartine was tried for peculation and for prolonging his personal rule. He was speedily acquitted, but the calumnies left their mark on him, just as the suppression of the workers left its mark on memories long after the barricades were down, the streets washed clean of blood and order restored.

Order indeed was the aim both of bourgeoisie and peasantry. They yearned for a firm government which would re-establish the economy and give them a security which they felt lacking. General Cavaignac's rule was strong, but it was a military government with little appeal to either businessmen or peasants. Was there, they asked themselves, no alternative?

One man believed that there was. Once again, Louis Napoleon, watchful, lynx-eared, felt that his chance had come. With commendable restraint he had not presented himself as a candidate at the elections in April but, when the new Assembly was debating the exile of former reigning houses, he had written a letter to the President of the Assembly, demanding his rights as a French citizen. He pointed out that he was not a foreigner, as rumor held; he had been born in Paris.

Persigny and his other friends had worked away to such good

effect that in the June by-elections no fewer than five Departments chose Louis Napoleon as their representative. A wave of Bonapartist feeling broke over Paris. The name stood for much; to the bourgeois it stood for order, to the workers a legacy of the old ideals of the Great Revolution.

The Cavaignac government, however, had no wish to accept Louis Napoleon as a member of the Assembly and announced that as soon as he set foot in France he would be arrested.

He made no fuss; with dignity he resigned the seat in the Assembly to which he had been legally elected and again settled down to wait.

The Constituent Assembly proceeded with its constitution-making. Lamartine's influence remained strong and it was his urging that led to the establishment of a single legislative Chamber and the election of the future President of the Republic by direct universal suffrage. The Chamber, elected by the same method, was to consist of 750 members, to serve for three years and enabled to initiate and pass laws. The President's term was longer, four years, but he would not be eligible for re-election. During his term of office he would appoint ministers and officials and control the armed forces. The new constitution, drawn up under pressure of fear from the workers, hopefully envisaged a strong executive power; undeterred, the French pursued the dream that had so far eluded them, a government strong enough to govern, popular enough to continue in power.

Lamartine still believed that universal suffrage, extended to the point where even the President was elected, was a cure for all ills. In February he had put into words the essence of democracy, the right of a country "to choose for itself when it has been consulted." But Jules Grévy, a firm Republican, thought otherwise; he feared that the direct election of a President might produce a dictator. He proposed that the Chamber, not the mass of the people, should choose the nation's head; but his warning and his amendment were disregarded. The way of Louis Napoleon was being "made plain" in the biblical sense.

In the autumn the by-elections took place and once again Louis Napoleon, whom few voters would have recognized had they met him in the street, was returned as representative for five Departments.

This time he took his seat. He was so quiet and unobtrusive in the Chamber that Lamartine called him "a hat without a head." Other people besides Lamartine underestimated Louis Napoleon, whose appearance was the reverse of impressive—a long body on short legs, dull hair and lusterless eyes, leaden pallor and nicotine-stained fingers. Another "funny little man" but, like his uncle to whom Josephine applied that term, he had a charm which had nothing to do with physical comeliness. Queen Victoria, prejudiced against him, succumbed when she met him and wrote, ". . . that he *is* a very *extraordinary* man, with great qualities, there can be *no* doubt . . . I might almost say a mysterious man . . . with a *power of fascination.*"

He sat quietly until November when the presidential election was due; and then he presented himself as a candidate, putting forward in his election address the need to maintain order and uphold the rights of property, exploiting the country's growing desire for a "strong man." The choice for the people was between Lamartine, who had ceased to be a real factor, Cavaignac, with the blood spilled in June hardly dry on his hands, and this unknown man, bearer of the magic name.

To the threadbare old soldiers gathering about his hotel in the Place Vendôme under the shadow of his uncle's great column, the name itself was enough; to them Louis Napoleon was already elected. Their enthusiasm was contagious, and Miss Howard's money helped the promotion of the Bonapartist cause. Some of the leading figures of the July Monarchy came to think that service with a Bonaparte might be preferable to remaining in the icy wastes of the opposition. Berryer, Guizot, Marshal Bugeaud, even Thiers suddenly discovered within themselves a leaning toward the Prince's candidature.

The Prince stood firm on his declaration that what France needed was "a firm, wise and intelligent government which would think more of curing the ills of society than avenging them." This far-from-original analysis—few countries at any time have asked much else—appealed to the people.

They gave him five million votes. Cavaignac polled a million and a half; Lamartine, never really in the running, fewer than twenty thousand.

The first President of the Second Republic offered Lamartine a ministry, which he refused, saying, "The people is sovereign; but the people is man, and man can err. The people are novices in sovereignty." He retired from politics and devoted himself to writing, though he never again equaled his earlier work.

Louis Napoleon's victory was welcomed as a victory over the Socialists and the red Republicans; he represented the order and authority that the moderate majority desired; there was nothing in his mild manner and hesitant manner of speaking to hint at immoderate ambition lying in ambush. Thiers said long afterward: "The French made two mistakes about Louis Napoleon; the first when they took him for a fool, the next when they took him for a man of genius." A neat pronouncement but one which ignores those five million votes; it is a little difficult to believe that in November 1848 five million Frenchmen deliberately chose a fool to govern them.

He devoted himself to consolidating his position. In May 1849, new elections returned a Legislative Assembly composed in the main of Royalist bourgeois determined to undermine the Republic and put back the clock. Unwittingly it was playing Louis Napoleon's game for him, and events in Italy offered him a chance to win over to his side an element which might have held aloof—the extreme Catholic right wing. Mazzini headed a rising against Pope Pius IX and declared a Roman republic. Louis Napoleon sent an expedition to protect the Pope—an expedition which was to remain in Italy until 1866; and when there were Socialist demonstrations in Paris in favor of Mazzini, the Assembly had the ringleaders arrested.

Three laws passed in 1850 showed the government's reactionary and anti-democratic tendencies. The Loi Falloux permitted the opening of both lay and ecclesiastic private schools and placed elementary schools under the surveillance of the Church, thus giving the Catholics, and particularly the Jesuits, a sphere of influence over French youth. There followed an electoral law which modified universal suffrage and disqualified three of the ten million voters; most of the disenfranchised were working-class men who became bitterly antagonistic to the régime that had robbed them of their votes. By that one act the Assembly had committed political suicide and opened the way for the President—in his own good time—to stand forth as the champion of universal suffrage.

The third act clamped down on the press and reimposed the old restrictions.

All this legislation had a definite object in view; the Royalist bourgeois Assembly was working toward the restoration of the monarchy. But they were faced by a strange question. Which monarchy? When you turn back the clock, how far should you go? Legitimists said back to 1830 and bring Charles X's grandson, the Comte de Chambord, to the throne; Orleanists said back to 1848 and restore Louis Philippe's grandson, the Comte de Paris. Men uncommitted to either side may have thought, "a plague o' both your houses." Neither Royalist side would compromise, so the question of restoration was shelved. But only temporarily, they assured themselves; a little postponement until things were sorted out and Legitimist or Orleanist gained the upper hand. Meanwhile there was the President, keeping the seat warm.

How many of them looked back to the year 1804 when the uncle of this President had held the crown of France in his gift and could have called back Louis XVIII to wear it, but had instead placed it on his own head? There was so little about Louis Napoleon, except the name, to remind men of his breed.

Louis Napoleon had his own plans and his own problems. He was President, and under the constitution ineligible for re-election. He tried to get that rule amended but the Assembly, intent upon the restoration—the Comte de Chambord? the Comte de Paris? —threw out the amendment. And that meant that in May 1852 a career barely under way would come to an abrupt end. Aged forty-two, after a brief taste of power and plenty, he would find himself back in obscurity and poverty.

When he looked out from the windows of the presidential palace of the Elysée, he could see the tree tops in the garden of another palace, the Tuileries, where he had been born in 1808, at the height of the Empire's glory. His father was King of Holland, his uncle Emperor of the French. Admittedly there were doubts about his paternity; his parents had been unhappily married and the existence of Auguste de Morny, the illegitimate son of Hortense and the Comte de Flahaut, himself the illegitimate son of Talleyrand, proved that Hortense's virtue had not always been unassailable; and when the King of Holland had brought a scandalous lawsuit against his wife in order to secure the custody of the two elder sons he had pointedly made no claim to the third, whom unkind rumor held to be the child of a Dutch admiral.

But Louis Napoleon recognized in himself the Bonaparte qualities; the readiness to gamble; the liking for intrigue; the capacity for silence; the exaggerated sensuality; the power to charm; the ambition. He looked at the Tuileries and was conscious of "Time's wingèd chariot hurrying near," as his term of office wore, day by day, away.

He knew the risk he took; he had sworn an oath to maintain the constitution; if he broke that oath and failed he could be executed, or again condemned to life imprisonment. Either, he decided, was preferable to relapsing into nonentity.

He could count upon his popularity; he had moved about outside Paris, lavishing promises to all in speeches that perhaps carried conviction because of their very lack of eloquence—to the end of his days he spoke French with a German accent, acquired in his youth in Augsburg. He varied his arguments to meet the aspirations of his audiences, the bourgeoisie, the Catholics, the peasants and the industrial workers, he made promises to them all.

"My power," he said, "is in an immortal name . . . It stands for order, authority, religion, the welfare of the people, national dignity, particularly in the country districts—my true friends are to be found not in palaces but in cottages."

He knew very well that in virtually every cottage a picture of Napoleon hung side by side with a crude engraving of the Virgin Mary and that they were revered almost to the same degree. He also believed in his own statement that France, "in the midst of confusion, seeks the hand and the will of the man it elected. . . ." And he too, like Napoleon, had faith in his star.

On December 2, 1851, the forty-sixth anniversary of the battle of Austerlitz, early risers in Paris, trudging to work in the drizzling rain, saw that all the newspaper offices and strategic points in the city were occupied by soldiers. The army had, once again, been asked to save the country. Posters everywhere announced the dissolution of the Assembly which had made itself unpopular by its reactionary program. The posters—the paste that held them still damp—promised the return of universal suffrage.

It was another *coup d'état,* following the classic pattern. Neither France nor the world could fail to observe that imitation rather than innovation had become the norm in bringing down French governments. December 2 was a repetition of 18 Brumaire. France, still lacking political stability, was vulnerable to any man or system of government which had sufficient energy and determination to impose upon her.

Between the two take-overs, that of uncle and nephew, there was one ironic difference; Napoleon the soldier, on his way to the throne, shed no drop of French blood; Napoleon III, the man of peace, who had publicly declared that he was interested only in industrial, commercial and humanitarian ideas, walked to his throne over several hundred corpses. It was again a single shot, fired by some unknown person that provoked a few nervous young soldiers to retaliate. It was all over in a few minutes, but it was a tragedy that Louis Napoleon, squeamish, humanitarian, fundamentally kindhearted, never quite forgot.

January days are short, but in 1852 three of them were sufficient to reorganize the French government. The President—now to be elected for ten years—would enjoy powers exceeding those bestowed on the King by the Charter of 1814. He had complete freedom in his choice of ministers and could cut across any conflict with the Assembly by a direct appeal to the nation by way of plebiscite.

Four bodies nominally shared the tasks of government with him; the Senate, nominated by him, was to guarantee and, if necessary, to complete the constitution and to legislate for the colonies: the Legislature, which the President had the power to dissolve, was to be elected for six-year terms by universal suffrage: the Council of State, nominated by the President, and the High Court of Justice.

It was in fact, with a few modifications, the structure of the First Empire, and with the elected Legislature able to vote only on propositions put forward by the government and its right of the address lost, was close to being a régime of personal rule.

Throughout the year 1852 the word "Republic" appeared less and less frequently on official documents. The President again toured the country and chose the old Royalist stronghold of Bordeaux from which to make a decisive speech, intended to calm anxieties abroad as well as at home.

"The Empire," he said, "means peace." Peace at home had already been secured by the severe control of the press, by the deterrents of prison sentences, exile and deportation, but it was essential that Europe be assured that, with another Bonaparte upon the throne of France, history would not repeat itself bloodily.

So, almost imperceptibly, the Second Republic slipped into the Second Empire. Appealed to by plebiscite in November 1852, seven million Frenchmen voted for the restoration of the Bonaparte dynasty; a quarter of a million voted against it; two million abstained.

France's second attempt at a Republic had failed and for that failure—although he took every advantage of it—Louis Napoleon was not responsible. Its weakness lay in itself, in its government's blindness to the interests of the people who had brought it into being. The Second Republic had been born out of an insurrection of workingmen; it had handled their social problems ineptly and lost their confidence. Now they, with the peasants and the bourgeois, tired of bloodshed and fear and insecurity, turned with varying emotions and differing hopes to an authoritarian régime.

Chapter 2. THE SECOND EMPIRE

Dynasties are continuous, and the boy who died in Vienna was in the eyes of Bonapartists Napoleon II so Louis Napoleon was proclaimed Napoleon III, Emperor of the French. In four years since his return to France he had achieved his ambitions; the question now was, could he, as Emperor, be as successful as he had been as President?

The new constitution made it clear what kind of government was envisaged; an enlightened despotism, what G. P. Gooch has called "an efficient and paternal autocracy resting on nation-wide assent." The working of such a system throws a heavy burden on the man at its head who assumes enormous responsibilities and must impose law without sacrificing his personal popularity.

Louis Napoleon came well-equipped to the task; he rated himself too modestly when he claimed that his power rested only in an immortal name; he had qualities of his own—intelligence, flexibility, patience learned during the long waiting, statesmanship, subtlety. His vision was wide, his interest in social matters genuine and compassionate; in many ways he was a man of his time. He was a figure of greater potential strength than any of his predecessors since 1814 and his accession seemed to promise the return of the "strong man" who would definitely re-establish France as a leading world power. At the same time his desire for peace was sincere, based on common sense; there was, he said, too much chance about war for his liking.

At the time of the *coup d'état*, he seemed to have every quality desirable in a monarch, but as time went on weaknesses appeared. In an autocrat stability and a capacity for firm decision are of greater importance than ideologies. As he aged, his inherent instability and indecision increased, so that some of his policies lacked forethought and some were not followed through. He was generous and grateful, qualities that can be inconvenient to an autocrat who must from time to time display ruthlessness. In the end Napoleon III revealed himself as an intellectual humanitarian rather than a man of action.

In 1854, Queen Victoria, with her innate common sense, put her finger on another of the Emperor's weaknesses—a lack of experience. "How could it be expected that the Emperor *should* have any experience in *public affairs*, considering that till six years ago he lived as a poor exile, for some years even in prison, and never having taken the slightest part in the *public* affairs of any country. It is therefore the more astounding, indeed almost incomprehensible, that he should show all those powers of Government and all that wonderful tact in his conduct and manners which he evinces, and which many a King's son, nurtured in palaces, and educated in the midst of affairs never succeeds in attaining." Perhaps as she wrote the last words she was thinking of her own rather unsatisfactory thirteen-year-old son, who was presently to say to Napoleon III, "I wish I were your son!"

The new reign opened under happy auspices, possibly happier than those attending any monarch since 1814; the Church and the Catholics supported the man who, as President, had given them proof of his good will. The army, naturally, was on his side; it cherished evergreen memories of its heyday under the old Bonaparte Empire and expected great things of the new one. The Royalists, still divided between Legitimist and Orleanist sentiments, were at least both in favor of the monarchical principle, and to the Legitimists the Empire offered an authoritarian rule not so very different from the one of their dreams. The Republican party was weakened by internal dissension and by the loss of its leaders, many in exile, some in prison.

As for the ordinary people, less concerned with political theory, the peasant with his crops, the merchant in his office, the workman at his bench, had they not given ample proof that they approved of Louis Napoleon's self-promotion? In return for seven million votes they expected peace and prosperity.

Almost, the Emperor seemed to have achieved his aim; one nation, united about himself: but he was far from stupid and despite his gambling streak not prone to overoptimism. Universal suffrage had been his friend, but if the opposition, now small, timid and ineffectual, ever revived, universal suffrage might become his enemy.

He did not repeat the mistake of the Second Republic and snatch away men's votes. He whittled away their effectiveness by the institution of "official candidates" and the prefectoral system. In each department the Prefect was a picked, trusted man, a necessary link between the central government in Paris and the province which he supervised. He was the eyes and ears of the Emperor; he exercised considerable power, not all of it in the open.

Universal suffrage remained, giving each man the right to vote as he wished, or to abstain; any man could offer himself as a candidate for election, but an opposition candidate would find himself confronted by some extraordinary difficulties; he might find that no one was willing to print his election addresses or, if he managed to get them printed, to distribute them. He would be handicapped in his attempts to bring himself and his program to the notice of the public. The Prefect had all kinds of local material favors in his gift; it was wiser not to offend him.

Control of this kind was less easily exercised in cities than in country districts and as a result the political climate in town and country differed and the gulf between them widened.

In 1852 eight opposition members were elected, in 1857, nine, of whom five were from Paris: but the nature of the opposition had changed in the five years. Legitimist in 1852, it was mainly Republican in 1857.

Having got himself elected, an opposition candidate still had another hurdle to face; this time a moral one. Every deputy, before he took his seat must swear an oath of allegiance. This eliminated any man not willing to commit perjury. In 1857, one of the five deputies for Paris, a young man named Emile Ollivier, thought it worth while to perjure himself and take the oath in order to sit and be able to speak in the Chamber to which he had been elected.

In 1858, in order to forestall the unfortunate publicity of an elected candidate's being compelled to resign because of the oath, the rule was amended and candidates were required to take it before they began their campaigns.

Such measures showed how little real love the Emperor had for parliamentary institutions. He held them, in fact, to be responsible for all the misfortunes that had overtaken the country since the end of the First Empire. By clever manipulation he allowed the people to retain the universal suffrage which they cherished, and which he had promised to them, and they had an illusion that they shared in the government; actually his power was almost as absolute as that of Louis XIV, since he held all executive authority and, thanks to the prefectoral system, any election or plebiscite would return him the result he wished for.

Not even an autocrat can rule without assistance, and in his choice of right-hand men Napoleon III was limited by his own reserve which made it hard for him to give his confidence except to those he knew well, and by his gratitude to those who had been his friends in less fortunate days. His personal and political entourage remained basically the same throughout his reign. When death made replacements necessary the Emperor was never at ease with the newcomers.

He had a preference, too—in common with many other princes—for men whose natural abilities were inferior to his own. There was Persigny, the faithful friend who had shared the adventures at Strasbourg and Boulogne, worked hard for the Bonapartist revival and been rewarded with a dukedom. His intelligence was limited; to him force was the answer to everything, and his manners were not of the best. There were Achille Fould, Minister of Finance, and Pierre Jules Baroche, the counselor who represented the government before the Legislature, both fiercely hard workers and docile lieutenants, but neither of them the stuff of which great ministers are made.

The most able of the Emperor's counselors and the one who exercised most influence upon him was his half brother, whom he made Duc de Morny. He was illegitimate, as his father had been, but he had inherited charm, elegance, worldliness and great political skill from his grandfather, Talleyrand. The half brothers had never met until Louis Napoleon returned to France where de Morny was an officer in Louis Philippe's army. Then, with as swift a switch as any executed by Talleyrand, de Morny turned Bonapartist and played a great part in the *coup d'état;* in fact he wrote that but for him it would never have taken place. After it, as Minister of the Interior, he helped to re-establish order and suppress the enemies of the new régime. His real interests, however, were not political; he preferred social life, amusement, business and speculation. In 1852, with the Empire on a sound footing, he resigned his post; but his business interests were not without influence of the Emperor's policy and so on the destiny of France.

Like Napoleon I, Napoleon III was victim to the family and tribal traditions of his Corsican breed; success for one member of the group implied comfort for all. As soon as Louis Napoleon was installed as President, back to the Elysée they came, like the symbolic bees buzzing to the home hive. Old King Jerome, the only survivor of the senior branch, was more an embarrassment than help to his nephew, and his son, Prince Napoleon, known as Plon-Plon, a vicious character, was actively hostile to the cousin whom he envied but whose money he was willing to accept. The Bacciocchis and the Murats were nothing more than hangers-on. Only one of the tribe, Princess Mathilde, was useful to Louis Napoleon; she undertook the duties of hostess for him as President and continued after he became Emperor.

They had once been in love and on the point of being engaged, but when the Strasbourg attempt failed, King Jerome had lost faith in his nephew's future and looked about for a rich husband for his daughter. He found one, a Count Demidoff, very rich but a boor, who beat his wife in private and in public slapped her face. That unhappy marriage had ended in a separation. Mathilde was now acting as hostess where, had things gone a little differently, she would have reigned as Empress.

This situation was not to last long. Napoleon III realized, as his uncle and many other men had done, that one man is not a dynasty. A man on a throne is haunted by the question, after me, what? As soon as he was firmly established the new Emperor began to seek a wife among the princesses of Europe, and found that the royal families were reluctant to give one of their daughters to a parvenu Emperor. What had happened to Marie Louise was a warning; four years of marriage and then dethronement and after that, with a husband still alive on St. Helena, unable to marry her lover and living scandalously.

The simplest marital course for Napoleon to have pursued would have been to marry Mathilde, who would not have found it difficult to obtain a divorce from her husband. Mathilde was, through her mother, Catherine of Württemberg, related to almost all the crowned heads of Europe. By such a marriage the Emperor would have gained entry to the charmed circle. But Mathilde was a love outgrown and the Emperor, now forty-five years old, had fallen under the spell of another charmer.

Despite his lack of obvious physical attractions, despite the short legs and dull eyes, he had always had success with women. As a prisoner for life, in the fortress of Ham, he had had a mistress who had borne him two sons. Miss Howard, a courtesan, who had exploited other men, had financed him. (To do him justice one should note that his power to fascinate was not confined to females; an Englishman as cool, as little likely to be dazzled as Lord Normanby, would, after half an hour's interview with him say, "A gentleman from the crown of his head to the sole of his foot.")

Now—while he was still making marriage offers elsewhere— he attempted to charm a beautiful, red-haired, half-Spanish, half-Scottish girl named Eugénie de Montijo, and would have made her his mistress. It should have been easy; emperors seldom meet with much resistance from young ladies whom they wish to favor or from their mothers; but this was an exceptional young lady with an exceptional mother, who despite lack of money and status —there was the shadow of "trade" in the background—had succeeded in marrying one of her daughters, Paca, to the Duke of Alba, and did not intend to waste the other on a mere liaison. The Emperor was never allowed to see Eugénie alone; nor could he write to her freely. ("I must warn you, my mother sees all my letters.") It was made clear that the only way to Eugénie's bed lay through Notre Dame.

The Emperor decided that a love match would appeal to the romantic element in the nation; it would also show the monarchs of Europe that a man with a great people behind him had no need to make an advantageous marriage. He announced his decision early in 1853 and pensioned off Miss Howard, giving her the title of Comtesse de Beauregard and entrusting her with the care of his two illegitimate children.

Of the wedding, which took place in a setting that rivaled the splendor of the First Empire, an English eyewitness said, "a magnificent theatrical representation and nothing more." Others, glimpsing Eugénie's beauty through the mist of transparent lace, thought that it, her grace and her engaging manners would win her popularity.

The London *Times* remembering Richardson's novel about virtue triumphant, said, unkindly, "The Imperial Pamela has received her reward." The royal families of Europe considered that the Emperor had done for himself socially: and there were Bonapartists who felt that, having failed to make a royal alliance, the Emperor should have chosen a Frenchwoman.

Eugénie never lived down her nationality; as Marie Antoinette and Marie Louise had each in turn been "the Austrian" so the new Empress was "the Spaniard." None of her efforts to identify herself with France could make her popular.

In announcing his choice of wife Napoleon had referred to "the kind and gentle wife of General Bonaparte . . . not of royal blood." But Eugénie was not a second Josephine; as a girl she had delighted in riding bare-backed horses and had patronized bullfighters; as Empress she showed an unfeminine interest in politics. The Emperor, a romantic sensualist, found to his dismay that her red hair belied her temperament. Her frigidity soon drove him back to extramarital adventures. Women were for him a necessity and a distraction, but except for Eugénie, not one of them was ever allowed to exert the slightest political influence over him. Now, paradoxically, as her physical and emotional hold on him weakened, he allowed her political influence to increase. Where politics were concerned she could be passsionate, indulging in grandiose dreams of national prestige and territorial aggrandizement; her meddling in this sphere did not endear her to the people.

The Court over which she presided was, however, appreciated. After the dull pedestrian years there was again splendor, display and ceremonial; the Emperor had a taste for such things, the Empress was beautiful and elegant.

Like the courts of the eighteenth century, or that of Louis XIV, this one moved to an appointed rhythm. Winter was spent at the Tuileries except for a hunting season at Compiègne where stag hunting alternated with charades, plays, archery contests and balls, all of which had the glitter and grandeur of the old days, but not the strictness and formality; manners were, indeed, sometimes relaxed beyond what was seemly. Summer saw the court at St. Cloud, and in September the Emperor and Empress went to Biarritz to live for a short time almost as private citizens.

From most of this gaiety and activity the old nobility held aloof, regarding this as just another parvenu court whose manners and morals were not above criticism. They were hardly missed, so many members of foreign aristocracies were anxious to sample the delights of Paris; the nobility of the First Empire rallied to another Emperor Napoleon, and the wealthy middle classes regarded an appearance at Court as the stamp upon their social status.

As Josephine had found her mentor of fashion in Leroy, so Eugénie's elegance was dictated by a boy from Lincolnshire in England who became the great couturier, Worth. Between them they made the crinoline fashionable, and since each crinoline skirt needed ten lengths of silk or velvet, the looms in Lyons worked to capacity. The fashion spread. What Eugénie wore must be copied by every woman with any pretension to stylishness. (And it was a fashion kind to the pregnant, of whom, in that philoprogenitive age, there were many. "Hitch your top hoop a little higher and it won't show.") French textiles enjoyed an export boom.

Worth's fabulous creations seemed to flow with the same rhythm as the Strauss waltzes to which Paris danced and to Offenbach's melodies, conducted by Jullien; the silk of the gowns still seems to slide and whisper in the canvases of Winterhalter, the fashionable portrait painter of the age.

What Worth was to fashion, Offenbach was to music and the theatre. With his great star, Hortense Schneider, he kept Paris amused with his brilliant operettas—*Orpheus in the Underworld*, which introduced the can-can; *La Belle Hélène; La Vie Parisienne* and the *Grand Duchess of Gerolstein*. His best-known work,

The Tales of Hoffman, was not enjoyed by the Second Empire. When those tunes came to the ears of the world, that gay society had been swept away, and Offenbach himself was dead.

The Second Empire liked to laugh and laughter was provided by dramatists like Labiche, Meilhac and Halévy; but at the same time Rachel was putting fresh life into old classics—and finding time to coach Eugénie in the deportment suitable to an Empress. Alexandre Dumas the younger produced a play that now seems gently romantic but was then regarded as the last word in realism, *La Dame aux Camélias.* To understand the impact made by this play, dealing with the life and death of a cocotte, it is necessary to remember that it was presented to the same people who were so shocked by Flaubert's *Madame Bovary* that they attempted to have it suppressed by official censorship. Flaubert was acquitted of the charge of immorality, but Charles Baudelaire, author of *Les Fleurs du Mal,* was less fortunate. The hardheaded businessmen of the Second Empire might be impatient with romance and eager for more naturalism and realism in art and literature, the court might be lax in its morality, but the French people as a whole maintained the same rigidly moral standard as they had done under Louis Philippe. There was also—out of power but still surviving —a hard core of stern Republicans who refused to approve either of the spirit of the age or the authoritarianism of the régime. A vast number of people, while admitting that there was visible improvement in the country's economy, wondered if so much show and extravagance were necessary. There were thousands of women to whom a crinoline would have been an encumbrance as they went about their work; thousands of men who could not fit Offenbach's tunes to their steps as they trod the furrows behind the laboring oxen. They worked on.

Napoleon III had no desire to play the sedulous ape to Napoleon I and he had said that the Empire meant peace: yet of a Bonaparte a vigorous foreign policy was expected. The revolution of 1848 in France had given tremendous impetus to the growth of nationalism all over Europe and, as a sovereign who owed his throne to a revolution, and as an idealist who genuinely believed in the principle of nationalism, Napoleon III was both ready and eager to support nations struggling for freedom. The French shared this willingness; they were conscious of the responsibilities inherited from the revolution of 1789, and they were still aware of the loss of face which they had suffered from the treaties of 1815.

Napoleon III, like Louis Philippe, realized the importance of an Anglo-French alliance, and was inclined toward it for personal as well as political reasons; England had welcomed him as an exile. He was fortunate to have, as his ambassador in London, Count Walewski, who succeeded in overcoming Victoria's reluctance to favor the sovereign who had taken Louis Philippe's place. The English people showed their usual half-magnanimous, half-masochistic tendency to befriend a foe—once he had fallen—and at the funeral of the Duke of Wellington had given their loudest cheers to the French representative, Marshal Soult, the Duke's old enemy.

Soon the two nations were to be allies, not in Europe but in the Near East, where the Czar's ambitions ran counter to French and British interests. Nicholas I was pursuing the ancient Russian dream of gaining an outlet to the Mediterranean and took advantage of the Turks' refusal to give the guardianship of the Holy Places in Palestine to the Orthodox Church, to offer himself as champion of the Russian Orthodox communities inside the Ottoman Empire. In 1853 he invaded Romania in the guise of protector, and in the West the bells of alarm and opportunity rang out. England was frenetically sensitive to any possibility of the expansion of Russian power; Russia lay just beyond the troubled North West frontier of India. Napoleon III saw an opportunity of endearing himself to the extreme Catholic right wing at home, by opposing the champion of the Orthodox Church. He was also motivated by the wish to avenge France for the humiliations of 1812 and 1814. So, on March 27, 1854, France and England, all their old differences forgotten, declared war on Russia, ostensibly to defend the Ottoman Empire, each in fact to further her own interests. A minor religious squabble had sparked off one of the most hideous wars in history.

Neither country was prepared; since 1815 their military exercises had been confined to a few punitive expeditions and colonial wars. Weapons and methods were outdated, commissariat and medical services lamentably inadequate. Both French and English armies were fighting far from home, and there was no co-ordinated command.

French mobilization was faulty; the value of the new railways as a means of moving troops and their gear was not appreciated, nor was the importance of up-to-date maps. In the middle of the nineteenth century men went off to war with the same equipment, often similar clothes as they had done in the early years of the early eighteenth.

Queen Victoria stood on the balcony of Buckingham Palace and watched "the beautiful and touching sight" of her Guards in their spectacular, impractical uniforms, marching off to embark; in Paris, Napoleon took the salute from his quick-marching regiments, swinging past to the tune that his mother had composed, a love song, "Partant pour la Syrie." Both monarchs were watching doomed men bravely going to death, sentenced less by enemy action than by miserable incompetence.

In neither army did the need of the hour call forth the man; this grew more apparent as the terrible months went on. Napoleon III had not been bred as a soldier and, now that war was here, he showed no sign of that inborn talent that can convert, overnight, a civilian into a military leader. Many experienced French generals had been purged in the *coup d'état;* Saint-Arnaud, a competent colonial commander, died in September 1854, immediately after the successful battle of the Alma; Canrobert, unwilling to shoulder responsibility, resigned, and MacMahon, courageous as he was, lacked initiative. The English were just as badly off; they had sound, experienced men, but the experience had been gained in India and, for social reasons, officers from India were despised, not listened to and forced to be subservient to leaders whose soldiering had been done on the parade ground and whose behavior, in some cases, seen in retrospect, varied between the mildly and the virulently insane.

The English press was free; Russell of *The Times* could report what he saw of horror and hardship and mismanagement; the French press was muzzled.

This particularly tragic war had its by-products, in the final analysis more important than any of the military actions of which it consisted. Florence Nightingale's work in the Crimea completely revolutionized hospitals and raised nursing from one of the most despised to one of the most respected professions. The lack of co-ordination between English and French in the Crimea resulted in a more sensible policy when French, English and American troops went into war side by side in later years. It was the beginning of the recognition of the common soldier as a human being with a human being's needs, and of the fact that those who lead armies need training for the job. And it also gave the world the first of something by which we all, almost unconsciously, shape our lives —weather forecasts.

Napoleon III should be remembered for his notion that weather could be, within certain limits, foreseen. One of the sudden storms, to which the Black Sea is prone, sent ships carrying men and stores, both urgently needed, to the bottom. Such catastrophe, the Emperor felt, could be guarded against and he established, in many places, weather stations to send in their observations to Paris, where they were correlated and the possible forecasts dispatched to the rest of the world.

While French and British soldiers fought and starved and thirsted and sickened and died in the Crimea, the Prince Consort made a visit to Boulogne, once again a mustering place. If the memories of two other occasions when fleets at Boulogne had gathered there to threaten England haunted this meeting, neither Napoleon III nor the Prince Consort was likely to be troubled by them for, dissimilar as they were in character and disposition, they were both inclined to think of the future rather than the past.

This meeting was so successful that in the spring of 1855, with the armies still besieging the apparently impregnable fortress of Sebastopol, Napoleon and Eugénie went to stay at Windsor. Even Louis Philippe, a cousin of kings, had felt it an honor to be entertained by the Queen of England; to the parvenu Emperor and Empress the invitation implied even more of recognition and acceptance.

The visit was a great success; Napoleon's strange charm cast its spell, and Eugénie, with charm of her own, had the perception to see that within the somewhat formidable little woman who was

Queen of England there existed a female creature, devoted wife and mother. Visiting Victoria's flourishing nurseries, Eugénie mourned her own childlessness. She had had two miscarriages, and Victoria is said to have advised her to avoid hot baths.

In August, when Victoria and the Prince Consort went to Paris to return the visits, Eugénie was being "very careful."

This was a memorable visit. The Paris Exhibition was on, the weather superb, and the Emperor exerted himself to entertain his guests and to indulge their two elder children. Victoria admired the improvements which had already been made in Paris, visited the Exhibition, to every aspect of which she gave tireless attention, and continued to find her host fascinating and her hostess "dear and very charming." Best of all, crowning felicity, came the news that Sebastopol was at last falling.

The winter of 1854–55 had been a long and hard one, recalling to superstitious minds the winter of 1812. Victor Hugo, rabidly opposed to the man whom he called Napoleon the Little, had sneeringly remarked that the new Emperor was beginning his career in 1812. The jibe had some justification for, when Sebastopol fell, the Russians withdrew in good order, systematically burning the city as they had burned Moscow.

The Allies were victorious, but they were also exhausted; the war, brief compared with many, had been very bitter, every victory hardly won; hunger, disease and cold and lack of cohesion as deadly as the enemy. Fortunately, Alexander II, who had succeeded Nicholas I in 1855, was himself ready for peace.

French prestige was now at its zenith. France was no longer the conquered and humiliated nation of 1815, but a triumphant power with England, her ancient enemy, her ally. The Peace Conference which met in Paris soothed the wounds left by the Congress of Vienna. Imperial policy had given France an exceptional place in international affairs. As Lord Palmerston said: "No one in Europe dares to undertake anything until he first knows the thoughts and wishes of the Emperor of the French."

Eighteen fifty-six brought another cause of joy and satisfaction; in March the Prince Imperial was born. The dynasty was established, though its continuity depended on this one young life. Eugénie could have no more children.

The Peace Conference was short, lasting only a month. Alexander was conciliatory and less ambitious than his predecessor. The Treaty guaranteed the integrity of the Ottoman Empire, neutralized the Black Sea by forbidding the riverine states to possess ports or warships on it, established the freedom of navigation on the Danube and held out hope of independence for the Romanian principalities formerly under Russian protection—a promise fulfilled in 1861.

In return for protection from Russian ambition, the Ottoman Empire was required to show sympathy toward desire for independence in her Balkan domains but there was a general opinion that too much reliance could not be placed on Turkish promises.

In one respect the Peace Conference disappointed Napoleon III. At the tail end of the Crimean War, Camillo Cavour, Prime Minister of Sardinia, had sent 10,000 Piedmontese troops to the support of the Allies. He hoped thus to win their sympathy for the liberation of Italy from Austrian domination; Napoleon III was willing to use the conference as a means to obtain a general revision of the European frontiers, but no one supported him, and he was frustrated.

Austria had remained neutral in the Crimean War and had thus lost prestige and possible friends. The young Emperor, Franz Josef, had come to the throne in 1848 and in the same year had dismissed Metternich who, for forty years, had guided his country's destiny and been the arbiter of Europe. Without him and his counsel Austrian foreign policy was all at sea, and Austria was drifting into a position where she was isolated, with no real friend, and faced with trouble from her Italian possessions.

In 1856 the old, fatal pattern began to show through; the vanquished foe not really such a bad fellow; the ally not quite the friend he seemed. Even before the Peace Conference was ended a coolness had developed between France and England. Neither had made any territorial gain; England had guarded the North West frontier of India; France, by undertaking to protect Christian communities in the Near East had extended her influence there, winning by policy what Napoleon I had failed to win by the sword. But England's foreign policy had for hundreds of years been dominated by the simple rule that nobody should be allowed to obtain *too* much power in Europe.

Napoleon III, riding on the crest of the wave, had no need to take to heart this slight lessening of friendship between him and his ally. His first war, though costly, had been successful, and he could turn his attention to other things. To an Emperor, foreign policy mattered, but, as in Queen Victoria, the wife and mother stood behind the royal façade, so behind Napoleon III, now Metternich's successor in Europe, stood the modern man. His interest in up-to-date developments was such that, scorning silver and gold, he ordered a dinner service made of the new material, aluminum.

Between them he and Haussmann changed the face of Paris and laid it out as it is today; twelve great avenues radiating, starlike, from the Arc de Triomphe, their names commemorating great victories of famous soldiers of the First Empire. Streets were lighted and 75,000 trees were planted, many of them chestnuts, most beautiful in spring.

How many people noticed that in this clearing away of old Paris, the day of the barricade, a heap of paving stones with two angry armed men behind it, was over? Along these broad new avenues a troop of cavalry could charge; or rifles at one end could threaten the whole length.

Why should anyone think in this fashion? Empire and Emperor were popular. People saw old, unsanitary dwellings demolished and something new and beautiful taking their place.

The Second Empire had not ushered in the millennium, but it had brought about an economic expansion which had made employers, through sheer self-interest, adopt a more liberal attitude toward workers if only to secure their co-operation. Wages were still low but work was plentiful; housing was deplorable, but the Emperor, who had once written a pamphlet on pauperism, was trying to improve the conditions under which the poor lived and to develop charitable institutions for their benefit. The events of 1848 had shown that revolt was not the infallible cure for proletarian woes; there was a feeling that parliamentary action was more effective; and already, overcoming all obstacles, five left-wing deputies sat in the chamber. The persevering efforts of the middle class to attain political power through liberalism encouraged the workers to hope that they might reach the same goal through socialism and thus improve their material conditions.

In 1858 an Italian named Orsini made an attempt to assassinate the Emperor; his bomb exploded when Napoleon and Eugénie were on their way to the Opera, just as Napoleon I and Josephine had been when they had their narrow escape. Again Emperor and Empress escaped, though there were many casualties and Eugénie's white dress was spattered with blood. With royal calm they proceeded to the Opera and were greeted with temendous cheering.

At his trial Orsini gave as reason for his action that Napoleon was not doing enough to help Italy to freedom. Since nobody else was doing anything at all, and Napoleon had shown sympathy with Italian liberation since his youthful days with the Carbonari, this seems somewhat illogical. Orsini and one of his accomplices were executed, the other two received severe sentences. The immediate effect of the plot was the passing of a law of general security which seemed to bang the door against more liberal attitudes. And, whether as a result of the plot or not, the Emperor's interest in Italian affairs quickened.

In July 1858 he went to drink the waters at Plombières and there he received a visit from Count Cavour, the Sardinian Prime Minister, an ardent Italian patriot. There were already links between the two men; Cavour was a godson of Napoleon's aunt Pauline and, whether the Emperor knew it or not, his most dazzling mistress, the Countess of Castiglione, had been chosen for him by Cavour and sent to Paris with the object of winning him over to the Italian cause.

In this secret interview the two men sized each other up. Cavour shrewdly laid emphasis on the magic name of Italy and the glory which the Italian campaigns had brought to the first Emperor. The spirit of Napoleon I brooded over this meeting, for it was impossible for Napoleon III to forget his uncle's dictum: "The first sovereign to embrace wholeheartedly the cause of peoples, will find himself master of Europe and can do as he pleases."

And here, offering itself as a cause of peoples to be embraced, was the question of Italian liberation. One sovereign was needed to support Italy in this latest attempt to cast off the Austrian yoke.

The prospect of being that sovereign was very appealing to Napoleon III. He was a Bonaparte and the Bonapartes were Corsican; Corsica had been, until just before the birth of the first Napoleon, an Italian island; there was the call of the blood, the memory of youth when he and his dead brother had been ardent members of the Italian resistance; and there was present expediency. The loss of her Italian provinces would be a blow to Austria still, despite her non-participation in the Crimean War, the giant power in Europe. To deliver that blow would be an immense boost to French prestige.

But to move in Italy meant a break with two principles which had hitherto governed his policies, the alliance with England and good relationship with French Catholics.

The Catholic question was particularly thorny. Few Frenchmen would object to a military operation that would free northern Italy but, when this aim was achieved, could Cavour and Victor Emmanuel be restrained from casting greedy eyes on the Papal States? Napoleon III knew that any encroachment on the Pope's temporal power would enrage the French Catholics. It would also enrage Eugénie, who was particularly attached to the Pope.

In this cleft stick Napoleon III wriggled uncomfortably. He was anxious not to give the impression that he—an Emperor—was supporting revolution against an Empire; he was equally anxious lest some other power should step in, help the Italians and reap the moral and material benefits. He had also to consider the condition of his army—not yet fully recovered from the horror of the Crimea. He had to visualize the effect of another war upon domestic opinion, upon the English and upon the Russians to whom, since the friendship with England had begun to cool, he had been making advances.

In the end his character and temperament shaped his decision. War, he had said had too much chance about it; but with other things he had always taken chances and always been, in the long run, lucky. He decided to chance his luck again.

The agreement reached at Plombières was that France should help Piedmont to annex Lombardy and Venetia and, as reward, should have Nice and Savoy. Cavour went back to make his military preparations and rack his brain for some good reason for war with Austria which would involve the French Emperor in whose good faith he lacked complete confidence. He provoked uprisings and made peaceful settlement of them almost impossible, though both Russia and England intervened. In April 1859 the young and inexperienced Franz Josef fell into the trap laid for him and declared war.

Cavour called upon Napoleon III to fulfill his undertakings and in Paris the Emperor issued a declaration, accusing Austria of violating her treaties and threatening the French frontiers, and promising that the French, aiding the oppressed Italians, would not move against the Papal States nor in any way undermine the power of the Pope.

Again no proper preparation for war had been made, and when the Emperor, this time in supreme command, joined his army he was horrified by its lack of equipment. Fortunately for the French the Austrians were ineptly led and the battle of Magenta was a victory for the French. Magenta had its effect upon the fashions of the day, giving its name to a color midway between beetroot and overripe plum.

Sixty-three years and one month after Napoleon I had ridden in triumph on his white horse through the streets of Milan, his nephew rode, side by side with Victor Emmanuel, through the same streets and the same wildly cheering crowds.

Three weeks after Magenta came another French victory, that of Solferino, a battle whose name deserves to be better remembered than it is, since on its field was born the idea that grew into the Red Cross Society. It was a particularly bloody battle; the Emperor looked upon the dead and the dying—10,000 of them Frenchmen—and was nauseated; but a young Swiss, Henri Dunant, on a tour, stopped his carriage and did what he could for a few wounded. He devoted the rest of his life to founding the Society which is today international and active in civil affairs as well as in war.

Napoleon's aversion to bloodshed undoubtedly played its part in his decision to propose an armistice, but there were other considerations too. At home the Empress, acting as Regent for the first time, was giving proof of her inexperience, and the ministers, alarmed by the general animosity in Europe toward France, were anxious for peace to come quickly. Prussia was mobilizing and adopting a threatening attitude; England was so alarmed by the Italian venture, which she took to indicate the Emperor's intention to make himself master of Europe, that she began to form a Volunteer Corps. And Napoleon III had been right in doubting his ability to control Cavour, who was already forgetting his promises and aiming beyond Italian liberation to Italian unity.

Since unification would involve the Papal States the French Catholics were shrieking that they had been betrayed and the commercial classes were afraid of the effect continued war would have on their prosperity. On the other hand the Emperor had pledged himself to liberate Italy as far as the Adriatic. However, he realized that he must ignore his inclinations and if necessary his promises and think of France.

He and Franz Josef met at Villafranca—a meeting reminiscent of that of Napoleon I and the Czar at Tilsit—and came to terms. Austria gave Lombardy to Piedmont, but retained Venetia, a compromise which did not please the Piedmontese. Even Napoleon felt that he had failed his ally and renounced the provinces of Nice and Savoy which had been his agreed reward; but, despite this gesture, when next he rode through Milan, on his way back to France, there was a stony silence, and in the streets portraits of Orsini were ostentatiously displayed. Yet the Italians must have been aware that Napoleon's intervention had been decisive and that nothing now could halt the coming of Italian unity. Shortly afterward Nice and Savoy were ceded by treaty to France and, in curiously traditional style for so modern-minded a man, the Emperor sealed the friendship between Piedmont and France by arranging an incongruous marriage between his libertine cousin Plon-Plon and the prim, very pious Princess Clothilde. (Eugénie tried to be kind to the stiff, shy, homesick girl and was rebuffed by the remark, "Madame, you seem to forget that I was born in a Court.")

For Napoleon III the dreams of the prison years and the exile's aspirations now seemed to be fulfilled. The Bonaparte dynasty was re-established, France again stood on a pinnacle—feared if not loved; he had helped to promote a cause dear to him, Italian liberty, and he had himself reached an eminence which few would have foretold for him when he took office as President in 1848. Abroad his stock stood high; at home the opposition was weak and confused and easily contained.

Prudence would have suggested that he should now proceed to consolidate his country's gains and allow it to pursue its peaceful economic expansion; but his career to date had proved that prudence was not one of his predominating qualities.

What, indeed, were these?

He was a man of paradox; an autocrat whose sympathies were essentially liberal; a man who loved power but lacked the ruthlessness needed to exercise it; a man who often seemed timid and vacillating yet who could plunge into enterprises that demanded energy and recklessness; a lecher who was a fond and indulgent husband and father; a promiser of peace, a promoter of war.

And aged fifty-two, a man already growing old. His health had never been robust and now, impaired by anxiety and sexual excess, it rapidly deteriorated.

Even so he could still astonish France and Europe and the world. In 1860 he almost completely reversed the policy which had been so successful by injecting into his virtual dictatorship a strong dose of liberalism that made considerable modifications to the constitution of 1852. At the same time he attempted to vitalize the French economy by concluding with England a commercial treaty which incorporated his own very liberal ideas of free trade. Here again he was well ahead of his time and came into conflict, as such men do, with vested interests.

France had for so long sat secure behind a high tariff wall that she found difficulty in meeting competition from the British, whose industry had been geared for much longer to full production by modern methods. In this field French adjustment had been slow, held back by the resistance of workers and peasants. The Emperor's hope that the treaty would lead to a lowering of internal prices came to nothing, and its main result was to ruin the good understanding which had hitherto existed between him and the rich middle classes with whom the treaty was immensely unpopular. The

Italian war too had been unpopular with them and their attitude had helped to bring about its inconclusive end. They could now point out that the Pope had lost territory when the Romagna had elected to join the new kingdom—which the Emperor had helped to establish.

In the face of this growing hostility, suspicion and discontent, out of which the old, tough growth of republican feeling drew nurture, the Emperor made reforms of a revolutionary nature which led the régime even further from authoritarianism toward parliamentary rule. The old right of address to the throne was restored; government commissioners were ordered to be present at debates to furnish whatever information or explanation was demanded by the deputies; ministers without portfolio were to have the right of entry to the Assembly in order to defend their proposals. The most sweeping change of all was the granting of the right of publication of the debates in both houses; this gave the Senate equal status with the Legislature and brought both bodies into close contact with the electorate and with public opinion.

Even more significant perhaps was the tacit recognition of the workers' right to strike, which opened the way to a new alignment of political forces in France in the future. With that, perhaps, the Emperor felt that he had gone too far but, having set reform in motion, he found it difficult to apply the brake.

The one defense against too great and too sudden change lay in the system of official candidates for election, a system which still worked, with greater energy and even less pretence at impartiality than before. But, in 1863, twenty-five opposition candidates were returned as deputies and though this was not a large proportion of the Legislature they represented a substantial increase in the opposition vote. It appeared that the liberal concessions had inspired instead of quietening discontent, and that the Emperor must withdraw or increase them.

Characteristically he hesitated, slightly modified his ministry and replaced the ministers without portfolio by a minister of state. The man he chose was Eugène Rouher who had been introduced to politics by de Morny and who, as Minister of Commerce, had shown great talent for organization and done excellent work for the development of the railways: but, like Guizot, he became too closely identified with his master and allowed his genuine ability to be minimized by blind devotion. His docile acceptance of Napoleon's policy earned him the nickname of Vice-Emperor.

The peasantry and the lower middle classes were now enjoying what Renan called "the greatest possible liberty without giving rise to excesses," but the wealthier section of the community distrusted the Emperor's growing liberalism. The commercial treaty was disliked by a nation nurtured on theories of protection, the concessions made to the workers roused suspicion, and the moderates in the Chamber were not mollified by being given increased power to control the budget. At the same time the opposition regarded the concessions as a sign of weakness, and a resurgent Thiers spoke out strongly in favor of yet greater liberty.

As for the Catholics, no domestic legislature could mollify them. They, to whom Napoleon III owed a great deal, possibly even his election as President, now looked upon him as a double dealer who, in 1849, had sent an expedition to protect the Papal States and ten years later allied himself with the Pope's enemies. Leopold of the Belgians remarked that Napoleon III seemed to be putting the ax to the root of the whole Catholic Church without the slightest provocation. The Emperor did not need Leopold or anyone else to tell him how the Catholics felt; he had a critic nearer home.

Eugénie had made a cult of the Pope, just as she had made a cult of the Austrian Empire and of the memory of Marie Antoinette. She was not pious in the same way as Princess Clothilde. It is possible that in her quarrel with Napoleon over the Papal States she was seeking an unconscious revenge for his flagrant infidelities to herself. There was no open rupture; Napoleon had married for love and in his ambivalent way seemed to love her to the end; he would never admit that their marriage was a failure; and from her point of view the position of Empress was not a thing to be lightly relinquished. Eugénie took a long holiday. In Scotland she brooded over Holyroodhouse, the home of Mary Stuart—queens who had come to sad ends had a fascination for her. In England she hunted recklessly. She also visited Queen Victoria who found her as charming as ever, but thought it surprising that the Empress should never once mention the Emperor.

Eugénie came home and the breach was healed. The quarrel between the Emperor and the Catholics was not so easily mended; further alarm had been created by the strong anti-clerical tone of the Republican press, and by the educational reform of Victor Duruy which tended to emancipate education from Catholic control and thus defeat the aims of the Loi Falloux. Increasingly the Church began to dissociate itself from the régime.

Nevertheless, if only peace could have been maintained, these dissensions should not necessarily have been totally disruptive, for most people in France were as happy and prosperous as they had ever been; and the several small foreign affrays had not affected them much. Missionaries and traders had been ill-treated in Syria and a punitive force had been dispatched to the tune of *"Partant pour la Syrie,"* more apt this time than when the departure had been to the Crimea; protection for other missions in Indochina opened the way to the conquest of Cochin China and French penetration to Tonkin. A joint Anglo-French occupation of Peking resulted in the opening of several Chinese ports to European trade.

The foundation of a vast colonial domain was being laid, but it all meant little to the peasant in the Lot, wresting a living from unproductive limestone, or to the industrial worker in the expanding area of the Pas de Calais. Even the completion of the conquest of Algeria did not immediately affect Jacques Bonhomme at his plow, his loom or his coal face, though he might be mildly gratified by his country's gains. To the Emperor and Empress, however, the acquisition of territory more than twice the size of metropolitan France was an intoxicating achievement and, when the chance came to take a hand in affairs in another part of the world, one where French influence had been non-existent for years, they welcomed it.

Pablo Juarez, fighting his way to the presidency of Mexico, had been obliged to borrow heavily from the United States, France, England and Spain. In 1861, safely elected and aware of his country's inability to meet its obligations, he announced that no debt could be repaid for two years. France, England and Spain organized a communal debt-collecting force and landed troops at Vera Cruz. The United States, fully engaged with its own Civil War, took no part in this attempt to extract blood from stone.

Napoleon, chain-smoking in Paris, brooded over every aspect of this pregnant situation. His half brother, de Morny, was heavily involved with one of the Swiss bankers who had lent money for investment in Mexico; Eugénie was Spanish and Catholic; Juarez had risen to power by trampling Spain and the Church and she was eager for intervention in Mexico. The United States was preoccupied by civil strife, and this might be an opportunity to defy the limitations of the Monroe Doctrine. To stand up for the Catholic Church in Mexico might regain the approval of Catholics at home . . .

Whatever else he lacked, Napoleon III had never lacked vision or the courage to take whatever steps were needed to make the thing visualized and desirable become actuality. He now saw Mexico as a vassal Empire, owing everything to France; he saw the ancient house of Hapsburg gratified by an extension of its domain, and the loss of the Italian provinces forgotten. He saw the brother of Franz Josef, the Archduke Maximilian, sitting on the throne of Montezuma.

Maximilian, handsome, well-meaning, happily married to Carlotta, daughter of Leopold of the Belgians, was living a private life, untroubled by ambitions, at Miramar. He had no great wish to uproot himself, to go to Mexico, or to be an Emperor; but Carlotta was ambitious, Napoleon III and some Mexican envoys very persuasive, and Maximilian went out to his doom.

French troops, battling against heat, fever and mosquitoes, and subject to a confused command, pushed on to Mexico City and proclaimed the new Emperor. Napoleon had promised that the French would remain in Mexico until Maximilian was firmly established. When he made this promise there was peace in Europe but, before Maximilian reached his Empire, a short sharp war had broken out between Denmark who held the duchies of Schleswig-Holstein, and the Prussians and Austrians who claimed them. While France and England were talking of intervention and the Princess of Wales, the King of Denmark's daughter, was saying plaintively, "But the duchies belong to Papa!" the Prussians acted and Denmark was defeated. Napoleon seemed less aware of the growing power of Prussia than alarmed by the military resurgence of Austria.

His health continued to worsen; he tired easily and was often in considerable pain. In 1865 de Morny died, and his death shocked Napoleon more than the assassination of Lincoln—he probably recognized violent death as a ruler's occupational risk. De Morny had seen the weaknesses of the imperial structure and urged reforms; his death left the aging, ailing Emperor more and more dependent upon the Empress who, though lacking political intelligence, was full of energy and zeal and violently opinionated. She was deaf to such warnings as that implicit in an article in *The Times* in April 1865:

"France is kept in equilibrium under the Empire, but it is an unstable equilibrium, maintained by a single force which keeps all others in check by acting in opposition to them. If the single force be impaired in efficiency, or if it be withdrawn, there remains nothing which can prevent the machine from being brought to destruction."

In Mexico things went badly. Maximilian had never been wholeheartedly welcomed there and he had not the capacity for ruling which might have impressed even those originally hostile. The Catholic bishops were against him; Bazaine, the French commander, engaged in intrigues that were damaging rather than helpful, and the liberal Mexicans under Juarez continued to fight. Then, with the Civil War over, the Americans, faithful to the Monroe Doctrine, sent in troops and demanded the withdrawal of French forces.

Hapsburg pride and honor demanded that Maximilian should remain where he was, but Carlotta came back to Europe to rush from one court to another, imploring help for her husband. No help was forthcoming, and after a final two-hour interview with Napoleon and Eugénie, she showed signs of the insanity which was to last until she died forgotten in 1927. The Mexican venture had always been dear to Eugénie and now, impotent in the practical field, she spent long hours on her knees, praying that Maximilian should be safe. But at Queretaro, in 1867, with dignity and calm, Maximilian faced a firing squad of Juarez' men, and paid with his life for ambitions not his own.

The failure of a venture which had been costly in men and

money was a severe blow to the Emperor and to his régime just at the moment when France needed unity and strength to face the emergence of Prussia as a formidable power in Europe.

Prussian intentions had been made clear to Napoleon in 1865 when, during a holiday in Biarritz, he was visited by Count von Bismarck, the big bald East German Junker who was minister to Frederick William, King of Prussia. The trend and the significance of that interview is revealed in Bismarck's own observation: "It would have been a good thing if the Emperor and Prussia could have got together—between us we could have swallowed Europe, while now one or the other of us will be devoured. What has he got out of his campaigns in the Crimea, in Italy and in Mexico? Nothing. Perhaps they have weakened him. The Emperor is deaf to all my offers. Nothing can be done with him."

Whoever was to be swallowed up, Bismarck, ruthless, realistic and opportunist, was determined that it should not be Prussia, for which he had other plans. In the war against Denmark, fighting alongside Austria, he had accurately assessed his ally's military strength; he also knew that when he made his next move he need not fear a violent reaction from France. He easily found cause for a quarrel with Austria over the administration of the duchies and, in the summer of 1866, declared war. Again it was short and sharp, lasting only seven weeks; Austria was defeated at Sadowa and lost the Danish duchies and several Rhineland states. More important and more significant was her loss of domination of the German-speaking peoples, which passed into Prussian hands with the formation of the North German Confederation.

The Treaty of Prague, which ended this brief war, gave Venetia to Italy and thus fulfilled one of Napoleon III's long-cherished dreams. The Confederation of German states was in line with his belief in national unification, but he would have been very blind not to see the threat to Europe in this shift of power from an old ramshackle, mainly peaceable Austria to Prussia, armed to the teeth and eager for war.

Had he been the man he was even five years earlier, he would not have let slip the opportunity offered to him at the Biarritz interview; nor would he have failed to turn, somehow, this new alignment of power to his country's advantage; but he was now

too sick a man to deal energetically with a situation which demanded, above all else, a vital reorganization of the French armed
forces. The army needed to be modernized, but the French people,
desiring a strong fighting force, did not wish to meet the necessary cost. With a perversity in which there seemed to be something of doom, France turned away from the dark threat looming
on her eastern frontier to nibble at, and bicker about, her domestic problems.

The Church and the Catholics had been alienated by the Emperor's Italian campaign and not, as he hoped, reconciled by the
Mexican venture. The working classes, whom he had done his
best to befriend and who owed to him the greater industrial
freedom and the toleration of the trade unions which they now
enjoyed, had been alienated by the efforts of the Republicans who,
at a time when they should have been alive to the importance of
sinking ideological differences, carefully fomented the innate sus-
picions of the proletariat. With an armed gang on the doorstep,
the French turned their attention to arrangements inside the house.

Little noted at the time but pregnant with significance for the
future was the presence of three French delegates at an international workingmen's association in London, an association there-
after to be known as the First International. The meeting was
addressed by Karl Marx, the German socialist and philosopher
who gave *Das Kapital* to the world. Like all messiahs he had his
forerunners; one of them, Pierre Joseph Proudhon, had issued the
startling statement that he who owned property was a thief.

The First International was something new and so in France
was the formation of a third party, led by Emile Ollivier, who had
once committed the perjury necessary to take the seat to which he
had been elected. He was a Republican, but he now gave his approval to a hereditary Empire and, if his *volte-face* was due to
vanity and calculation rather than conviction, it did offer leadership to a middle group, loyal to the Emperor but bent upon constitutional reform. This Ollivier continued to demand, though it
brought him into conflict with Rouher, still faithfully devoted to
the ideas and methods of the authoritarian Empire.

That was a thing which had gone forever. So long as Napoleon
could offer the nation success, either military or diplomatic, it was

prepared to give him a free hand. Lately his luck seemed to have deserted him; even his offer to act as mediator between North and South in the American Civil War had been rebuffed, and now his foreign policy faltered. As it did so opposition to him strengthened.

Yet superficially Paris was as gay, as prosperous and as frivolous as ever. The Great Exhibition of 1867 was an unprecedented success, attended by royalty from all over the world, even from Japan, as brilliant a company as had gathered about Napoleon I at Erfurt. The Emperor had invited each monarch to bring a battalion of his own army; nobody accepted this invitation, and the troops which paraded were all French; 30,000 picked men in colorful uniforms. Watching them as they went by was the huge, white clad, eagle-helmeted man who was himself one of the show pieces of the Exhibition, Count von Bismarck. There were cheers for him from the crowd. The Empress was pleased when he took her son on his knee.

In the elegant quarters of Paris the tunes from Offenbach's latest success, *The Grand Duchess of Gerolstein*, were on everyone's lips, and visitors to the city greatly admired Haussmann's new streets; but in poorer parts there was less gaiety. The apparently healthy economy had received a jolt when the Crédit Mobilier, which had done so much to finance industry and enterprise, went into liquidation and brought a rise in prices and in unemployment. There were unrelated misfortunes; the Civil War in America had caused a crisis in the cotton trade; the silk industry upon which Lyons so largely depended had been injured by a disease which killed silkworms; and in the vineyards the scourge known as phylloxera had made its first appearance. In succeeding years it was virtually to wipe out the French vineyards and compel owners to buy new stock from America and South Africa.

In addition, there were strikes in the coal-mining regions in the Massif Central and in the North; the government replied to them by repressing workers' organizations and dissolving the French branch of the Workers' International.

Darkening skies at home were matched by those outside. Once Napoleon had recovered from his surprise at Austria's defeat by Prussia, he tried to claim the "compensations" vaguely promised

by Bismarck at Biarritz; all his claims were rejected, and his proposal to form a customs union with Belgium, and to purchase
Luxembourg met with the same fate. Bismarck had taken the
place of Napoleon III as the strong man in Europe.

At such a moment it would have seemed wise for the Emperor
to maintain control of the press, but he chose to relax it, thus
inviting attacks—many of them irresponsible—upon the régime.
Again liberalism was interpreted as weakness, of which full advantage was taken by a passionate young lawyer, Léon Gambetta,
who become prominent overnight by his defense of a journalist
who had overstepped even the relaxed boundaries.

Even in this troubled atmosphere there were gleams of comfort; 1869 was the centenary of the birth of Napoleon I, and a
Bonaparte was still on the throne of France. The same year
saw the opening of the Suez Canal, planned, built and largely
financed by the French. The Emperor did not go to Egypt, but
Eugénie set off, with two hundred and fifty dresses in her trunks,
to perform the opening ceremony and to grace the attendant
festivities. There was one hitch. The Khedive of Egypt had
commissioned Verdi to write a great, spectacular opera, *Aida*, in
which live elephants and camels would appear. It was not ready in
time and, when it was first performed in 1871, there had been
great changes in Europe.

There was tension already. "Everyone is afraid," wrote Prosper
Mérimée, "without knowing why." In proper literary style he
likened the feeling of unease in France to that in Mozart's *Don
Giovanni* just before the entrance of the spectral Commendatore.
When the results of the elections of 1869 began to come in, some
people at least knew why they were afraid.

This election, fought without the force that had hitherto been
behind the approved candidates, was a campaign of great violence
and although the government scored a nominal victory the opposition made substantial gains which brought new faces and the
prospect of new policies to the Chamber. The thin ranks of old
stalwarts like Thiers who had gone on demanding more parliamentary liberty, were reinforced. Gambetta, bitterly hostile to the
Emperor, was elected for Belleville, one of the working-class
districts of Paris, and was ready to champion a program of radical

democracy. Votes in favor of the Emperor had dwindled to four and a half million; the opposition amounted to three million. Rouher resigned and was succeeded by Emile Ollivier, who was largely responsible for the reforms of 1869 and 1870.

History should have taught France that, with her vulnerable frontiers, her internal policies must, to a large extent, be dictated by what was happening outside. This was a lesson she refused to learn and, just when it was most vital that all her forces and energies should be united to face the enemy without, her politicians concentrated their attention on constitutional change. In this respect Ollivier showed as little percipience as his predecessors.

In May 1870 the new constitution was ratified; it incorporated reforms against which even the most rabid Republican could not vote. The country was moving toward parliamentary democracy; the Republicans wanted it without the Emperor at its head, the Imperialists were willing to accept it provided the Emperor remained, even with limited powers. The difference between them could have been bridged; but France was restless. The First Empire had lasted for eleven years; the Restoration monarchies for fifteen; the July Monarchy for eighteen; now the Second Empire was eighteen years old and *"La France s'ennuie."* The single force which *The Times* had said held the whole machine together was now a failing force, one man, aging, sick, bereft of such advisers as de Morny and Walewski and, perhaps worst of all at this juncture, dependent upon military chiefs inferior to those of the plainly seen but not yet openly declared enemy.

Rather more than two thousand years earlier a Greek slave named Aesop had told some simple stories with a moral content. One of his fables concerned a wolf and a lamb and proved that anyone determined to pick a quarrel can do so. Bismarck was out to pick a quarrel; the blood of martyrs is the seed of the church; the blood of soldiers is the seed of empire, and Bismarck had dreams of empire; he also had soldiers.

Once again in this sad, repetitive history, Spain was the sparking point. Despite all Louis Philippe's machinations the throne of Spain was again vacant and the Germans put forward as a candidate a cousin of their King, Prince Leopold von Hohenzollern.

Europe still believed that family *mattered*. A Danish princess' English marriage had brought no support from England for Denmark in 1864; Maximilian's relationship to the Emperor of Austria had not saved him from the firing squad in Mexico in 1867, but some residual belief in the virtue or the danger of family reinforcements remained. To France a Hohenzollern on the throne of Spain meant her encirclement by Prussian-dominated territory. England and Russia, far less geographically concerned, were hardly less anxious. They added their protests to that of France, and Leopold's candidature was withdrawn; but that was not the end of the affair.

Had the outcome not been tragic, the next development could be regarded as absurd. It is all ancient history now but it is positive proof of how matters of life and death for ordinary men can be decided by a manipulation of words.

The King of Prussia was staying at Bad Ems, a pleasant watering place; there Count Benedetti, Napoleon's ambassador, accosted him and asked for assurance that Prussia would never again support a Hohenzollern candidate to the Spanish throne. The King said that he was unable, by himself, to make any such promise and then, acting under advice, announced that he would hold any further communication with the French ambassador through an adjutant. An account of the interview and the King's decision was sent in a long telegram to Bismarck, who released to the press a subtly doctored version which made it appear that King and ambassador had exchanged insults. Moltke, Bismarck's colleague and equally eager for war, saw both versions of the telegram and remarked with satisfaction upon the second, "Ah, it sounds different now." Publication in Berlin and Paris produced exactly the effect that the Prussian minister had calculated.

In France the Empress, the majority of the Legislature, Ollivier and the people were all clamorous for war. Some were ignorant of, some ignored the fact that the French army had not profited by the breathing space allowed it to correct the weaknesses so glaringly exposed in the Crimea. Thiers' protesting voice was lost in cries of *"A Berlin! A Berlin!"* In Berlin people cried, *"Nach Paris! Nach Paris!"*

Paris bubbled with excitement and enthusiasm. At the Opera,

where Auber's *La Muette de Portici* was being performed, the leading soprano, wearing a mantle embroidered with the Imperial bees, came down to the footlights with the *tricolore* in her hand and began to sing the "Marseillaise," the battle song of the Revolution, banned these many years. Everybody sang, and when the singing ceased they shouted *"Vive la France! Vive l'Empereur!"* Possibly they were confusing the Emperor of the legend with the aging man at the Tuileries, suffering agonies from stone in the bladder.

The French embarked upon the war confidently. What did it matter that despite feverish diplomatic activity France had found no ally? What if England stood aloof and Italy remained ungratefully absorbed in the business of her own unification? Napoleon I had scored glorious victories against the Prussians; Napoleon III would do the same.

Napoleon was prepared for a long-drawn-out, difficult war, but Bismarck knew the advantages of a blitzkrieg; both his wars had been short and sharp, and Prussia was stronger now than when she fought against Denmark or against Austria.

Eugénie imagined that the war would re-establish the glory and prestige of France and restore to the Emperor the popularity and power which recent events had nibbled away. In true Roman matron style she saw her menfolk off to the front; the man of sixty-two, whose failing health was obvious to everyone but her, the boy of fourteen who only yesterday had abandoned his Little Lord Fauntleroy clothes and coiffure for the uniform of a sub-lieutenant and a military haircut.

Fighting began in early August, in northern Alsace. The French fought with their usual courage, but they were hampered by bad organization; hastily mobilized troops from distant places arrived exhausted and were unable to find their units; there were men without tents or blankets or cooking equipment, horses without harness. Against a ruthlessly efficient war machine, long and carefully prepared, courage was not enough. Marshal MacMahon, hero of Sebastopol, was forced to fall back. Bazaine, who had been a thorn in the flesh to Maximilian in Mexico, was trapped in Metz to face a long siege unless relieved. On September 2,

MacMahon made a heroic attempt to relieve Metz and was surrounded and forced to fight the battle of Sedan.

In theory that should have been the end of Bismarck's blitzkrieg,
for Sedan brought the surrender of 80,000 men, and of the Emperor.

He, too, had displayed enormous courage. He was in such pain
that he could no longer sit in his saddle but, lest his sickly face
should discourage his troops, he had rouged his cheeks. At Sedan,
where once again the bloodshed had nauseated him, as he wrote to
the King of Prussia, tears made tracks through the false color on
his face: "Monsieur my brother; Not having succeeded in dying
at the head of my troops, nothing remains for me but to hand
over my sword to Your Majesty."

Then, in pain and desolation of spirit, he drove out of Sedan to
meet Bismarck and Frederick William of Prussia in a nearby village. He was sent to Wilhelmshöhe—in what had once been his
uncle Jerome's kingdom of Westphalia—to remain as a prisoner
for the rest of the war. Bearing in mind his fundamental kindness
of heart one is glad to note that the circumstances of his imprisonment were not rigorous.

Defeat upon the field usually leads to the hunt for a scapegoat
at home; in this case the scapegoat was Ollivier. He, with the
Emperor, had virtually ceased to exist; an excited mob crowded
into the chamber to hear Léon Gambetta announce that a provisional government would take up the defense of the country.
Bismarck's blitzkrieg, very successful up to a point, was now to
be confronted with another obstacle. The Emperor was a prisoner,
the Empress and the Prince Imperial on the exiles' road to England;
but the people of France were prepared to fight on.

Book V

Chapter 1. THE THIRD REPUBLIC

Within three weeks of the defeat at Sedan the siege of
Paris had begun. The hated Prussians in their hated pointed helmets
had tramped again over northeastern France and established their
headquarters at Versailles.

The city was defended by seventeen forts strategically placed
outside its boundaries, manned mainly by 15,000 sailors and naval
gunners. Of trained and experienced soldiers there was a dearth—
Bazaine and his army were still trapped in Metz—but there was
an ample supply of citizen-soldiers, for the National Guard had
been joined by men from every part of France, hurrying in to the
defense of the capital. Untrained they might be, but they were
fired by patriotism and willing to fight.

The unanimity of the spirit of the men under arms did not
extend to those in high places or to politicians as a whole. Sedan
had been more than a physical defeat; it had sparked off a political
crisis of the kind that is damaging enough in time of peace, in
time of war often fatal. The Third Republic had been proclaimed,
a provisional government set up, but for people in the provinces
the new régime bore the suspect stamp, "Made in Paris." It took
little account of the country people, still largely conservative, or
of the clergy with their considerable influence, who had Legitimist leanings. Paris had chosen its new leaders; would the country
rally to them in strength sufficient to enable them to organize the
Republic and save the country?

Gambetta was the man of the hour; it was he who on September 4 announced to the Chamber that Napoleon III's dynasty had

ended, and proclaimed the Third Republic. It was he who, determined that the war must go on, persuaded his less resolute colleagues, General Trochu and Jules Favre, to share his view, and in early October left Paris by balloon for Tours, from which city he hoped to organize the provinces to resistance and eventually to bring the Army of the Loire to the relief of the capital.

Winter closed in on a Paris whose sole means of communication with the outer world was by carrier pigeon or balloon and whose food supplies were growing low. Hunger fought for the Prussians as winter weather had fought for the Russians in 1812, and again during the Crimean War. Strange things began to go into the stew pots, not merely horses, including two famous trotters which the Czar had presented to Napoleon III, but cats and dogs and rats and camels, yaks, peacocks and elephants from the zoo. Even such delicacies were for those who could afford them; rats, said to taste halfway between partridge and pork, cost fifteen sous each. For the poor there was bread made of hay and chaff and clay. The problem of finding something to eat troubled the Parisians more than the shells from the Prussian guns.

Thiers, who had been so opposed to the war and pleaded so eloquently against it, was not in Paris; he was traveling through Europe seeking from one government after another help for France. None was forthcoming. Thiers had not joined the Provisional Government; he knew it would not survive the military defeat which he saw as inevitable; he had been in the political wilderness for so long that, though he was seventy-four, he felt he could afford to wait a little longer.

Gambetta still tried to govern and organize resistance from Tours and then, for greater security, from Bordeaux: in Paris conditions worsened. An attempt by the desperate Parisians to break a way out of the beleaguered city failed, and in late January a mob of hungry, cold and angry people invaded the Hôtel de Ville, trying to organize a revolutionary government which they hoped might bring some relief. They were fired on and dispersed, but the riot showed that the external struggle of French against Prussian was evolving into an internal struggle of left against right, of revolution against officially constituted Republic.

In that same month, January 1871, in the Great Hall of Mirrors at Versailles, Bismarck's dream took shape and substance; the King of Prussia was proclaimed Emperor of Germany. Out of a loose federation of small German states led by an old and tiring Austria, a new nation had been forged, dominated now by Prussia, vigorous, aggressive, truculent and efficient. Napoleon III had always believed in the principle of nationality and done much to foster it; that his Second Empire should be destroyed by a new nation and that its death pangs should coincide with the new nation's christening was the supreme irony of his career.

Ten days later a famished and divided Paris capitulated. Jules Favre asked for an armistice which Bismarck granted, and the starving Parisians rushed out into the countryside in search of the food from which they had been cut off for four long months, proper bread, rabbits, chickens and potatoes.

Bismarck had consented to an armistice, stipulating that a peace treaty should be negotiated with a new government, representative of the French people. In the hurried elections that produced the new Assembly the voters knew that the attempt at revolution in Paris had failed, that Gambetta'a attempts to continue war to the death had failed, that only peace could rid the country of a hated enemy and that whatever the price demanded for peace it must be paid.

The Assembly elected in this mood and meeting at Bordeaux in February 1871 was as unexpected in its make-up as the *Chambre Introuvable* of 1815 and surprisingly similar. It was overwhelmingly Royalist, though divided between Legitimists and Orleanists. Republicans were in a minority and of Bonapartists there was a mere handful. Most of the deputies had never before sat in an Assembly; these newcomers were mainly of noble or wealthy bourgeois stock. There were a few familiar faces; Victor Hugo, returned to France after twenty years of exile in opposition to Napoleon III, Louis Blanc and Ledru-Rollin. One of the new men was young; his name was Georges Clemenceau; he was an ardent Republican and an atheist, a strange product of the Vendeé, always Royalist and Catholic.

This Royalist Assembly chose for its President Jules Grévy an out-and-out Republican who had been an outspoken enemy of the Empire and equally hostile to Gambetta. The choice, surprising on the face of it, was in its way true to pattern; both the Empire and Gambetta had failed, therefore the man who had opposed them appeared, by hindsight, to be wise and worthy.

Gambetta resigned his seat in the Assembly, but he continued to exert his influence and energy as vigorously in consolidating the Republic as he had done in the attempt to organize national defense. With his temporary eclipse, one man stood out from the ruck of the new and the untried—Adolphe Thiers.

Thiers enjoyed a nationwide popularity—he too had been a critic of Napoleon III's policies, especially of the war with Prussia: he was also an experienced politician, the one man, people felt, who could negotiate a peace as favorable as possible after so total a defeat. He was nominated as Chief of the Executive power and entrusted with the discussion of terms of peace with Bismarck.

He fought very hard and that he failed to do as well for France as Talleyrand had done at Vienna in 1814 was not his fault; he was facing not three divided allies but one power, represented by a man who knew exactly what he wanted and was in a position to obtain it. The Peace of Frankfurt, signed on May 10, 1871, imposed terms which to the French seemed grueling—Alsace and Lorraine, including Metz, were to be handed over to the Germans, a war indemnity of five billion francs was to be paid and a German army of occupation in the northern and eastern Departments was to be maintained at French expense.

In the "lost" provinces the adult population, though they retained their homes, suffered the spiritual misery of displaced persons, watching their children learn an alien tongue and, with the adaptability of youth, grow up to be German rather than French. In the Assembly there were touching scenes when the deputies representing Alsace and Lorraine took their leave. In the Place de la Concorde, where eight great statues represented the most important cities of France, that of Strasbourg was draped in crape and mourning wreaths. And in French hearts the spirit of *revanche* was born.

The people of Paris, by their attack on the government in January, had contributed toward the psychological defeat of France. They had been cold and hungry and anxious for a change which would bring about a betterment in their conditions and, in the circumstances, only peace could do this. Now they had peace, but with it humiliation which proved to be as intolerable as hunger. They were infuriated by Thiers' order that the cannon on the heights of Montmartre should be dismantled and the National Guard disarmed. The guns on Montmartre, they insisted, belonged to the people of Paris, and this was true, for they had been bought with money raised by public subscription. They hanged the generals sent to take away the guns and proceeded to take power into their own hands. The Paris Commune formed itself into a government, the Republican government formed itself into an armed force of repression, the wealthier, soberer or more timid citizens hastily evacuated the city, and from the suburbs the Germans watched stolidly while for ten dreadful days, May 18–28, 1871, Frenchmen fought Frenchmen. Of all the street fighting that Paris had seen this, in the bright spring sunshine, was the bloodiest and most savage.

When the government troops at last gained control and the red flag was hauled down, the public buildings over which it had fluttered were half in ruins; in the Place Vendôme, Napoleon's great column lay toppled on the cobbles and the palace of the Tuileries was a blackened shell. Twenty thousand people had been killed and half that number were to be deported to penal colonies. The Commune had achieved nothing of its aims; the Communards were as far as ever from the political power which alone would alleviate their social frustrations and economic miseries. All that was left to them was to put their hope and trust in the Workers' International and the solidarity of the proletariat.

What those May days had done was to bring about the virtual extinction of socialism in France for three generations and to lay up a hoard of bitter memories which poisoned the relationship between the classes for even longer. To this day there is an annual pilgrimage to the great wall of the cemetery of Père Lachaise in Paris, where 140 Communards were lined up and shot.

Once again France showed her amazing recuperative power; she had been humiliated, she had lost territory and revenue, she had no friend in Europe, but she set to work under Thiers, as under Richelieu in 1815, to rehabilitate herself and meet the heavy indemnity. In 1873, two years ahead of schedule, the indemnity was paid off and the last German soldier withdrew, to the discomfiture of Bismarck, who had hoped that France would be kept subject and impoverished for a long time. A grateful nation endowed Thiers, whose brilliant policy was responsible for the country's liberation, with the title of "Liberator of the Territory."

He already held the title of President of the Republic, an office to which he had been elected in August 1871. It was as yet a shadowy republic without constitution or institutions, but Thiers, a practical politician, bothered less with such things than with the re-establishment of France's position in Europe. In a great speech he rallied the nation to meet its obligations:

"To pacify, to re-organize, to raise credit, to re-animate work, this is the only policy possible and even suitable at the moment . . . when this work of repair has been carried out, then the time to discuss and weigh theories of government will have to come."

Richelieu's ability to pay off the war indemnity in 1818, ahead of time, was due in part to the sound financial basis of the First Empire. Similarly, in 1873, France, despite decennial cycles of economic crisis, still enjoyed real prosperity, inherited from the Second Empire, when major industries had established themselves firmly. The merging of small firms into large ones, such as the Comité des Forges, producing iron and steel and dominated by the family of Schneider at Le Creusot, resulted in greater strength and efficiency, helpful to the country's economy: but it had another side; it also resulted in an increasingly uneven distribution of wealth, for larger firms could afford mechanization which led to less demand for labor and a consequent lowering of wages.

Externally France's policies were dominated by her fear of Germany and by her memories of Thiers' futile search for help in 1870. She looked hopefully to Russia for an allegiance since England, deeply preoccupied with her own colonial expansion, had withdrawn from European affairs. But Germany also looked to Russia. Germany's geographical position made her vulnerable on two fronts, and to Bismarck the rapid recovery of France was alarming; by 1875 she could, by a heroic effort, have put an army

of two and a half million men into the field. So the keystone of
the "Bismarckian system," which governed European policies until 1890, was the isolation of France and alliance between Germany, Russia and Austria.

Whatever their discord on other matters, French statesmen
were at one in their determination that war should never again
catch them napping. Gambetta supported Thiers in his wish to
see obligatory military service.

"War," he wrote, "is not only a matter of courage, it is also
a matter of industrial and economic production. To foresee war
is not a desire to provoke it. Is the question not first of all that
France must live, that she must live in dignity, independence and
honor?"

Over the desirability of military readiness there was no dissension; over other matters the old wranglings went on. France
was a Republic with an Assembly made up of Royalists, some of
them Legitimist, some Orleanist. What Thiers' preference was
nobody quite knew; he had been an Orleanist all his life, but he
might be coming round to the Legitimist view.

In July 1871 there were some partial elections and, of the 117
deputies elected, 112 were Republicans, with Gambetta at their
head. This was plain indication of a change of climate. And the
great financiers and powerful industrialists were now taking the
view that a conservative Republic would serve their interests better than a monarchy. Slowly there began to emerge yet another
political group with close associations with the great finance
families like the Rothschilds and the Germains, who founded the
bank, the Crédit Lyonnais.

By November 1872, Thiers was able to say: "The Republic is
in being. It is the legal government of the country; to desire
anything else would be a new revolution and the most redoubtable of all."

Throughout his long political life Thiers had been devoted to
furthering the interests of the comfortable middle class, and the
Republic he had promised was to be a conservative republic, yet
now he was suspected of yielding too much to the radical element
and of seeking support from the left. Even his great prestige
could not withstand the combined attack made upon him by

the conservative monarchists and Bonapartists, who sank their own differences in order to bring him down. "The Liberator of the Territory" was forced to resign his office as head of state and return to the Chamber as deputy for Belfort.

The movement to displace Thiers had been headed by the Duc de Broglie who, by virtue of his name, his rank and his traditions was a monarchist, and it was an avowed monarchist, Marshal MacMahon, who was chosen to succeed Thiers as Provisional President. His role was to keep the seat of government warm for a king who, at the appropriate time, would slip into it.

MacMahon was well cast for the part: he was of Irish stock, a descendant of one of the many Irish soldiers who, after the expulsion of James II, had joined the French and fought in the Irish Brigade: he was tall and handsome and had behind him a splendid military career; he had won fame outside Sebastopol, a dukedom and a marshalate at Magenta; he had served as governor of Algeria, been wounded and captured at Sedan, and he had commanded the troops which suppressed the Commune.

MacMahon chose the Elysée as the official residence of the President of the French Republic. The Tuileries stood in ruin— and was to remain so, a visible reminder of the Commune, until the 1880s when the site was laid out as a public garden, but even had it been habitable it had too many associations with royalty to make it quite acceptable as the official home of a President. The Elysée did not lack associations of its own, it had once belonged to Madame de Pompadour; it had briefly housed, in magnificent splendor, Napoleon's sister, Caroline Murat, and her husband; Napoleon himself had used it occasionally and had there signed his second act of abdication after Waterloo.

Now, under MacMahon, the old Elysée regained some of the brilliance of the Second Empire and its salons, where people of every shade of Royalist opinion rubbed shoulders and only Republicans felt ill at ease, became the focal point of Parisian society. As the humiliations and distresses of the war receded, Paris recaptured its old luster, largely through the efforts of the President and his wife who might be said to be consciously creating a climate in which monarchy would flourish. Being head of the Republic in no way diminished MacMahon's royalism; on the

contrary he was happily confident at the outset that his tenure of
the Elysée would be short, despite the new law which gave the
President a seven-year-term, for outside France there had been
a rapprochement between the two claimants to the French throne
which seemed to promise a political union between Legitimists and
Orleanists.

The Comte de Chambord, the Legitimist claimant, had no children; it was said that his marriage to a princess likely to be sterile
had been maneuvered by Orleanist interests. The senior Bourbon
line would die with him, and his natural heir was the Comte de
Paris, the Orleanist claimant, grandson of Louis Philippe and
twenty years younger than Chambord. At Frohsdorf in Austria, the
place of Chambord's exile, the two counts met and reconciled
their differences, agreeing that the older man should have the
privilege of restoring the monarchy and that he should recognize
Paris as his heir.

A restoration now seemed more of a probability than a possibility with so large a Royalist party in France and with two
avowed monarchists, MacMahon and de Broglie at the head of
affairs, though de Broglie entertained some fears about de Chambord's stubborn nature.

Those fears were well justified. Some time earlier, when restoration was less likely, the Comte de Chambord had issued a statement that he would not accept the tricolore but would, if restored,
bring back the Bourbon flag; and now, over a piece of rag which
to him represented a principle, he threw away his chance of becoming King of France. He would have nothing to do with the
tricolore, so symbolic and so beloved of the French people. So
rigid an adherence to principle was perhaps inevitable in a man
brought up by the austere Duchesse d'Angoulême, many of
whose characteristics he shared. His most ardent supporters in
France might deplore his unswerving loyalty to the flag of his
house and its régime, but even they could not withhold admiration
for his steadfastness. "All devotion," Napoleon said, "is heroic,"
and there is something, if not heroic, romantic, about a man weigh-
ing a throne against a flag and making what seemed to be a fantastic decision. It is just possible that there was more to it; the
Comte de Chambord could hardly be ignorant of the fate of Louis

XVI, Charles X, Louis Philippe. And two Emperors had ended badly . . .

The devotion of the French aristocracy to the cause of monarchism survived for a time, but when de Broglie's ministry, so aristocratic that it was called, with irony, "the Republic of Dukes," fell, the aristocratic element went with him, deserting the political arena. The nobly born would serve in the army, they would become distinguished in the world of letters, dukes would sit in the French Academy and a de Broglie would win a Nobel Prize for physics, but in the actual government of their country the old, solid families of France would henceforth play little part.

In January 1875, the Assembly, tired at last of delays and intrigues, passed by one vote those laws which together form the constitution of the Third Republic. It was a constitution designed to be a compromise between widely differing views and was capable of working under a king as well as under a president since, in effect, it vested deputies and senators with supreme authority and absolute power; the head of state became a mere figurehead, retaining one great prerogative—the right to dissolve, with the consent of the Senate, the whole Assembly. In the whole life of the Third Republic this right was exercised only once.

There was now no parliament in the world with so much authority as the two French houses whose members were henceforth to be paid for their labors, a logical extension of the system of allowances for traveling and other expenses instituted in 1789, allowed to lapse, revived, discontinued and revived again.

The Third Republic made a tentative start, but it lasted for sixty-five years, partly because the recent bloody experience of the Commune seemed at last to have taught the French that changes as fundamental as those wrought by the Revolution of 1789 can rarely be repeated; partly because of the threat represented by Bismarck. But for the intervention of Russia and Britain, war between France and Prussia might have broken out again in 1875. Thus, threatened from without, stable government within was essential, and gradually men came to accept the Third Republic as a stable and viable form of government.

Within its framework changes were frequent; fear of the one

"strong man" continued to result in bewildering reshufflings of office, each of which gratified the endemic French restlessness but had little effect on a country which could afford the luxury of superficial change because, below the superstructure, lay the solid base of good law, as expressed in the Code Napoleon, and an efficient administrative system.

It was in the early years of the Third Republic that France acquired the national nickname of Marianne, the equivalent of the American Uncle Sam, the English John Bull. The name was derived from a secret society formed to overthrow the government of Napoleon III. In every official building and for a long time on postage stamps and coins the new Republic was represented by a female figure, wearing the Phrygian cap of liberty. Marianne might be taken as a symbol of the femininity of the French self-image, except that she represented the *father*land, called, curiously, *la patrie*, just as John Bull represented the England of whom her poet could write, "Oh Motherland, we pledge to thee. . . .

As the years passed France faced the realities of the nineteenth century—growing industrialization with its accompanying social problems, a declining birth rate, the slow but steady drift of population from country to town. The shock of the defeat of 1870 had long-lasting results, the more so because this shock had been sustained in part by men with memories of 1815. All were certain that the country's security must be assured and such bitter experiences never repeated, but there was no agreement as to how this security could best be achieved. Unity of purpose might exist but the country was still divided between clerical and anti-clerical feeling, by the conflicts between employed and employer, and by differences between convinced Republicans and those who still clung to the idea of monarchy.

MacMahon, the President, was monarchist, the Chamber predominantly Republican. Disagreement between them was inevitable, and when, in 1876, the result of the elections which he had hoped would bring a larger proportion of monarchists to the Chamber disappointed him, MacMahon dismissed first the ministry constitutionally chosen from a parliamentary majority and then the Assembly itself.

This was a test for the young constitution; the President had been given the right to dissolve the Assembly but, in exercising that right, the victor of Magenta was considered to have acted in a manner certainly high-handed and verging perilously near to a *coup d'état*. There was violent opposition and a new electoral campaign of great bitterness inflamed by anti-clerical passions, resulting in another Chamber with a Republican majority. Mac-Mahon was forced to accept a ministry chosen by the new Chamber and the political power of the presidency was thus sharply defined and seen to be limited. Henceforth the President of the Republic, with certain rare exceptions, was a representational figure, much like the constitutional monarchs of England, bound like them to accept as ministers those chosen by the parliament of the day. But the President's lost power did not pass into the hands of the Premier and his cabinet; they remained the servants of the Assembly, nor did MacMahon's act of dismissal institute a precedent: henceforth any threat of dissolution was regarded as a threat of the Republic itself. No other President dared to exercise the power of dismissal which gradually fell into desuetude.

Thus freed from presidential interference and guaranteed by the constitution a period of seven years' life, the French parliament might easily have degenerated into an oligarchy, save for the moderating influence of the Senate and the highly developed individualism of the French, which led to a multiplicity of parties; very rarely could any party claim an absolute majority. Governments were inevitably coalition governments, involving the inevitable "horse-trading" and corruption that compromise demands.

Thiers did not live to see the triumph of the Third Republic over the presidency; he died two months before MacMahon was forced to submit to the will of the people's chosen representatives; he had a magnificent public funeral which was made the occasion of large Republican demonstrations. His monarchical affiliations, his mistakes, were all buried with him, and his name remains as that of one of the great architects of the Third Republic.

There was another death, too. As all but the most stubborn monarchical hopes had foundered on a bit of colored cloth, so in

1879 Bonapartist dreams ended with a broken stirrup strap. Since the death in 1873 of Napoleon III, the Bonapartists, few in number, but important because they stood between Republican and monarchist parties, had centered their hopes on the Prince Imperial, young and charming. Eugénie shared their hopes. There is little evidence that the boy ever did; his ambition was to be a soldier and, his path smoothed by Queen Victoria, he had undergone military training in England. In 1879 he insisted, against everyone's wishes, on joining an English expedition sent out to Africa to quell Cetewayo, the Zulu chief. Meticulous precautions were taken to ensure his safety, but he and a small party were ambushed while they were dismounted. Everyone else got away but, as the Prince Imperial went to mount, his stirrup strap broke. When his body was recovered it bore eighteen assagai wounds, all in front. He had died in a manner becoming to a Bonaparte and even Eugénie derived some comfort from the thought that her son had met death in heroic fashion. In his will he had passed over the unpopular Plon-Plon as his heir and named Plon-Plon's son; no one took the bequest seriously. In France there were new dynasties, the dynasties of parliamentarians, of industrialists and of financiers.

In 1878 France gave new proof of her astonishing recuperative power. Sixteen million people came to see the great new Universal Exhibition which showed what benefits France had gained from new industrial methods and from scientific discoveries and inventions. She had lost the iron, steel and coal of Alsace and Lorraine, but she had compensated herself by development in the northern Departments and in the Paris region. For the gap between the demand for labor made by expanding industry and the falling birth rate she had compensated herself by importing foreign workers, Italians, Poles and Spaniards, who were to leave their mark on national physique and characteristics in later generations.

The ordinary tourist, impressed by the Exhibition with its emphasis on mechanical progress, would not see that modernization was still being firmly resisted by the peasant cultivators, or that the legislation for the good of the industrial worker had been timid, or that the workers were slowly recovering from their eclipse after the Commune. Communards had been amnestied and one of them, Jules Guesde, returning from exile, had translated into French Karl Marx' *Das Kapital*.

What the tourist saw was evidence of revival in social life and in the arts. There was a new school of painters, headed by Edouard Manet, whose *Déjeuner sur l'Herbe* had shocked the conformists. Renoir, Degas, Cézanne were lumped together as "Impressionists" and were mocked, but were to outlive the derision. In the world of music Georges Bizet's genius was in full swing, and a new name was being heard—César Franck, both at the moment outranked by the German Richard Wagner, but nevertheless important. And in the theatre, where the plays counted for less than the players, there was Sarah Bernhardt.

Visitors to Paris in 1878 had, like most visitors, a thoroughly enjoyable time and went away with schizophrenic nostalgia, homesick for two places, their own and Paris.

The French had contributed to this happy atmosphere by observing a political truce as long as the Exhibition was open; France had wished to exhibit not only material progress but internal harmony to the watching world. But, as soon as the doors of the Exhibition closed, leaving the twin minarets of the Palais du Trocadéro to stand as landmarks for years, political dissension broke out again, the more hotly because of the enforced truce. Under pressure MacMahon resigned from the presidency and his place was taken by Jules Grévy, seventy-one years old, a cold and austere Republican. With Grévy at the Elysée the Republicans felt that at last they had room to maneuver and that the future was secure.

"Since yesterday," Gambetta wrote on the day after the elections of 1879, "we are a republic." Nine years had passed since the fall of the Second Empire and four since the framing of the constitution of the Third Republic. Gambetta's "Since yesterday" holds something of the inner significance of the proverb, coined, after all, by the French, "The more things change, the more they remain the same."

One man watching the swift French revival was Bismarck, apprehensive of war in western Europe but, throughout the 1880s, trouble centered in the east, with Russia at war with Turkey, and England on the brink of intervention on Turkey's behalf.

In 1878, Bismarck, taking upon himself the role which in 1856 had been filled by Napoleon III, that of mediator, called a Congress to Berlin to settle the Eastern Question. As a result Russia's encroachments were checked and the "unspeakable Turk" was given a new lease of life in return for reforms in his Empire. Romania, Serbia and Montenegro gained their independence, Bulgaria was granted autonomy, and Austria was given protective power over Bosnia and Herzegovina. France was not greatly concerned with these arrangements, yet her future was affected, for in one of the Austrian protectorates was to be fired the shot that was to have a million echoes on the Somme.

More important, in the eyes of most people, was the new factor which affected international relationships, the competition for markets overseas for the surplus goods which mechanized industry produced. Colonial possessions, formerly a matter of prestige, an outlet for the spirit of adventure, or merely a dumping ground for undesirable characters, took on a new aspect and assumed a new importance. France joined in the exploitation and development of backward countries, led by Jules Ferry, who served first as Minister of Public Instruction and then as Premier. Ferry never became President, he was not sufficiently popular, but he was one of the outstanding figures of the Third Republic.

He was a gift to the caricaturists, having a nose that could be elongated into an elephant's trunk, but there was nothing else comic about him. His determination that education should become a strictly secular matter revived all the old clerical-anti-clerical strife. Ferry had a long hard struggle ahead of him. Catholic France had its partisans in the fashionable quarters of Paris, in the Vendée, in the army and among the remaining monarchists and Bonapartists who were opposed to the Republic. A Catholic journal could write bluntly, "Catholic France will beat Republican France," as though two separate entities were involved.

In the Chamber deputies came to blows, and undignified sessions had to be terminated. When Gambetta was speaking against the clergy he was silenced by another deputy who cried, "You're the first to send for the priest when you are dying. Be logical to the end. How many of you only went through a civil marriage?"

That shot went home for it was generally known that Gambetta's devoted mistress, Léonie Léon, refused to marry him unless the marriage was solemnized by a priest.

Similar scenes took place in many towns and villages where opinion was divided into two camps, a division that continues to this day. From pulpits, Ferry was denounced as being Attila, Nero, Satan and anti-Christ. Blood was shed; in Lyons, Orléans, Marseilles, Lille and Le Havre people died for this opinion or that and when, after a final battle in the Senate, Ferry succeeded in passing his laws there were hundreds of official resignations. One of Ferry's measures was to abolish the observation of Sunday as a day of rest.

One of those who resigned because of Ferry's militant anti-clericalism was the Premier, Waddington. He was succeeded by Charles de Freycinet who altogether held office four times during the eighties and nineties. Already the Third Republic was showing one of its chief characteristics—the inability of any ministry to remain in office for any length of time. In the twenty-five years between 1877 and 1902 France had twenty-eight premiers, but the effect of these constant changes was mitigated by the fact that many men went on serving under different premiers. Most of these men made little mark on their times and today are merely half-forgotten names.

On July 14, 1880, the French for the first time celebrated the anniversary of the taking of the Bastille in 1789 as a public holiday. The President of the Republic took the salute at a grand military parade and in the working-class quarters the evening was given over to fireworks displays and dancing in the streets. Monarchists ostentatiously refrained from taking part in the celebrations and, even today, there are the irreconcilables who will leave Paris rather than witness scenes that recall a two-hundred-year-old humiliation.

In November 1881, Ferry, who had been Premier for a year, resigned, mainly as the result of the violent attacks made on his foreign policy by Gambetta. President Grévy had no alternative but to call upon Gambetta to form a ministry. It was just over ten years since Gambetta, organizing the defense of France, had been a national hero, and time had done its work on him both mentally and physically. He had been a handsome man, despite the glass eye he wore as the result of an accident. Now aged forty-four he looked far older; his hair was receding, his beard going gray, and he had become careless in his dress. He had retained his fine features and a warm, vibrant voice which exercised charm, especially upon women.

The premiership should have set the seal upon a brilliant career of the man who helped to destroy the Second Empire and establish the Third Republic, who was acknowledged as the defender of his country, who had been President of the Chamber. His ministry should have been a notable one. It collapsed in less than two months. His colleagues, seemingly blind to the fact that the years had brought him closer to the moderates, suspected him of grandiose ideas and President Grévy was alarmed by his suggestion of revising the constitution.

Disappointed and unhappy, Gambetta retired to his little villa, Les Jardies, outside Paris, where, in 1882, he died as a result of a mysterious accident with a revolver. There was no question of suicide.

The plans made during his sixty-six days of office bore evidence of wisdom and foresight; his fall, his death before he could make a political comeback, were a loss to France; but they served his reputation well. His memory as a patriot, as an organizer of resistance in the dark days, even as an intrepid balloonist, remains unclouded. In many squares in provincial towns his statue stands, streets bear his name, and he has his great monument in Paris between the Louvre and the gardens of the Tuileries.

Three other governments followed in rapid succession; in 1883 Jules Ferry was again in office in a country whose internal condition had deteriorated. Bad harvests had compelled her to import wheat, of which generally she had a surplus to export. One of the leading banks, the Union Générale, failed, bringing ruin to thousands of small investors. The budget suffered from a decrease in the returns from indirect taxation. There was unemployment; there were strikes.

Ferry brought about a few administrative changes, making every commune in France conform to the same rules and increasing the power of every mayor; then he turned his attention abroad because he believed that France could recoup the losses in territory and in self-esteem of 1871 by conquests overseas and at the same

time improve her economic situation. Here again, as with his secu-
larization of education, he ran into opposition. There were those
like Clemenceau who believed that all French effort should be concentrated upon meeting the potential threat from Germany; and
there were others who saw colonial expansion as a manifestation of
capitalist greed, of militarism and clericalism, for the colonial road
was being opened by Catholic missions.

Bismarck approved of French activities in far places; in his
opinion they diverted attention from lost Alsace and Lorraine and
the spirit of *revanche*. He saw that any country with interests
overseas must maintain a large navy and he believed that any
country with a mounting naval power would incur the enmity of
England. Bismarck himself was European-minded, and it was not
until his influence waned that Germany really scrambled for a share
in the colonial cake.

Clemenceau continued to keep his eye upon the Rhine and the
potential enemy beyond. When Arabi Pasha, in 1881, raised a revolt
in Egypt against the dual control by England and France, which
Egypt's bankruptcy in 1879 had brought about, Clemenceau said,
"No French soldiers in Egypt." So for a time England became
paramount there. France compensated herself by taking Tunisia
under her protection, an act which strengthened her hold on North
Africa, but which also roused resentment in the Italians who regarded Tunisia—immediately across the Mediterranean from their
own shores—as their natural area of expansion. The French move
in Tunisia did a great deal to throw Italy into the arms of Germany and into the Triple Alliance of Germany, Austria and Italy
—all pleasing to Bismarck as forwarding his aim to isolate France
in Europe.

In Indochina, where the French were also active, things were
different. Ever since the seventeenth century the French had
been interested in the country and during the Second Empire had
occupied the South of it. In 1873 they took Hanoi and signed a
treaty with Annam which gave them the right to penetrate as far
as Tonkin. In the event this right had to be fought for as the
Emperor of Annam regretted and refused to honor the treaty.
Ferry sent an expeditionary force, gaining himself the nickname

of "le Tonkinois." Its initial setbacks cost him his ministry. In the end the French were successful, and by the Treaty of Tien-Tsin, in 1876, France was recognized as the protector of Indochina and given rights of economic exploitation in Yunnan.

There followed the expansion—with small outlay of men and money—in North, West, and Equatorial Africa and later the conquest of Madagascar and the neighboring small islands of Réunion and Mauritius. The acquisition of territory was less the result of a preconceived plan than of circumstance, yet, by 1914, France was second only to England as a colonial power and her colonies contributed to her economic prosperity and to her military power.

Ferry understood the value of colonies, but the work of exploration and consolidation was done by individuals, and France was fortunate to have so many energetic and gifted men, both civil and military, capable of bringing a fresh outlook to an age-old enterprise.

Already, in Senegal, under the Second Empire, Faidherbe had recognized the importance of co-operation with the native population, a policy which produced battalions of Senegalese troops of great military value.

Another gifted colonial administrator was General Galliéni who in the course of a long career held to a coherent policy. He believed in pacification and development; ideally a conquered village should have a market by noonday, a hospital in the evening, and on the following day a school. To him and the men who came after him, often trained by service under him, France owes its reputation for being the colonial power least conscious of difference of color, most inclined to take France with them wherever they went, and to hanker less for "home." Ironically, this attitude was to rebound and lead to trouble, especially in Algeria. England could free herself of India and Kenya and a dozen other places with far less fuss; her colonists were "home" orientated and came home in thousands; the French in Algeria were French, but they were Algerian too.

That the French should be such successful colonizers was the more remarkable because the average Frenchman was not even an enthusiastic traveler, had little interest in far places and was concerned with his land, or his business; he was ready to defend his country, happy to reap the benefit of colonial expansion, but ready to leave overseas development to the devoted minority. In part this attitude was due to the diverse climate of France—no Frenchman need go abroad to feel the sun—and in part to the fact that France was underpopulated.

Many of the French colonists were from Alsace and Lorraine, men unwilling to see their children brought up as Germans; to them Algeria, in particular, owes its growth and its prosperity.

During this period, too, France saw an expansion not to be measured in miles or in numbers. All around the Mediterranean French became the language of the educated classes; the French governess, like the English "nanny," became a recognized export; families with any pretension to style, even in remote Balkan fastnesses, employed both: the English nurse with her devotion to fresh air and soap-and-water, reared a healthy child who then began his education under his French governess and proceeded to French school and university, to return home with an undying nostalgia for everything French.

Ferry's political power did not survive the elections of 1885, which brought to the Chamber some two hundred solidly united conservative members, and also a new deputy, a young man of twenty-six named Jean Jaurès, a socialist who was destined to have a great influence on the political development of France. His time was not yet ripe and, on the whole, Ferry's successors brought little change, since they pursued much the same domestic policy. Yet the following years were not uneventful. Louis Pasteur made his first successful injection against rabies—an advance difficult for us, in the post-Pasteur age to estimate. Ferdinand de Lesseps, who had constructed the Suez Canal in his old age, made an attempt to construct a similar passage at Panama, and was defeated by malaria, which killed at least two thousand skilled French technicians and ten times that number of native laborers. Paris got her first dustbins and electric trams. Victor Hugo was given a funeral almost as magnificent as that of Napoleon I. And glamour, so long absent from French public life, made a brief return in the person of General Georges Boulanger.

This handsome young man became Minister of War at the moment when the anti-military mood, bred by the defeats of 1870, was declining and soldiers were becoming popular again. He carried out a few minor army reforms which benefited the rank-and-file; he professed Republican principles; he had been the representative of the French army at the centenary celebrations of the American War of Independence and had acquired something of the aura of the young Lafayette. He was chivalrous and, when called upon to put down the violent strikes among the miners, he had used great moderation. Yet his enormous popularity derived less from what he had done than from what people hoped he would do. He was known to be a bitter enemy of Germany and was openly called *"General Revanche,"* and looked upon as the man who would restore the lost provinces.

The politicians did not share the people's enthusiasm: they remembered another popular general whose name also began with B, who had also been the darling of the people. The Republicans wanted no repetition of the 18 Brumaire. Boulanger was maneuvered out of office and sent into virtual exile from Paris to command an army corps at Clermont-Ferrand in the heart of France. His departure was accompanied by extraordinary scenes. The people would hardly allow his carriage to pass to the railway station; they lay down on the tracks to prevent his train from leaving. Everywhere there were cries of *"Vive Boulanger"* and "He will come back." Some people added, "To the Elysée."

Clemenceau had actually launched Boulanger on his career, but scenes and slogans such as these were unacceptable, even alarming to the true Republican, and Clemenceau turned against the man he had helped to raise. To combat the dangerous element in this Boulanger-worship he founded the League of the Rights of Man whose purpose was "to defend the Republic against any reactionary or dictatorial enterprise."

Boulanger did not lack champions. Paul Déroulède, a fiery character, retorted by founding the League of Patriots whose aim was to foster patriotism and the spirit of *revanche*. While they squabbled about him in Paris Boulanger, in Clermont-Ferrand, was spending his time with his adored mistress, the Vicomtesse de Bonnemains, who was to have a great effect upon his future.

Then in 1887 came the Wilson scandal. Old President Grévy
was a model husband, a virtuous Republican, a man who, in the
interests of economy, copied Charles X's habit of having his shoes
resoled, but late in life took a mistress who was the sister of a
deputy named Daniel Wilson. Wilson was of English extraction,
extremely respectable in appearance, but of dubious reputation.

Grévy, however, had a daughter, unmarried at the age of thirty-
two, perilously near to becoming an old maid in a period when
spinsterhood was a thing no woman would wish upon herself, no
responsible father willingly see inflicted upon his daughter. When
Wilson presented himself as a suitor he was, despite his reputation,
gladly accepted. The position of son-in-law to the President offered
temptations quite irresistible to one of Wilson's character, and soon
there was talk about sales of orders and decorations and in the
cafés the most popular song was, "Oh, what a misfortune to have
a son-in-law."

For as long as possible the old man at the Elysée—he was now
eighty—turned a blind eye, a deaf ear, though his personal reputation was closely concerned, for if Wilson had sold the orders
who but the President could have signed the awards? By a large
majority the Chamber of Deputies voted for the setting up of a
commission of inquiry and finally the matter found its way into
the hands of the public prosecutor.

It was a field day for the politicians; the anti-Republican right
hoped that the prestige of the Republic would be irretrievably
smirched: the leftists hoped that Grévy would resign. There were
impatient men ready to move into the Elysée, Jules Ferry among
them; and Clemenceau had no love for the old man who had
consistently kept him out of office. The desire of the people was
simple and straightforward—they wanted Wilson's head.

The old President tried to divert the course of justice, but in
vain. Clemenceau was too formidable an enemy. Already he had
won for himself the nickname of "Tiger," applicable both to his
looks, the prominent cheekbones, yellowish complexion and bris-
tling eyebrows, and to the manner in which he could launch an
attack. His fierce oratory on the Wilson scandal was received by
a storm of applause from the left who heard in it the death knell
of Grévy; it was equally welcome to the right who heard in it

the death knell of the Republic. The center hesitated: obviously the Chamber as a whole could neither ignore nor connive at such a scandal.

Grévy made countermoves. He invited Clemenceau to form a ministry; this the Tiger was unable to do. Then Grévy argued that if he now yielded to popular clamor and resigned, he would be setting a bad precedent. Future Presidents of France would feel obliged to resign whenever public opinion moved against them. This argument failed to move Clemenceau to whom the interests of the Republic were paramount and who believed that those interests were endangered by Grévy's continuance in office.

In the end Grévy resigned, expressing the hope "that the Republic should not suffer from the blows dealt at me . . ." The date was December 2, 1887, the anniversary of Austerlitz and of Louis Napoleon's *coup d'état*. Wilson was brought to trial and sentenced to two years' imprisonment, a sentence quashed by the Court of Appeal and, after a brief withdrawal from public life, was again elected as a deputy and held his seat until 1902.

The disgust engendered by the Wilson scandal refocused public hopes on the "strong man," General Boulanger. His return to Paris was marked by scenes as unrestrained as those caused by his departure. His fighting of a duel—in which Clemenceau seconded the other man—gave the caricaturists an opportunity to foretell the future. They drew him, sword in hand, with his foot on the body of the young Republic and with the shadow of Napoleon in the background. The caption read, "Boulanger the First, Emperor."

Why then, with France and the presidency ready to fall into his hands, did he not snatch his opportunity? Partly through weakness—his mistress had once said that she would be unhappy on the day that saw him master of France; partly through strength —he would not use illegal means to gain power, he would have no truck with a *coup d'état*; partly, perhaps mainly, through confidence—he was convinced that the next elections would carry him, without opposition, to the Elysée. But that was not to be; too many people feared him. A warrant for his arrest on a charge of conspiracy was made out, and he fled. For two years he lived in Brussels, political ambition abandoned, his only preoccupation his nervous and excitable mistress' health. In 1891 she died and, two months later, the man upon whom the ordinary people of France had fixed their hopes of *revanche* made his will.

"In leaving this world I have but one regret, of not having died for my country as a soldier on the field of battle. The country will at least allow one of her children, about to enter the void, to utter the two rallying cries of those who love our dear fatherland—*Vive la France, Vive la République!*"

Then, carrying a bunch of the red roses that Marguerite had loved, he went out and shot himself on her tomb.

Fickle France was too busy celebrating yet another anniversary of the fall of the Bastille to pay much attention to her erstwhile hero's death. Another distraction was the great Universal Exhibition, dominated by the Eiffel Tower, over 980 feet high, named for the engineer who built it.

But Boulangism survived Boulanger and was to be heard of again. In the meantime nothing in French political life seemed to have changed; ministry succeeded ministry until 1892 when a new scandal broke, one of such proportions as to cause men to question seriously the structure of the society in which they lived.

It involved the method by which funds for the Panama Canal had been raised; and where, when raised, half those sums had gone. It is sad that a project which abroad showed the French at their best—inventive, imaginative, incredibly determined in the face of monumental difficulties and brave to the point of recklessness—should at home have led to large scale bribery, corruption and cheating. Rumors of these things had been current when Boulanger's popularity was at its peak and, had exposure come then, he would have undoubtedly been borne in triumph to the Elysée; that made his removal and the hushing-up of scandal essential, and the hushing-up had continued for four years after his eclipse; but when the scandal broke it was overwhelming; over a hundred deputies were involved and few men in public life escaped entirely from the mud that was flung.

Clemenceau bore the brunt of the accusations because he had many enemies glad to believe the worst of him, eager to denounce him as the paid agent of England. He had some difficulty in

exonerating himself and was forced for a time into political retirement. For other men retirement was permanent. Even old de
Lesseps and his son, guilty only of overenthusiasm and the un-
derestimating of difficulties, were charged and sentenced. The
older man did not serve his sentence, he was well over eighty
and, from being a man phenomenal for his age, he became senile
overnight; his son went to jail for a year.

After such a purge of deputies new faces appeared in the
Chamber; some bore well-known names, like Casimir-Périer, who
became President of the Chamber, and Cavaignac, who became
Minister of Marine and made violent attacks on corruption and
"international finance agents." There was also a group of Opportunists (like Gambetta)—Louis Barthou, Raymond Poincaré and
Paul Deschanel.

Parliament, though so largely preoccupied with its own short-
comings, did find time for other things, notably the institution of
a tariff barrier, called by the name of the man who introduced it,
the Méline tariff. During the 1880s the fall in prices had brought
bitter complaints from French producers and this act, passed in
1892, was as stiffly protectionist as those in force in Russia or
America. Sheltered by it from foreign competition, French industry expanded and production was quickly stepped up, but the
result was not industrial peace.

Imperceptibly socialism was making great strides in the country;
the government had no longer to fear the Boulangism of the
extreme right but the radicalism of the left. The Republicans were
no longer the vital force that they had been; they had grown
indolent, and the Wilson and Panama scandals had done great
damage, showing the deputies as venal and self-seeking, too easily
exploited in the cause of capitalism, more intent upon their own
ambitions than on promoting the country's well-being. All this
produced a climate of opinion favorable to the Socialist cause.
In 1894, fifty Socialist deputies, headed by Alexandre Millerand
and Jean Jaurès, were returned to the Chamber and their presence roused the hope that attention would be drawn to, and some
solution proposed for, some urgent social problems. And indeed
after this influx of Socialists, successive governments were obliged

to pay serious consideration to the workers and the division between left and right became more sharply defined.

In 1890, William II, often called simply "the Kaiser," succeeded his father, who had reigned only a few months. William has been called arrogant and ambitious, which he was, but psychologically he was more interesting than such simple adjectives imply. He had been born with a withered arm, of an English mother, and about this disability he was acutely and humiliatedly conscious. As compensation and also because of his envy of his uncle, Edward VII, handsome, whole and popular, heir to the greatest Empire of the time, William was determined to assert himself. He began by dismissing Bismarck, an act to which a caricaturist gave the name of "dropping the pilot." The French saw in him a more dangerous enemy than Bismarck, who had at least cherished no overwhelming colonial ambition. As a result they moved closer to Russia; there were reciprocal visits of the French and Russian fleets to Kronstadt and Toulon, followed by the signing of a pact of friendship. The Germans retorted by renewing the Triple Alliance with Italy and Austria.

Except when war threatens, the French do not concern themselves overmuch with foreign affairs and now, satisfied that they were no longer isolated in Europe, that the prospect of regaining Alsace and Lorraine was remote, they turned their eyes inward again. And almost immediately they found plenty to occupy them.

The year 1893 opened with the death of Jules Ferry as a result of a maniac assassin's attack, and it ended with the hurling of a bomb into the Chamber of Deputies. Blood spurted everywhere and debris fell all over the Chamber. The Premier, Charles Dupuy, one of those obscure politicians chosen for office for his negative rather than his positive qualities, uttered the only memorable phrase in his career. "Gentlemen," he said, "the sitting continues."

The man who had thrown the bomb, Vaillant, was himself wounded. At his trial he announced that he was an anarchist who hated society and that his action had been dictated by the hope that the deputies would be shocked into passing laws which would benefit the underprivileged.

In February 1894, shortly after Vaillant's execution, another bomb exploded in Paris near the Gare St. Lazare, causing twenty-one injuries, only one of which was fatal. This time the bomb-thrower was Emile Henry, son of a condemned Communard; the harvest of history was ripening. Henry, too, professed himself an enemy of bourgeois society which he castigated in his final speech in court before he was condemned to death.

In June 1894, the whole of France—and the world—was shocked by the assassination at Lyons where he had gone to visit a new Universal Exhibition, of the President of the Republic, Sadi Carnot. The crime was especially appalling because of the character of its victim.

When Grévy was forced to quit the Elysée, the office of President had been brought into such disrepute that its integrity and prestige could only be restored by a man of irreproachable character. Sadi Carnot, grandson of "the organizer of victory" was such a man. He was a sincere Republican whose public life gave every evidence of probity; for seven years he had carried out his duties with dignity and integrity; he was everywhere regarded with respect and affection. The assassin's dagger was not directed at the man who was recognized as an incarnation of the virtues of the Republic; the target was the office itself, but it was the man who died.

The assassin was an Italian anarchist named Caserio. Unlike his predecessors, Orsini and Fieschi, he had been successful but, at his trial, he admitted that he had been motivated by no political conviction; he had killed Carnot to avenge Vaillant's death. French anger was not appeased by this and there was a brief demand for war against Italy. It soon died down. Inevitably the assassination was followed by repressive laws which just as inevitably provoked alarm, suspicion and riots, since the left felt that any repressive measure was aimed especially at them.

Casimir-Périer, who had served a brief term as Premier, was elected President in Carnot's place, but he resigned after seven months, saying that he found the campaign of defamation against the army, the magistracy, the government and himself as head of state insupportable. It is more likely that, after a lifetime spent in the rough and tumble of political life, he found the office of President insupportably dull.

His place was taken by Félix Faure, a young man, amiable and vain enough to enjoy all the aspects of presidential life which had so irked Casimir-Périer. He was happy with the near-puppet, representational rôle which all heads of state, presidential or royal, were increasingly called upon to play as the nineteenth century drew toward its close. But into his circus round of cere-monial dress, official visits and receptions, the exercising of tact and charm, exploded the worst crisis yet; worse than the scandal of Wilson or of Panama; the Dreyfus affair.

In 1894, Captain Alfred Dreyfus, a French army officer, and a Jew, thirty-five years old, was convicted by a secret military tribunal of having divulged state secrets to a foreign power. The main evidence in the case was the so-called *bordereau*, a file of papers which, it was alleged, Dreyfus had handed over to Ger-many. A court of army officers, most of them anti-Semitic, sentenced him to degradation and life imprisonment on the in-famous Devil's Island off French Guiana.

On Saturday, January 5, 1895, Alfred Dreyfus was marched out under escort into the great square of the Ecole Militaire, where the snow lay deep, to hear the words, icy as the weather, "Alfred Dreyfus, you are no longer worthy to carry arms. In the name of the French people we degrade you."

They ripped away his gold braid and his buttons; his com-manding officer, Colonel Sandherr, took Dreyfus' sword and broke it across his knee. Dreyfus, holding himself erect, said, "Soldiers, an innocent man is being degraded. I am innocent. *Vive la France! Vive l'Armée!*"

He was led away, repeating in a flat, emotionless voice, "I am innocent."

Afterward an eyewitness of the scene remarked, "They should have drowned his voice in a roll of drums."

Louis XVI's last words had been thus drowned; but Dreyfus' words went on echoing and re-echoing around the civilized world.

Dreyfus' family and certain members of the public were firmly convinced of his innocence, but it took them eleven years to prove it. During this time France was bitterly divided into Dreyfusards and anti-Dreyfusards, and the campaign of the former was com-plicated by increasing anti-Semitism. The issue speedily became a political one with all the forces opposed to the Republic using the conviction of a possibly innocent man as a stick with which to beat the government.

Conditions on Devil's Island, where Dreyfus dragged out a miserable existence, were extremely harsh and unhealthy. In 1897 a Colonel Picquart of the French Military Intelligence, aided by Dreyfus' brother, made public a discovery which Picquart in the course of his ordinary duties had made—the writer of the incriminating *bordereau* had been another French officer, Major Esterhazy. This revelation sparked off an agitation for the case to be re-opened.

In the following year, Emile Zola wrote a series of pro-Dreyfus articles, the famous *J'Accuse,* and thus earned for himself a prison sentence for summing up the evidence against the army's procedure and conclusions in 1895. Among others who rallied to the cause of the man they thought innocent were Jean Jaurès, fast making his name as a socialist leader, the great writer, Anatole France, and Clemenceau. They boldly attacked the members of the right who were in favor of letting sleeping dogs lie, even at the expense of an innocent man; the right, with the aid of Paul Déroulède and Maurice Barrès, repelled the attacks. The war between the two sides, if bloodless, was grim.

Then Colonel Henry of the Army Intelligence branch who, with Esterhazy, had been responsible for fabricating evidence against Dreyfus, was arrested, and while awaiting trial committed suicide in his cell. A revaluation of the case could no longer be postponed, Dreyfus was brought back to France and given a second trial, once again condemned and sentenced, this time to ten years' imprisonment. This, not unnaturally, astonished and shocked France and the watching world, and the President gave Dreyfus a free pardon. Dreyfus' partisans were far from satisfied with this half-hearted vindication and renewed their efforts to prove his complete innocence.

At last, in 1906 the Court of Appeal quashed the sentence, and Dreyfus returned to the army with the rank of major. He lived to serve his country in the Great War, to receive the Legion of Honor and to retire with the rank of lieutenant colonel, and in

1930 to see irrefutable evidence brought to light to prove the guilt of Esterhazy.

Dreyfus had suffered a long and savage ordeal, but he was not the only sufferer. The moral health of the Republic, already undermined, was severely affected. The whole affair, with the passions it aroused and its indications of attempts to divert the course of justice, made a sorry episode in the history of France. The dark picture it presents of the ethical state of the country is only relieved by the unflagging efforts of those who supported the man victimized by errors and chicanery in high places.

The Dreyfus case was not the only scandal of the 1890s. In 1898 there was an echo of the Panama affair when one of the men who had been implicated was extradited from England. This gave René Viviani, one of the new generation of orators, an opportunity to make a great speech in which he attacked the magistracy, the police and the politicians for the parts they played in financial operations and negotiations.

Despite so much domestic trouble, France's international position had improved: her alliance with Russia was no longer merely diplomatic, it was military, and Russia was pledged to come to her aid in any future conflict. William II had abandoned Bismarck's policy of trying to conciliate Russia and thus threw her into the arms of France even though an alliance with a Republic did not seem wholly desirable to the autocratic Czarist régime.

The President, Félix Faure, had enjoyed the visit of the Czar, Nicholas II, to France, and his own return visit to Russia. He was a man who enjoyed all the good things which life and his office had to offer, which included the society of pretty women. He was entertaining one at the Elysée when apoplexy struck him. Even a country which looked more indulgently than most upon extra-marital activities thought the circumstances of his death unbecoming. (His successor managed to scandalize a great number of people in a different, and worse, way. When he visited the King of Italy, as a sop to the anti-clericals, he did not seek the customary interview with the Pope. Every Catholic in France felt affronted.)

When Félix Faure died, Déroulède saw an opportunity to make a successful attack on the Republic with the aid of his League of Patriots; but there was now no Boulanger, no immensely popular general, whom the soldiers could carry to the Elysée as in old days Roman legions had carried their commanders to the throne. Déroulède's attempt collapsed in a storm of ridicule and, for the part he had played, he was exiled for ten years but amnestied after five. The anti-Republican movement had over-reached itself, and the country reacted by electing, in 1899, the men who formed the Bloc des Gauches.

Chapter 2. *LA BELLE EPOQUE*

In 1900 Paris became once again the place to which all roads lead. The Universal Exhibition of that year was the biggest and most brilliant of all. Like ordinary people, kings and emperors and eastern potentates flocked to Paris, willing to overlook, for the sake of the sights to be seen and the gaieties to be enjoyed, the fact that the French Republic was the only great power in Europe to have done away with their breed.

There was Emile Loubet, the new President, to welcome them; there was a new bridge by which to cross the Seine. It was called, in honor of the late Czar, the Pont Alexandre III, had huge allegorical figures at each end and was embellished with the arms of Paris and St. Petersburg, symbolic of the Franco-Russian alliance. The two great buildings in which the Exhibition was held were to remain as permanent features in Paris, the Grand and the Petit Palais des Beaux Arts.

The Exhibition marked the beginning not only of a new century but of a period which the French call *la belle époque;* it matched with a deadly exactitude those years immediately preceding the Revolution which Talleyrand had called the years of the *douceur de vivre*, the sweet, the golden years. This reveling in a sunset, unrecognized as such, was not peculiar to France. Innumerable books of memoirs and autobiographies bear witness that in England, in Austria and in Russia, the sunset was glorious, that before the lights went out all over Europe, they glowed with an unprecedented brilliance.

The world of entertainment catered to every taste. Sarah Bernhardt was no longer young, but she played in *La Dame aux Camélias* and in *L'Aiglon*, a play which was received in a way which proved that, though as a political force Bonapartism might be dead, the Napoleonic legend lived on. As Bernhardt dominated the legitimate theatre so Mistinguett dazzled those who frequented the music halls. For lovers of opera there was Charpentier's new success, *Louise*, with its realistic background of working-class Paris. Maxim's restaurant in the Rue Royale offered discreet private rooms as well as an opportunity to see the fabulous *grandes cocottes*, the courtesans who dissipated the fortunes of their admirers and whose beauty, elegance and luxurious way of life made them the real queens of Parisian society. Their humbler sisters offered their charms at the promenades of the music halls, of which a disapproving Baedeker wrote that they were "mostly unsuitable for ladies," but the music-hall world was immortalized by the genius of Toulouse-Lautrec, a cripple of aristocratic birth in whose posters and canvases the night life of Paris, the stars of the Moulin Rouge and the circus, still seem to live and breathe. The Folies Bergère attracted then, as now, the foreign customer and the gaping provincial; the real Parisian preferred the *cafés concerts* which were cheap and where the *chansonniers* in their topical songs planted barbs of wit and satire in the flanks of the great, especially the politicians.

Paris was still a city embracing many small separate worlds. In Montmartre there were the *apaches*, the roughs and toughs of the capital, distinguished by their huge berets and corduroy trousers: they waged war among themselves; they sometimes terrorized ordinary people. The decent working-class man had his own world and his uniform, cap and blue blouse, and his womenfolk wore black as they had done since the eighteenth century, when carriages passing along streets without pavements threw up so much mud that clothes of any other color were impractical.

There was another world, too; that of writers, artists and musicians, for Paris was still the acknowledged center of intellectual and artistic activity. The great man of letters of the period was Anatole France; Verlaine, Mallarmé, André Gide and Paul Valéry were making their way into the place formerly occupied by Flaubert and Zola. Watching the manners of *le tout Paris* was a sickly young dilettante who later recorded his impressions of that vanished society in a long psychological novel which he called *Remembrance of Things Past*. His name was Marcel Proust.

In art and in music there were innovations. Franck, Fauré,

Ravel and Debussy were using new themes and fresh techniques not always immediately appreciated. Around Debussy's opera *Pelléas and Mélisande* waged a battle of opinion as fierce as that fought over Victor Hugo's early dramas. The new school of painters—Matisse, Derain and Vlaminck, were dubbed *les fauves*, the wild ones. Their work was regarded as outrageous. The Cubists, Picasso and Braque were ridiculed; Toulouse-Lautrec, highly regarded now, was little thought of then. And working away in this period, unrivaled as a breeding ground of genius, were Monet, Renoir, Gauguin and Van Gogh.

There were distractions on a different level. Little did M. Garcin, propelling his hobby horse past the jeering spectators in 1806, dream that in 1903 there would be a bicycle race in France—the first of many annual events which hold the whole of France breathless as the grueling race goes on, or that men would literally die of exhaustion in the competition for the supreme distinction of the right to wear the leader's yellow jersey.

The Tour de France of 1903 was an immediate success and became an institution, but on the whole the Frenchman had as yet little interest in organized sport, and the second Olympic Games, held in 1900 in Paris, roused little enthusiasm, though when France beat Germany at rugby football the victory went some way to avenging Sedan.

Less successful than the bicycle race was that of the relatively unknown machine, the motorcar, which should have run between Paris and Madrid but had to be stopped halfway because of the fatal casualties. So far as the race went it was won by Louis Renault, whose young motor-car factory was to expand into one of the greatest industrial concerns in France.

In France pure research suffered, as it seems fated to suffer everywhere and at all times, from a chronic shortage of funds; nonetheless scientific discovery and development went ahead. Marie and Pierre Curie made their world-shaking discovery of radium; Louis Lumière produced the color film and it was Edouard Branly's work in physics which made possible Marconi's first experiments in wireless telegraphy which, with a successful transmission across the Atlantic in 1901, completely revolutionized communications over the world's wide surface.

These advances, of universal importance, seemed less to the Parisian of the day than the opening of the underground railway, the Métro, which enabled him to reach his work in a wider area and with greater ease than before.

The discoveries and the inventions which brought countries and continents closer together produced their own problems. Improved methods of agriculture made the fields of France, and of Europe, more productive, but they worked the same magic on the wider fields of America, Canada and Australia. The conquest of disease made populations expand; hundreds of thousands of people left Europe for younger countries in which they could have elbow room and opportunity, but of this great flood of emigrants few were French. France was still underpopulated and very largely self-sufficient. Even the French exporter need seek no customers, they came to him; his wine, his silk, his fashionable clothes were sought after. This economic self-sufficiency was reflected in the national character and in its policies. Before 1914 the average Frenchman was indifferent to the outside world, even to that part of it which made up the vast and growing French Empire. He was still aware of the enemy across the Rhine, yet he resisted any efforts of his politicians to improve Franco-German relationships. To any rallying call save *la patrie en danger*, he was apt to turn a deaf ear. He cherished memories of days of glory under Louis XIV and Napoleon I, but they bred in him no desire to see them repeated in his own lifetime.

The focus of French attention was the family, its home, its property: when guidance was needed it was sought not from the lawyer or the bank manager but from the *conseil de famille*, a gathering of the whole clan. The home was sacrosanct; few strangers were ever invited to cross its threshhold; in peasant families it was also the treasure-house, for savings—and the thrift of the French is proverbial—were not to be trusted in other hands; money went into an old woolen stocking or was stuffed under a mattress, or buried under a tree. The bourgeois, particularly in towns and cities, did invest his savings, but only in things which seemed to have the State behind them, government bonds, Suez Canal shares and the railways.

The bourgeoisie was still jealous of its political rights and reluctant to see them extended to the growing working class, and its attitude was, if anything, even more self-contained and self-satisfied than that of the peasantry. The provincial Frenchman of the middle class was reserved, austere, thrifty and difficult to know. His aims were to make suitable marriages for his daughters and to send his son to Paris to study law, law being the best springboard for a successful career.

The life of the middle-class girl was hard; marriage was the aim, and her chances of marriage depended not upon her looks or her charm, but on the size of the dowry which her father could afford; so, heavily chaperoned, clad in insipid white or pastel-colored dresses, she must wait for marriage to release her from a boring, semi-cloistered life.

The satisfaction with things as they were, shared by the middle class and the peasantry—despite the latter's inborn tendency to grumble, was absent in the industrial worker and the underpaid minor official. Despite the efforts of the socialist deputies, legislation to benefit the underprivileged was slow and timid, hampered by the fact that the right and the center, composed mainly of the middle class, still held a majority and were reactionary, believing that charity was the answer to poverty. It was at a charity bazaar in Paris in 1897 that a terrible fire broke out, causing more than a hundred deaths and plunging many families into mourning.

The workers themselves were divided in their opinion as to how their condition could be bettered; they agreed that political power was essential, but some believed that it could only be reached through revolutionary action, others pinned their faith to legitimate parliamentary measures. Nevertheless some progress was made; in 1910 the system of old age pensions was introduced. The greatest exponent of socialism—and one who still holds a revered place in French left-wing ideology—was Jean Jaurès, who was both an intellectual and a man of action. His powerful personality, acknowledged integrity and moral courage earned him immense popularity, and his influence was extended through the paper which he founded, L'Humanité.

The Republic, as an institution, had suffered from the scandals, the crises, and the constant change of ministries. In 1899 Waldeck-Rousseau became Premier and set himself the task of strengthening and reforming it. He was in a strong position because he was the leader of the Bloc des Gauches, the left-wing group who had sunk all their differences in order to present a united front. His ultimate aim was to strengthen the Republic for purposes of defense, and between him and his aim his cold lawyer's eye—one enemy likened him to a fish in aspic—saw one obstacle, the influence of the Church in education.

Twenty years had passed since Ferry had passed his anti-clerical acts; they had been consistently evaded and the evasion of law was, in itself, enough to rouse the lawyer in Waldeck-Rousseau. Monks and nuns might be banned from taking any part in the education provided by the State, but great Catholic private schools had been established and were flourishing. Catholic schools produced Catholics who, politically, tended to be reactionary. Waldeck-Rousseau was determined to root them out and proceeded to pass a law which was intended to put an end, once and for all, to the dual system of education. He was undeterred by an absurd incident at the races at Longchamp, when a Catholic conservative bashed in the silk hat of President Loubet with his umbrella.

But Waldeck-Rousseau was already a sick man and, in 1902, he resigned, naming Emile Combes as his successor. President Loubet, though not in sympathy with Waldeck-Rousseau's anti-clericalism, which his chosen successor might be expected to sustain, was mindful of his constitutional limitations and asked Combes to form a government.

Combes himself was the product of the discredited Catholic education, but he had lost his faith and become virulently anti-clerical, as venomous as the ex-priests of the Revolution. During a premiership of record length for any man under the Third Republic, he devoted himself almost exclusively to the cause of anti-clericalism. He broke off diplomatic relations with the Vatican, relations which had lasted a hundred years, ever since Napoleon I made his Concordat; he expelled monks and nuns by the thousand. Once again that stronghold of Catholic feeling, the Vendée, rose in open rebellion, and once again army officers, charged with the expulsion of monks and nuns, refused to carry out their orders, and resigned their commissions. But Combes and the Republic triumphed. When the "diabolical Combes" resigned in 1905 he left, as his legacy to France, a complete dissociation between state and religion which, finally, even Catholics came to recognize as not entirely disadvantageous to the Church.

Throughout the many changes of Premier, shifts which might have been damaging to the nation's interests, a certain continuity was maintained by men who remained at their posts under successive governments. One of these was Théophile Delcassé who was Foreign Minister from 1898 to 1905, a period when his chiefs were so engrossed in domestic affairs that he had more than usual freedom in shaping outside policies. He set himself to strengthen France's position in Europe and to encourage colonial expansion. Neither aim was easily achieved and, in pursuing the second, Delcassé came into conflict with other powers, notably England.

In 1890 a Franco-British agreement had defined the two countries' spheres of influence in Africa, but those Frenchmen who gave thought to colonial matters dreamed of a French Africa extending from the Atlantic to the Indian Ocean. In pursuit of this dream Colonel Marchand, with a mere handful of companions, set out in 1897 from Brazzaville in the French Congo to cross the continent. After an eighteen-month journey he reached Fashoda in the Sudan and was there met by Kitchener, the British general, advancing up the Nile into the southern Sudan after his victory at Omdurman. The southern Sudan in itself was not particularly covetable territory, but whoever held it had power of life or death over Egypt, since the damming of the Nile could reduce Egypt to desert. England, then in occupation of Egypt, was not prepared to see the French paramount in the Sudan but the French claimed, with some justice, that they were there first. The situation looked ugly, but Delcassé was not prepared to go to war; France was being torn by the Dreyfus affair and there was no certainty of support from Russia. He ordered Marchand to withdraw; France ceded all claims to the valley of the Nile and the French and British zones in the Sudan were clearly defined. The French regarded the Fashoda incident as a

humiliation and to Delcassé it was particularly unwelcome since
he was planning to strengthen France by cultivating friendship
with England in order to counterbalance the growing power of
Germany.

He had an uphill task; a few fashions, a few phrases, the attitude
of a few people might hint at anglophilia, but in the main French
opinion was still resolutely anglophobe. France might join England,
even Germany, in order to put down the Boxer rebellion in
China in 1900, but that was purely a matter of expediency; her
real attitude toward England was shown when the Boer War
broke out in South Africa; she was passionately on the side of
President Kruger and the Boers, though she took no part in what
was then regarded almost as a family affair, a squabble between
a colony and the mother country; one sided, one sympathized,
but one did not intervene. The heyday of the "escalating war"
had not quite dawned.

Delcassé, only too well aware of the general feeling toward
England, pressed on with his scheme for an Anglo-French *entente*
and in an unseasonably chilly May, in 1903, saw his dream begin
to take shape. Edward VII paid his first state visit to France.

He had made, during his long years as Prince of Wales, many
visits; he had fallen in love with France on that long ago summer
when Napoleon III had been so kind and indulgent; later, a
connoisseur of food and wine and people, he had spent some of
his happiest days in Paris, but always unofficially. This, his first
official visit, began badly; people shouted, "Long live the Boers!"
"Long live Marchand!" and "Fashoda!" The hostility of his reception was in the sharpest possible contrast to that given his
cousin, Nicholas of Russia, two years earlier.

Edward's parents had despised and often despaired of him, but
he had a quality that neither of them possessed, a vast, buoyant
bonhomie which enabled him to carry off this difficult situation
as few other men could have done. He was deaf to the catcalls
and to the even more ominous silences; he smiled, he bowed, he
shook hands; his charm, so envied by his nephew William of Germany, his good will and the desire that everybody should be
comfortable made their impact, and within three days he had
earned his name of Edward the Peacemaker. Fashoda was for-

gotten, anglophobia had melted away, and when he left the crowds acclaimed him. More important, in private talks with Delcassé, he had laid the foundations of a genuine *entente cordiale*.

In 1904, President Loubet and Delcassé made a return state visit to London. Edward, with what may have been a touch of malicious humor, but was more likely his innate sense of what was seemly, asked that on state occasions they should wear the regulation knee breeches, the *culottes* which the Revolution had banished. Loubet and Delcassé, stoutly republican, went to Buckingham Palace *sans-culottes*; and nobody minded in the least.

More than fifty years had passed since Louis Philippe had made tentative approaches toward an Anglo-French alliance; during those years the two countries had fought side by side in the Crimea and they had, from time to time, come perilously near to fighting each other. Now they saw that their interests were mutual and began to make concessions. France was to have a free hand in Morocco, England a similarly free hand in Egypt. Fashoda was given a new name, so that no mention of it should irritate national susceptibilities. This Franco-British entente was a great triumph for Delcassé but, before French ambitions could be realized in Morocco, it was necessary to come to terms with Italy, equally interested in that area. This he did by making a pact whereby Italy recognized French occupation of Morocco in return for French recognition of Italian rights in Tripolitania.

The Kaiser looked with a jaundiced eye upon French approaches to Italy—Italy was allied to him in the Triple Alliance; upon the Franco-British entente he looked with fury. In 1905 he made a visit to Tangier and there, in a speech, declared German support for the Moroccans and for the independence of the Sultan. To round off this aggressive speech, he demanded Delcassé's resignation.

France was in no position to go to war with Germany, and Delcassé was forced to resign. His policy—highly successful in steering France out of isolation in Europe and in solving the delicate problem of Franco-British relationships—failed because he had not taken into account two vital considerations; he had not backed a vigorous foreign program with a strong military and naval force so that, when a showdown came, as at Fashoda and

Tangier, he could only make concessions and withdraw. And he had made no attempt to enter negotiations with Germany, which lent some credence to Germany's belief that she was being encircled. It is true that, could Delcassé so far have overcome his own hatred of Germany as to suggest friendship, the idea would have been unacceptable to France as a whole. The scars of Waterloo were growing old and, under pressure of expediency could be, if not forgotten, ignored; memories of 1870 were still vivid and painful.

Delcassé's part was not yet over; as Minister of Marine and again as Foreign Minister he still had a vital role to play. And although he was not present at the conference of European powers which met at Algéciras to settle the problem of Morocco, it was his policy which triumphed there. French interests in Morocco were recognized, and Germany received a severe rebuff. The Kaiser's hopes of inflicting a diplomatic defeat on France and of undermining her understanding with England were disappointed. The ties between France and England were strengthened by their growing suspicion of Germany and her increase in naval armament. The Tangier speech and the Algéciras conference paved the way to the Triple Entente of England, France and Russia.

Alliance with Russia was still highly valued, and nobody doubted her real strength, but her situation at the moment was not a very happy one. She had just been soundly beaten by Japan in the Russo-Japanese War, a result which astonished and shocked a world which could accept Japanese victory over the Chinese but had up to now always believed that when West confronted East, victory for the former was certain.

Russia had internal troubles, too. The defeats of the Russo-Japanese War brought into the open the discontent which had been long smoldering; there was mutiny on the battleship *Potemkin*, and there were strikes. One, in St. Petersburg, directed by the first workers' soviet, lasted for ten days; the Czar was forced to yield to the revolutionaries and grant Russia a constitution and a legislative assembly, the Duma. This first tentative step toward democracy in Russia was warmly welcomed in France. The year 1906 seemed to presage a great swing toward liberalism. In England the Liberal party came to power after a landslide election; in

France the left increased its power. Emile Loubet came to the end of his seven years as President and was succeeded by a jolly, bearded Gascon, Armand Fallières, who was soon called to face changes and developments which were strongly to influence the future.

The Bloc des Gauches began to disintegrate, split by two opinions. Jules Guesde held that it was wrong for a Socialist to take office in a bourgeois ministry; to do so was incompatible with the aims and objects of socialism. Jean Jaurès held the opposite view, a Socialist in any government could do his party useful service but he bowed to majority opinion and refused to take office. Whether the Socialist party gained or lost by his decision is debatable; what is certain is that France was deprived of the services of an enlightened humanitarian of great personal integrity.

The differences were healed and the new, unified Socialist party, drawing into itself men of various shades of opinion, was henceforward known as the S.F.I.O., the *Section Française de l'Internationale Ouvrière*. Its members continued to refuse to take office, but they fought elections and occupied seats in the Chamber.

Almost at the same time the General Confederation of Labor, the C.G.T., held a conference at Amiens which declared that the best means of fighting a capitalist régime was the general strike. About this resolution there was something of the spirit of the Tennis Court Oath; it underlined the fact that "the principles of '89" were still the core of all left-wing political belief in France. The immediate result of this conference was the intensification of serious working-class agitation. It was to be a feature of French social life for the next half-dozen years.

Strikes were nothing new; they had been bedeviling governments for some time. At Monceau-les-Mines, the miners had held out for three and a half months in an attempt to establish the principle, if not the immediate practice, of an eight-hour day. Principle in fact mattered more to the pure Socialist than substance.

In 1906 Clemenceau became first Minister of the Interior and then Premier. He was sixty-five, had thirty-six years of political life behind him and his great years were still to come. French politicians enjoy an extraordinary longevity; Aristide Briand, for example, was expelled from the Socialist party for taking office under Clemenceau, and he was forty-four then; he was still active in 1932.

The Tiger's involvement in the Panama scandal had been entirely wiped out by the part he had played in the vindication of Dreyfus. He planned a program of wide reforms which he could never fully implement because of his day-to-day concern with economic problems and social agitation. In the southwest there was a particularly ugly affair, involving three million people engaged in wine making, protesting against overproduction and fraudulent practices. In Narbonne disturbances led to bloodshed; in Perpignan the prefecture was burnt down and the local regiment mutinied. Several strikes were only put down by military action. In one strike, that of the Paris waiters, there was something at once comic and significant. Waiters were forbidden to wear mustaches. The chef's hat, the waitress' little cap are evidences that people like their food to be dealt with by people whose hairy growths are concealed. But at the time the mustache was an essential sign of respectability and of sexual attractiveness. (Who said, "Kissing a man without a mustache is like eating an egg without salt"?) The Paris waiters saw no reason why they should be deprived of the right to wear this status symbol; so they went on strike.

Clemenceau's government was distinctly leftist and the increase in left-wing representation produced by the elections of 1906 did result in socialist legislation; night work by women was banned; one day of rest for every worker was obligatory; Friendly Societies were not merely recognized but organized by the state. Nevertheless strikes continued to occur; now among the post office workers, now among the school teachers, but there was a lack of cohesion; in May 1909 an attempt by the C.G.T. to promote a general strike failed.

The same year brought an immense boost for French prestige, when Louis Blériot made the first cross-Channel flight in an airplane. It was not Clemenceau as Premier who publicly congratulated him. Clemenceau had quarreled with Delcassé and been succeeded by Briand.

In 1909 all France rejoiced over Blériot's achievement; in 1910

all France mourned over the loss from the Louvre of a picture by
Leonardo da Vinci, called the *Monna Lisa*, or *La Gioconda*.

It had been, since the sixteenth century, the property of the
Kings of France and, since the Revolution, one of the chief
glories of the Louvre, but an Italian, caught trying to sell it two
years after the theft, excused his action by saying that Napoleon
had stolen it and that he had merely tried to restore it to Italy. It
was a trivial incident, unworthy of note, except that the concern
it caused was symptomatic of French mentality at the time. The
French newspapers said that the theft was intended to humiliate
France. Today they take our pictures, tomorrow they will take
our colonies!

Newspaper outcries, however absurd, usually reflect something that exists in the public mind; and the French, now that
they had come round to the idea of France as a colonial power,
had some reason for concern. Germany was fomenting trouble
in Morocco. A German consul in Casablanca was encouraging
desertions from the French Foreign Legion. The decisions of the
Algeçiras Conference were threatened. But when a dynastic crisis
occurred, the Sultan of Morocco sought French, not German,
aid. The French moved and occupied Fez, and the Kaiser sent a
gunboat, the *Panther*, to Agadir on a saber-rattling expedition,
allegedly to protect German interests menaced by French expansion.

The *Panther* and what it implied in this "send a gunboat"
age, alarmed the English even more than it did the French. From
London David Lloyd George, Liberal though he was, issued a
warning to Germany which would have done credit to Palmerston.
Germany withdrew and there were talks; head-on conflict was
averted and in return for the cession of some territory in the
Congo, Germany agreed to recognize French rights in Morocco.

Morocco, with Algeria and Tunisia, became a valuable asset
which gave France a position of privilege in the western Mediterranean. For thirteen years the office of Resident-General was
held by Marshal Lyautey, France's greatest colonial administrator.
He was a native of Lorraine and probably found some compensation for the loss of his homeland by establishing a new
Empire for France. He had served under General Galliéni in

Madagascar and learned something of his methods. Although a soldier, Lyautey believed that nothing durable is founded on force, and he pursued a policy of associating the native population with French culture and civilization through education, economic development and social services. French colonization owed a great deal to the teachings of Lyautey.

In 1911 the French were not happy about the concessions made to Germany, and the scapegoat of their dissatisfaction was the Premier, Joseph Caillaux. He was the third Premier that France had had in a year; Briand's government had fallen, and his successor, Ernest Monis, had been obliged to resign because of the injuries he had received when an airplane crashed near him. The period of relatively long ministries, like those of Waldeck-Rousseau, Combes and Clemenceau was over; with Briand's short government came an era of repeated ministerial crises, complicated by mounting external problems.

Joseph Caillaux is one of the most ambivalent characters to have figured on the French political scene. He became a deputy in 1898 and served as Minister of Finance under Waldeck-Rousseau, Clemenceau and Monis. A professor of political science, he was both democratic and authoritarian and rallied to himself all the parties of the left except the Socialists. He was regarded as a financial genius and a potential "strong man," but his government could not survive the unpopularity engendered by the Moroccan affair and in 1912 he resigned to be succeeded by Raymond Poincaré.

Poincaré was another Lorrainer, an ardent and uncompromising patriot, a barrister by profession, possessed of an irreproachable character and great intellectual abilities—he was a cousin of the distinguished mathematician, Henri Poincaré, and a member of one of the upper-middle-class families which are the backbone of France. If he lacked anything it was an easy cordiality of manner.

Poincaré had been a deputy since 1887 and had served brief terms as Minister of Education and Minister of Finance. Now, as Premier, leading a coalition government, he set himself a program calculated to increase French prestige. Reform was confined to the recasting of the electoral system and securing the regular voting of the budget.

His term of office proved to be short, for in 1913 he was elected to succeed Armand Fallières as President of the Republic. Over Europe the storm clouds were gathering fast and it was an advantage for France to have at this moment a head of state to whom the national interest was paramount and who, having been a parliamentarian, knew every move in the political game. It was plain that Poincaré, while strictly observing the limits of his constitutional powers, would be a more active President than any since MacMahon.

Poincaré's first Premier was Briand, whose most important task was to bring before the Chamber a measure to increase the length of compulsory military service to three years. The increase in German armed forces and armaments had alarmed the French, always haunted by the fear of a surprise attack which might put them out of action before reserves could be mustered. Yet to this suggestion the left reacted so violently that Briand's ministry fell. Louis Barthou took over and the law was passed with a large majority voting in its favor. Barthou's ministry was short, he was succeeded by Gaston Doumergue—the third Premier to hold office in 1913.

Once again Caillaux became Minister of Finance and, it was while holding this office, that he became involved in one of the greatest scandals of the Third Republic.

The editor of that influential paper, *Le Figaro*, a man named Calmette, accused Caillaux of misconduct in connection with his proposal to levy income tax; in his campaign against Caillaux Calmette did not hesitate to make use of a letter written by Caillaux to his first wife. The second Madame Caillaux became obsessed by the fear that Calmette might also publish some letters which she had written to Caillaux while she was still the wife of another man. On March 16, 1914, she bought a revolver, went to Calmette's office and shot him five times. Caillaux' enemies thought that, in killing Calmette, she had finished her husband's career. They were mistaken.

The affair, political, with sexual undertones, roused great interest and the trial was eagerly awaited. Compared with the noise of Madame Caillaux' five shots, another, fired in a place no one then had heard of, merited, at the time, small attention.

This, the shot that changed the world, was fired in Sarajevo, by a tubercular Serbian student named Prinzip. It killed the Archduke Franz Ferdinand, heir to the Austrian empire, and his morganatic wife, whom he had taken with him on his visit to the provinces because at home, in court circles, her status was lowly and she had been subjected to humiliations. In Bosnia she could enjoy, briefly, the position of first lady which he, a loving husband, thought her due. On the morning of Sunday, June 28, 1914, Prinzip fired his shots and they died together, her last act an attempt to shield him with her body, his last words a plea to her to live for the sake of their children.

When, in 1908, Austria annexed the territories of Bosnia and Herzegovina, the Serbs in Bosnia began a terrorist agitation against Austrian rule. The Emperor of Austria, Franz Josef, was already old and the personal tragedies of his life had done nothing to soften his rigid conservatism. He had hated the dead man, his nephew, but this was an outrage which must be paid for. The Emperor and the Austrians insisted that the murder was not the work of a secret terrorist organization, but a political move, backed by the Serbian government, to whom the Austrian government issued an ultimatum on July 23. On the twenty-fifth the Serbians sent a reply which went to the extreme limit of concession, but Austria was out to make an example from which other restive provinces, fired by nationalism, might learn a lesson. On July 28 Austria declared war on Serbia.

On that day at the Paris assizes, Madame Caillaux, brought out of privileged imprisonment, was defended by the same man, Labori, who had defended Dreyfus, and acquitted. All who sympathized with her were elated. Her husband had resigned, however, and his resignation brought about the fall of Doumergue's ministry.

Far from France on that day events had taken a turn that would make a change of ministry, Madame Caillaux' acquittal and every other purely domestic affair less than dust on the wind.

Austria was allied to Germany; Austria, in her negotiations with Serbia, in her eluding any offer of mediation by the other great powers, had had one aim in mind—the gaining of time during which Germany could mobilize. Germany had mobilized and so, in fear and self-defense, had Russia. Germany now demanded Russian demobilization, at the same time claiming that she was threatened and must proceed with her own mobilization. And Germany mobilized was a threat to France, the fructification of an old, deep-rooted fear.

The man who had most passionately opposed the three-year compulsory military service was Jean Jaurès, a pacifist whom even his opponents recognized as a genuine idealist; even his opposition to the three-year measure had been dictated by his belief that the whole military structure was in need of remodeling. When he realized that Germany and Russia had mobilized, that France was on the brink of mobilization, Jaurès rushed to the office of his paper, *L'Humanité*, and wrote a broken-hearted, impassioned appeal for peace. The danger lay, he said, not in what had already taken place but in the war-fever whose temperature was mounting. He then went to a café intending to take a hasty snack before returning to the office to keep in touch with developments.

For twenty years people had been shouting. "Death to Jaurès!" He had taken no precautions and suffered no harm but, on this evening, July 31, 1914, he was shot down by a half-wit with the apt name of Villain, who had never read a word that Jaurès had written and understood nothing of his ideals. Motivated by his own form of patriotism, Villain deprived France of a great man.

People of all political parties were shocked by the assassination and the next day the Premier, Réne Viviani, issued a proclamation in which he paid tribute to Jaurès' real patriotism and merit; at the same time he appealed to the workers for their support in the difficult days through which the country was passing. Internal unity was of vital importance, for on August 2 the Germans were in Luxembourg, violating the Grand Duchy's neutrality, on the third they declared war on France and began to move into Belgium, while in the Mediterranean the cruisers *Goeben* and *Breslau* started to bombard Bône and Philippeville. The Great War had begun.

In Berlin the British ambassador sought assurance that the

neutrality of Belgium would be respected. The German Chancellor, Von Bethmann-Hollweg, said, "Just for the word 'neutrality,' a word which in wartime has so often been disregarded, just for a scrap of paper Great Britain is going to make war."

The scrap of paper contained Britain's guarantee to defend Belgian neutrality, pledged in 1839. The German advance into Belgium continued, and on August 4, Britain declared war.

Perhaps to France, after the brooding threat and the alarms of the last ten years, open warfare brought some element of relief. The spirit of *revanche*, which had been nurtured even in schools, where maps showed the lost provinces Alsace and Lorraine colored in mourning purple, the spirit of '92, with its attachment to the principle of French support for small nations against great empires, sprang up, powerful enough to fuse the nation into one. Poincaré's call for a *union sacrée*, a sinking of all differences in the face of the country's danger, met with an almost unanimous response. Viviani broadened his cabinet to make it truly national, calling back Delcassé to take charge of Foreign Affairs, Millerand to become Minister of War, Briand to become Minister of Justice, and even bringing out of retirement the old fighter, survivor of the Commune of 1871, Jules Guesde.

For the Germans, again crying "*Nach Paris,*" this was the long awaited moment, "*Der Tag,*" the day when France would be crushed as she had been in 1870, when German naval superiority would be proved and, with the Pax Germanica taking the place of the Pax Britannica, Germany would move into that "place in the sun" to which she felt entitled.

In France the cry was again, "*A Berlin!*" Soldiers wearing horizon blue instead of baggy red trousers and marching to "La Madelon" and "Sambre et Meuse," instead of "Partant pour la Syrie," crowded into trains that carried them to the frontiers, north and east. The mood was confident. In 1870 France had fought alone; this time she had powerful allies, England and Russia; her prestige was high, she was prosperous, she had a vast colonial empire whose troops would come to fight side by side with Frenchmen born.

"*A Berlin! A Berlin!*" by way of Alsace and Lorraine of which

Gambetta had said, "Let us speak of them never, think of them always." The French did not know it then, but the road to Berlin was a long one; it was to take them twenty-six years, Alsace and Lorraine were to be regained and lost again before French troops, swinging into the triumphant strains of the "Marseillaise" through the Brandenburger Tor, were actually to be in Berlin.

The *belle époque* ended abruptly; Stravinsky's tunes gave way to martial music, Poiret's clinging gowns to sober nurses' uniforms. The English are regarded as an inarticulate people but, as the younger Pitt had summed up the situation after Austerlitz ("Roll up that map, it will not be wanted these ten years."), so Sir Edward Grey summed up the end of the *belle époque* ("The lamps are going out all over Europe; we shall not see them lit again in our lifetime.").

Under the hot August sun, corn still waved in fields soon to be brilliant with poppies, red as the blood which would drench them. The ordinary French soldier, the *poilu*, went through this smiling countryside to war, resolute and determined, responding to the cry, "*la patrie en danger*," as thousands of his like had done. He did not dream that he and a million and a half of his fellows, millions of his allies must die; that his country would be devastated, ruined financially and suffer spiritual damage as well. The war to end all wars began in sunshine and movement. Trench warfare, with lice-ridden men living underground, with undefined fronts moving a few yards this way or that over ground where corpses rotted in the mud that waited to engulf living men, was a thing of the future.

Fighting men on both sides believed that the war would be over by Christmas.

The German High Command shared the belief that this would be a brief war. They had a plan, prepared well in advance, named after the man who had worked on it, General von Schlieffen, who had been helped by General von Moltke, a nephew of the von Moltke of the Franco-Prussian war. The line of French fortifications at the frontier was to be by-passed by the invasion of Belgium—a mere walk-through—and German forces would be at the rear of the French defense, and heading for control of the Channel ports. The planners visualized a repetition of 1870.

Like Napoleon before them, and with better reason, the Germans discounted Russia; she was a country with troubles of her own; she was vast, and like all great things, slow to get into motion. If the Schlieffen plan worked the war would be over and won before Russia was mobilized.

France's other ally seemed equally negligible. England had what the Kaiser called "a contemptible little army." In numbers and terms of heavy equipment it was contemptible, but the British Expeditionary Force which landed in France on August 9, 1914, was made up of men who by their performance converted the gibe into a title of honor. For more than half a century survivors, proudly calling themselves "the Old Contemptibles" were to go on parade, in dwindling numbers, age and infirmity defied, the Mons Star shining on their often shabby, though well-pressed, jackets.

The France which the Germans visualized as going into action with these two ineffectual allies was the France of the public image which she had for so long presented to the world, full of revolutionaries and pacifists who could be relied upon in a crisis to stir agitation and dissension. The France which actually took the field was fired with the old spirit of '92, further inflamed by resentments nourished since 1870.

And Belgium, instead of opening the door and allowing the invaders free passage, resisted this violation of her territory with the valor and determination that gained her the name of "gallant little Belgium." In places the resistance might hold up the German advance for no more than a day; but the Schlieffen plan foresaw the complete overrunning of France in forty days. On so tight a schedule every day counted.

Economists and their kin also reckoned on a short war; modern economic life was too complex, they reckoned, to support for long the upheavals and demands of full-scale war. Countries were now too interdependent: modern warfare demanded that behind the fighting army there must be another of munition workers; no country could for long recruit for both. Nobody, as yet, realized how little food a human being actually *needs*, or remembered that, until very lately in the history of mankind, most of the heaviest work had been done by men who ate meat seldom, and luxuries not at all.

So, for military and economic reasons this must be a short war. It turned out to be, "war on an unimaginably bigger scale than all the wars of previous history. It was an altogether unprecedented exhibition of human energy, human destructiveness, and human endurance."* On the Western Front it was to be virtually one battle, prolonged for four and a half years. It was to introduce new weapons—the Zeppelin, the airplane, poison gas and the submarine.

In the Vosges, the battle at first went well for the French. They took the heights of the Donon on August 14, and an advancing *poilu* scrawled, *"On les aura* [We'll get them]." Four terrible years were to pass before another could add a postscript, *"On les a eu* [We did]."

The Schlieffen plan, meeting so many unexpected obstacles, failed in its entirety; but by August 20 the Germans were in Brussels, and the British had retreated from Mons—despite the angelic intervention, in which at the time many people honestly believed. On September 2 Germans were in Senlis, only forty miles

* D. C. Somerville, *A History of Western Europe 1815–1926.*

from Paris; and from the Eastern front came news that the Russians, lumbering into action, had been defeated at Tannenberg, with prisoners rounded up "like cattle."

The French government moved, as once before, to Bordeaux. And there were other more painfully accomplished movements from East to West. Just ahead of the advancing German army were the refugees, people from Artois and Picardy, from the sandy region of the Boulonnais and from the rich vineyards of Champagne, making for what they regarded as the safe regions, for sun-baked Provence, the country of the Tarn and the Dordogne, where rivers ran swiftly through limestone gorges, not like the rivers at home and everything else was almost equally alien, dialect, customs . . .

The Germans were feared; Prussian behavior a hundred years previously had become part of the tales old men tell; the *pickelhaube*, the pointed helmet of 1870, had become a symbol of fear, not only in France but in countries that had never seen one except in pictures. And now there were terrible stories of atrocities in Belgium. It was rational to suppose that Belgium, which had placed the first obstacle in the path of the German advance, should suffer the weight of German displeasure. Nobody waited to ask whether anybody had actually seen a Belgian baby hung from a hook in a butcher's shop, or whether an advancing army would pause to play a game that involved throwing Belgian children into the air and catching them on bayonet points. German—and the word now included the sentimental, good-natured Bavarians—meant Prussian, and Prussians were now Huns, a term of terror since Attila, dead these fifteen hundred years. Some old race memory revived on that word and even in England, safe behind the Channel and the Fleet, rumors were shudderingly believed. Those with the enemy on the doorstep loaded up farm wagons, horses, mules, their own shoulders, and set off, the thunder of the guns speeding their progress. Women heavily pregnant trudged beside a heavily laden horse or handcart; and presently some man, fighting in the northwest would be the father of a child he would never see.

With a population one third less than that of Germany, France could only bring an army inferior in numbers to meet the invaders; Belgium, overrun, could help little and, though in England the recruiting offices were crowded, volunteers must be provided with uniforms and arms and given some training, however sketchy. Retreat was inevitable but, under the command of General Joffre, it was disciplined, and on the Marne he was able to make a stand and score a victory.

Joffre, known to his troops as "Papa Joffre," was sixty-two, short in stature, with a swelling paunch over which his tunic stretched tightly. His career proved that under the Third Republic advancement was open to all; he was one of an artisan's eleven children and by way of the lycée and the Ecole Polytechnique had entered the army; in the colonial service he had worked alongside men like Galliéni and Lyautey and acquired method, the ability to remain calm in crisis, a taste for responsibility and the self-confidence essential in a commander.

Like other French commanders he was haunted by the memory of Metz, of Bazaine being shut up there, useless, finally to emerge and be looked upon as a criminal. Joffre believed in the war of movement, in the value of railways and any other form of transport. In his memoirs he wrote, "The art of war consists of doing that which in normal times appears impossible." Not an original thought since wars have always demanded the impossible of their participants, but perhaps when he wrote the sentence Joffre was remembering the day when, with the railways blocked with trains full of wounded and evacuees, and no army vehicles available, the French went to war by taxicab.

In Paris, in a shadowy corner at the end of the Cour d'Honneur of the Invalides, there stands an ancient motorcar with a high chassis and a tarpaulin stretched over the driver's seat—a Paris taxicab of 1914, which will stand there in a place of honor until it falls apart from sheer age. It represents 250 of its kind which, crammed with men sitting on one another's knees, carried the necessary reinforcements to Joffre at a critical moment and enabled him to win the battle of the Marne. In all, the taxis transported nearly 4000 men; their drivers were thanked by General Galliéni, who had organized them, and they were given a citation for their zeal, but they were not paid the full charge registered on their meters because in their effort to save France they had committed an offense. They had carried more than three passengers at a time!

The Schlieffen plan had failed; the opposing armies dug in and men began to lead a troglodyte life in trenches and holes. The digging and the heavy shelling disrupted all drainage systems and with winter came the mud, deep enough in places to engulf a man who fell wounded, or even an active one who chanced to slip off the duckboards. On the Western Front the war was at a standstill, but it was not quite static; men died horribly and in great numbers in order to advance a few yards, usually only to be driven back again. On the barbed-wire entanglements, wounded men hung until they stank. Rats and lice added misery to a way of life so inimical to human existence that the enemy, the man suffering similar wretchedness in the opposite trench, often seemed, by comparison, a friend. Brief periods of fraternization at Christmas and innumerable war poems bear witness to this attitude, a new one in the history of conflict and one which was not to be without its effect on future thinking and policies.

In other places there was a war of movement. Turkey had entered the war early on the German side, and now, to compensate for the stalemate on the Western Front and in compliance with the Russian request that something should be done to establish direct communication through the Black Sea, French, English and Australian forces made an attempt to strike at what, in a later war, was called "the soft underbelly of Europe." But the attempt on the Dardanelles failed, and the Gallipoli campaign, though it added to the roll of magnificent deeds—the Australians and New Zealanders particularly distinguished themselves—made no appreciable contribution to the furtherance of the war.

In December 1914, the French government returned to Paris, and the Assembly resumed its sittings. During the early weeks of the war Joffre had been given almost unlimited authority and national life had been almost suspended, but this was not a state of affairs that could continue indefinitely. Though the needs of the army were paramount the civil population and many non-military matters must be given some consideration. It was realised that any runaway rise in the cost of living would damage the war effort, so rationing and controls must be imposed; and the colossal cost of the war must be met. To pay for armies in the field and the armaments they needed France gradually spent all her foreign investments; then taxes were increased and enormous sums borrowed from abroad. The French people were asked to make unprecedented sacrifices, and they responded magnificently. In industry and in agriculture women took the place of men and everybody worked long and hard for *les braves poilus*.

The resumption of parliamentary sittings added complications because the politicians felt that war was too serious a business to be left entirely to the generals, but every attempt of the civilians to direct operations brought head-on conflict with the High Command. Joffre, so far as he was able, by-passed politicians and in so doing roused animosity that was to redound on his head. Between Millerand, Minister of War, and the Chamber so much hostility developed that it brought down Viviani's government, in which the people had already lost confidence as they realized that this war might be indefinitely prolonged.

Briand became Premier and faithfully adhered to the idea of the "sacred union," but no lip-service to unity could prevent political disputes, to which now was added the question as whether parliament or the army should dictate military strategy. And in the army itself there was dissension. Joffre remained attached to the principle of the war of movement; Pétain and Foch held that the aim should be to wear down the enemy, that the war of attrition could be won. Pétain in particular pinned his faith to fire-power and the famous French '75s; he believed that artillery should win the ground which the infantry could then occupy.

As 1915 drew to its close France and her allies were not alone in wishing to end the stalemate. Von Falkenhayn, the German chief of the general staff, was equally anxious to come to a speedy decision and planned to attack his enemy where he had no line of retreat and could be destroyed where he stood. This could be done if the line of French fortifications could be breached at Verdun, its center; once a gap was made the Germans could swoop round and take the French from the rear. But Verdun held out for six months under massive assault, one of the longest and bloodiest battles of the war. Von Falkenhayn had been right about the French dying where they stood, 362,000 of them, but they yielded no more than a few yards of ground and the survivors gritted their teeth on the words, "*Ils ne passeront pas* [They shall not pass]." Once again the German advance was halted; for attempting and failing von Falkenhayn was dismissed.

The hero of Verdun was Philippe Pétain who, by his defense, won the respect of his men and the admiration of the world. Through "the hell of Verdun" he had shown his capacity for organization by the arrangements made behind the front line to bring up supplies and relief forces; he had also shown a marked distaste for the wastage of men's lives; he was a defensive rather than an aggressive tactician, and most of the dead had died in defensive positions.

Pétain, like Joffre, came of humble stock but had succeeded in reaching St. Cyr—the French equivalent of West Point and Sandhurst. When he took command of an Army Corps in 1914 he was fifty-eight.

After Verdun came the Somme, an allied attack which opened in June 1916 in fine summer weather and died down in the next winter's mud. The total casualties, French, English and German, numbered almost a million, and there were no victors. The senselessness and futility of mass slaughter were becoming apparent. Men asked themselves how long such wholesale massacre could continue; how long before there were no men left to fight.

The war-weariness and the impatience which were afflicting both sides evidenced themselves in changes of government and of High Commands. Field Marshal von Hindenburg and General von Ludendorff replaced von Falkenhayn, and in France "Papa" Joffre was dismissed and the command given to Nivelle. The victor of the Marne was retired with every possible outward mark of admiration and respect, but the trimmings could not conceal the fact of dismissal.

In England Asquith resigned from his post as Prime Minister

and was succeeded by the fiery little Welshman, Lloyd George, who set himself, among other things, the aim of improving the output of munitions.

In Russia the sinister monk Rasputin, who had exercised so dominant, and often fatal, influence upon the Russian royal family, was assassinated.

In the United States there was no change. She endeavored to stand aside from the squabbles of Europe and many of her citizens, though English-speaking, were by blood or by history, anti-English in sympathy. America's invitation to the world, "Give me your poor . . ." had brought Germans, Austrians, people from the Balkans, and the Irish whose dislike of the English was inborn. There were vast spaces in America from which Europe seemed as remote as the moon. Public sentiment had been outraged by the sinking, in 1915, of the passenger ship *Lusitania*, with the loss of over a hundred American lives, but the re-election of Woodrow Wilson on a program of strict neutrality was indicative of the general feeling. He had made one attempt to mediate and bring the combatants to the conference table; he made another, equally abortive.

Gradually anti-German feeling hardened; the promise that submarine war should not be waged on neutral ships was not kept. Then Germany tried to entice Mexico into the war, promising in return help in the recovery of territories, once Mexican, now part of the United States. Wilson's neutrality was severely criticized. A public speaker who declared that "the Kaiser should be boiled in oil," was wildly acclaimed. In April 1917, the United States declared war on Germany and that was the real turning of the tide.

Yet for the Allies the year which was to see the entry of a new ally, fresh and full of vitality, had opened badly. The Germans had started the unlimited submarine warfare which was intended to starve out the British, and nearly attained its objective. In Russia the long overdue revolution was about to break out. From the very start of the war the German aim had been to put such pressure upon Russia that she would sue for a separate peace and thus release German forces for the Western Front. The Russian peasant, most patient of creatures, had been mobilized in tens of thousands and thrown, ill-equipped—even rifles were in short supply—into battle against the best prepared modern army in the world; he had fought with unbelievable bravery and died. But there is an end to patience. "On March 8th, 1917, riots broke out in Petrograd. They began with the sacking of bakers' shops; they ended with the overthrow of world order."* Nicholas II, Czar of all the Russias, was forced to abdicate, and a provisional government, willing to make terms with the Germans, was set up.

Speed, always important, now became the paramount issue—in March for the Allies who must do what they could before the German forces from the East could be deployed on the Western Front; in April for the Germans who must demolish the Allies before America's vast resources of men and material could be mobilized and effective.

In April 1917, two offensives were launched; one in Champagne, by the French, one in Artois, by the British. General Nivelle planned a frontal attack upon the Germans and he had the support of President Poincaré; the attack promised the liberation of Lorraine, Poincaré's native soil. Before Nivelle's preparations were complete the Germans feinted a withdrawal and Nivelle gave pursuit, thinking that the war of movement had begun. The weather was foul, the rain so incessant that guns were bogged down, the visibility so poor that air activity was hampered. Nivelle, however, stuck to his plan and incurred enormous losses.

He had reckoned that his wounded would be cared for in the hospitals of the towns he captured; but he had taken no towns and he had 120,000 casualties. The wounded were sent by train, not to Paris, where plenty of beds were available, but to other places reached by by-passing Paris at the cost of some deaths and much pain. It was felt that the hospital trains would have a deplorable effect upon the morale of the capital. However, generals who had opposed Nivelle's plan, among them Pétain, did not fail to inform their parliamentary friends of the extent of the disaster and news of the losses aroused fury in the Chamber. Nivelle, undeterred, opened another offensive which resulted in 150,000 casualties. Following upon previous severe losses, a battle in which

* John Terraine, *The Great War 1914–1919.*

more than a quarter of a million men were killed or wounded seemed more than any country could stand, or any army bear.

The diversion of the hospital trains held a hint that the army had doubts about civilian morale and a cartoon expressing the doubts has passed its caption into the French language and national tradition. Two *poilus* were depicted discussing the war. One said, "If only they hold out." "If who holds out?" "The civilians."

Actually, in 1917, it was not the civilians who failed to hold out. At the end of May mutinies began in the French army on the Chemin des Dames sector. The soldiers had borne thirty-four months of misery and slaughter, they had seen a massive offensive badly prepared and badly directed result in trivial gain and ghastly loss of life; in many corps there were complaints about an unjust system of granting leave; but above all the soldiers had lost faith in Nivelle, who stubbornly persisted in his own ideas and gave no regard to the realities of the situation.

There was no lack of excellent officers, commissioned and non-commissioned, no lack of courage or of material; blame for the defeat fell on the generals, above all on the Commander in Chief. The parliament intervened to stop the battle, and a commission of inquiry was set up to investigate Nivelle's handling of the battle. It found that he did not measure up to the task that he had undertaken.

Once again the truth of Rochambeau's words, written nearly 150 years earlier, was proved: "There are no men easier to defeat when they have lost confidence in their leaders, and they lose it once they have been endangered through personal and selfish ambition."

It was not only in their military leaders that the soldiers had lost confidence; the ordinary civilian, overworked and underfed, was holding out staunchly, but the same could not be said for the parliamentarians. Pacifism had not died with Jaurès, and in the Chamber an anti-militarist and defeatist attitude was increasingly evident. Louis Malvy, who had held the post of Minister of the Interior since 1914, and Caillaux—back in political life—were suspected of favoring a negotiated peace with Germany, even of meditating a *coup d'état* which would make Caillaux master of France.

In his slimy, stinking trench the French soldier was virtually cut off from the outside world and, lacking real news, gave a ready ear to rumor. There were stories that Paris was in revolt and that crowds were being shot down in the streets; there were stories of the luxury in which munition workers lived, while soldiers rotted away in filth. Subversive and pacifist literature found a way into the trenches, was read, handed on and talked about.

Soldiers knew that America had declared war in April, but America was far away; and news from Russia was disappointing when it reached the ears of men accustomed since childhood to stirring stories of the wars of their revolution, of the *leveé en masse* and the volunteers of '92. They expected that the Russians, having made their revolution, would fall upon the Germans and overcome them as the soldiers of revolutionary France had fallen upon the Austrian invaders. This did not happen; Lenin brought peace and anarchy, not the revival of the martial spirit.

No single factor would have led to mutiny, but the cumulative effect was overwhelming. Beginning in May when a colonial division refused to re-enter the line, the contagion spread and lasted into June. In all 115 regiments were affected. Nobody cried "To Berlin!" Berlin and the determination to get there were forgotten: the cry was, "Peace, peace, down with war!" If anybody sang, it was not the "Marseillaise," it was the "Internationale." The form the mutiny took varied from unit to unit; whole battalions refused in some places to re-enter the front line, but were willing to defend their rear-line positions if attacked; some groups planned a march on Paris; others simply deserted and went to live like vagabonds upon what they could find; some turned upon their officers. It was the nearest France had come to revolution since 1848.

Nivelle was removed, Pétain took his place and proved himself to be an excellent restorer of calm and confidence. A peasant born, he understood the ordinary man and his reactions; he was known to be careful with the lives of those he commanded. He also understood the need for tempering justice with mercy; of the many who had mutinied only twenty-three were executed. He also had the virtue of patience; he was prepared to let the army recoup its strength and hold its positions to wait until the impact of American participation could make itself felt.

The truly astounding thing about this mutiny of the French army is that it took place and collapsed without the German High Command learning what was afoot.

Pétain waited for the Americans; English soldiers around Arras, their tenuous hold endangered first by the mutiny and then by Pétain's go-slow tactics, had a new song, "The Yanks are coming." Yankee had never been a term of particular approbation; it had connotations of newness, brashness, money-grubbing. Now, when the old world had literally fought itself to a standstill, the word acquired an almost messianic quality.

They landed in June 1917, an advance contingent under the command of General Pershing, who on arrival said, "Lafayette, we are here."

Lafayette had fought and shed his blood in the War of American Independence and helped to bring the United States into being; now the debt was about to be paid off.

The very appearance of the newcomers was impressive. A whole generation of French and English—and German—youth was dead, or maimed or old before its time. Contemporary photographs record the haggard, dogged, ill-fed faces of men who had been schoolboys when the war began and had yet to see—if they lived—their twentieth birthday; and the faces of older men who had by chance survived, gone into battle, been withdrawn, even granted leave, sent back again. It was a long time since Europe had seen a really young man, looking young and not hungry. Surface and submarine warfare had sent countless tons of food to the sea's bottom, and though in every army the ration was better than that allocated to the civilian, before it reached the mouth for which it was intended it ran the hazard of interrupted supply routes and the activities of the army cook. Real food, like all genuine things, ages and decays, but an article known as a biscuit, issued to a soldier about to come on leave and brought home as a curiosity, "this we eat," was bored through, not without difficulty, and hung from a kitchen beam. In seven years it never changed its consistency.

The sight of the Americans was heartening; but their build-up was slow, and Pershing held out on his point that his should be a separate army, under its own command, a point justified by the quibbling and dissensions rampant in the Anglo-French alliance.

American entry into the war—though Château-Thierry and Belleau Wood and the Argonne were still a year distant—had as deep a psychological effect upon Germany as upon the Allies, but in the reverse direction. No new country with infinite resources was coming to *her* rescue and what allies she had were becoming more of a liability than an asset. Also her civilian front was weakening. (Snap judgments are to be avoided; perhaps some Frenchwomen, some Englishwomen, did write to their men in the trenches in such terms as were contained in a letter found on a German soldier's body, "I have lost 10 pounds' weight. I am afraid it will soon be all over with us . . ." Firsthand experience supplies the memory of packing up, from the meager civilian ration, a food parcel for the relative in the trench and the resolute suppression of any discouraging piece of news.)

One possible reason for this weakening of the German civilian front was the great distinction always made there between soldier and civilian. The professional soldier was a member of a privileged class, given priority even on the street pavement and now, though the army was made up of ordinary men, fathers, husbands, brothers, something of the long-suppressed resentment made itself felt in this critical hour. Also, the army, so much revered, so greatly privileged, had failed to achieve the swift victory that had once seemed so certain. To the French and to the English and to the Americans, soldiers had never meant quite what they had been to the Germans; nor perhaps had food, despite the French reputation for cookery, fundamentally based on the principle of "make do." German housewives needed solid ingredients. They wrote to men in the trenches about the potato shortage.

In July 1917, the Crown Prince of Germany, the "Little Willie" so beloved of the cartoonists, wrote to his father: "If Germany does not achieve peace before the end of the year the dangers of revolution are imminent." On two ships of the German navy mutinies occurred.

The French Premier, Ribot, who had succeeded Briand in March 1918, was in turn succeeded by Paul Painlevé, a moderate Republican who failed to bring order into a government now afflicted with lassitude. An international Socialist congress met in Stockholm to call for a negotiated peace, but it met without any French delegates (they had been refused passports); as a result the French Socialists abandoned the *union sacreé* and took no further part in the government. There was a press campaign which attacked the President, the British—who had borne the brunt of the war in Flanders—and by implication the war itself, and paradoxically, the two Radical ministers, Malvy and Caillaux, who were suspected of trying to bring the war to an end.

In such a muddled mental climate the spy mania flourished. Even in stolid England to own a dachshund dog was to be suspect, but France had something specially exotic in the spy line—Mata Hari. Her story has been fully exploited. In real life she was a Dutchwoman who performed Indonesian dances—inexpertly, say those qualified to judge—and possibly her espionage was equally unimportant. Some spectacular example was needed, however, and Mata Hari was executed and given a crumb of immortality.

Painlevé could not hold out against the criticism and the scandals, especially those involving Malvy and Caillaux; Malvy was convicted of using public funds to subsidize a defeatist paper, Caillaux was imprisoned for treason. In October Painlevé resigned, and President Poincaré called upon Georges Clemenceau to form a government.

In the choice of Clemenceau Poincaré showed that for him national interest overrode any personal consideration. He and Clemenceau were mutually antagonistic, but it was plain that for the prosecution of the war the services of a strong man were needed. Poincaré would probably have liked to take up the role of strong man, but he was President and subject to constitutional restrictions and he played the political game by the rules. He and Clemenceau had one thing in common; they were both completely opposed to the idea of a negotiated peace that might leave the fate of Alsace-Lorraine in jeopardy.

Clemenceau stands head and shoulders above the rest of the brilliant men which the Third Republic, for all its weaknesses, produced. He was the last survivor of those men of the early Republic who had refused mentally to accept the loss of Alsace-Lorraine as final. Throughout the war years he had been a constant and trenchant critic of military incompetence; he had been eloquently scornful of the weak, the hesitant and the defeatist. Now, with the massive support of the Chamber behind him—his appointment had been approved by 418 votes to 65—the Tiger moved into battle, an old tiger, seventy-six years old, growling, *"Je fais la guerre."* Nothing else mattered and nobody was allowed to interfere with this one-line program.

Clemenceau was thirty-three years older than Churchill whose career was, in so many ways, to follow the same pattern—long years in the political wilderness, clinging tenaciously to certain beliefs, emergence in old age to save a country where he had been treated with neglect and scorn.

In those winter months of 1917–18 France had need of a strong man; in October the Russian revolution flared with even greater violence, and in December the Germans attained what they had long wanted, a separate peace, which would release men and armaments for the west. Italy, an ally since 1915, had been defeated at Caporetto. The northeastern Departments of France were now a bloody morass, "a lunar landscape" marked by the ruins of Gothic cathedrals and the stumps of blasted trees. Hundreds of thousands of people were homeless in their own country. And for every dead man there was at least one woman wearing mourning crape, which was so much in demand for widows' veils and armbands that the textile factories worked overtime to meet the demand.

The civilians continued to hold out; the army, purged of the defeatism that had bubbled to the surface earlier in the year, fought on with courage and determination, and Clemenceau, while making war, cleansed political life of its worst elements. Malvy was tried for treason and acquitted on that charge but sentenced to five years' banishment for subversive activities. (In 1924 he received a full pardon and was re-elected as a deputy; in 1926 he was back at his old post as Minister of the Interior. He died in 1949.) Malvy had been weak and defeatist rather than treacherous, but Caillaux' case was rather different because politically he was both more prominent and more powerful than Malvy. He was imprisoned and after the war tried on a charge of corresponding and associating with the enemy while on a government mission in South America. He, too, was amnestied in 1924; he, too, showed the phoenixlike quality shared by so many French politicians; he returned to political life as a senator in 1928 and died in the middle of another war at the age of eighty.

The year 1918 opened with a message from President Wilson in which he laid down his Fourteen Points, his war and peace aims. They included renunciation of secret diplomatic negotiations, freedom of the seas, reduction of armaments, evacuation of countries overrun by Germany and her allies, the liberation of France and the restoration of Alsace and Lorraine and, final point, the formation of a general association of nations to guarantee the political independence of all states.

A clear statement of war aims was necessary, since it was now obvious that the war was entering its final phase. Hindenburg and Ludendorff realized that if the decision was to be made in their favor it must be made quickly. In March 1918, with men brought from the Russian front after the Treaty of Brest-Litovsk, and from the Italian front after Caporetto, they were numerically superior, able to put into the field twenty more divisions than the Allies. They must seize their chance before the influx of American forces tipped the balance of numbers against them.

The new attack, launched in March, had as its aim the driving of a wedge between the British in Flanders and Picardy—mainly concerned with covering the Channel ports so that, if the worst happened, retreat by sea was assured—and the French, whose preoccupation was the protection of Paris.

In two days' battle on the Somme the German aim was achieved and they broke through into the open country northwest of Saint-Quentin. Now the British were in trouble, wholly exposed on their right flank, and Haig, the British commander, who had no reserves, appealed to Pétain to throw in his. Pétain, cautious and pessimistic by nature, refused.

Clemenceau had always been aware that one of his most urgent tasks was to bring about closer unity between the Allies; and it was no easy one. "Differences of language, temperament, weapons, and command and supply systems always made close co-operation between French and British very chancy."* Hitherto the two armies had fought under separate commands but now Haig, seeing that war might well be lost in a matter of days, telegraphed to London, asking that "General Foch or some other determined general, who would fight," should be given supreme control.

Foch had fought his first battles in 1870; aged sixty-seven, he was regarded as an old man, fit only for minor posts; but he came from a family of fighting men, one of his grandfathers had been an officer in Napoleon's Grand Army, and Haig knew him as "a man of great courage and decision." Once brought out of the armchair which the French command had deemed to be his place, he showed by his magnetism and determination how wrong they had been, and how right was Haig.

Under the unified command the Allies halted the Germans once more, but not for long. In April Ludendorff launched another desperate offensive, and Haig issued his famous Order of the Day: "Victory will belong to the side that holds out longest. There is no other course open to us but to fight it out. Every position must be held to the last man; there must be no retirement. With our backs to the wall and believing in the justice of our cause, each one of us must fight on to the end."

His battered forces, English, Australian and Canadian, fought on to the end, with frightful losses and the advance was halted. There were however signs that the Germans were wearying, too.

The years 1914–18 produced a new element of terror—bombardment from the air, which threatened the entire civilian population.

* John Terraine, *The Great War 1914–1919.*

Things had changed very swiftly since the time when the founder of the Red Cross, because he was a civilian, could drive his carriage across the field of Solferino, where battle had raged so recently that its wounded were not yet dead. Beginning with raids from Zeppelins and followed by those from the swifter and more deadly airplane, war was now waged directly upon people far from any front. Paris and London had already been targets, and when the great German offensive was launched in the spring of 1918, Paris braced herself to meet massive bombardment from the air. It did not come. Instead, with no air-raid warning, no sight or sound of aircraft, came loud explosions and the identification of fragments of a large shell. People were incredulous. In order to shell Paris the Germans must be within a range of twenty miles, yet were known to be at least three times that distance away. They must, then, be using guns of unprecedented range. For 139 days the people of Paris lived under this new menace which did not, however, bring about the demoralization which the Germans had hoped. The civilians still held out.

On August 12 the shelling suddenly ceased. Under pressure of a big French offensive—the second victory of the Marne—the Germans withdrew, taking with them their long-range guns, one of which was nicknamed Big Bertha, after the daughter of the armaments manufacturer, von Krupp. The massive gun emplacements, with the ranges neatly written on the walls, remained, but nobody ever found Big Bertha. In the area from which she vanished, after her attempted reign of terror, there is a pool where now children fish and frogs croak in the weedy water, and nearby is a clearing in a little wood which local legend holds was Big Bertha's site.

By now the Germans had lost the initiative, the Americans were pouring into France. Every French and English ship that could possibly be spared had been helping with the transport of American soldiers, and every ship was bringing men only; the Allies could provide equipment. In airplanes and in that new weapon, the tank, the Allies had superiority. France was one vast arsenal.

By September the German High Command was thinking about an armistice; they had no ally now, it was said, but the French politicians who clamored for peace gained nothing but contempt from Clemenceau.

The old Tiger, with a stick to help support the burden of his seventy-seven years, went with Poincaré to the front, where he said, "The situation is improving hourly. Our reserves are intact and we are separated from the enemy by a formidable iron curtain which no human force can penetrate."

To Lloyd George he telegraphed: "You can cross the Channel peacefully. We are calm, strong and sure of what tomorrow will bring."

On his return to the Chamber Clemenceau was met with an ovation designed to frustrate a manifestation of the Socialist left. One Socialist turned on his fellows and cried, "The Boches will not pass even if you insist on opening the door to them. I have just come back from the front. My confidence is absolute."

On September 3 the Chamber held its last sitting before dispersing. Of its members elected in 1914, twelve had been killed in action and thirteen seriously wounded, among them a young man named André Maginot.

One by one Germany's allies collapsed dramatically, Bulgaria, Turkey, then Austria. The Allies rolled forward across the plains of Picardy and Flanders, through the poor, broken villages with immortal names, Beaumont-Hamel, Bapaume, Saint-Quentin, the Argonne—taken by the Americans—on and on, to be greeted tumultuously by those who, through it all, had clung to their shattered homes and ruined acres.

As the Germans retreated revolution broke out in Germany; it was no longer safe for a soldier to appear on the street in the uniform which he had done nothing to disgrace. On November 9 a Republic was declared in Berlin, and the Kaiser fled to Holland. In Austria the Emperor Charles, who had succeeded his old great-uncle, Franz Josef, in 1916, abdicated. The Russian Czar and his family had been murdered in July; so, with the millions of casualties of this war, could be reckoned three empires.

Germany, though beaten, was thinking of an armistice in terms which might permit the regrouping of her forces and the renewal of the struggle. Such delusive ideas were soon dispelled. With white flags flying and a trumpet sounding, the German delegates drove through the Allied lines and came to Rethondes in the forest of Compiègne—once the scene of gay hunting parties. There General Foch had made a railway train his headquarters.

The newly appointed German Secretary of State, Erzberger, told Foch that they had come to receive the Allied proposals.

"I have," Foch said coldly, "no proposals to make."

"We ask the conditions of an armistice."

"I have no conditions to make."

But every day's fighting, the Germans urged, increased the danger of Bolshevism sweeping over Europe. Foch was unimpressed. It was the German, not the Allied soldier who was hoisting the red flag and throwing away his weapons. No one was even very sure if any government now existed in Germany. It was Hindenburg who had told Erzberger that there was no alternative but to ask for, and sign, an armistice on any terms.

At the eleventh hour of the eleventh day of the eleventh month of 1918 the cease-fire sounded all along the front, and the four-and-a-half-year war was over. By a freakish chance, just before eleven o'clock that morning, the British had entered Mons, where they had fought their first battle in August 1914. Between the two dates 12,000,000 people had died—some authorities reckon this too low an estimate.

Hindenburg had said, "The side which has the best nerves will win." The French, fighting on their own soil, had shown nerve, tenacity and endurance; civilians as well as soldiers had held out. France had also had stout Allies; the fighting retreats, the hold-on-to-death-and-three-days-after defenses of the British and of men from the Dominions had often saved the day, and the effect of American intervention should not be underestimated.

On November 11 the world went mad with joy. In Paris the crape was ripped from the statue representing Strasbourg in the Place de la Concorde, and the flowers at its feet were no longer mourning wreaths. Of all the terms of the Armistice—the evacuation of occupied territory, the surrender of all German submarines, the internment in Allied or neutral ports of all German fighting ships—the return of the "lost provinces" probably meant most to the average Frenchman. The wound that had ached for almost half a century was healed.

In the Chamber, Clemenceau, now with a new popular name, "*le Père la Victoire*," struck a somber and realistic note. In announcing the Armistice he said, "We shall have to win the peace and that perhaps will be more difficult."

Chapter 4. BETWEEN THE WARS

Winning the peace meant building a new world from ruins, and this, from the material point of view alone, was something to daunt all but the staunchest heart. In France 5,000,000 acres of land lay waste, for four and a half years plowed only by the tramping feet of soldiers, knowing no wheel but those of the gun carriages and yielding no harvest save dead men. A year, two years, might see them partially recovered; the recovery of land upon which poison gas had fallen would take longer, perhaps an incalculable time. Almost 10,000 factories had been destroyed or badly damaged; the railways were in ruin, cattle and other live-stock reduced to a bare minimum, coal and steel supplies exhausted.

Worst of all was the loss of men. This damage must be repaired by a population from which 8,000,000 able-bodied men had gone to war. A million and a half would never come back; 3,500,000 had been wounded and many of these were permanently disabled. This was a desperate situation for a country which had, by 1914, barely made up her loss of men in an earlier war, had suffered a falling birth rate, and now lost a generation and the children that men of that generation should have fathered. The hands that should have guided the plow, garnered the grapes, done intricate jobs in factories were stilled forever. The ghost of Arthur Young, riding through France in this postwar time, would have observed the preponderance of old men and women in the fields, and how few children played in the streets.

A fictional Frenchman with only one leg spoke for many—as fictional characters do—"Je m'en fiche de ma jambe. Elle reste en Alsace regagnée, ou elle se trouve fort bien."* He did not care a straw for his leg; it lay in regained Alsace and it was happy. But France now needed able-bodied men.

* Tennyson Jesse, A Pin to See the Peepshow.

Other combatants were in similar need; and all were smitten by the final blow, the aftermath of war. When the red horse of the Apocalypse prances into battle, the pale horse of pestilence is never far behind. Across stricken Europe stalked the pestilence known as "Spanish influenza." On people already debilitated by malnutrition, anxiety and fear, it worked havoc and in the end killed more people than the war itself; but it was less selective and did not confine itself to men in their prime.

The loss of men could never be made good, but material damage could be paid for, and Germany must pay. Twice in a little more than a hundred years France had been loaded with heavy indemnities and she had paid them, swiftly and with pride. She had no doubt that her beaten enemy would show the same national dignity nor that, however enormous might be the sum exacted, she would pay. France had yet to learn.

On January 19, 1919, the Peace Conference opened at Versailles. It was attended by hundreds of delegates, but only four really counted, the Big Four: President Wilson, in person, representing the United States; Lloyd George, England; Orlando, Italy; and Clemenceau, France. That *le Père la Victoire* should speak for the country he had done so much to lead to victory was only fitting, and the nation put its trust in the man whom it knew to be devoted entirely to its interests.

Throughout the war Clemenceau had cherished one aim—the total defeat of Germany; that attained, his plan for peace was equally simple. Any further aggression by Germany must be made impossible and compensation must be paid. He was not alone in this; Sir Eric Geddes, a member of the British Imperial War Cabinet, spoke of squeezing Germany like a lemon, "until you can hear the pips squeak."

By May 7 the text of the Treaty was ready to be handed to the Germans, whose delegates had been allowed to take no part in the negotiations. (The world had changed since Talleyrand attended the Congress of Vienna and spoken for defeated France.) Being allowed no voice, Germany could afterward claim that she had been the victim of a *diktat*, an ultimatum which she must accept and, since the German nation would not agree to the "war guilt" clause which held them culpable of starting the war, the seeds of the next one had begun to germinate before the ink was dry on the signatures.

Alsace and Lorraine returned to France, which was also to occupy for fifteen years the Saar region, rich in iron and coal; at the end of the term the Saar was to settle its own future by means of plebiscite: parts of East Prussian territory were to be ceded to Poland, with Danzig an internationally administered port; the German army was limited to 100,000 men with no heavy weapons, no aircraft, no General Staff; the navy was to consist of small ships, no submarines, no air auxiliaries; provision was made for the trial of the Kaiser and other war leaders; and all German colonies were to be distributed among the other powers under a system of mandates.

People yet to be born were to judge these terms as both harsh and provocative; the men who dictated them had just emerged from the worst war in history and were dedicated to the belief that they were guarding against a recurrence. Neither England nor America had grieved over lost territory within living memory; but Clemenceau had felt very strongly about Alsace and Lorraine. Did he never speculate on what the loss of the Saar, East Prussia, and those lately-come-by colonies would mean to Germany? He was probably more concerned, at the moment, with the concessions which he had been obliged to make to President Wilson. The system of reparations and the use of the Saar mines for fifteen years seemed a poor substitute for the war indemnity upon which France wished to insist.

Of even graver consequence for the future was her Allies' refusal to allow France to fix her frontier on the natural boundary of the Rhine. Clemenceau fought hard for this, but was overruled and forced to accept instead an Anglo-American guarantee of aid to France should she ever again become the subject of direct aggression. Clemenceau came to occupy an invidious position; Wilson and Lloyd George considered him harsh in his demands; his own people thought him too lenient and were disappointed.

Disappointment turned to dismay when the United States Senate refused to ratify the Treaty of Versailles and the Anglo-American guarantee of security. Although the League of Nations was a direct growth from one of President Wilson's Fourteen Points, America did not become a member. Nevertheless, the League of Nations struggled on without American support for almost twenty years; it was not entirely unsuccessful in regulating causes of disagreement and conflict among its members but its greatest achievement was realized through its subsidiary organizations working to improve social conditions throughout the world.

In the immediate postwar period France and England entertained differing attitudes toward Germany. Once the fight was over—and won—the English showed their usual tendency to be magnanimous. Lloyd George made himself vastly unpopular in France by saying, "We cannot both cripple Germany and expect her to pay." He was Welsh, and the Celts, often regarded as the most romantic of races, are actually the sternest realists. To the French the Germans were still the enemy, to be repressed and held in a state of subjection until they had fulfilled their obligations. The watchwords of the French veterans were, "Never again" and "Our dead shall not have died in vain."

France was very conscious of being alone in Europe; Russia, so long regarded as an ally, was wholly preoccupied with revolution's aftermath, and her future course was unpredictable; the ramshackle Austro-Hungarian empire had been broken down into a tiny Austria, surrounded by new independent states with mixed populations—for again boundaries had been arbitrarily drawn, with little regard for ethnic and lingual differences. It was with these new states, Czechoslovakia, Yugoslavia and Romania that France joined in an organization known as the "Little Entente." For although Germany was no longer the Germany of the General Staff and the war lords, but of the social democratic Weimar Republic, she was still Germany, to be guarded against.

Not everyone in France shared this attitude; people with leftist leanings showed a laudable if unrealistic belief in the new "good" Germany, and thought that the Weimar Republic would uphold the democratic principles that they themselves cherished and that Germany should be given every chance. They also supported the new institutions to promote universal peace. People on the right, by nature more skeptical and cautious, could not shake off a hereditary suspicion of Germany, and had little confidence in the efficacy of international bodies.

Meanwhile the business of reconstruction began. Back to the ravaged northeastern departments trudged the evacuees to begin, with furious energy, to rebuild houses, villages, towns and to bring the waste land back into cultivation. In the repairing of a home, in bringing fields back under the plow their strong family bonds served the French well; even robbed of its best the unit was still a unit. Industry was more complicated; the return of Alsace and Lorraine brought France a highly populated and industrialized region, but it could not make up for what she had lost in men and in damage. For the needed manpower France turned to foreigners who presently numbered 3,000,000 who, like all immigrants, brought problems, but, for all their efforts, French industry continued to lag behind that of Germany.

The war had brought social change. Prior to it only women of the poorest classes had sought gainful employment; during it women of all classes had played an important part in economic life, and after it their work was still needed. Emancipation followed naturally and produced a revolution within the family, particularly in the middle classes. A daughter who was self-supporting could no longer be kept in a protective cocoon, waiting for marriage to release her. The ultimate stamp of emancipation, the franchise, was, however, to be witheld from the Frenchwoman for many years.

Another change in the social structure was more serious because it underlined the difference between rich and poor. All wars produce their quota of "new rich," people who have taken advantage of the situation, or simply been lucky. Those whom aggressiveness has enriched often show it in their manners and "profiteer" is an ugly word. Those who had come worst out of the war were the *petite bourgeoisie*, the backbone of France—small landowners, minor civil servants, professional people and those who lived on small pensions and modest investments. They had become almost a depressed class, with little hope of improving their position in a period when goods were scarce and prices high. Comparatively the position of those who worked on the land or in factories had

improved. In a country virtually besieged and partly out of cultivation, prices had risen with scarcity and industrial wages had
risen with prices. For those able and ready to grasp the opportunity
there was still wealth to be made out of the business of reconstruction.

At the end of 1919 came the legislative and presidential elections.
By now the nation was heartily tired of the left-wing and pacifist
Chamber which had been elected in 1914 and whose performance
during the war had not been conspicuously good. There was the
inevitable rebound, such a swing to the right that the new Chamber was more like the *Chambre Introuvable* of 1815 than any
France had seen for many years. It included so many veterans who
had worn the blue uniform of the fighting man that it quickly
received the nickname of *Chambre bleu horizon*.

The first act of the new Assembly was to "drop the pilot."
Poincaré, after his seven-year term of office, was only too ready to
quit the Elysée and turn with relief to active political life again.
As President he had shown great energy but he had, despite all
temptations, kept strictly within constitutional bounds. Who was
to succeed him? The obvious choice was Clemenceau, *le Père la
Victoire*, with his brilliant wartime premiership to his credit. But
in the course of a long and uncompromising career Clemenceau,
like any man worth his salt, had made enemies and been misunder-
stood. At the peace negotiations he had been intransigent but,
when they ended, people thought that he had yielded too much to
American opinion and dealt too kindly with the Germans. Other
things counted against him too; during the war he had acted
virtually as a dictator and, though he had done so in French interests and though as President he would fill only a nominal role, the
Assembly, anxious to exercise its own powers, decided to deny
him the highest honor the Republic had to bestow.

There was another reason, and one that did the Assembly little
credit. Clemenceau was old; he might die during his presidency
and rate a public funeral. He was a lifelong atheist and would
certainly have simply a civil, not a religious, ceremony. The pre-
ponderantly right-wing Chamber, numbering many practicing
Catholics, looked ahead and visualized scandal. So they chose a

nonentity, Paul Deschanel; and the repudiation of Clemenceau by the right, like the repudiation of Churchill by the left twenty-six years later, proves that there is one common human characteristic, ingratitude.

There was one person, however—perhaps the least expected—who wrote to Clemenceau enthusiastically, begging him to call for a plebiscite, to let every ordinary man speak for himself and not through his official representative. Eugénie, once Empress of France, now very old, reached out from the shadows and wrote Clemenceau a letter which he did not answer; her last political gesture. In a few months she was dead.

Clemenceau, now eighty-two, was, for all his white hair and mustache, a still sturdy figure. He set out to stump the United States, but he was too late to persuade the Americans to revoke their embargo on the Treaty of Versailles. He returned to his native Vendée to write. Neither old age nor retirement nor bitter disillusion had impaired his judgment, and his experience reached back to 1870. In the memoirs upon which he was engaged when he died, *The Splendors and Miseries of Victory*, he looked forward, too, and with singular prescience foretold that the year 1940 might be a year of crisis. (He lived until 1929, so he could have served his seven-year term as President without embarrassing France by the nature of his funeral.)

The passing over of Clemenceau was avenged: Paul Deschanel became so mentally unstable that it was impolitic to allow him to remain in office and Millerand, who had been Premier, became President.

Millerand, like many other men, had started his political life as a Socialist and moved steadily toward the right as he aged. When the difficulties, both social and economic, which accompanied demobilization resulted in strikes, first among railwaymen, then among miners, building workers and dockers, he did not hesitate to follow Briand's example and take a firm stand against the left.

The left itself suffered from disunity. At the Socialist congress held in Tours the party split in two, one section adhering to the Third International, the Comintern, set up by Russia to work for Communist revolutions, the other retaining the name and the policies of the S.F.I.O. At the same time some trade unionists broke away from the General Confederation of Labor to form the C.G.T.U., the Unitary Confederation of Labor, which, like the Communist Party, took its orders from Moscow.

The old days, when a country's internal problems were her own affair and her foreign policy ran on traditional lines, were gone forever. Increasingly international ideologies were taking over. The growth of Communism—and presently of Fascism—had repercussions everywhere. From 1920 to 1939 internal affairs in France were largely governed by external considerations—the question of reparations, of security, of the world economic crisis in 1931, the efforts to achieve world disarmament through the League of Nations.

France in the immediate postwar period possibly had more than her fair share of the general world malaise. The emergence of the Communist Party, small as yet but sturdy, a body that looked abroad for its orders, created a situation without precedent and one to which older politicians could not readily adapt themselves. There was a dearth of younger, more flexible men; names that should have been written in the annals of their country were engraved on war memorials. Aristide Briand, Raymond Poincaré, Paul Painlevé and Alexandre Millerand were all born before 1870 and continued to dominate the political scene not only because of their extraordinary longevity but because there was no one to replace them. Not until 1924 did France have a Premier born after 1870—Edouard Herriot who, in time, was followed by André Tardieu, Camille Chautemps, Albert Sarraut, Pierre Laval and Léon Blum.

The preponderance of the old and the elderly in places of power accounts for the essentially conservative nature of the Third Republic which, for the greater part of its life, was governed by center-party coalitions such as the Bloc National, for twenty years by the right wing and for ten only by the left. Nor did the constitution of the Chamber of Deputies change much; it always contained a high proportion of journalists, among them Briand, Millerand, Clemenceau, Delcassé and Tardieu, a certain number of landowners and industrialists and, on the extreme left a few workingmen, but the vast majority were lawyers. To the French it seemed logical that laws should be made by men of law; and the filling of the Chamber with intellectuals was not regarded as undemocratic. In fact it was considered to be a sign of the good sense of the French peasant that he did not wish to be represented exclusively by working men.

When Millerand left the premiership to become President, Aristide Briand became Premier for the seventh time. Since 1917, when he clashed with Clemenceau over the question of a negotiated peace with Germany, Briand had been in eclipse; now he emerged and until his death in 1932, with only one brief gap, his was the guiding hand on French foreign policy which he directed according to the principles of his own firm beliefs—support for the League of Nations, international arbitration and the vital necessity for Franco-German reconciliation. On the last point he was as insistent as Louis XVIII had been on reconciliation with all former foes in 1814—and the climate was equally unfavorable to this lofty ideal.

Briand was born and brought up in humble circumstances. His parents kept a squalid music hall in St. Nazaire, and all his life he felt at home in the world of theatre and music hall, in the company of actors—and actresses.

The contempt and cold-shouldering of his bourgeois schoolfellows at the Lycée made him a Socialist. Although he did not attend a university he became a barrister but soon turned to journalism. It was through the brilliance of his speeches at congresses of the Socialist party—speeches distinguished by simple eloquence and delivered in a musical voice that has been likened to a violincello—that he came to be noticed and he was elected as a deputy in 1902. In his first ministry, when he was charged with the carrying through of the law separating Church from State, he already showed the qualities of moderation and conciliation which were to be so effective in the future.

Now, beginning to go gray, beginning to stoop a little, he took up his first post-war ministry and gave his time almost exclusively to international conferences with their recurrent preoccupation of adjusting reparation payments to Germany's willingness to pay, and to the first of the disarmament conferences in Washington.

Not every gun had ceased to fire on November 11, 1918. A joint Franco-British and White Russian force continued until 1919 to oppose the Bolsheviks in Russia. (It is still possible to find, here and there, aging men who say disgruntedly that this sub-war, waged more vigorously, would have been successful.) There was fighting between Russians and Poles and, in 1920, a French mission, headed by General Weygand, Foch's distinguished aide, was sent to help the Polish leader, Pilsudski. Weygand took with him two young officers both of whom were to be heard of again—Colonel de la Rocque and Captain Charles de Gaulle.

That Clemenceau's atheism had helped to bar him from the presidency was proof that the religious issue was not yet dead in France, though the sharpest edge of anti-clericalism had been blunted by the heroic behavior of priests in the front line. Now the canonization of Joan of Arc was a Catholic triumph and the clerical party was strengthened by the restoration of Alsace and Lorraine. The French in the lost provinces had clung to their Catholicism as part of their national identity—though many Germans were Catholic, too—and now, restored to France, they wished for a resumption of diplomatic relations with the Vatican. This, despite the Senate's reluctance, Briand brought about, hoping that the move would make the extreme right of the Chamber more amenable to his conciliatory policy toward Germany—a kind of tit-for-tat and also that it would help toward the complete reintegration of Alsace and Lorraine with France.

The Germans had done a thorough job of Germanizing the two provinces. Older people had their memories, their resentments, their religion, their Frenchness; but the young had gone to German schools and become bilingual—French at the dinner table, German in class. Some of them had served in the German army; many, if consulted in 1919, would probably have preferred to become members of an autonomous state, neither French nor German. While Strasbourg's representative statue stood in the Place de la Concorde draped with crape and heaped with mourning wreaths, the actual city had been growing, the new buildings German rather than French in style, the increasing population including many German families who now, in their turn, must adapt. (Europe had been the world's leader in the abolition of slavery, the trading of men like cattle and the separation, in the market, of parent from child; it was to be the world's leader back into another form of man-marketing, nationality by decree and the rift in families between those too old to change and the adaptable young.)

In December 1921, Germany made a first reparations payment, the equivalent of fifty million pounds sterling; after that she suspended payment on account of the devaluation of the mark. The currency landslide had begun and was to reach such fantastic depths that a German workman, paid bi-weekly, had to take a suitcase in which to carry home his almost worthless wage. The devaluation excuse was regarded as a piece of typical German chicanery; then the franc fell too and other currencies followed; 1922, financially, was a calamitous year.

Millerand, pursuing the hard French line and intervening unwarrantably in politics, complicated the delicate negotiations in which Briand and Lloyd George were engaged at a conference in Cannes, and Briand resigned, content to retire and wait for public opinion to come around to his way of thinking. Millerand invited Poincaré to form a government—the first ex-President to re-enter the political arena as Premier.

Further conferences on reparations, all equally unsatisfactory, and the continued decline of the franc, led Poincaré to revert to the basically sensible principle of barter; specie being worthless, France must be paid in kind. He took over the great German industrial region of the Ruhr. England protested—never kick a man when he's down. Briand who had fought so hard for reconciliation with Germany, rallied the left, which made Poincaré the target of a campaign of vilification. He was denounced as a warmonger, "a man who laughs in graveyards," an accusation with as little real substance as that brought against Napoleon I saying that he was indifferent to the numbers of dead and wounded in his wars.

The Ruhr was not the gold mine that Poincaré had hoped for; the Germans waged a war of passive resistance, troops for the occupation cost money. The franc continued to fall, but not as the mark did. In July 1923 one American dollar was worth 160,000 marks; in November one American dollar was worth 4,200,000,-000,000 marks.

In spite of all that Poincaré tried to do to bring order into what was rapidly becoming financial chaos he failed, hampered by vehement opposition to any attempt he made to investigate widespread tax avoidance, or to increase taxation. His government fell.

In August 1924, both France and Germany accepted the Dawes Plan, named after the American financier who had drawn it up. It provided for a scale of annual payments, the reorganization of the German Reichsbank and the raising of a large foreign loan in order to enable Germany to meet their obligations. These measures were of considerable aid to Germany, but reparation payments continued to lag. In 1929 the Young Plan slashed her commitments by 75 per cent, and then the general economic depression of 1931 put a stop to all reparation payments. In all, Germany had paid an eighth of the sum she was supposed to pay and that eighth was largely provided by foreign loans. The sorry thing was that without collecting from the Germans, France, so scrupulous about paying her indemnities after 1815 and 1870, now could not pay off the debts she had incurred, openly borrowed money.

Throughout the life of the Third Republic, experiments were made with various electoral systems. The *scrutin de liste*, used in 1919, provided for lists of candidates and a form of proportional representation and in the elections of 1924 this system gave an overwhelming victory to the left, a coalition of Radicals and Socialists, called the Cartel des Gauches. This success for the left was not entirely due to the electoral system; it was helped by the failure of the Bloc National to solve domestic and foreign problems and by a revival of anti-clerical feeling, provoked by the concessions which the Bloc had made to the Catholics.

Immediately after these elections came a constitutional crisis. Edouard Herriot, the leader of the Radicals, refused to take office under President Millerand. Millerand had never quite accepted the passive role demanded of a President, his interference had caused Briand to resign, but Millerand had made clear from the first that he did not believe that a President must be politically neutral. Faced by Herriot's refusal to take office under him, Millerand said that he had been elected for seven years and no mere change of party dominance could affect his position. But when he had tried—and failed—to form a government not led by Herriot, he resigned from the presidency, and Gaston Doumergue, a moderate Radical, a smiling, amiable southerner, took his place. Doumergue was acceptable to Herriot, he became Premier and set to work.

Herriot had fought his way up from humble, indeed rather mysterious origins, into the *Ecole Normale Supérieure*, nursery of so many of France's best brains, and become a teacher, first at Nantes, then at Lyons, of which town he became mayor, a position he held for forty-two years. He had a delicate appreciation of literature and had he not become a politician he would probably have made an even greater mark as a writer than he did. (Time was speeding up and becoming compressed; it was no longer so easy to pursue two lines as earlier writer/politicians had done.)

Herriot was devoted to France; it was natural that throughout his ministry he should be concerned with security. He signed the Geneva Protocol to outlaw war; he recognized the U.S.S.R. He was a man of his age, a generation which truly believed that adjuration of war meant its end. ("I do not have leprosy, I do not believe in leprosy, therefore leprosy does not exist!")

Like many another idealist, Herriot fell, brought down by religion and money; his attempts at laicization—all abortive—induced extreme agitation on the right, and there was a monetary crisis.

Paul Painlevé, the other chief of the Cartel des Gauches, took over the premiership and chose Joseph Caillaux as Minister of Finance. Caillaux' past was murky and he had only recently been rehabilitated, but as a financier he still enjoyed great prestige. He advocated a program of austerity which was not welcomed by the public who wished to see the franc restored by financial wizardry, not by their own sacrifices.

France believed that she had a moral right to link the repayment of her debt to the United States with the reparations that Germany owed to her; the United States did not share this view.

President Coolidge said coldly, "They hired the money, didn't they?" The failure to reach agreement over the debt brought Painlevé's ministry down: between October 1925, and July 1926, no fewer than five ministers tried, and failed, to halt the headlong collapse of the franc.

In France, as elsewhere during this time, one must penetrate to the back streets in order to see the grim reality of the financial situation. In the fashionable quarters it was cloaked by the merry-making, the feverish postwar gaiety. People on their way to see Diaghilev's Ballets Russes or to hear Maurice Chevalier sing, straw hat tilted over the knowing wink in the eye, or to gloat over Mistinguett wearing a twenty-foot train of feathers and with ai-grettes in her hair would stop and toss a charitable coin to the armless, legless or blind beggars. There were many peglegs to be seen, France could not afford to provide the *grands mutilés* of the war with artificial limbs.

As well as regaining her place at the center of fashion and enter-tainment, Paris could claim to be the leader of all that was modern in letters and art. Picasso, Braque, Léger and Matisse were at the peak of their talent, and cubism all the rage. Sophistication was the keynote, but even sophistication could go too far, as Victor Mar-gueritte proved when he published a book called *La Garçonne*. Not since the prosecutions of Flaubert and Baudelaire had there been such a literary scandal. *La Garçonne* reflected the do-all and dare-all spirit of the twenties, but its revelations of degeneracy in Parisian society proved too much even for the tolerant French. It lacked the literary merit of *Madame Bovary* or *Les Fleurs du Mal*, nevertheless it sold in its hundreds of thousands. Margueritte was accused of damaging the image of France by calumniating French womanhood, and he was cast out of the Legion of Honor. The storm and the scandal, similar to that which was to greet D. H. Lawrence's *Lady Chatterley's Lover*, soon died out. More solid contributions to French literature were being made by men such as André Gide who had become the leader of a young genera-tion of writers.

The war was still too near for its realism to be in favor as a sub-ject, but Freud's work had opened up the world of the subconscious, and Marcel Proust came into his own. Paul Valéry was doing his best work and Romain Rolland producing his master-piece serial novels. The spirit of the period was best expressed, however, by Jean Cocteau, the many-sided genius who survived until 1960, by Jean Giraudoux, and by that supreme interpreter of chromium civilization and the "wagon-lit" complex, Paul Morand, who wrote brilliantly about the glamorous life of grand hotels, luxury liners and fashionable resorts and night clubs.

Statesmen were still aware of the possibility of threat from across the Rhine but few saw much danger in the attempt of an Austrian ex-corporal and General von Ludendorff to overthrow the Bavarian government. In fact the election of Field Marshal von Hindenburg, now so old and solid and slow-moving that he looked like a wooden idol, to be President of the German Republic was regarded by many as a sign of stability.

The Locarno Treaties, signed in 1925, were a triumph for Briand, Austen Chamberlain of England, and Stresemann of Germany, and a hopeful signpost to the world. It was genuinely believed that the decisions reached at Locarno would usher in a new era of peace. The Treaties provided for the inviolability of the Franco-German and Belgo-German frontiers and for the permanence of the demilitarized zone of the Rhineland. At the same time Franco-Polish and Franco-Czechoslovakian treaties of mutual guarantee were signed. Already France had begun to evacuate the Ruhr, and altogether the international climate looked healthier.

French colonies, however, presented problems. Turkey's siding with Germany in the war had resulted in the collapse of her empire in 1918 and France had taken over Syria on a mandate which proved to be no sinecure since there was a rebellion of the Druses that lasted until 1927. Lebanon was peaceful, and Algeria should have been prosperous. It had a large European element which had worked hard to produce large quantities of wheat, wine and minerals: but, with increased productivity, came an increase in native population for which even expanding agriculture, industry and trade could not provide.

People began to leave the country and drift into cities, to Algiers, to Oran, to Casablanca in French Morocco, and finally to

France. The immigrants were not adapted to life or work in urban areas and lived wretchedly. Algerian carpet sellers were to be seen everywhere in Paris, peddling their wares at sidewalk cafés; in the evening they returned to the shantytowns which they had made in the outskirts, slums which soon became hives of discontent.

An organization called the North African Star began an agitation for Algerian independence, but its influence was small. Another group of native Algerians, but French in education and culture, claimed political rights. There were opportunities for agreement and compromise, but time and again they were missed and trouble for the future ensured.

The French concept of colonization was based on the Roman model and the general aim was to create a number of small Frances entirely dependent upon metropolitan France. She transported her administrative institutions and her public services to the colonies and set them to work with only the minimal adaptation to local conditions. The granting of full political rights to natives was something vaguely visualized for the future.

Indochina, with its own highly developed civilization, had refused to be assimilated and was now acutely conscious of the Revolution taking place in China and the agitation for independence at work in India. The great decolonizing movement had begun, and the colonizers, clever and stupid, good and bad alike, were on their way out. But in the nineteen-twenties this over-all trend was not recognized.

Lyautey, one of the best colonial administrators, had trouble in Morocco where, in 1922, Abd El Krim set up an independent state in the mountains of the Rif, and threatened Fez. It took a full-scale military operation commanded by Marshal Pétain to defeat him. Lyautey fell out with Pétain and left Morocco to return to France to find, as so many of his kind have found, before and since, that his life work was not appreciated. His departure led to the growth of Moroccan nationalism and the decline of French prestige.

By July 1926, the constant change of government had exhausted the Cartel des Gauches. Poincaré had kept clear of party strife, and was now able to form a government of national union wide enough to include Herriot and Painlevé from the left, Louis Barthou and André Tardieu from the center. Briand, naturally, filled the post of Foreign Secretary.

Danger of war seemed to have receded with the admission of Germany to the League of Nations and the first preparatory meeting of the Disarmament Commission, but the franc was still in trouble. The Chamber had been unwilling to grant Caillaux almost dictatorial powers to deal with financial problems, but Poincaré, a man of extreme personal probity, was able to launch a determined campaign which included a poster on every blank wall, appealing, SAUVEZ LE FRANC.

So many governments had tried and failed that the people now saw the saving of the franc as a vital necessity; they responded to the appeal and made the inevitable sacrifices and Poincaré was able to arrest the inflation.

The Radical ministers left his government, but it survived until July 1929—an exceptional life span for any postwar ministry. Poincaré then resigned on account of ill health and was briefly succeeded by Briand, who in the previous year had once again scored a great diplomatic victory with the Kellogg-Briand Pact. In all, sixty-five states had signed the Pact, which renounced war as a means of settling disputes, and, since the signatories included Germany, the U.S.S.R. and the United States, the future looked hopeful.

There were other favorable signs; by grim determination and effort the ruined farmlands in the north and east had recovered and were once again in production; the manufacture of French cars had become a principal industry. On the whole France remained a country of small or medium enterprises, apart from a few great industrial combines such as the long-established Comité des Forges, popularly supposed to have a sinister influence upon politics. French prestige was boosted by the successes of the aviator Coste, who made the first non-stop flight from Paris to Buenos Aires, and then from Paris to New York. Even the triumphs of French tennis players meant something to national consciousness and pride.

Briand's term of office was short, and then France fell into the hands of a thoroughly modern man, André Tardieu, a product of the Ecole Libre des Sciences Politiques. He wished to see France prosperous and progressive, with agriculture mechanized, industry modernized and vast new schools, hospitals and laboratories built to serve a people enjoying social security and family allowances. Since Poincaré had succeeded in stabilizing the franc, such ambitions were not immoderate, but Tardieu ran into violent opposition, even from the left who accused him of stealing *their* program. Today the things he dreamed of are regarded as commonplace and, had his ideas been adopted in 1930, they would have done much to soften the impact of the approaching economic depression. Tardieu was ahead of his time and his manner, unconciliatory and arrogant, aroused the dislike of the Senate. It was poor consolation to him to be the minister under whom the long-planned line of defense-in-depth began to come into being; it was called the Maginot Line after the Minister of War, André Maginot, a *grand mutilé* of the Great War.

Tardieu, like his predecessors, left the conduct of foreign affairs to Briand who, in 1930, produced a memorandum in which he advocated a United States of Europe. Napoleon had dreamed the same dream, but of a Europe united by conquest. Briand, too, was before his time, and the idea made no impact in his day though it foreshadowed the Council of Europe and the Common Market. Briand's more practical work went on, and his last years were crammed with activity. Allied troops began to leave the Rhineland; there was a Naval Disarmament Conference in London, an Economic Conference in Geneva; the question of reparations was finally agreed.

Yet before Briand died he was to see his unwearying efforts to improve relationships between France and Germany brought to nothing; by September 1930, the National Socialist party in Germany, with Adolf Hitler at its head, was the second largest political party and hourly gaining strength.

Hitler, by his treatment of the Jews and other minorities, placed himself outside the bounds of what human beings like to think of as *human;* but he was merely a man, he was born and he died, and when enough time has elapsed his career will be seen as illustrative of two truths, both distasteful; one that no matter with how much good will and idealism the would-be peacemakers go into the conference chambers, they cannot legislate for the tiger outside; the other that certain circumstances produce the man, rather than the man shaping circumstance.

The general depression, with its resulting unemployment, the hunger marches and the spirit of disillusion with things as they were, brought the German Nationalist Socialist party to power. Even the name was cleverly chosen, implying a kind of patriotism, a kind of reform. It appealed to all who felt that Germany had been ill-done-by at Versailles; it appealed to the leading figures of industry who feared Communism; it appealed to the boy who lurks in most men by its special passwords, salute and songs; and by its anti-semitism it appealed to the thug element, of which Germany does not hold the monopoly, alas.

The Treaty of Versailles had limited the German army to 100,000 men at any one time; the purpose of this clause was easily defeated by a system of short-term engagements which brought men in, trained them intensively and sent them home, part of a powerful reserve force. By contrast, France, putting her faith in the international agreements she had signed, reduced her obligatory military service, and England had a relatively small standing army.

Tardieu's first ministry lasted a year. It was followed by Laval's, whose program was very similar, and Tardieu was again briefly in office until the legislative elections of 1932 produced a decisive victory for the left, and Herriot formed a government, essentially radical in nature, which was doomed to grapple with mounting financial difficulties. The economic blast under which, with the briefest intermissions, Europe had shivered through the postwar years, reached the United States in 1929, and men who had been millionaires one day were paupers on the next. Budgetary weakness hampered Herriot's program, and Briand, with all his gifts and experience, was no longer at the Foreign Office.

The presidency eluded Briand as it had eluded Clemenceau. Doumergue, who had been a competent and popular President, would not offer himself for re-election in 1931, explaining his refusal in words which any constitutional head of state might echo: "Do you think it is amusing to be a prisoner in that house, unable to take a step into the street without watchdogs clinging to you like limpets?" So the presidency lay between Briand and Paul Doumer, a man of great probity and the object of much popular sympathy because he had lost four sons in the Great War. Doumer was elected.

The watchdogs failed Paul Doumer; he was shot and killed by a crazy Russian at a book sale organized by the Association of Veteran Writers. The next President was Albert Lebrun, who so strictly interpreted the constitutional limits of his office that he made no attempt to influence events between 1932 and 1940 (he was elected for a second term), though these years were some of the most unruly and disturbed that the Third Republic had faced. Lebrun was so deeply affected by a railway accident in 1933 that his name became part of a slang expression. The three hundred dead were laid out in the great hall of the Gare du Nord and the President went to pay his last respects, raising his silk hat to each coffin. *Lebrun travaille du chapeau*—Lebrun makes his hat work, became an expression to be applied to anyone not quite right in the head. Lebrun was sane enough at the time, but afterward he became very melancholic.

Herriot's government fell, after only six months in office, over the question of repaying war debts to America. Herriot hoped to obtain a moratorium on the installment due; America, herself now in deep water, could not agree. Amid so many changes one more was of no special significance, yet Herriot's fall marked the end of an epoch because it almost coincided with the installation of Adolph Hitler as Chancellor of the German Reich.

Hitler had made no secret of his intention to abolish the Treaty of Versailles and to rearm Germany. French leftists were alarmed and suspicious, but the general feeling in France was influenced by a desire to give Germany better treatment than had been meted out at Versailles, by an increasingly international outlook, by the pacifism bred by the horrors of the Great War, by the image of the Soviet Union as the most threatening enemy and, in some cases, by a nostalgic sympathy with the rule of a strong man. France, which had once led Europe in political ideas, now seemed bankrupt of them and more and Frenchmen turned to the two ideologies which were fast making headway: those with conservative and authoritarian views looked admiringly at Mussolini's achievements in Italy; the advanced left wing became passionately devoted to what they believed to be the rule of the proletariat in Russia. Few people realized that there was little difference between the two régimes except that communism had room for expansion without interfering with western Europe.

In October 1933, Germany left the League of Nations to which she had been admitted in 1926. This was a real blow to all those who had looked upon the League as a bulwark against war.

In France politically flavored organizations flourished, some new, some developing from existing bodies, some fascist, some communist. The old Royalist Action Française, anti-semitic and reactionary, gained new adherents, especially from the younger generation who formed themselves into a sub-group, noisy and aggressive, called the Camelots du Roi (the King's Newshawks). The Croix de Feu also recruited from the young, though it had originally been set up as an association of ex-servicemen who had been decorated for valor. The leader of the Croix de Feu was Colonel de la Rocque, who had gone with General Weygand on the mission to Poland. Their companion on that mission, Colonel Charles de Gaulle, published in 1933 a small book, *Vers l'armée de métier* (*Toward a Professional Army*). It aroused little interest in France but had been most carefully studied in Germany, where it had its effect upon military thinking.

Other leagues, of less importance but noisier, were formed to protect France against internal revolution, against the Jews, against the Communists. The already divided Socialist party split again when a group calling itself Neo-Socialist, broke off and took for its slogan, "Order, authority, nation."

This was a period—not only in France—of the most dangerously muddled thinking and feeling; relatively unimportant factors swayed men's minds. Punctual people admired Mussolini for making Italian trains run on time; humane people approved of his order to a callous nation to treat their beasts of burden more kindly. Hitler had helped German agriculture, set unemployed men to work on fine new roads, and given aim and purpose to a people demoralized by defeat and failure. It was not without significance that the various leagues in France adopted the outward symbols that served the dictatorships so well, the colored shirts, the parades. (In England there were Oswald Mosley's Blackshirts, contributing to the mental muddle; everybody deplored their anti-semitism; all but a few admired the way they went to assist in gathering in the harvests of small farmers besieged by the Tithe Commissioners.)

The winter of 1933 was very cold, the coldest that Paris had known for thirty years. And with the biting cold and the ice-covered puddles there came a spiritual chill, something akin to the "great fear" of 1789. Without any open acknowledgment of the fact, people felt that democracy, under the critical and skeptical eyes of the non-democratic world, was about to go on trial.

Scandal was nothing new to the Third Republic; latterly it had known nothing comparable to the Wilson and Panama affairs but there had been enough minor scandals to justify the setting up of a parliamentary commission in 1930 to inquire into parliamentary corruption. Now, in this cold winter, there were rumors of another.

It began when an adventurer named Serge Stavisky was accused of issuing fraudulent bonds on the security of a municipal pawn-shop in Bayonne. In January 1934, before he could be brought to trial, he was found dead—an ostensible suicide. Then the public learned that he had been engaged in dubious activities for at least six years and had enjoyed the protection of people in high places. The logical question presented itself—had Stavisky killed himself, or had he been "suicided" so that whatever exposure his trial might bring about could be avoided?

Chautemps, the Premier of the moment, did himself and democracy as a whole poor service by trying to hush the matter up. His ministry fell and the name of the Third Republic was tarnished. Inside France there were angry demonstrations.

Edouard Daladier, the new Premier, was thought of as a strong man; it was hoped that he would act swiftly to end public uncertainty and deal rigorously with this evidence of corruption. He had fought with distinction in the Great War, been a deputy in the *Chambre bleu horizon*, and occupied several cabinet posts. In appearance he bore a marked likeness to Mussolini.

The Camelots du Roi had for days been demonstrating in the

streets and the Paris Prefect of Police was suspected of showing too much indulgence to right-wing agitators. Daladier dismissed him, hoping to mollify the left, but the Prefect, Jean Chiappe, was popular, and his dismissal displeased people.

There was confusion in a telephone call between Daladier and Chiappe. Had the latter said, "*Je serais à la rue*," meaning that he would be unemployed, or "*Je serais dans la rue*," meaning that he would join the demonstrators? No one knew, but a demonstration was planned for the evening of February 6.

For that evening the piece billed at the Comédie Française was Victor Hugo's *Ruy Blas*, in which occurs the famous scene where Ruy Blas, the valet forced to masquerade as a grandee of Spain, turns on a council of corrupt and incompetent ministers with a scathing speech that begins: "Good appetite, gentlemen, O worthy ministers, virtuous counselors—this is the way in which you serve, servants who rob their masters . . ."

On this drear evening on those round kiosks that carry advertisements of entertainments available in Paris, yellow stickers were posted over the announcement of *Ruy Blas*. *Relâche*—No performance. Did anyone remember the remark of that observant old man? "When the Comédie Française shuts its doors . . . there is mischief brewing."

Mischief was brewing.

At the corner of every street leading into the vast Place de la Concorde there were squads of the Gardes Mobiles, the sinister riot police, called in from outside Paris for fear that the Paris police, indignant over Chiappe's dismissal, might prove unreliable.

The demonstration was led by the *grands mutilés*, veterans of the war, all proudly wearing their medals, some in their wheelchairs. Once again they were made the spearhead of attack. Not all who walked behind them were motivated by innocent intentions and, as the crowd pressed forward over the stones which had once been part of the walls of the Bastille, ugly scenes developed. The Gardes Mobiles opened fire. Demonstrators who stood their ground were killed or wounded, those who fled were pursued in vicious baton charges.

The demonstration had been a spontaneous gesture of disapproval at the way in which the country's affairs were being handled; many governments in the past had yielded to mass sentiment thus expressed, but this was the first time the Third Republic had been obliged to do so.

Next day, in an atmosphere of gloom and apprehension far worse—according to those who had lived through both—than the days when Paris was bombarded by Big Bertha, Daladier resigned. And in the evening the disorderly elements, the successors of the Apaches, came into the center of Paris to riot and loot. A few days later there was a general strike.

To meet the crisis old Gaston Doumergue, unsullied by involvement in the Stavisky or any other scandal, was called out of retirement. Once again France put her faith in old men. Doumergue formed a government of national union, its breadth evidenced by the inclusion of both Herriot and Tardieu.

Political passions were cooled but, like his predecessors, Doumergue faced the seemingly insoluble problem of finance. Paul Reynaud, one of the youngest men in the new government, urged the devaluation of the franc, but the public was not prepared to face the renewed sacrifices that this would demand. Instead, taxes were increased and civil service salaries and pensions reduced, a double-handed blow at the least well-defended members of the community.

Doumergue, called to power as a result of political scandal, was anxious to introduce some constitutional reforms. He proposed that the President should be given the power to dissolve a discredited Chamber without the need of consent from the Senate. But the Chamber asked to accept this proposal was already a discredited Chamber, had no intention of yielding up its power and patronage and refused to "suicide" themselves. The Radicals reacted violently and left the government, and Doumergue was obliged to resign.

The merry-go-round of governments began again, to the old tune of "The more it changes the more it remains the same."

In 1935 Laval became Premier, the choice largely dictated by the need for some continuity in foreign affairs. (He had been Foreign Minister in the previous government.) He came from the Auvergne, the poorest and dourest part of France. As a young man he had been so poor that he possessed only one tie, white, but washable, and later in life when he had prospered he still wore white ties, a sharp contrast with his dark and saturnine countenance. He had started life as a Socialist but had voluntarily left the party though he represented, as mayor or deputy, the working-class Parisian suburb of Aubervilliers for thirty years. In the Great War his pacifism had almost brought him to prison. As Premier he tried to follow in Briand's footsteps, but in the few years since Briand's death things had changed.

While France was occupied with the aftermath of the Stavisky scandal a Nazi *putsch*, in July 1934, had led to the murder of the Austrian Chancellor, Dollfuss. In October of the same year King Alexander of Yugoslavia on a state visit to France was assassinated at Marseilles. The French Foreign Minister, Louis Barthou, died with him, but this fact did not prevent a coolness developing between France and Yugoslavia. A Disarmament Conference had failed. The people of the Saar, in the plebiscite promised at Versailles, had opted to rejoin Germany, a blow to French pride and to her economy.

The democracies were not blind to what was implied by Germany's withdrawal from the League of Nations, and her now open rearmament. In April 1935, a conference was called at Stresa to discuss the formation of a common front against Hitler. France began a frantic search for new allies and concluded a pact with Soviet Russia.

In October 1935, Italy invaded Abyssinia and, despite the sanctions imposed by the League of Nations, went on to conquer the whole country. The Italians had been there before and suffered the defeat of Aduwa in 1896. The new invasion was recognized as an act of aggression, but it was against a barbarously backward country, where slavery still existed and soldiers defeated in battle were mutilated on their return. A great many fundamentally good people comforted themselves with the thought that it was high time that some civilizing influence was brought to bear on Abyssinia. Yet, when the British Foreign Secretary, Sir Samuel Hoare, and Laval produced the pact for the division of Abyssinia, it was proved that they had both underestimated the weight of anti-Fascist opinion in their countries. They were both forced to resign. Laval defended his policy; he claimed that he had wished to preserve peace and to remain on good terms with Italy—in case of war: he had particularly feared what might happen in Tunisia, where Italians had special privileges, if some concession were not made to Italy. The left forced him to resign and he remained in the background for four years. When he re-entered the political scene, the Third Republic had ceased to exist.

On March 7, 1936, German troops moved into the Rhineland zone which had been demilitarized by international agreements to which Germany had been a signatory. The French General Staff advised mobilization and, if the Germans refused to withdraw, the declaration of war, but the majority of ministers in the government—led by Sarraut since Laval's fall—was unwilling to act except in concert with England, and the English would not act at all. Every anti-military sentiment current in France was present also in England where, although the threat was seen and recognized, there was a good deal of the don't-look-and-perhaps-it-will-go-away attitude. It is probable that action taken at this moment might have arrested Hitler's expansionist schemes; as it was, the supine acceptance of a violation of agreements seemed to promise that whatever Germany did in future France and England would remain passive. Work on the rebuilding of the wartime fortifications of the Siegfried Line began immediately.

In France political action took the place of military action; faced with the growing menace of Fascism and the rapprochement of the two Fascist countries, Germany and Italy—a rapprochement which by the end of the year had culminated in the "Rome-Berlin Axis," the French left rallied and sank its differences to form a Popular Front. The S.F.I.O held the majority of seats, and it fell to them to form a government. As a party, the S.F.I.O had never before held power, and its members had no experience of ministerial responsibility, even participation in government had long been contrary to party principles.

On June 4, 1936, Léon Blum formed a coalition left-wing government made up of pure Socialists and Radicals; for the first time women were included in the ministry—an anomaly, since women in France were still denied the vote.

Blum looked what he was, an intellectual and a man of letters.

He was an Alsatian Jew and had been drawn into the Socialist cause by Jaurès because of his sympathy with Dreyfus; he entered political life as a member of the *Chambre bleu horizon* in 1919 and by 1925 was leader of the party. When he took office he was the first Socialist premier France had known, and the hundredth premier of the Third Republic, then in its sixty-sixth year, but this figure is less astounding than it seems since some men held office more than once. Briand was Premier eleven times.

Blum, Chautemps and Daladier who succeeded him, based their program on extensive social reform and the repression of fascism. The masses saw, in this victory of the left, an opportunity to react against the results of deflation, against reduced salaries and wages, against unemployment. Before Blum had even formed his government there were stay-in strikes which spread until a million and a half workers were involved and daily life in France was threatened with paralysis.

Blum acted with energy and determination, calling together the representatives of labor and management and hammering out the Matignon Agreement—named after the Premier's official residence. There was to be a general rise in wages, the introduction of collective bargaining, a forty-hour week—so long the working man's dream, and holidays with pay.

The bourgeoisie feared that the working man would not be able to organize his new leisure and that it would lead to drunkenness and debauchery: they were wrong. Soon the roads were full of tandem bicycles on which people were making their way to beaches and camping sites and country places where relatives still lived and worked in the fields. In time paid holidays radically changed French social life.

Just before he became Premier, Blum had been severely beaten up by right-wing extremist toughs, so it was natural that he should legislate for the dissolution of those para-military leagues of the right whose ranks were now swollen by the forming of a new organization, the Secret Committee of Revolutionary Action, known as the *Cagoulards* or hooded men. But the leagues were like quicksilver; pressed upon, they broke up, then reformed and continued their existence.

In this imperfect world everything, even social reform, must be paid for, and the policy of the Popular Front resulted in expenditure which increased the chronic budget deficits. In September 1936, the long-dreaded devaluation of the franc could no longer be avoided, unemployment had increased and the whole economy seemed stagnant. Even Socialists halted between two opinions: the Popular Front had gone too far and too fast; the Popular Front had gone too slowly and not far enough. What everyone felt was a deep dissatisfaction with things as they were, and an almost superstitious dread of trying anything new.

In March 1937, there was a clash between supporters of the Croix de Feu and supporters of the Popular Front. Police guns were needed to quell it, and it was followed by a twenty-four-hour strike. Throughout the year there were others. Domestic events, however, were overshadowed by the beginning of the Spanish Civil War, which brought conflict between opposing ideologies into the open. In Spain another Popular Front had been challenged by a revolt of army commanders, headed by General Franco. Outside powers hastily decided not to intervene, but Italy, Germany and Russia saw Spain as a useful training ground and sent troops and air crews to help this side or that. There were unofficial volunteers, too, young men of a supposedly disillusioned and cynical generation who, between 1937 and 1939, went to Spain to fight for the Catholic right or the Republican left.

France viewed with concern this conflict just beyond her Pyrenean border; the policy of nonintervention was strongly attacked from the left, siding passionately with the Republicans, and from the right; Catholics were outraged by accounts of atrocities suffered by monks and nuns.

There were inevitable repercussions in the Mediterranean territories. Blum promised independence within three years to Syria, a promise strenuously opposed by the die-hard military leaders. Tunisia tried to exact a similar promise, but Tunisia was more economically valuable and, however sympathetic Blum might be toward national aspirations, he could not be blind to what the loss of Tunisia would mean to France. In 1938 there was a rising in Tunisia, brought to a truce by the outbreak of war in the following year.

With Algeria Blum was more successful. In 1936 the various Algerian organizations combined to demand complete integration with France—but with the maintenance of their own Muslim laws. In response to this demand, certain categories of Muslims, small at first but gradually increasing, were granted full French citizenship.

As a diversion from all her internal and external problems, from the second and third devaluation of the franc, France planned yet another Universal Exhibition, sited, like the last, on the heights of Chaillot. The old Palais du Trocadéro whose twin-minareted towers had since 1878 been part of the Parisian scene, was torn down and in its place arose a new concourse of buildings, designed to be permanencies. There was the new Palais de Chaillot, a naval museum, a museum of Man, of modern art, of costume. It was estimated that the Exhibition would bring millions of visitors to Paris.

Alongside all this, Blum pressed on with his program of reform which included the partial nationalization of the Banque de France and the nationalization of railways and the armament industry. The big industrialists—particularly those who controlled cartels like the Comité des Forges—undoubtedly exercised, through their control of the press, great influence on political life, and they maintained close economic links with Germany. They also had a large share in the control of the Banque de France whose General Council of 200—the famous "200 families"—were the heart of the right-wing industrial and financial oligarchy that was commonly believed to direct the destinies of the Republic. Such concentrations of power were anathema to Socialists; equally any proposed curtailment of such power was anathema to those who enjoyed it. Blum ran into massive opposition, especially from the Senate. He would have been willing to pause in his plans, but the Popular Front was steadily losing ground, and he resigned, to be succeeded by Camille Chautemps, a typical Radical Socialist of postwar vintage and in character and ability decidedly inferior to Blum.

It is often possible to state, through the medium of some art, things that no politician would dare to say outright. In 1937 Jean

Renoir—son of the great painter—produced a film called *La Grande Illusion*, its theme that class solidarity can override nationality. It made people ponder over the links formed between industrialists, French and German, the sympathy that existed between officers wearing different uniforms and workers speaking different languages.

Chautemps' fall, mere routine in French parliamentary life, coincided with an event of the greatest importance. On March 11, 1938, Hitler's forces marched into Austria and the *Anschluss*, expressly forbidden by the Treaty of Versailles, was accomplished. Germany and Austria were united. What next?

In France Blum tried to direct a new Popular Front government; it lasted a month. Daladier then took office and faced a menacing international situation. It had for a long time been glaringly apparent that Hitler was deaf to words and that, if action must be taken, armaments would be needed. But France's industrial and financial resources had been strained to the limit, constant strikes had weakened her and in France, as in England, anyone who dared mention the need for strengthening the country's defenses was liable to be howled down as a warmonger. The whole history of these years holds the hint of events being foredoomed, dictatorships and democracies alike taking somnambulist strolls.

In 1938 King George VI and Queen Elizabeth paid a state visit to France, regarded as a tightening of Franco-British bonds. It was the more welcome because France had just made a new agreement with Belgium, whereby Belgium instead of calling on France—as by former agreement—when she was threatened, thus giving the French army time to organize, would now only cry "help" when actually attacked. The difference was significant and was to prove disastrous to the French.

The world waited. As early as February 1938, Hitler had indicated his next move, the "rescue" of the Sudentenland Germans who, in 1919, had been citizens of Czechoslovakia, learning Czech, outwardly conforming, helping with their industry and skills to make Czechoslovakia the most prosperous of the "new" countries, but preserving their ethnic identity. In September they were "rescued" by military occupation, and the question was: Would Europe go to war for Czechoslovakia?

It seemed possible and, all through the warm September days in big cities, trenches were dug, air-raid precautions practiced, gas masks distributed, food cupboards stocked by people who remembered the shortages of a former war. People remembered other things too; the last war had seen the beginning of war in the air, and in the intervening twenty years airplanes had improved and proliferated. In any future war there would not only be "no discharge," there would be no front line.

There was a general feeling of relief, shared by all but a few foresighted people, denied now by hypocrites, when Neville Chamberlain, the British Prime Minister, decided to fly to Germany for a face-to-face talk with Herr Hitler. It is fashionable to decry Chamberlain and to make derisive mention of his umbrella—at that time as much a part of any respectable man's equipment as his handkerchief—but at that moment Chamberlain was the "Everyman" of the old morality plays; he represented the overwhelming weight of public opinion. Let there be no war; come to terms if possible.

The result of Chamberlain's visit was a conference at Munich on September 29, 1938. Daladier, Chamberlain and Mussolini, reached an agreement with the Germans which made Czechoslovakia the sacrificial lamb—but it was a young country and since the time of Isaac, son of Abraham, the gods have always favored young victims. Germany was to have the Sudentenland; Hungary and Poland were to have back some territory that they had lost in 1919. The poor remnant of Czechoslovakia was guaranteed against any further aggression.

Hitler said that this was "the last territorial claim" he would make in Europe. Chamberlain said the agreement meant "peace in our time." People threw away their gas masks and danced in the streets.

But in the still independent part of Czechoslovakia stood the great Skoda works, producing heavy engineering machinery, and armaments.

In France the Popular Front collapsed after Munich; Daladier no longer subscribed to its principles and Socialists no longer figured in his government. All parties were in disarray, torn between those who felt that Czechoslovakia should have been defended and those who believed that a dangerous corner had been rounded. In March 1939, Hitler occupied the remainder of Czechoslovakia, and even the most self-deluded optimists saw that appeasement had failed.

Immediately afterward the Chamber granted full powers to Daladier until the end of November, and amid the general dismay and confusion the presidential elections passed almost unnoticed. Albert Lebrun was elected for a second term.

On August 23, 1939, came the profoundest shock of all: Hitler, whose anti-communism had helped him to power and made him tolerated in some quarters, had signed a non-aggression pact with Soviet Russia. Nine days later, with passivity on her eastern front assured, Germany moved into Poland. Another era was ended.

Chapter 5. AGAIN WAR

France and England declared war on Germany on September 3, 1939. There was little of the enthusiasm of 1914; the mood was rather of resignation. There had been a war "to end war," followed by twenty years of sustained effort to avoid a recurrence; the effort had failed, hope was shattered.

By October Poland had ceased to exist and Hitler offered peace; the offer was rejected by Daladier who retorted that the French would lay down their arms only when they had the guarantee of a security which could not be called in question every six months.

As yet, however, the French had barely taken up their arms. Their plan was to sit down behind the seemingly impregnable Maginot Line and to wage a war of attrition. The national obsession with defense had produced the "Maginot mentality" which was, in fact, ill-suited to the national temperament. The Germans had different ideas, they had learned the value of tanks in warfare—largely through studying Charles de Gaulle's thesis; a blitzkrieg had taken Poland, another would take France, if necessary, and in due time.

So began the "phony" war, which continued for eight months and gave the Germans time to realign the forces that had overrun Poland and to wage psychological warfare; the bombing of Warsaw had shown what modern warfare meant. Let the Allies think about it. Did they want bombs on Paris, on London?

Life went on in a kind of abnormal normality. In Paris the myriad lights were not extinguished but dimmed blue, giving the city an almost unearthly beauty and, after the initial shock, the capital regained its gaiety; there were men on leave, there were members of numerous Allied missions in need of entertainment, and the uniforms to be seen everywhere looked like a kind of fancy dress.

In December 1940, the Chamber voted the government full

powers for the duration of the war, but Daladier was out of office
by March 1941, his place taken by Paul Reynaud who, with
Gamelin, was in favor of something more than mere defensive
action, though the means for attack were lacking. Reynaud's
position, based on a small majority, was bolstered by his making
an agreement with Britain that neither Allied country would entertain any proposal for unilateral peace negotiations.

In April 1940, the Germans invaded Norway and Denmark. In
May Belgium, Holland and Luxemburg were overrun. In places
the Dutch breached their dykes and let the seawater flood in to
render barren land that had been most painfully won, but the
bombing of Rotterdam was decisive; the Queen and her government fled to England.

French and English forces left their prepared positions to go to
the aid of Belgium which had put up such gallant resistance in
'14–'18. This time she surrendered unconditionally on May 28;
once again the French defenses were breached at Sedan and the
bulk of the British army, and part of the French, found themselves
trapped at Dunkirk. They were rescued by the "little ships"
manned often by amateurs, "Sunday seamen"; 233,039 British
troops and 112,546 Allies—mainly French, were evacuated in
an operation regarded by the world as a miracle and by the
English as a triumph. All their equipment, which would take time
to replace, was left behind. The men owed their lives to Hitler's
order that the German advance should be halted. For this out-of-
character order various explanations are offered; Hitler, remembering the First World War, feared that his tanks might be bogged
down; Hitler hoped that England, not subjected to the ultimate
humiliation, might be willing to come to terms. Whatever his
reason he took it to the grave with him—a dictator is under no
obligation to explain or discuss his policies—and thinking of the
evacuation of 345,000 men who were going to live and fight
another day one is forced back upon Euripides, "Whom the gods
would destroy, they first make mad."

At this moment, when it looked as if France was destroyed,
Italy, so wooed and cajoled over Abyssinia "in case of war,"
stabbed France in the back and declared war on the Allies. Chur-

chill in London said, "Well, *we* had them last time!" and there was laughter.

The British, with the Channel between them and the panzer divisions, could lick their wounds, draw breath and prepare for a siege and presently a comeback. The French were in a far more desperate situation; the German tanks were rolling on. There was a little comfort to be taken from the dismissal of General Gamelin and the appointment of Weygand, and the recall of Marshal Pétain from the French embassy in Madrid to take office as Vice-Premier and chief military adviser. Both Weygand and Pétain bore names that were associated with victory and the nation's morale rose to meet them, but they were only men. Other things being equal, since the beginning of time war has gone in favor of the best-armed; arrows had triumphed over battleaxes, however bravely wielded, firearms over bows, however bravely bent. . . . The rule still held; while France had been concerned with the Stavisky affair, Germany had been building the tanks, the heavy guns, the bombers. Weygand and Pétain were called in to fight a battle already lost.

Where they could, French troops held out heroically, but they were disorientated, often in isolated groups separated from their headquarters and all too often opposing vulnerable human flesh to steel. On the roads there were repetitions of the scenes of 1870 and 1914, but far more dreadful; a tired horse could be prodded or dragged into action, a car, run out of gas, stayed where it was and blocked the road; guns could be fled from, but there was no escape from the pitiless Stukas, sweeping low with bombs and machine-gun fire. The chaos on the roads reflected the state of the nation and the government, which moved first to Tours and then to Bordeaux.

Reynaud had accepted Churchill's offer of a union between the two countries and was anxious to take the government of France to London or North Africa, but there was no time. The panzer divisions advanced swiftly, and on June 14, 1940 the Germans entered Paris, which had been declared an open city. Half its inhabitants had fled, those who remained wept quietly. A few could just remember the occupation of 1871. The dreaded spiked helmets were no longer there to revive childhood fears, but with this invasion something worse came to Paris. Despite the vast material progress made in the last seventy years, in countries where Fascism and Communism had taken root men as individuals had lost value: to the Gestapo, which came into France alongside the fighting men, the French were not merely a beaten enemy, they were things to be used and exploited and ruthlessly suppressed, if necessary by means of physical torture long outlawed by all civilized communities.

The end came quickly. In Bordeaux Reynaud resigned and Marshal Pétain, "hero of Verdun," became Premier. He immediately broadcast to the nation his intention to seek an armistice, and make an honorable peace with Germany, as between soldiers. He was eighty-four and used the language of a more chivalrous age.

The French had preserved, as a museum piece, the railway carriage in which the Armistice of November 11, 1918, had been signed. In that same carriage, on June 22, 1940, Hitler backed by Marshals Goering and Keitel, Admiral Raeder and Foreign Minister von Ribbentrop, dictated his terms.

They were stiff. France was to be divided into Occupied and Unoccupied Zones, the former to include the Channel and Atlantic ports, the northeast and part of western France. What remained was to be administered by the French government. France was to pay the unlimited cost of an army of occupation and Germany was to retain the vast army of French prisoners of war. Alsace and Lorraine were again annexed by Germany, but France was to be allowed to retain her fleet. The English, deeply concerned about their own safety, could not view without alarm the possibility of the French fleet passing into German hands and, as a measure of self-preservation, found themselves obliged to put the French ships at Mers-el-Kebir in North Africa out of action.

The French nation was stunned by the swiftness and completeness of the catastrophe; two million French soldiers were in enemy hands, between six and eight million people were homeless refugees; normal life was entirely disrupted, and the gray-green troops, as they poured over France sang confidently, *"Wir fahren gegen England* [We are marching against England]." The invasion of

England seemed likely, the bombing was actuality, and though Churchill had said that England would hold out, if necessary alone, if necessary forever, who but the British could believe that? There was another question, too; even if England held out, how could it benefit France, writhing under the enemy heel?

The Germans moved to occupy Bordeaux and the French government moved inland to what, only last summer, had been a fashionable spa—Vichy—and there the Third Republic came to its end. The Assembly, glad enough to shelter behind the great moral prestige of Marshal Pétain, and influenced, but not compelled by Laval, voted:

"The National Assembly hands all powers over to the government of the Republic, under the authority and signature of Marshal Pétain, so that by one of several acts he can promulgate a new constitution for the French state. This constitution should guarantee the rights of work, of the family and of the fatherland. It will be ratified by the nation and by the assemblies which it will have brought into being."

President Lebrun had to make a decision more difficult and agonizing than had ever faced any of his predecessors, but he believed that in investing Marshal Pétain with the constituent power he was acting constitutionally—and there were many who agreed with him. So on November 11, 1940, the fourteenth President of the French Republic signed the death warrant of the Third Republic and a new régime was established—the Etat Français.

For a hundred years France had exerted herself to make a nation out of a state; now, at one stroke, the nation became a state and a virtual dictatorship. The powers of the National Assembly were abolished, the Assembly itself adjourned, and no new constitution was ever proposed by what became known as the Vichy régime. The Third Republic, born of internal struggle and bloodshed and brought into being by one French soldier, Marshal MacMahon, was brought to an abrupt and brutal end with another, Marshal Pétain. Liberty, equality and fraternity, the watchwords of France since 1789, were jettisoned in favor of a new concept—work, family, the fatherland.

The mass of the French people held that the Third Republic,

with its scandals and corruptions, was responsible for the disaster. To think in this fashion was natural—some scapegoat is always needed—but it is also to be blind to the truth. The Republic died, not as a result of its own errors, nor from natural decline, it was killed by an overwhelming military defeat for which many factors were responsible.

France had never fully recovered, either materially or psychologically, from what she had endured in the Great War. For the last twenty years her military policy had been based on the necessity of avoiding, in any future war, such senseless waste of men's lives as the last had seen. This policy inevitably led to a defensive mentality and a widening gulf between the nation and the army—the High Command would have moved against Hitler earlier, before he was so well-prepared. When the brutal moment of truth came the democratic belief in individuals and in human liberty was no defense against the tanks and bombers of a ruthless and cynical dictator. Nonetheless, the ideals, wounded and defeated, were far from dead.

The Vichy government was allowed a standing army of 100,000 men—exactly the number allowed to Germany by the Treaty of Versailles. The Third Republic had always been suspicious of the army because its officers tended to be conservative and Catholic. Now, with its elderly leaders, Weygand and Pétain, given over to defeatism, the army, disciplined and patriotic, set an example to the nation desperately in need of guidance and inspiration.

Hitler, having wiped out, in the railway carriage, the humiliation once inflicted there and looking down with satisfaction on conquered Paris from the heights of Sacré-Coeur, saw that some measure of conciliation would be to his advantage. He made the theatrical gesture of bringing back from Austria the body of the Duc de Reichstadt to lie beside that of his father, Napoleon I, in the Invalides. The French ignored the gesture; it was badly mistimed; the people were stunned and despairing, any reminder of the faraway days of glory smacked of sadism, emphasizing that Hitler now controlled both Vienna and Paris. Melancholy prevailed, and with it a reluctant attraction toward the mysticism of defeat which was all that Pétain had to offer.

Then, in the midst of the misery a new voice was heard. It came from London, it was not familiar, and it first spoke on what, for the French, was an ill-omened date, June 18, the anniversary of Waterloo.

"France," the voice said, "has lost a battle but France has not lost the war." It went on to speak of governments, hastily assembled, yielding to panic and capitulating, forgetful of honor, delivering the country to slavery. Nevertheless nothing was lost. One day the immense forces of the free world would crush the enemy. On that day France must be present at the victory, then she would once again find her liberty and her greatness.

Charles de Gaulle invited Frenchmen, wherever they might be, to join him in action, in sacrifice and in hope. *Vive la France!*

Not everybody heard the voice or was able to read reports of what it had said, but something new had started; gradually those Frenchmen who refused to accept defeat as final joined with this almost unknown general to carry on the fight and made a force, small in numbers but strong in determination and in readiness, to sacrifice everything in order to free France of the enemy.

Like the Gaul which Caesar described, "divided into three parts," the fighting men of France now made separate forces. There was the army, recognized by Hitler, the army of France, ruled by Marshal Pétain and his associates. There was the army of Free France, headed by General de Gaulle, momentarily on the fringe of the conflict. And there was a third army, the army of shadows, the army of the Resistance, working in secrecy and risking not death on the battlefield or incarceration in a prisoner-of-war camp, but torture in the Gestapo headquarters or the slow death of a concentration camp, where no rules held. (Hell, someone once observed, is the place where there are no rules.) Innumerable memorials, some of them touchingly humble, outside French towns and villages, bear witness to how many members of this third army died, men and women who not only refused to collaborate with the enemy but went into action against him.

Courage, however, is a rare virtue, and heroes are few. The mass of people, led by Pétain—still respected for his victory at Verdun and for his restoration of order after the mutinies on the

Chemin des Dames front—tried to settle down. Behind Pétain at this point was Laval, and it was he who, in October 1940, arranged a meeting between Pétain and Hitler. After the meeting Pétain issued a manifesto. It read: "It is in honor and to maintain French unity, a unity a thousand years old, within the cadre of a constructive new European order that I today embark on the road of collaboration. Follow me and keep your confidence in eternal France."

What Pétain meant by collaboration was never quite clear; the Germans knew, and the French soon learned. It meant the complete subordination of French manpower and economic life to the insatiable demands of the German military machine. It meant queuing for what food remained after the bulk of supplies had gone to Germany; it meant managing without motor transport and riding bicycles, presently without tires; it meant no stockings, bare feet in wooden shoes; and a black market where astronomical prices threw the poor back on the official ration to see their children grow pale and emaciated. Worst of all, it meant forced labor, the deportation to Germany of those capable of work; and in the darkened streets the heavy tramp of German patrols, and the knock of the dreaded Gestapo on the door.

Under Pétain the authoritarian elements which have always existed in France found free rein; Laval acted as Premier, was dismissed and replaced by Admiral Darlan, and then reinstated. Laval claimed that he was a patriot, but after the liberation of France he was tried and executed for treason. A question mark still hangs over his name. When some members of the government, among them Daladier, attempted to leave France for North Africa —from which they were ignominiously sent back—Laval argued that to leave France without a government would be to expose her to the fate of Belgium, Holland and Poland, all ruled by the Germans and their puppets. He believed that a French government in Unoccupied France protected French interests, made provision against the risk of Britain's being totally defeated and made possible negotiations which eased hardships. Pétain's view was simply that to go to Africa or elsewhere was to desert in the face of the enemy. For this crime Charles de Gaulle was tried *in absentia* and condemned to death by a Vichy court. So far from being a deserter, he was anxious to meet the enemy when and where he could. He tried first at Dakar in West Africa, and failed. The hostility of the Germans and of some of the French colonies was not the only difficulty he had to face; he had to struggle hard to obtain recognition for himself and his Free French Forces. He was not regarded as an easy man to deal with; single-minded men seldom are; de Gaulle was very single-minded; he could have said, with Clemenceau, "*Je fais la guerre*," and he made it until he succeeded.

The war went on and in September 1940, reached one turning point. The Germans launched 3000 aircraft into the Battle of Britain, round-the-clock bombing as a prelude to invasion. The British had only 800 planes, manned by men who often had time neither to eat nor sleep between affrays; but German losses were heavy. In the smoking ruins of London streets newspaper placards used the laconic terms of cricket scores—"24 for 5," and the nation of shopkeepers, behind glassless windows, announced "Business as usual." Massed daylight raids proved too costly and ceased; night bombing went on for two more years. Plans for invasion were shelved.

Elsewhere German victories continued; Yugoslavia and Greece were overrun, and then, in June 1941, came another turning point. Hitler turned on Russia, and his armed divisions made a whirlwind advance across the terrain over which Napoleon's Grand Army had plodded. They reached the outskirts of Stalingrad and Moscow, but not quite soon enough; they had the Russian winter to face and, for once, German efficiency had failed. The invaders of 1941, like those of 1812, lacked sufficiently warm clothing. The Russians started a counter-offensive and, from the losses and strain of that winter, the German troops never fully recovered.

In December came news from the far side of the world. The Japanese made a sudden sneak attack on the American naval base at Pearl Harbor. That brought America into the war, and on the following day China declared war on her old enemy, Japan, and on Germany and Italy. The war was now global.

In France the ordinary Frenchman suffered and endured as Laval had predicted in an interview with Hitler. Laval did not lack courage; he said bluntly, "You can crush us because you are the stronger; we shall suffer, we shall endure and, because it is a natural law, one day we shall rise in revolt. You have beaten us, yes, but in the past we have beaten you."

But the day of hope seemed far away. It looked as though America's major effort must be directed against Japan, and on France the steely grip of fascism tightened. French Jews, like their co-religionists all over conquered Europe, were first distinguished by the yellow star that branded them as something less than human, and then herded in thousands into extermination camps. Freemasons were persecuted. Politicians of the Third Republic, among them Blum, Daladier, Reynaud and General Gamelin, who had been imprisoned, were brought to trial as warmongers. The Treaty of Versailles had included a clause which provided that the Kaiser and others could be tried for war guilt. It had never been put into effect and the ex-Emperor had ended his days in Holland, peacefully chopping firewood. Still, the existence of the clause made the trials possible. Some of the best brains in France went into the dock and so turned the tables upon the prosecution that the trials were stopped before they could do further injury to the régime.

Below the surface the army of the Resistance was at work. It was forbidden to listen to English broadcasts, but they listened and spread the truth from the outer world by word of mouth or in clandestinely printed and circulated papers; they committed acts of sabotage, they smuggled Allied airmen who had been brought down to safety, passing them from contact to contact much as American people had once passed on runaway slaves; they picked up and passed on the encouraging pamphlets dropped from Allied planes. They were ordinary men and women of all ages and conditions, operating under the eyes of the most ruthless organization the world had yet seen; the torture chambers at Gestapo headquarters had methods of which the Inquisitors never dreamed. The Scarlet Pimpernel of the story, organizing his rescues, had wealth, neutral nationality, and a waiting yacht; the Pimpernels of the Resistance, harboring an Allied airman, were often hard

put to it to feed him, and ran risks never before faced by people—
in cold blood.

The Communists of France had been shattered by the Russo-
German non-aggression pact; they still thought Fascist and Communist ideologies were opposed. Then, when Germany invaded
Russia, they rallied under the leadership of Jacques Duclos. It was
a Communist resistance group, the Francs-Tireurs et Partisans, who
on the anniversary of the battle of Valmy issued a leaflet, "*La
Patrie en danger 1792–1943.*" It consisted of a rough woodcut of
the volunteers of Valmy and an appeal, "To save France like our
great ancestors, the volunteers of the *levée en masse*, to arms, Parisians! Forward and death to the *Boches!*"

In 1942 the Free French Army recognized the potential value
of this other army inside France and decided that co-ordination of
the various scattered groups would give them greater strength.
A National Council of Resistance was formed. Its first leader,
Jean Moulin, was caught by the Gestapo and died under torture.
Georges Bidault took his place and the fight went on.

Resistance, however determined and heroic, was not in itself
capable of lifting the Nazi yoke; the hopes of liberation centered
upon Britain and America. Britain had held out, made good the
loss of equipment at Dunkirk and proved her superiority in the
air. America had not—as once was feared—concentrated her whole
attention on the war with Japan. With her immense resources of
men and material she was able to wage war in the Pacific and
send men and supplies for the relief of Europe. Great American
air bases had been established on the eastern side of England, from
which planes flew almost nightly to bomb key points of industry
and communication in Germany and in German-held territory.

Nineteen forty-two was a decisive year. First came the Allied
raid on the submarine pens at St. Nazaire, then the Commando
landing at Dieppe. The latter was a failure, but even the sight of
English and Canadian soldiers being marched off as prisoners
brought reassurance of a kind. Outside France there were still
free people intent upon the liberation of Europe.

French spirits soared again when they learned of General Koenig's defense of Bir Hakeim in the Western Desert and the routing

of Rommel's army. Then, in November 1942, came the Allied landings in North Africa.

President Roosevelt had found General de Gaulle an uncomfortable ally and, when the Allies took Algiers and found that Admiral Darlan was in the city, they felt that—could he be persuaded to abandon Pétain and the Vichy government—he would make a more amenable chief for the Free French Forces. The admiral agreed but a month later was assassinated by a young Royalist fanatic. Deprived of their leader, the French scuttled their fleet at Toulon.

It was then proposed that General Giraud should take de Gaulle's place, and he was smuggled out of France for this purpose. But the attempt at substitution failed; Charles de Gaulle continued to lead Fighting France and to head the French National Committee, which was already making preparations for the liberation of France.

But the end was not yet. As a riposte to the North African landings, the Germans occupied the whole of France, introducing all the machinery of repression that they employed in the Occupied Zone. Increasing pressure was brought to bear upon Laval for more positive collaboration and the provision of French workers for German factories. The campaigns in Russia and North Africa had drained German resources.

A million and a half French prisoners were still in German hands, but even under its corrupt administration Germany made some distinction between men taken wearing their uniform and civilian labor. (The Japanese worked thousands of prisoners of war to death.) Laval was realist enough to know that Hitler was in a position to enforce his demand for laborers and that point-blank refusal would be useless. So he temporized and bargained on a system of exchange, so many workmen for so many returned prisoners. His tactics spared a number of Frenchmen from exile and exploitation, but about half a million men were taken.

Slave laborers of other nationalities were herded into France to work for the Todt organization, which was building the Atlantic Wall, "a belt of strong points and gigantic fortifications from Norway to the Pyrenees." German-held Europe was preparing to meet invasion.

There was other building going on too, particularly in the Calais area, mysterious erections which were to be the launching pads of a new weapon, unmanned missiles, the V1 and V2. Though unidentifiable they were suspected and regularly bombed by Allied planes, and as regularly built up again.

One result of the labor drafts was to send more and more young men into the army of the Resistance; better a hunted life as a member of the *maquis* than that of a slave laborer in a German factory, now being bombed by day and by night. (The word *maquis* came from Napoleon's birthplace.) At the end of 1943 the troops of Fighting France landed in Corsica and with the help of local resistance groups, liberated the island. The maquis was the thyme-scented scrub which had sheltered the Corsican resisters, and the name was adopted, so that a man was a *maquisard* whether he operated in the woods and forests of Savoy and the Vosges, in the country of sunken roads in the west of France, where once the Vendéens had defied the Revolution, or in some dreary street where the smell of a green thing growing was unknown.

To this swelling army, supplies and weapons were dropped by parachute by Allied planes and distributed through devious channels. A boy on a rattling bicycle might carry stuff that a little later would blow up a German supply train; harmless-looking old women handed and received strange things across counters. The army without uniform was in constant danger; the Germans realized that when invasion came—it was no longer a question of "if"—the maquisards would strike from within; so they redoubled their precautions and their penalties. They were aided by spies, and by the brutal French militia, composed of men dredged up from the worst elements in France, natural thugs, social misfits, kin to the anti-Bolshevik legion fighting alongside the Germans in Russia. Not the least agonizing part of France's long ordeal, and one that was to have a bitter aftermath, was this undeclared civil war between Frenchmen. When liberation came at last whole communities and individual families split over the question of who had resisted, who had endured passively, who had collaborated.

In June 1944, the Allied Expeditionary Force, under the overall command of General Eisenhower, was ready to make the assault on *"Fortress Europe."* For months workmen—most of them without knowing the end product of their labors—had been toiling away at the construction of two artificial harbors, each capable of dealing with the traffic of a sizable port. Every harbor in the southeast of England was crowded with ships of all descriptions and, through the long days and short nights of summer, masses of men and all that men need for modern warfare had been on the move. Green boughs were favored as camouflage—Birnam wood was moving to Dunsinane.

The artificial harbors had to be towed across the Channel, a tricky business in any weather, and the whole operation had to be deferred for two days because of unfavorable conditions; then on June 6 the world learned that D-day had come and that Allied troops were disembarking on the coast of Normandy.

Today, in summer, Arromanches, like any other little seaside town, sleeps in the sun, its tranquillity disturbed by nothing more than the voices of children playing and the cries of gulls—once believed to be dead seamen reincarnated. Offshore there floats a broken breakwater, all that remains of Mulberry, the artificial harbor which made possible the landing of the Allied troops on that June morning. The dead have been decently interred, the tides and the rains have washed away the blood; in June, Arromanches sleeps in the sun . . .

In southwestern France an even warmer sun shines on another place, Oradour-sur-Glane: there, lest the French should think that liberation was a foregone conclusion, the Germans massacred the entire population, and then set fire to the village.

General de Gaulle had not even been informed of the date of D-day, though a general call had been sent out to the army of resistance, asking it to support the Allied landings; the response had been energetic and enthusiastic. The Allies intended to set up a temporary military government in France. They underestimated both the determination of the man himself—sometimes they had been inclined to look upon him as a negligible nuisance—and the devotion which he inspired in many French hearts. On June 14 he was rapturously welcomed in Bayeux—the town where hangs the tapestry which commemorates another invasion, that of England by Normandy—and close behind him were his chosen administrators, Frenchmen to govern France. It may be a peculiarity of the twentieth century, when more words are bandied about than ever before, that words seem to have lost value. Hitler put his intentions into words, so did Churchill, so did de Gaulle. When he said, *"Vive la France,"* he meant France, freed from her foes, independent of her friends.

The Allied advance continued, violently resisted; before Caen was liberated half the city was razed to the ground. In Provence, General Patch landed, and with him came General de Lattre de Tassigny, known to the Resistance as *Père La Violette;* Marseilles once again heard its own song, the "War Song of the Army of the Rhine"— the "Marseillaise"—as French troops entered the city.

The forces of liberation were now pushing from the north, the west and the south and, though the Germans fought on stubbornly, they were driven backward. Where they could, they picked up French government officials, old Pétain, out-and-out collaborators like Déat and Doriot. They took Laval, but he managed to escape and fled to Spain.

On August 1, 1944, the Second Armored Division of Frenchmen, commanded by General Leclerc de Hautecloque, who used General Leclerc as his *nom de guerre,* landed in France and was given a rapturous welcome. Their tanks and armored cars bore, in addition to the *tricolore,* the double cross of Lorraine, Joan of Arc's emblem, which had been adopted as the symbol of Fighting France. To Leclerc, General Eisenhower, in a delicate and chivalrous gesture, left the actual liberation of the capital, and Leclerc, from the suburbs, two days later, issued his order, "Take possession of Paris."

There was still danger that Paris, when taken, would be as derelict as Moscow in 1812 or Warsaw in 1940. Hitler, in a frenzy, ordered that the city should be set on fire; but the people of Paris had a long history of street fighting. German tanks still patrolled streets, but up went the barricades again, manned by anyone who could lay hands on a weapon. Paris was not burned. Today, in humdrum streets, a plaque on a wall, a little vase of flowers, and the legend MORT POUR LA FRANCE commemorate those who, in the eleventh hour, gave their lives.

Anxiety and uncertainty as to the city's fate still hung heavily, when suddenly the bells rang out after a four-year silence, carrying the news from steeple to steeple; "Leclerc is here—he has come, Leclerc, Leclerc, Leclerc!" Indifferent to snipers and pockets of German resistance, Paris went mad with joy. "Everyone suddenly burst out singing . . ." This sad war had bred no songs, and it was the songs of long ago which were sung: "Marche Lorraine," "Sambre et Meuse," "La Madelon" and the "Marseillaise," the battle hymn of the old republic.

At four o'clock on the afternoon of August 25, 1944, General von Choltitz, who had been Governor of *"Gross Paris"* met General Leclerc at the Hôtel de Ville, where so many stirring scenes of French history had been enacted, and there accepted the terms of an armistice. The worst experience that the country had yet been called upon to endure was over.

The next day, August 26, saw the birth of a new life and a new period. Through a human sea, and flanked on one side by General Koenig, on the other by General Leclerc, Charles de Gaulle marched from the Arc de Triomphe, down the length of the Champs Elysées, past the river Seine and on until he reached Notre Dame, the cathedral church which for eight hundred years had been the heart of Paris. Its old walls had echoed to many Te Deums, some for victories long forgotten, some long remembered —Wagram, Friedland, Austerlitz—but this Te Deum was unique. It brought together two of the strands that had been separated in 1940, the French who had fought from abroad and who had come to Notre Dame by way of Chad, Fez, Tripolitania, Tunisia, Morocco and England and those who had fought at home.

Nobody doubted the magnitude of the tasks that lay ahead; this war had inflicted more than death, more than material damage; upon a nation already suffering from so many divisions, it had made a cleavage far more difficult to repair than broken walls and bridges and railway lines. There would be—in French tradition—purges, bitter recriminations and accusations, conflicting policies, irreconcilable claims. But all that was for the future, when France must once again resume one entity.

Now the mood was one of joy and thankfulness. Thanks be to God for the liberation, for survival; for the fighting spirit that had shown itself on named battlefields, in little places too numerous to be named; for that other spirit that enables humans to live on hope and cabbage water.

Thanks and praise be to God. Heads which the Germans had failed to batter down, bowed. When they lifted, many eyes turned toward one who had been a disembodied voice, a name, a symbol, an inspiration, one to whom this war had dealt many invisible wounds, borne with fortitude, but not forgotten, one whose single-minded *"Vive la France"* was a motto for peace as well as for war—General Charles de Gaulle.

INDEX

Abd-el-Kader, 126
Abd El Krim, 281
Aberdeen, George Hamilton-Gordon, Lord, 134
Aboukir, 34
Abrantès, Andoche Junot, Duc d', 52
Abrantès, Laure Junot, Duchesse d', 71, 118
Abyssinia, 290
Acre, 34
Adelaide, Madame, 110, 139
Aduwa, 290
Aesop, 190
Afghanistan, 52
Africa, 134, 207, 213, 232–33. *See also* North Africa; specific places
Agadir, 238
Aida, 189
Aide-toi-et-Dieu-t'aidera, 99, 100, 120
Aiglon, L', 226
Aix-la-Chapelle, Congress of, 90
Alba, Duke of, 166
Albert, Prince, 135, 172, 173
Albert (in Provisional Government), 149
Albuera, 56
Alexander I, Czar, 46, 52–53, 57, 58, 65ff., 84; and Richelieu, 85
Alexander II, Czar, 173, 174
Alexander, King of Yugoslavia, 290
Algeçiras, 235, 238
Algeria(ns), 125, 153, 183, 213–14, 238, 280–81, 294
Algiers, 102, 309
Alma, 171
Alsace and Lorraine, 83–84, 99, 192, 198, 220, 243–44, 253, 266, 268, 270 (*See also* Revanche); Algerian colonists from, 214; and strengthening of clerical party, 275; and World War II, 301
America. *See* United States
Ami du Peuple, L', 12
Amiens, 39, 41, 42, 236
Ampère, André Marie, 89
Ancona, 51
Angoulême, Louis Antoine de Bourbon, Duc d', 68, 78, 92, 97, 105, 106
Angoulême, Marie Thérèse, Duchesse d', 23, 72, 75, 78, 97, 99, 203
Annam, 212
Anti-Semitism. *See* Jews and anti-Semitism
Apaches, 227
Arabi Pasha, 212
Arago, Dominique François, 149
Arc de Triomphe, 81, 175
Arcola, 31, 80
Argonne, 263
Arras, 255
Arromanches, 311
Artois, Charles Philippe, Comte d', *See* Charles X
Artois, 247, 253

Arts, the, 27, 88–90, 132, 168–69, 208, 226–28, 279–80. *See also* Music; Painting
Aspern-Essling, 54
Asquith, Herbert. *See* Oxford and Asquith, Herbert Henry Asquith, Earl of
Assembly. *See* Parliament, houses of
Atala (Chateaubriand), 90
Atlantic Wall, 309
Auber, Daniel, 132, 192
Aubervilliers, 290
Augsburg, 44
Augusta of Bavaria, Princess, 45
Aumale, Duc d', 111, 114, 144
Austerlitz, 44, 51, 80, 97, 217
Australians, 249, 261
Austria, 18ff., 114, 116, 126, 174, 201, 209, 212, 220, 226; and Great War; aftermath, 241–42, 269; Louis XVIII and, 76, 81, 84; Napoleon I and, 29, 31, 39, 44, 52, 54ff., 60ff., 65ff.; Napoleon III (2nd Empire) and, 177, 178, 184, 186, 188, 197
Automobiles (motorcars), 228
Auvergne; Auvergnats, 88, 289

Babeuf, François, 30
Bad Ems, 191
Badajoz, 58
Baedeker, 227
Balkans, 214, 252. *See also* specific countries
Ballets Russes, 279
Balzac, Honoré de, 118
Bank of France (Banque de France), 36, 294
Bapaume, 236
Barbizon school, 132
Baroche, Pierre Jules, 164
Barras, Paul François Nicolas, Comte de, 25, 28–29, 30–31, 35, 37
Barrès, Maurice, 223
Barthou, Louis, 151, 219, 240, 282
Bastille, the, 9, 14, 210, 218
Baudelaire, Charles, 169
Bautzen, 60
Bayeux, 311–12
Bayonne, 287
Bazaine, Achille, 185, 192, 195, 248
Beauharnais, Eugène de, 30, 43, 44, 60, 62; marriage, 45
Beauharnais, Hortense de, 30, 39, 43, 124, 158
Beauharnais, Josephine de. *See* Josephine, Empress
Beaumarchais, Pierre de, 6
Beaumont-Hamel, 263
Beets, 51–52
Belfort, 202
Belgium, 19, 20, 29, 79, 84, 115, 280, 295; coal from, 123; and Great War, 242–43, 245ff.; Louis Philippe and, 113–14;

Napoleon III and, 189; World War II and, 299
Belle Hélène, La, 168
Belle Poule (ship), 128
Belleville, 189
Benedetti, Vincent, Count, 191
Berezina River, 59
Berlin, 45, 191, 209, 242ff.
Berlioz, Hector, 132
Bernadotte, Jean-Baptiste, 61
Bernhardt, Sarah, 208, 226
Berri, Caroline Fernande Louise, Duchesse de, 86, 91, 117
Berri, Charles Ferdinand, Duc de, 68, 86, 91, 112, 134
Berryer, Louis Napoleon and, 155
Berthier, Louis Alexandre, 34
Bertier de Sauvigny, G., 89n
Bethmann-Hollweg, Theobald von, 243
Biarritz, 168, 186, 189
Bicycles, 228; forerunner of, 87
Bidault, Georges, 308
Big Bertha, 262, 289
Bir Hakeim, 308
Bismarck, Otto von, 86, 188ff., 197, 200–1, 204, 212, 224; dismissed, 220; and Eastern Question, 208–9
Bizet, Georges, 208
Blacas, Duc de, 77
Black Sea, 172, 174, 249
Blanc, Louis, 121, 149, 150, 151, 197
Blériot, Louis, 237
Bloc des Gauches, 225, 231, 236
Bloc National, 273, 277
Blücher, Gebhart Leberecht von, 79, 81
Blum, Léon, 273, 291–92, 293, 295, 307
Boer War, 233
Bolshevism; Bolsheviks, 264, 275. *See also* Russia: Revolution
Bonaparte, Caroline (Caroline Murat), 39, 44, 45, 46–47, 202
Bonaparte, Elisa, 44
Bonaparte, Jerome, 43, 165
Bonaparte, Joseph, 31, 34, 43, 45, 47, 53, 58
Bonaparte, Letizia, 45
Bonaparte, Louis (King of Holland), 43, 45, 46, 57, 124, 158; wife (*See* Beauharnais, Hortense de)
Bonaparte, Lucien, 35, 43
Bonaparte, Napoleon. *See* Napoleon I
Bonaparte, Napoleon Eugène Louis Jean Joseph (son of Napoleon III) 173–74, 188, 193, 207
Bonaparte, Napoleon Joseph Charles Paul. *See* Napoleon, Prince
Bonaparte, Pauline (Pauline Leclerc; Princess Borghese), 41, 44, 45, 76, 176
Bonaparte and the Bourbons, 68
Bonaparte, Lieutenant of Artillery, 118
Bonapartes, 77, 86, 115, 116, 177, 179–80. *See also* specific family members
Bonapartists, 86, 93, 96, 97, 149, 197 (*See also* specific persons); facial hair of, 131
Bône, 242
Bonnemains, Marguerite, Vicomtesse de (mistress of Boulanger), 214, 217, 218
Bonnie Prince Charlie, 117
Bordeaux, Duc de. *See* Chambord, Henri

Charles Ferdinand Marie Dieudonné, Comte de
Bordeaux, 24, 78, 88, 160, 196, 197, 247, 300, 301, 302
Borghese, Prince Camillo, 45
Borghese, Princess Pauline. *See* Bonaparte, Pauline
Borodino, 58
Bosnia, 209, 241
Bougainville, Louis Antoine de, 133
Boulanger, Georges, and Boulangism, 214–15, 217–18, 219
Boulevard du Temple, 81
Boulogne; the Boulonnais, 42, 172, 247
Bourbon, Duc de, 110–11
Bourbons, 4, 36, 38, 41–42, 67, 82, 86, 90ff., 96, 107, 203. *See also* Royalists; specific family members
Bourmont, Louis Auguste, Comte de, 100
Bourrienne, Louis Antoine Fauvelet de, 33
Boxer rebellion, 233
Branly, Edouard, 228
Braque, Georges, 228, 279
Brazil, 52
Breslau (cruiser), 242
Brest-Litovsk, 260
Briand, Aristide, 236–37, 239, 240, 243, 250, 258, 273ff., 280, 282ff., 290, 292
Brissot, J. P., 18, 22
Britain. *See* England
Broglie, Jacques Victor Albert, Duc de, 202, 203, 204
Brunswick, Charles William Ferdinand, Duke of, 19
Brussels, 246
Buckingham Palace, 171
Bugeaud de la Piconnerie, Thomas Robert, 155
Bulgaria, 263
Busaco, 56
Byron, George Gordon Byron, Lord, 117

C.G.T. (General Confederation of Labor), 236, 237, 273
C.G.T.U., 273
Cadiz, Duke of, 136
Cadoudal, Georges, 42
Caen, 313
Café de Paris, 132
Café Riche, 132
Cagoulards, 292
Caillaux, Joseph, 239ff., 254–55, 258, 260, 278, 282
Caillaux, Mme. Joseph, 240, 241
Calais, 310
Calendar, new, 21
Calmette (editor), 240
Cambacérès, Jean Jacques Régis de, 36
Camelots du Roi, 286, 287–88
Campagne de Russie, 118
Campo Formio, Peace of, 31
Canadians, 261, 308
Cannes, 77, 276
Canrobert, François Certain, 171
Caporetto, 259
Carbonari, the, 116
Carlotta, Empress, 184, 185
Carnot, Lazare, 25, 37
Carnot, Nicolas Léonard Sadi, 89
Carnot, Sadi, 221

Caroline of Brunswick, 70
Cartel des Gauches, 277, 278, 281
Casablanca, 238
Caserio (assassin), 221
Casimir-Périer, Jean Paul Pierre, 219, 221
Castiglione, Countess of, 176
Castiglione, 31
Catherine of Württemberg, 160
Catholicism; Catholics (the Church; anti-
    clericalism; etc.), 209–10, 212, 223, 231–
    32, 271–72, 275, 277 (See also specific
    adherents); Charles X and, 95ff.; Louis
    XVI, the Revolution, and, 14–15, 19, 24,
    40; in Louis Philippe's reign, 112, 133–34;
    Napoleon I and, 40, 42, 50–51; Na-
    poleon III and, 156, 162, 170, 182–83ff.
Caulaincourt, Armand Augustin Louis, Mar-
    quis de, 57
Cavaignac, Godefroy, 106, 121
Cavaignac, Louis Eugène, 152, 153, 154, 155,
    156, 219
Cavour, Camillo, 174, 176, 177, 178, 179
Cayla, Zoë Talon, Comtesse du, 92
Cazamian, Louis, 89
Cetewayo, 207
Cézanne, Paul, 208
Chamber. See Parliament, houses of
Chamberlain, Sir Austen, 280
Chamberlain, Neville, 296
Chambord, Henri Charles Ferdinand Marie
    Dieudonné, Comte de (formerly Duc de
    Bordeaux; known as Henri V), 91, 106,
    107, 117, 125, 157, 203–4
Champ de Mai, 78–79
Champ de Mars, 14, 16
Champagne, 65, 247, 253
Champs Elysées, 129
Charivari (paper), 119
Charlemagne, 44
Charles I, Emperor of Austria, 263
Charles I, King of England, 22
Charles X, 95–107, 112, 116, 144; as Comte
    d'Artois, 4–5, 10, 11, 16–17, 68, 69, 75,
    83, 84, 91–92, 94; death of, 125
Charles William Ferdinand, Duke of Bruns-
    wick, 19
Charpentier, Gustave, 227
Château d'Eu, 135, 136
Chateaubriand, François Renë, Vicomte de,
    27, 51, 68, 89–90, 93, 95, 117
Châtillon, 65, 67
Chautemps, Camille, 273, 287, 292, 294, 295
Chemin des Dames, 254
Chénier, André, 27
Chevalier, Maurice, 279
Chevaliers de la Foi, 68
China, 183, 233, 281, 306
Choltitz, General von, 313
Chopin, Frederic, 132
Church, the (See also Catholicism; Cath-
    olics): Orthodox, 170
Churchill, Sir Winston, 259, 272, 299–300,
    302
Cisalpine Republic, 31, 37
Ciudad Rodrigo, 58
Clemenceau, Georges, 197, 212, 236–37, 258–
    59ff.; 263, 265, 271–72, 275; and Bou-
    langer, 215, 217; and Dreyfus, 223; and
    Panama Canal scandal, 218–19; and Ver-

sailles, 267, 268; and Wilson scandal,
    216–17
Clermont-Ferrand, 215
Cleves and Berg, Grand Duchy of, 45
Clive, Robert, 69
Clothilde, Princess, 179
Clovis, 15
Cochin China, 183
Cocteau, Jean, 280
Code Napoléon, 37, 205
Coke of Holkham, 87
Combes, Emile, 231–32
Comédie Française, 59, 143, 288
Comité des Forges, 200, 282, 294
Committee of Public Safety, 24, 25
Commune; Communards, 10, 199, 207–8
Communists, 272–73, 308. See also Bolshe-
    vism; Socialism; specific individuals
Compiègne, 168, 264
Condé family, 42
Congo, 232, 238
Constant, Benjamin, 90
Consulate, 33–43
Continental Decrees; System, 45, 50, 56, 57,
    64
Cook, James, 133
Coolidge, Calvin, 279
Copenhagen, Battle of, 40
Corday, Charlotte, 24
Cordeliers, 17
Corot, Jean Baptiste Camille, 132
Corsica, 177, 310
Coste (aviator), 282
Councils, 28, 31–33
Crédit Lyonnais, 201
Crédit Mobilier, 188
Crimean War, 135, 170–72, 173, 174
Croix de Feu, 286, 293
Cromwell (Hugo), 89
Curie, Marie and Pierre, 228
Czechoslovakia, 269, 280, 295, 296–97

Daguerre, Louis, 89
Dakar, 306
Daladier, Edouard, 287ff., 292, 295ff., 305,
    307
Dame aux Camélias, La, 169, 226
Danton, Jacques, 17, 20, 23, 25
Danube River, 174
Danzig, 268
Dardanelles, the, 249
Darlan, Jean François, 305, 309
Daumier, Honoré, 119
David, Jacques-Louis, 27, 48
Davout, Louis Nicolas, 82
Dawes Plan, 277
D-day, 311
Déat (collaborationist), 312
Debussy, Claude, 228
Decazes, Elie, 91, 92
Declaration of the Rights of Man, 11
Degas, Edgar, 208
Dego, 31
Déjeuner sur l'Herbe, 208
Delcassé, Théophile, 232, 233, 234–35, 237,
    243
Demidoff, Count, 165
Denmark, 184, 186, 299
Derain, André, 228
Déroulède, Paul, 215, 223, 224–25

Deschanel, Paul, 219, 272
Desmoulins, Camille, 17, 23
Devil's Island, 222, 223
Diaghilev, Sergei, 279
Dieppe, 308
Directory, the, 30–32, 33–35
Disarmament Commission, 282
Divorce, 28, 130, 131
Dollfuss, Engelbert, 290
Donon, the, 246
Dordogne, the, 247
Doriot, Jacques, 312
Doumer, Paul, 285
Doumergue, Gaston, 240, 241, 278, 284–85, 289
Dresden, 58, 60, 61
Dreyfus, Alfred; Dreyfus affair, 222–24, 232, 237
Druses, the, 280
Duclos, Jacques, 308
Duma, the, 236
Dumas, Alexandre, *fils*, 169
Dumouriez, Charles François, 20, 24, 109
Dunant, Henri, 178
Dunkirk, 299, 308
Dupuy, Charles, 220
Duruy, Victor, 183

Ecole Normale, 26
Ecole Polytechnique, 26
Education, 36, 97, 120, 156, 183, 231
Edward VII (son of Queen Victoria), 162, 220, 233–34
Egypt, 33–34, 40, 98, 126ff., 133, 189; Clemenceau and, 212; and Fashoda incident, 232, 234
Eiffel Tower, 218
Eisenhower, Dwight D., 309–10, 312
Elba, 69, 70, 75–76, 77, 90
Elchingen, 44
Electoral law. *See* Suffrage
Eliot, George, 132–33
Elisabeth, Madame (sister of Louis XVI), 19, 23
Elizabeth, Queen Consort of England, 295
Elysée, 202, 203. *See also* specific occupants
Empire. *See* First Empire; Second Empire
Enghien, Louis Antoine Henri de Bourbon-Condé, Duc d', 42, 51, 85
England and the English (the British; Great Britain), 11, 19, 23, 123, 132–33, 200, 204, 205, 208, 212, 213, 226, 232ff. (*See also* specific battles, leaders, places, refugees in, etc.); between World Wars, 267ff., 275, 279, 284, 287, 291, 295; in Charles X's reign, 98; Continental Decrees against, 45, 50, 56, 57, 64; and Great War, 242–43, 244, 245, 247ff., 256ff., 261, 262, 264; Louis XVIII and, 74, 76, 81ff., Louis Philippe and, 109–10, 114–15, 125ff., 133ff.; Napoleon I and, 26, 33, 34, 39, 42ff., 52ff., 67ff., 79, 117; in Napoleon III's reign, 170ff., 174–75, 179, 180, 183, 184, 191, 192; in World War II, 298ff., 306, 308, 311
Erfurt, 52–53
Erzberger, Matthias, 264
Essay on Revolutions, 27
Esterhazy, Ferdinand Walsin, 223

Etat Français, 302ff.
Eugénie, Empress, 166–68, 169, 172–73, 176ff., 185, 188, 189, 191ff., 207; and Clemenceau, 272; pregnant; bears son, 173–74
Euripides, 299
Eylau, 46

Faidherbe, Louis, 213
Falkenhayn, Erich, von, 250, 251
Fallières, Armand, 236, 240
Families, 28, 123, 130–31, 229–30, 270
Fascism, 273. *See also* specific countries, leaders
Fashoda, 232–33, 234
Faubourg St. Germain, 83, 131
Faure, Félix, 222, 224
Fauré, Gabriel, 227
Favre, Jules, 196, 197
February Revolution (1848), 141–46, 150
Ferdinand I, King of the Two Sicilies, 86
Ferdinand VII, King of Spain, 92
Ferry, Jules, 209, 210, 211–12ff., 216, 220
Fersen, Axel, 15
Fez, 238, 281
Figaro, Le, 240
First Empire, 43–68, 190, 200
First International, the, 187
First Republic, 21–43
Flahaut de la Billarderie, Auguste Charles Joseph, Comte de, 158
Flanders, 258, 260, 263
Flaubert, Gustave, 169
Fleurs du Mal, Les, 169
Foch, Ferdinand, 250, 261, 264, 275
Folies Bergère, 227
Fontainebleau, 51, 67, 70
Foreign Legion, 238
Fouché, Joseph, 25, 37, 40, 47, 57, 82, 83
Fould, Achille, 164
Fourteen Points, 260, 269
Fox, Charles James, 39–40
France, Anatole, 223, 227
Franchise. *See* Suffrage
Francis II, Emperor (Francis of Austria), 17, 55, 66–67
Francis Ferdinand (Franz Ferdinand), Archduke, 241
Francis Joseph (Franz Josef), Emperor, 174, 178, 179, 241, 263
Franck, César, 208, 227
Franco, Francisco, 293
Francs-Tireurs et Partisans, 308
Frankfurt, Peace of, 198
Franz. *See* Francis
Frederick the Great, 14
Frederick William, former Crown Prince. *See* William I
Frederick William II, King of Prussia, 20
Frederick William III, King of Prussia, 66
Free France; Free French, 304ff.
Freemasons, 307
Fréjus, 34
French Guiana, 32
French Revolution 1788–1792, The, 13n
Freud, Sigmund, 279–80
Freycinet, Charles de, 210
Friedland, 46, 118
Frohsdorf, 203
Fuentes de Oñoro, 56

Galliéni, Joseph Simon, 213, 238–39, 248
Gallipoli, 249
Gambetta, Léon, 189–90, 193, 195–96, 197, 201, 208ff., 244; retirement; death, 211
Gambling, 132
Gamelin, Maurice Gustave, 299, 300, 307
Garcin, M., 87
Garçonne, La, 279
Garnier-Pagès, Louis Antoine, 149
Gaudin (financier), 37, 48
Gauguin, Paul, 228
Gaulle, Charles de, 275, 286, 298, 304, 305–6, 309, 311–12ff.
Gavarni (artist), 119
Gaza, 34
Geddes, Sir Eric, 267
General Confederation of Labor (C.G.T.), 236, 237, 273
Geneva, 283
Génie du Christianisme, 90
Genlis, Madame de, 109
Genoa, 37
George IV, 114; as Prince Regent, 70
George VI, 295
George, Mademoiselle, 118
Germains, the, 201
Germany and the Germans, 114, 117, 186, 190–91, 197ff., 215, 228, 229, 233ff., 238ff. (See also Prussia and the Prussians; specific leaders, places); between World Wars, 267ff., 274ff., 280, 282ff., 290, 291ff.; Great War, 241–42ff., 245–64; in Triple Alliance, 212, 220, 234; World War II, 298–314
Gestapo, the, 301, 307, 308
Ghent, 78, 80
Gibraltar, 137
Gide, André, 227, 279
Gioconda, La, 238
Giradoux, Jean, 280
Giraud, Henri Honoré, 309
Girondists, 18, 19–20, 24, 25
Goeben (cruiser), 242
Goering, Hermann, 301
Goethe, Johann Wolfgang von, 117
Gogh, Vincent van, 228
Gooch, G. P., 161
Gouvion-Saint-Cyr, Laurent, Marquis de (Marshal St. Cyr), 82, 92
Goya, Francisco de, 52
Grand Army, 57–60, 64
Grand Duchess of Gerolstein, The, 168, 188
Grande Illusion, La, 295
Great Britain. See England and the English
Great War, the, 242–65
Great War 1914–1919, The, 253n, 261n
Greece and the Greeks, 98, 306
Gregoire, Abbé, 21
Gregory XVI, Pope, 116
Grenoble, 77, 79
Grévy, Jules, 154, 197–98, 208, 210, 211, 216–17
Grey, Sir Edward, 244
Guastalla, Duchy of, 45
Guesde, Jules, 208, 236, 243
Guillotin, Dr., 7
Guillotine, the, 7, 23, 24–25, 72. See also specific victims
Guizot, François, 88–89, 90, 116, 120, 124, 125, 128, 155; dismissal, 142; as Louis

Philippe's chief minister, 133, 134, 137, 138, 140, 141, 142, 145

Haig, Douglas Haig, Earl, 261
Hair, facial, 131, 237
Halévy, Jacques, 132, 169
Ham, 129, 138–39, 166
Hanoi, 212
Hapsburgs, 55, 184, 185. See also specific family members
Hari, Mata, 258
Haussmann, Georges Eugène, Baron, 178, 188
Heine, Heinrich, 117
Henri V. See Chambord, Henri Charles Ferdinand Marie Dieudonné, Comte de
Henry, Colonel, 223
Henry, Emile, 221
Herriot, Edouard, 273, 277, 278, 282, 284, 285, 289
Herzegovina, 209, 241
Hindenburg, Paul von, 251, 260, 264, 280
Histoire des Girondins, 139, 147
History of Western Europe 1815–1926, A, 246n
Hitler, Adolf, 280, 283–84ff., 290, 291, 295ff., 298, 299, 303ff.; and burning of Paris, 312
Hoare, Sir Samuel, 290
Hohenzollerns, 191. See also specific family members
Holland (Netherlands), 23, 24, 29, 34, 42, 57, 113, 115; King of (See Bonaparte, Louis); and World War II, 299
Holy Roman Empire, 44. See also specific rulers
Holyroodhouse, 182
Hôtel de Ville, 145, 196, 313
Howard, Miss, 149, 155, 166, 167
Hugo, Victor, 89, 119, 173, 197, 288; funeral, 214
Humanité, L', 230, 242
Hundred Days, the, 77–80, 82, 83, 84–85
Hungary, 296

Imperial Guard, 71
India, 33, 34, 170, 171, 174, 281
Indians, American, 90
Indochina, 183, 212–13, 281
Industry, 87, 123, 200, 270. See also Socialism and socialists; specific places
Influenza, 267
Ingres, Jean, 132
Institute of France, 26
Invalides, the, 129, 248, 303
Irish, the, 252
Isabella II, Queen of Spain, 136–37
Italy, 224, 238, 286, 290–91, 293 (See also specific leaders, places); in Louis Philippe's reign, 113, 116; Napoleon I and, 29, 31, 34, 37, 44, 117; Napoleon III (Louis Napoleon) and, 156, 174, 176–78ff., 186, 187; in Triple Alliance, 212, 220, 234; in World War I, 259, 267; in World War II, 299–300, 306

J'Accuse, 223
Jacobins, 17, 18, 19, 20
Jaffa, 34
James II, 101

Japan, 188, 235, 306, 307, 308, 309
Jaurès, Jean, 214, 219, 223, 230, 236; as-
    sassination of, 242
Jefferson, Thomas, 91
Jemappes, 20
Jena, 80, 118
Jesse, Tennyson, 266n
Jesuits, 156
Jews and anti-Semitism, 283, 286, 287, 307;
    Dreyfus case, 222–24, 232, 237
Joan of Arc, 275
Joffre, Joseph, 248, 251
John VI, King of Portugal, 52
"John Bull," 205
Joinville, Prince de, 128, 144
Josephine, Empress (Madame Bonaparte),
    29–30, 34, 37, 38–39, 44, 46ff., 53, 65;
    death, 79; divorce, 55–56
Josephine, or the Return from Wagram, 118
Juarez, Pablo, 183–84, 185
Jullien (conductor), 168
July Monarchy. See Louis Philippe
July Revolution, 104–6. See also Trois
    Glorieuses, Les
Junot, Andoche, 52
Junot, Laure, Duchesse d'Abrantès, 71, 118

Kapital, Das, 187, 208
Keitel, Wilhelm, 301
Kellogg-Briand Pact, 282
Kitchener, Horatio Herbert Kitchener, Earl,
    232
Koenig, General, 308, 313
Kronstadt, 220
Kruger, Paul, 233
Krupp, Friedrich Alfred, 262

Labiche, Eugène Marin, 169
Labori, Ferdinand, 241
La Bourdonnaye (Minister of the Interior),
    100
Laënnec, René, 89
Lafayette, Marquis de, 10, 12, 13, 15, 16,
    20, 65, 105, 106, 116–17; and Aide-
    toi-et-Dieu-t'aidera, 99, 100; and Louis
    XVIII, 90, 91
Lafitte, Jacques, 90, 101
Lâiné (legislator), 63
Lamarck, Jean de Monet, Chevalier de, 89
Lamarque (commander), 118
Lamartine, Alphonse de, 90, 102, 118, 139,
    143, 147–48ff.
Lamballe, Marie de Savoie-Carnignan, Prin-
    cesse de, 20
Lammenais (socialist), 122
Lannes, Jean, 34
La Rochefoucauld-Liancourt, François, Duc
    de, 1, 3, 9
La Rocque, Colonel de, 275, 286
Latin Quarter, 131
Lattre de Tassigny, General de, 312
Laval, Pierre, 273, 284, 289–90, 291, 302,
    305, 306–7, 309, 312
Law, John, 5
League of Nations, 268–69, 273, 274, 282,
    286, 290
League of Patriots, 214, 224–25
League of the Rights of Man, 215
Lebanon, 280
Lebrun, Albert, 285, 297, 302

Lebrun, Charles François, 36
Leclerc, Charles Victor Emmanuel, 41
Leclerc, Jacques Philippe (de Hautecloque),
    312, 313
Leclerc, Pauline. See Bonaparte, Pauline
Le Creusot, 123, 200
Ledru-Rollin, Alexandre, 122, 151, 197
Léger, Fernand, 279
Legislature. See Parliament, houses of
Legitimists, 117, 125, 131, 134, 141, 157, 162,
    163, 197, 203
Le Havre, 210
Leipzig, 61
Lenin, Vladimir Ilyich, 255
Léon, Léonie, 210
Leonardo da Vinci, 238
Leopardi, Giacomo, Conte, 117
Leopold I, King of Belgium, 107, 114, 126,
    127, 182
Leopold von Hohenzollern, Prince, 190
Leroy (dressmaker), 48, 96
Lesseps, Ferdinand de, 214, 219
Le Tréport, 135
Lieven, Dorothea, Princess, 121, 125
Ligny, 79
Ligurian Republic, 31
Lille, 210
Lincoln, Abraham, 185
Lisbon, 52
Literature, 27, 89–90, 132–33, 169, 227, 279–
    80; on Napoleon, 117–18
Little Entente, the, 269
Lloyd George, David, 238, 252, 263, 267ff.,
    276
Locarno Treaties, 280
Lodi, 31
Loi Falloux, 156, 183
Loire, the, 196
Lombardy, 177, 179
Longchamp, 231
London, 115, 121, 125, 170, 187, 234, 238,
    304 (See also specific refugees in); and
    bombing, 262, 306; Naval Disarmament
    Conference, 283
London Missionary Society, 133
Longwy, 20
Lorraine. See Alsace and Lorraine
Loubet, Emile, 226, 231, 234, 236
Louis XIII, 3, 85
Louis XIV, 5, 50, 164
Louis XV, 4, 5
Louis XVI, 1–24, 55, 74, 86, 102, 103, 109,
    144, 222
Louis XVII (Dauphin; son of Louis XVI),
    13, 15, 19, 23, 30
Louis XVIII, 38–39, 41–42, 43, 68–78, 80,
    81–94, 96, 97, 107, 157; as Comte de
    Provence, 4, 16, 17, 30
Louis, Baron, 76, 82, 100
Louis Napoleon. See Napoleon III
Louis Philippe, 107–8, 109–44ff., 148, 149,
    153; as Duc d'Orléans, 24, 96, 101, 105–
    6, 107–8
Louise, Queen of Belgium, 114, 134, 145
Louise (opera), 227
Louisiana, 41
Louvre, the, 31, 39, 83, 238
Ludendorff, Erich, 251, 260, 261, 280
Lumière, Louis, 228
Lunéville, Treaty of, 39
Lusitania (ship), 252

Lützen, 60
Luxembourg, 29, 189, 242
Lyautey, Louis, 238–39, 281
Lyonnais, 65
Lyons, 26, 88, 168, 188, 221, 278; riots,
    disorders, 24, 112, 121, 210

Macartney, Lord, 73
MacDonald, Alexandre, 82
MacMahon, Marie de, 171, 192, 193, 202–
    3, 205–6, 208
Mâcon, 147
Madagascar, 213
Madame Bovary, 169
Madrid, 52, 53
Magenta, 178
Maginot, André, 263, 283
Maginot Line, 283, 298
Mainz, 20
Maison du Roi, 75, 79
Malet, General, 59–60
Mallarmé, Stéphane, 227
Malmaison, 79
Malta, 42
Malvy, Louis, 254–55, 258, 260
Manet, Edouard, 208
Manzoni, Alessandro, 117
Maquis. See Resistance
Marat, Jean-Paul, 12, 17, 23, 24
Marchand, Jean Baptiste, 232
Marconi, Guglielmo, Marchese, 228
Marengo, 37
Margueritte, Victor, 279
Maria Theresa, 5
"Marianne," 205
Marie Amelie (wife of Louis Philippe), 110,
    134, 144
Marie Antoinette, 4, 5, 8, 11, 13ff., 19, 20,
    23, 55
Marie Louise, 55–56, 57, 59, 66, 67, 165–66
Marie-Thérèse. *See* Angoulême, Marie-Thé-
    rèse, Duchesse d'
Marmont, Auguste de, 34, 67, 69, 88, 103–4,
    105
Marne, the, 248, 262
Marriage, 230. *See also* Divorce; Families
Marriage of Figaro, 6
"Marseillaise," the, 18, 192, 312
Marseilles, 24, 210, 290, 312
Martignac, Jean Baptiste Sylvère Gay, Vi-
    comte de, 99, 100
Marx, Karl, 187, 208
Mary Stuart, 22, 182
Masefield, John, 80
Massif Central, 188
Mata Hari, 258
Mathilde, Princess, 165, 166
Matignon Agreement, 292
Matisse, Henri, 228, 279
Mauritius, 213
Maximilian, 184, 185
Maxim's, 227
Mazzini, Giuseppe, 156
Méditations Poétiques, 90
Mehemet Ali, 126, 128
Meilhac, Henri, 169
Méline tariff, 219
Mémoires d'Outre-Tombe, 90
*Memorial of St. Helena, The (Mémorial de
    Ste. Hélène),* 79, 118

Mérimée, Prosper, 189
Mers-el-Kebir, 301
Métro, the, 229
Metternich, Clemens Wenzel Nepomuk Lo-
    thar, Prince von, 55, 60, 67, 76, 116,
    117, 129, 174
Metz, 192, 193, 195, 198, 248
Mexico, 183, 184, 185–86, 187, 252
Mexico City, 184
Meyerbeer, Giacomo, 132
Mignet, François, 100
Milan, 31, 37, 44
Millerand, Alexandre, 219, 243, 250, 272ff.,
    276, 277–78
Mirabeau, Honoré Gabriel Riquetti, Comte
    de, 7, 8, 10, 12, 13–14, 15; on Danton,
    25
Miramar, 184
Mistinguett, 226–27, 279
Mode, La (journal), 119
Molé, Louis Mathieu, Comte, 124, 125, 142
Moltke, Helmuth Johannes Ludwig, Count
    von, 245
Moltke, Helmuth Karl Bernhard, Count von,
    191
Monarchists. *See* Royalists
Moncey, Marshal, 69
Mondovi, 31
Monet, Claude, 228
Monis, Ernest, 239
Moniteur, the, 103
Monna Lisa, the, 238
Monroe Doctrine, 184, 185
Mons, 264
Montenegro, 209
Montijo, Eugénie de. See Eugénie
Montijo, Paca de, 166
Montmarte, 199, 227
Montpensier, Duc de, 136
Morand, Paul, 280
Moreau, Jean Victor, 42
Morny, Auguste, Duc de, 158, 164–65, 181,
    184, 185
Morocco, 234, 235, 238–39, 281
Morris, Gouverneur, 14
Mortemart, Duc de, 105, 106
Mortier, Edouard, 121
Moscow, 58, 59, 273, 306
Mosley, Oswald, 287
Motorcars, 228
Moulin, Jean, 308
Moulin Rouge, 227
Muette de Portici, La, 192
Mulberry harbor, 311
Munich, 44, 296
Murat, Caroline. *See* Bonaparte, Caroline
Murat, Joachim, 29, 34, 35, 44, 45, 47, 52,
    57, 60ff., 202
Music, 168–69, 208, 227–28. *See also* Opera,
    the; specific pieces
Muslims, 294
Musset, Alfred de, 132
Mussolini, Benito, 286, 287, 296
Mustaches, 131, 237

Naples, 60, 61; King of (*See* Bonaparte,
    Joseph; Murat, Joachim)
Napoleon I, Emperor (Bonaparte), 3, 28–
    30, 31, 33–68ff., 74, 78–80, 81, 90, 97,
    98, 125, 157, 228; body brought to

Paris, 128–30; centenary, 189; column toppled, 199; on devotion, 203; and Elba, 69, 70, 75–76, 77, 90; and the Elysée, 202; Hitler brings son's body to lie beside, 303; Hundred Days, 77–79, 82, 83, 84–85; L'Aiglon, 226; as material for writers and artists, 117–18; picture in cottages, 158; and St. Helena, 79, 128, 166; statue torn down, 119; Talleyrand's will and, 115; Wellington on, 93

Napoleon II. See Reichstad, Napoleon, Duc de

Napoleon III, 161–94, 195ff., 205; as Louis Napoleon, 124–25, 129, 138–39, 149, 150, 153–60

Napoleon, Prince (Plon-Plon), 165, 179, 207

Napoleon at Brienne, 118

Narbonne, 237

Natchez, Les, 90

National, the (paper), 101, 102, 103, 124

National Guard, 13, 14, 16, 151, 195; Charles X and, 98; formation, 10; Louis Philippe and, 112, 116, 121, 140, 142, 143, 153

National Workshops, 150, 152

Nations, Battle of the, 61

Navarino, 98

Necker, Jacques, 6, 8, 10, 15

Nelson, Horatio Nelson, Viscount, 33–34, 40, 44, 80

Nemours, Louis d'Orléans, Duc de, 114

Neo-Socialists, 286

Netherlands. See Holland

New Zealanders, 249

Ney, Michel, 58, 69, 78, 85, 88

Nice, 20, 178, 179

Nicholas I, 134, 135, 170, 173

Nicholas II, 224, 253, 263

Niemen River, 58, 59

Niepce, Joseph, 89

Nightingale, Florence, 172

Nile, the, 34, 232

Nivelle, 251, 253, 254, 255

Normanby, Lord, 166

Normandy, 311

North Africa, 301, 308–9. See also specific places

North African Star, 281

North German Confederation, 186

Norway, 299

Notre Dame, 40, 72, 313

Offenbach, Jacques, 168–69, 188

Ollivier, Emile, 163, 187, 190, 191, 193

Olympic Games, 228

Opera, the, 132, 191–92. See also specific works

Opportunists, 219

Oradour-sur-Glane, 311

Orfila, Mathieu, 89

Organization du Travail, L', 122

Orlando, Vittorio, 267

Orléans, Duchesse d' (wife of Ferdinand Philippe Louis Charles Henri), 144, 147

Orléans, Ferdinand Philippe Louis Charles Henri, Duc d', 134–35

Orléans, Louis Philippe, Duc d'. See Louis Philippe

Orléans, Louis Philippe Joseph, Duc d' (Philippe Egalité), 9, 12, 23ff., 109

Orléans, 210

Orleanists, 100, 101, 157, 163, 197, 203; and whiskers, 131

Orpheus in the Underworld, 168

Orsini, Felice, 176

Orthodox Church, 170

Ottoman Empire, 170, 174

Oxford and Asquith, Herbert Henry Asquith, Earl of, 251

Paine, Tom, 23

Painleve, Paul, 258, 273, 278, 279, 282

Painting, 27, 118, 132, 208, 228, 279

Palais Bourbon, 81

Palais Royal, 81, 96, 132

Palais du Trocadéro, 208, 294

Palestine, 170

Palmerston, Henry John Temple, Lord, 126–27, 128, 134, 136, 173

Panama Canal, 214, 218, 219, 237

Panther (gunboat), 238

Papal States, 51, 116, 177, 178, 179, 182

Paris, Louis Philippe Albert d'Orléans, Comte de, 135, 144, 147, 157, 203

Paris, passim (See also specific buildings, incidents, inhabitants); in "la belle epoque," 226–27, 230, 233–34, 237; Charles X's reign and, 96, 101, 103–4, 105; Consulate; First Empire and, 33, 56, 59; Exhibitions, 173, 188, 207, 208, 218, 226, 294; and fall of First Empire; Restoration; Hundred Days; reign of Louis XVIII, 65, 66, 71, 72, 81ff., 88–90; and Great War, 247, 248, 249, 253, 255, 260, 264–65; and Louis XVI; Revolution, 6–8ff., 19ff., 28; and Louis Philippe's reign, 112, 119, 121, 123, 126, 128–30, 131–32, 141–43; Napoleon's body to, 128–30; Peace conference of 1855, 173–74; and Second Empire, 168, 171, 173, 175, 188, 199; and Second Republic, 148, 150ff., 158; Second Treaty of, 84; in Third Republic, 195, 196, 198–99, 202, 208, 211, 214, 221, 226–29ff., 247ff., 298ff.; waiters' strike, 237; in World War II, 298, 300–1, 303, 312–13

Parlements, regional, 6

Parliament, houses of (and legislative bodies) (See also specific individuals, parties): between World Wars, 271–72, 273–74, 282, 289, 297; Charles X and, 99, 101–2, 103; Consulate; First Empire and, 36, 43, 50, 60; and fall of First Empire; Restoration; Louis XVIII, 68, 73–74, 81ff., 86, 88, 90–91, 93; and Great War, 249–50, 253–54, 259; and Louis XVI; Revolution, 5ff., 11, 12, 14ff., 20–22ff.; Louis Philippe and, 106, 112, 127; and Second Empire, 163–64; and Second Republic, 147, 151, 153–57, 159, 160; and Third Republic, 197–98, 204ff., 209–10, 214, 216, 219, 220, 240, 249–50ff., 271ff., 298–99ff.; World War II and, 298–99, 302

Pas de Calais, 123

Pasteur, Louis, 214

Patch, General, 312

Pearl Harbor, 306

Peking, 183
Pelléas et Mélisande, 228
Père Lachaise, 199
Périer, Casimir, 90, 115, 120
Perpignon, 237
Pershing, John, 256, 257
Persia, 52
Persigny (companion of Louis Napoleon), 149, 153, 164
Pétain, Philippe, 250, 251, 253, 255–56, 261, 281; and World War II, 300ff., 309, 312
Petrograd, 253
Philippe Egalité. *See* Orléans, Louis Philippe Joseph, Duc d'
Philippeville, 242
Picardy, 247, 260, 263
Picasso, Pablo, 228, 279
Pichegru, Charles, 42
Picquart, Georges, 223
Piedmont, 42, 177, 179
Pilsudski, Joseph, 275
Pin to See the Peepshow, A, 266n
Pitt, William, 67, 244
Pius VII, Pope, 40, 41, 51, 90, 98
Pius IX, Pope, 156, 177, 181, 182
Plombières, 44, 46, 176, 177
Poincaré, Henri, 239
Poincaré, Raymond, 219, 239–40, 243, 271, 273, 276, 277, 281–82, 283; during Great War, 253, 258–59, 263
Poland and the Poles, 45–46, 57, 113, 114, 151–52; between World Wars, 268, 275, 280, 296, 297; World War II and, 298
Polastron, Louise d'Esparbès, Comtesse de, 95, 98
Polignac, Jules, Prince de, 92, 100, 102–3, 104, 112
Polignacs, the, 11
Pompadour, Jeanne d'Etoiles, Madame de, 202
Pont Alexandre III, 226
Pont d'Arcole, 104
Pope, the. *See* Gregory XVI; Pius
Popular Front, 291–96
Portugal, 52, 54, 58, 115
Potemkin (battleship), 235
Prague, Treaty of, 186
Praslin, Duc and Duchesse de, 139
Press, freedom of the, 103, 157, 171, 189
Pressburg, Peace of, 44
Prinzip (assassin), 241
Proudhon, Pierre Joseph, 187
Proust, Marcel, 227, 280
Provence, Comte de. *See* Louis XVIII
Provence and Provençals, 88, 247, 312
Prussia(ns), 29, 44, 52, 60, 61, 76, 195ff., 204; and fall of First Empire, 65ff.; and Louis XVIII's reign, 81, 83; Louis Philippe's reign and, 114, 120, 126; Napoleon III and, 179, 184ff., 191ff.; and World War I, 247, 268
Pyrenees, 61, 65, 136

Quadruple Alliance, 126
Quatre-Bras, 79
Queretaro, 185

Rachel, 132, 169
Radicals, 141, 277, 291
Raeder, Erich, 301

Rasputin, 252
Ravel, Maurice, 228
Red Cross Society, 178
Reichstadt, Napoleon, Duc de (Napoleon's son; King of Rome), 59, 67, 80, 116, 117, 135, 161, 303
Religion, 170. *See also* Catholics and Catholicism
Remembrance of Things Past, 227
Renan, Ernest, 182
Renault, Louis, 228
René (Chateaubriand), 90
Renoir, Jean, 294–95
Renoir, Pierre Auguste, 208, 228
Republic. *See* First Republic
Republicans, 64, 106, 116–17, 118, 122, 137, 141, 151, 197, 199, 201, 206, 219 (*See also* specific persons, Republics); and beards, 131; and Second Empire, 162, 163, 169, 183
Resistance, the, 304, 307–8, 310, 311
Restauration, La, 89n
Restoration, the, 68–108, 130, 190
Rethondes, 264
Réunion, 213
Revanche, 198, 215, 218ff., 243. *See also* Alsace and Lorraine
Revolution, French, 1–32, 40, 113; 1838 (February), 141–46, 150; July, 104–6 (*See also Trois Glorieuses, Les*)
Reynaud, Paul, 289, 299, 301, 307
Rheims, 97–98
Rhine, the, 83, 212, 268
Rhineland, 186, 280, 283, 291
Ribbentrop (Prussian official), 83
Ribbentrop, Joachim von, 301
Ribot, Premier, 258
Richardson, Samuel, 167
Richelieu, Armand-Emmanuel du Plessis, Duc de, 85–86, 88, 90–91, 200
Richelieu, Armand Jean du Plessis, Duc de (Cardinal Richelieu), 85
Rif, the, 281
Rights of Man, The, 23
Rivoli, 31
Roads, 87–88
Robespierre, Maximilien de, 7, 17, 22, 23, 25, 27, 28
Rochambeau, Jean de Vimeur, Comte de, 65, 254
Rolland, Romain, 280
Romagna, 181
Romania, 170, 174, 209, 269
Rome, 51, 77, 156; King of (*See* Reichstadt, Napoleon, Duc de)
Rommel, Erwin, 309
Roosevelt, Franklin D., 309
Rothschilds, the, 201
Rotterdam, 299
Rouge et le Noir, Le, 107
Rouget de Lisle, Claude Joseph, 18
Rouher, Eugène, 181, 190
Rousseau, Jean-Jacques, 6, 128
Royal Household Corps, 74–75
Royalist Action Française, 286
Royalists (monarchists), 24, 34, 38–39, 42, 64, 67, 72, 81ff., 92, 110 (*See also* Legitimists; Orleanists; specific families, individuals); in Second Empire, 162; in

Second Republic, 157, 160; in Third Republic, 197, 202, 203, 210
Rue de Rivoli, 81
Ruhr, the, 276, 280
Russell (journalist), 171
Russell, John Russell, Lord, 145
Russia (Soviet Union; U.S.S.R.), 26, 29, 46, 52, 57–60, 61, 63ff., 76, 81ff., 98, 127, 178, 200–1, 204, 208–9, 220, 224; absorbs Poland (1830), 114; in *la belle époque*, 226, 232, 235; between World Wars, 272, 275, 282, 285, 286, 293; Comintern, 272; Crimean War, 135, 170–72, 173, 174; and Fashoda, 232; and Great War, 242, 243, 245, 249ff.; Japanese war, 235; and Kellogg-Briand Pact, 282; in Quadruple Alliance, 126; Revolution, 252, 253, 255, 259, 269; and Spanish Civil War, 293; in Triple Entente, 235; in World War II, 306, 308, 309, 310
Ruy Blas, 288

S.F.I.O., 236, 273, 291
Saar, the, 268, 290
Sadowa, 186
Saint-Arnaud, Armand de, 171
St. Cloud, 35, 43, 104, 105, 168
St. Cyr, Marshal. *See* Gouvion-Saint-Cyr, Laurent, Marquis de
St. Cyr, 251
St. Germain-l'Auxerrois, church of, 112
St. Helena, 79, 128, 166
Saint-Just, Antoine de, 21, 22
St. Nazaire, 308
Saint-Quentin, 261, 263
Saint-Simon, Claude de Rouvroy, Comte de, 122
Salamanca, 58
Salvemini, G., 13n
Salzburg, 44
San Domingo, 41
Sand, George, 132
Sandherr, Colonel, 222
Sanson the executioner, 23
Sarajevo, 241
Sardinia, 174
Sarraut, Albert, 273, 291
Savona, 51
Savoy, 20, 178, 179
Schleswig-Holstein, 184
Schlieffen, Alfred, Count von; Schlieffen plan, 245, 246, 249
Schneider, Hortense, 168
Schneider family, firm, 123, 200
Schönbrunn, Palace of, 44
Science, 228. *See also* specific scientists
Scotland, 182
Scott, Sir Walter, 89, 117
Sebastopol, 172, 173
Second Empire, 160–93, 200, 212
Second Republic, 145–60
Secret Committee of Revolutionary Action, 292
Sedan, 193, 195, 299
Ségur, Philippe Paul, Comte de, 118
Seine River, 128–29
Senegal, 213
Senlis, 246–47
Serbia and the Serbs, 209, 241
Shelley, Percy Bysshe, 147

Siegfried Line, 291
Sieyès, Abbé, 7, 36
Skoda works, 296
Slavery, 134
Smith, Sir Sydney, 34
Smolensk, 58
Socialism and Socialists, 122, 187, 199, 219–20, 230, 236, 272–73, 274, 277, 285 (*See also* specific individuals, places); and Popular Front, 293, 296; and World War I, 258, 263
Société des Droits de l'Homme, 121
Society of Equals, 30
Solferino, 178
Somerville, D. C., 246n
Somme, the, 251, 260–61
Soult, Nicolas Jean de Dieu, 61, 116, 118, 120, 170
South Africa, 233
Soviet Union. *See* Russia
Spain and the Spanish, 24, 29, 44, 52, 54, 56, 58, 60, 61, 92–93, 190–91; Civil War, 299; and Louis Philippe's reign, 115, 124, 136–37; and Mexico, 183, 184
Splendors and Miseries of Victory, The, 272
Sports, 228
Staël, Germaine de, 51
Stalingrad, 306
Stanhope, Lady Hester, 151
States-General, 3, 5–6ff.
Stavisky, Serge, 287
Stendhal, 107, 118
Sterne, Laurence, 128
Stockholm, 258
Strasbourg, 198, 264
Strauss, Johann, 168
Stresa, 290
Stresemann, Gustav, 280
Strikes, 181, 188, 235, 237, 289
Stuart, Charles Edward (Bonnie Prince Charlie), 117
Stuart, Mary, 22, 182
Stuarts, the, 101
Sudan, the, 232
Sudetenland, 295, 296
Sue, Eugene, 143
Suez Canal, 189, 214
Suffrage (electoral law; the franchise), 82, 88, 103, 131, 151, 156–57, 159, 162–63
Sugar, 51–52
Sweden, 60, 61
Swiss Guards, 19
Switzerland, 125
Syria, 126, 128, 183, 280, 293

Tahiti, 133–34
Talavera, 54
Tales of Hoffmann, The, 169
Talleyrand-Périgord, Charles Maurice de, 9–10, 13–14, 57, 66–67, 68, 73, 82, 84, 90, 98, 100, 116, 226; and Alexander I, 66–67, 84; illegitimate son; grandson, 158, 164; last days; death, 115; and Napoleon I, 33, 37, 38, 40, 47, 52–53, 53–54, 75, 76, 115; and *Les Trois Glorieuses*, 104, 105
Tallien, Thérèsa Cabarrus, 37
Tangier, 234, 235
Tannenberg, 247
Tardieu, André, 273, 282, 283, 284, 289

Tarn, the, 247
Taxicabs, 248–49
Telegraphy, 228
Temple, the, 19, 20, 23
Tennis Court Oath, 7
Tennyson, Alfred Tennyson, Lord, 18
Terraine, John, 253n, 261n
Terror, the, 24–25, 26, 27
Theatre, 118, 132, 168–69, 208, 226–27. *See also* Comédie Française; specific works
Thiers, Adolphe, 90, 100, 103, 105, 106, 116, 118, 123, 124ff., 139, 142, 143, 155; death, 206; and Second Empire, 182, 189, 191; and Third Republic, 196ff., 206
Third Estate, 7ff., 146
Third International, 272–73
Third Republic, 195–303
Three Glorious Days. *See Trois Glorieuses, les*
Tien-Tsin, Treaty of, 213
Tilsit, 46, 57
Times, The, 138, 167, 171, 185, 190
Tobolsk, 58
Tocqueville, Alexis de, 3
Todt organization, 309
Tonkin, 183, 212
Torres Vedras, 54
Tortoni's, 132
Toulon, 26, 220, 309
Toulouse-Lautrec, Henri de, 227, 228
Tour de France, 228
Tours, 196, 272, 300
Trafalgar, Cape, 44
Trianon, the, 105
Tricolore, the, 10, 12, 17, 79, 93, 104, 105, 192, 203
Triple Alliance, 212, 220, 234
Triple Entente, 235
Tripolitania, 234
Trochu, Louis Jules, 196
Trois Glorieuses, Les (Three Glorious Days), 104–6, 112, 113, 119, 121
Tuileries, the, 13, 15–16, 19, 37, 39, 72, 77, 78, 80, 92, 94, 129, 143, 157, 158, 168; burned; in ruins, 199, 202
Tunisia, 212, 238, 291, 293
Turkey and the Turks, 33, 52, 98, 126, 170, 174, 208–9; in World War I, 249, 263, 280
Tussaud, Marie, 27

Ulm, 44
Union Generale, 211
Unitary Confederation of Labor, 273
United States (America and Americans), 41, 79, 115, 120, 122, 125, 188 (*See also* specific travelers); and Mexico, 183, 184, 185; and World War I; Versailles; aftermath, 252, 255ff., 267, 268–69, 272, 278–79, 282, 285; and World War II, 306ff.

V₁ and V₂ rockets, 310
Vaillant (assassin), 220–21
Valéry, Paul, 227, 280
Valmy, 20, 308
"Velocipede," 87
Vendée, the, 24, 28–29, 117, 197, 209, 232
Venetia, 177, 179, 186

Venice, 31, 44
Vera Cruz, 183
Verdi, Giuseppe, 189
Verdun, 20, 251
Verlaine, Paul, 227
Vernet, Horace, 118, 138
Vers l'armée de métier, 286
Versailles, 4, 5, 7, 9, 11ff., 129, 195, 196–97; Treaty, post-World War I, 267–68, 272, 284, 285, 290, 295, 307
Vichy government, 302ff.
Victor Emmanuel I, 177, 178
Victoria, Queen, 21, 126–27, 131, 134ff., 145, 170ff., 182, 207; on Louis Napoleon, 155, 162
Vie Parisienne, La, 168
Vienna, 44, 54; Congress of, 76, 84, 113, 173
Vigée-Lebrun, Elisabeth, 27, 71
Vigny, Alfred Victor, Comte de, 118
Villafranca, 179
Villain (assassin), 242
Villèle, Jean, Comte de, 92, 93, 96, 98, 99, 101
Vimeiro, 52
Vineyards, 188
Vittoria, 60
Viviani, René, 224, 242, 243, 250
Vlaminck, Maurice, 228
Voltaire, François Marie Arouet de, 6
Vosges, the, 246
Voting. *See* Suffrage

Waddington, William Henry, 210
Wagner, Richard, 208
Wagram, 54, 80, 118
Waiters, 237
Walcheren, 55
Waldeck-Rousseau, René, 231
Walewska, Maria, Countess, 46
Walewski, Alexandre Colonna, Count, 170
War of the Spanish Succession, 52, 136
Warsaw, 46, 57, 298
Washington, George, 40–41, 109
Washington, D.C., 274
Waterloo, 79, 100, 115, 133, 202
Weather, 172
Weimar Republic, 269–70ff.
Wellington, Arthur Wellesley, Duke of, 54, 56, 58, 60, 61, 65, 79, 170; on Bourbons, 93–94; on Richelieu, 85
West Indies, 41
Weygand, Maxime, 275, 300, 303
White Terror, 82, 84, 100
Wilhelmshöhe, 193
William, Crown Prince of Germany, 257–58
William I, Emperor of Germany (formerly Frederick William), 186, 193, 197
William I, King of the Netherlands, 113
William II, Kaiser, 220, 224, 233ff., 238, 263, 268, 307
Wilson, Daniel; Wilson scandal, 216–18, 219
Wilson, Woodrow, 252, 260, 267, 268, 269
Windsor Castle, 135, 172–73
Winterhalter, Franz, 168
Women, 12–13, 230, 257, 270, 291. *See also* Marriage
Workers' International, 188, 199. *See also* First International; Third International
World War I (Great War), 242–65

World War II, 298–314
Worth, Charles Frederick, 168

Young, Arthur, 2–3, 265
Young Plan, 277

Yugoslavia, 269, 290, 306
Yunnan, 213

Zola, Emile, 223
Zollverein, the, 114